Thomas Mann

DEATH IN VENICE, TONIO KRÖGER,

and

Other Writings

The German Library: Volume 63

Volkmar Sander, General Editor

Thomas Mann

DEATH IN VENICE, TONIO KRÖGER, and Other Writings

Edited by Frederick A. Lubich

Foreword by Harold Bloom

CONTINUUM · NEW YORK

1999
The Continuum Publishing Company
370 Lexington Avenue, New York, NY 10017

The German Library
is published in cooperation with Deutsches Haus,
New York University.
This volume has been supported by Inter Nationes.

Printed in the United States of America

Library of Congress Cataloging-in-Publication Data

Mann, Thomas, 1875–1955.
    [Selections. English. 1999]
    Death in Venice, Tonio Kröger, and other writings / Thomas Mann ;
edited by Frederick A. Lubich ; foreword by Harold Bloom.
    p.   cm. — (The German library ; v. 63)
    Includes bibliographical references.
    Contents: Tonio Kröger — Tristan — Death in Venice — The blood
of the Walsungs — Mario and the magician — The tables of the law –
– Freud and the future — A brother — Germany and the Germans.
    ISBN 0-8264-0970-9 (alk. paper). — ISBN 0-8264-0971-7 (pbk. :
alk. paper)
    Mann, Thomas, 1875–1955—Translations into English.
    I. Lubich, Frederick Alfred. II. Title. III. Series.
PT2625.A44A2   1999
833'.912—dc21   98-53761
                                                      CIP

Acknowledgments will be found on page 321,
which constitutes an extension of the copyright page.

Contents

Foreword

The greatest of modern German literary scholars, Ernst Robert Curtius, observed that European literature was a continuous tradition from Homer through Goethe, and became something else afterward. Thomas Mann is part of that something else, which begins with Wordsworth and has not yet ended. Mann, too ironic to study the nostalgias, nevertheless was highly conscious of his lifelong agon with his true precursor, Goethe. It was a loving agon, though necessarily not lacking in dialectical and indeed ambivalent elements. From his essay on "Goethe and Tolstoy" (1922) through his remarkable triad of Goethe essays in the 1930s (on the man of letters, the "representative of the Bourgeois Age," and *Faust*) on to the "Fantasy on Goethe" of the 1950s, Mann never wearied of reimagining his great original. The finest of these reimaginings, the novel, *Lotte in Weimar*, was published in Stockholm in 1939. We know it in English as *The Beloved Returns*, and it is surely the most neglected of Mann's major fictions. Mann is renowned as the author of *The Magic Mountain*, the tetralogy *Joseph and His Brothers*, *Doctor Faustus*, *Death in Venice*, and *Felix Krull*, while even the early *Buddenbrooks* remains widely read. But *Lotte in Weimar*, after some initial success, seems to have become a story for specialists, at least in English-speaking countries. Perhaps this is because Goethe, who exported splendidly to Britain and America in the time of Carlyle and Emerson, now seems an untranslatable author. Or it may be that Goethe's spirit has not survived what happened in and through Germany from 1933 until 1945.

In his essay on *Faust*, Mann remarks that the poem depicts love as a devil's holiday. The meditation upon Goethe's career as a man of letters centers itself in a remarkable paragraph that is as much on Mann as on Goethe:

> But this business of reproducing the outer world through
> the inner, which it re-creates after its own form and in its

own way, never does, however much charm and fascination may emanate from it, quite satisfy or please the outer world. The reason is that the author's real attitude always has something of opposition in it, which is quite inseparable from his character. It is the attitude of the man of intellect toward the ponderous, stubborn, evil-minded human race, which always places the poet and writer in this particular position, moulding his character and temperament and so conditioning his destiny. "Viewed from the heights of reason," Goethe wrote, "all life looks like some malignant disease and the world like a madhouse." This is a characteristic utterance of the kind of man who writes: the expression of his smarting impatience with mankind. More of the same thing than one would suppose is to be found in Goethe's works: phrases about the "human pack" in general and his "dear Germans" in particular, typical of the specific irritability and aloofness I mean. For what are the factors that condition the life of the writer? They are twofold: perception and a feeling for form; both of these simultaneously. The strange thing is that for the poet they are one organic unity, in which the one implies, challenges, and draws out the other. This unity is, for him, mind, beauty, freedom— everything. Where it is not, there is vulgar human stupidity, expressing itself in lack of perception and imperviousness to beauty of form—nor can he tell you which of the two he finds the more irritating.

We would hardly know that this aesthetic stance is that of Goethe rather than Flaubert, of Mann rather than T. S. Eliot. It seems Mann's shrewd warning to us is that the true man or woman of letters always exists in opposition to the formlessness of daily life, even when the writer is as socially amiable and spiritually healthy as Goethe and his disciple, Thomas Mann. That spiritual health is the subject of the grand essay by Mann on "Goethe as Representative of the Bourgeois Age," which nevertheless makes clear how heroically Goethe (and Mann) has to struggle in order to achieve and maintain such health:

As for Goethe, I may make an observation here having to do with certain human and personal effects and symptoms of the anti-ideal constitution; an observation which, indeed, leads me so far into intimate and individual psychology that only indications are possible. There can be no doubt that ideal faith, although it must be prepared for martyrdom, makes one happier in spirit than belief in a lofty and completely ironic sense of poetic achievement without values and opinions, entirely objective, mirroring everything with the same love and the same indifference. There are in Goethe, on closer examination, as soon as the innocence of the youthful period is past, signs of profound maladjustment and ill humor, a hampering depression, which must certainly have a deep-lying uncanny connection with his mistrust of ideas, his child-of-nature dilettantism. There is a peculiar coldness, ill will, *médisance,* a devil-may-care mood, an inhuman, elfish irresponsibility—which one cannot indulge enough, but must love along with him if one loves him. If one peers into this region of his character one understands that happiness and harmony are much more the affair of the children of spirit than of the children of nature. Clarity, harmony within oneself, strength of purpose, a positive believing and decided aim—in short, peace in the soul—all this is much more easily achieved by these than by the children of nature. Nature does not confer peace of mind, simplicity, single-mindedness; she is a questionable element, she is a contradiction, denial, thorough-going doubt. She endows with no benevolence, not being benevolent herself. She permits no decided judgments, for she is neutral. She endows her children with indifference; with a complex of problems, which have more to do with torment and ill will than with joy and mirth.

Goethe, Mann, and nature are everywhere the same; their happiness and harmony are aesthetic constructs, and never part of the given. Contradictory, skeptical, and full of the spirit that denies, Goethe and Mann triumph by transferring "liberal economic principles to the intellectual life"; they practice what Goethe called a "free trade of conceptions and feelings." The late "Fantasy on Goethe" has a delicious paragraph on the matter of Goethe's free trade in feelings:

Goethe's love life is a strange chapter. The list of his love affairs has become a requirement of education; in respect-

able German society one has to be able to rattle off the
ladies like the loves of Zeus. Those Friederikes, Lottes, Min-
nas, and Mariannes have become statues installed in niches
in the cathedral of humanity; and perhaps this makes
amends to them for their disappointments. For the fickle
genius who for short whiles lay at their feet was never prepared to take the consequences, to bear the restriction upon
his life and liberty that these charming adventures might
have involved. Perhaps the fame of the ladies is compensation to them for his recurrent flights, for the aimlessness of
his wooing, the faithlessness of his sincerity, and the fact
that his loving was a means to an end, a means to further
his work. Where work and life are one, as was the case with
him, those who know only how to take life seriously are
left with all the sorrows in their laps. But he always re-
proved them for taking life seriously. "Werther must—must
be?" he wrote to Lotte Buff and her fiancé. "You two do
not feel *him,* you feel only *me* and *yourselves.* . . . If only
you could feel the thousandth part of what Werther means
to a thousand hearts, you would not reckon the cost to
you." All his women bore the cost, whether they liked it
or not.

It is to this aspect of Goethe as "fickle genius" that Mann returned
in *The Beloved Returns,* which can serve here as representative both
of the strength and limitation of Mann's art of irony.

2

After forty-four years, the model for the heroine of Goethe's notorious *The Sorrows of Young Werther* goes to Weimar on pilgrimage,
not to be reunited with her lover, now sixty-seven to her sixty-one,
but rather in the hopeless quest to be made one both with their
mutual past, and with his immortal idea of what she once had been,
or could have been. For four hundred pages, Mann plays out the all
but endless ironies of poor Lotte's fame, as the widowed and respectable lady, who has her limitations but is nobody's fool, both enjoys
and endures her status and function as a living mythology. Mann's
supreme irony, grotesque in its excruciating banalities, is the account
of the dinner that the stiff, old Goethe gives in honor of the object
of his passion, some forty-four years after the event. Poor Lotte,

after being treated as a kind of amalgam of cultural relic and youthful indiscretion shrived by temporal decay, is dismissed by the great man with a palpably insincere: "Life has held us sundered far too long a time for me not to ask of it that we may meet often during your sojourn."

But Mann was too cunning to conclude his book there. A marvelous final meeting is arranged by Goethe himself, who hears Lotte's gentle question, "So meeting again is a short chapter, a fragment?" and replies in the same high aesthetic mode:

Dear soul, let me answer you from my heart, in expiation and farewell. You speak of sacrifice. But it is a mystery, indivisible, like all else in the world and one's person, one's life, and one's work. Conversion, transformation, is all. They sacrificed to the god, and in the end the sacrifice was God. You used a figure dear and familiar to me; long since, it took possession of my soul. I mean the parable of the moth and the fatal, luring flame. Say, if you will, that I am the flame, and into me the poor moth flings itself. Yet in the chance and change of things I am the candle too, giving my body that the light may burn. And finally, I am the drunken butterfly that falls to the flame—figure of the eternal sacrifice, body transmuted into soul, and life to spirit. Dear soul, dear child, dear childlike old soul, I, first and last, am the sacrifice, and he that offers it. Once I burned you, ever I burn you, into spirit and light. Know that metamorphosis is the dearest and most inward of thy friend, his great hope, his deepest craving: the play of transformation, changing face, graybeard to youth, to youth the boy, yet ever the human countenance with traits of its proper stage, youth like a miracle shining out in age, age out of youth. Thus mayst thou rest content, beloved, as I am, with having thought it out and come to me, decking thine ancient form with signs of youth. Unity in change and flux, conversion constant out of and into oneself, transmutation of all things, life showing now its natural, now its cultural face, past turning to present, present pointing back to past, both preluding future and with her dim foreshadowings already full. Past feeling, future feeling—feeling is all. Let us open wide eyes upon the unity of the world—eyes wide, serene, and wise. Wouldst thou ask of me repentance? Only wait. I see her ride toward me, in a mantle grey. Then once more the hour of Werther and Tasso will strike, as at midnight already midday strikes, and God give me to say what I suffer—only this first and last will then remain to me. Then forsaking will be only leave-taking, leave-taking for ever, death-struggle of feeling and the hour full of frightful pangs, pangs such as probably for some time precede the hour of death, pangs which are dying if not yet death. Death, final flight into the flame—the All-in-one—why should it too be aught but transformation? In my quiet heart, dear visions, may you rest—and what a pleasant moment that will be, when we anon awake together!

In some complex sense, part of the irony here is Mann's revenge upon his precursor, since it is Mann who burns Goethe into spirit and light, into the metamorphosis of hope and craving that is *The Beloved Returns.* Mann and Goethe die each other's life, live each other's death, in the pre-Socratic formulation that so obsessed W. B. Yeats. But for Mann, unlike the occult Yeats, the movement through death into transformation is a complex metaphor for the influence relationship between Goethe and his twentieth-century descendant. What Mann, in his "Fantasy on Goethe," delineated in his precursor is charmingly accurate when applied to Mann himself:

> We have here a kind of splendid narcissism, a contentment with self far too serious and far too concerned to the very end with self-perfection, heightening, and distillation of personal endowment, for a petty-minded word like "vanity" to be applicable. Here is that profound delight in that self and its growth to which we owe *Poetry and Truth,* the best, at any rate the most charming autobiography the world has seen—essentially a novel in the first person which informs us, in the most wonderfully winning tone, how a genius is formed, how luck and merit are indissolubly linked by an unknown decree of grace and how a personality grows and flourishes under the sun of a higher dispensation. Personality! Goethe called it "the supreme bliss of mortal man"— but what it really is, in what its inner nature consists, wherein its mystery lies—for there is a mystery about it— not even he ever explained. For that matter, for all his love for the telling word, for the word that strikes to the heart

of life, he never thought that everything must be explained. Certainly this phenomenon known as "personality" takes us beyond the sphere of purely intellectual, rational, analyzable matters into the realm of nature, where dwell those elemental and daemonic things which "astound the world" without being amenable to further elucidation.

The splendid narcissism of Mann, at his strongest, is precisely demonic, is that profound delight in the self without which works as various as *The Magic Mountain* and *Doctor Faustus* would collapse into the weariness of the irony of irony.

3

In his remarkable essay, "Freud and the Future" (1936; included in the present volume), Mann wrote the pattern for his own imitation of Goethe:

> The ego of antiquity and its consciousness of itself were different from our own, less exclusive, less sharply defined. It was, as it were, open behind; it received much from the past and by repeating it gave it presentness again. The Spanish scholar Ortega y Gasset puts it that the man of antiquity, before he did anything, took a step backward, like the bullfighter who leaps back to deliver the mortal thrust. He searched the past for a pattern into which he might slip as into a diving-bell, and being thus at once disguised and protected might rush upon his present problem. Thus his life was in a sense a reanimation, an archaizing attitude. But it is just this life as reanimation that is the life as myth. Alexander walked in the footsteps of Miltiades; the ancient biographers of Caesar were convinced, rightly or wrongly, that he took Alexander as his prototype. But such "imitation" meant far more than we mean by the word today. It was mythical identification, peculiarly familiar to antiquity; but it is operative far into modern times, and at all times is psychically possible. How often have we not been told that the figure of Napoleon was cast in the antique mould! He regretted that the mentality of the time forbade him to give himself out for the son of Jupiter Ammon, in imitation of Alexander. But we need not doubt that—at least at the pe-

riod of his Eastern exploits—he mythically confounded himself with Alexander; while after he turned his face westward he is said to have declared: "I am Charlemagne." Note that: not "I am like Charlemagne" or "My situation is like Charlemagne's," but quite simple "I am he." That is the formulation of the myth. Life, then—at any rate, significant life—was in ancient times the reconstitution of the myth in flesh and blood; it referred to and appealed to the myth; only through it, through reference to the past, could it approve itself as genuine and significant. The myth is the legitimation of life; only through and in it does life find self-awareness, sanction, consecration. Cleopatra fulfilled her Aphrodite character even unto death—and can one live and die more significantly or worthily than in the celebration of the myth? We have only to think of Jesus and His life, which was lived in order that that which was written might be fulfilled. It is not easy to distinguish between His own consciousness and the conventionalizations of the Evangelists. But His word on the Cross, about the ninth hour, that *"Eli, Eli, lama sabach-thani?"* was evidently not in the least an outburst of despair and disillusionment; but on the contrary a lofty messianic sense of self. For the phrase is not original, not a spontaneous outcry. It stands at the beginning of the Twenty-second Psalm, which from one end to the other is an announcement of the Messiah. Jesus was quoting, and the quotation meant: "Yes, it is I!" Precisely thus did Cleopatra quote when she took the asp to her breast to die; and again the quotation meant: "Yes, it is I!"

In effect, Mann quotes Goethe, and thus proclaims "Yes, it is I." The ego of antiquity is simply the artist's ego, appropriating the precursor in order to overcome the belatedness of the influence process. Mann reveals the true subject of his essay on Freud just two paragraphs further on:

Infantilism—in other words, regression to childhood—what a role this genuinely psychoanalytic element plays in all our lives! What a large share it has in shaping the life of a human being; operating, indeed, in just the way I have described: as mythical identification, as survival, as a treading in footprints already made! The bond with the father, and the transference to father-substitute pictures of a higher and more developed type—how these infantile traits work upon the life of the individual to mark and shape it! I use the word "shape," for to me in all seriousness the happiest, most pleasurable element of what we call education *(Bildung)*, the shaping of the human being, is just this powerful influence of admiration and love, this childish identification with a father-image elected out of profound affinity. The artist in particular, a passionately childlike and play-possessed being, can tell us of the mysterious yet after all obvious effect of such infantile imitation upon his own life, his productive conduct of a career which after all is often nothing but a reanimation of the hero under very different temporal and personal conditions and with very different, shall we say childish means. The *imitatio* Goethe, with its Werther and Wilhelm Meister stages, its old-age period of *Faust* and *Diwan,* can still shape and mythically mould the life of an artist—rising out of his unconscious, yet playing over—as is the artist way—into a smiling, childlike, and profound awareness.

The profound awareness is Mann's own, and concerns his own enactment of the *imitatio* Goethe. Subtly echoed and reversed here is Goethe's observation in his *Theory of Color* to the effect that "even perfect models have a disturbing effect in that they lead us to skip necessary stages in our *Bildung,* with the result, for the most part, that we are carried wide of the mark into limitless error." This is also the Goethe who celebrated his own originality as well as his power of appropriating from others. Thus he could say that: "Only by making the riches of the others our own do we bring anything great into being," but also insist: "What can we in fact call our own except the energy, the force, the will!" Mann, acutely sensing his own belatedness, liked to quote the old Goethe's question: "Does a man live when others also live?"

The Goethe of *The Beloved Returns* is not Goethe, but Mann himself, the world parodist prophesied and celebrated by Nietzsche as the artist of the future. E. R. Curtius doubtless was accurate in seeing Goethe as an ending and not as a fresh beginning of the cultural tradition. Mann too now seems archaic, not a modernist or post-Romantic, but a belated Goethe, a humanist triumphing through the mystery of his own personality and the ironic playfulness of his art. Like his vision of Goethe, Mann too now seems a child of nature rather than of the spirit, but laboring eloquently to burn through nature into the transformation that converts deathliness into a superb dialectical art.

HAROLD BLOOM

Introduction

Thomas Mann, who had feared in the middle of his life that his work might have become outdated and outmoded, has experienced in recent years an astonishing renaissance of scholarly attention and appreciation. In 1995 and 1996 alone, no less than four voluminous biographies by German, British, and American authors appeared.[1] Why the sudden renewed international interest in this quintessentially German author? Of the several reasons that might be advanced, the most obvious one is biographical. Throughout his life, Mann meticulously kept diaries. Some of them he destroyed later; the remaining portion he stipulated should be kept sealed until twenty years after his death. Accordingly, they were opened in 1975 and subsequently edited and published in ten volumes, the last of them in 1995. In size, this posthumous oeuvre comes close to matching the thirteen volumes of the standard German edition of his work proper. These diaries have yielded a veritable *embarras de richesse* of personal and political, literary and historical observations, and constitute a running commentary on the most turbulent decades in German history. Thus, a generation after his death, the former *praeceptor et arbiter Germaniae* had made an impressive comeback, this time around as a private paterfamilias, his family saga successively serialized into an intellectual soap opera of national and international proportions. The new insights these diaries afford obviously play a major role in the recent proliferation of Thomas Mann biographies.

Other reasons can only be surmised. For example, Germany's fairly recent unification has refocused the world's attention on a country and its culture, whose most respected literary interpreter and representative had once been the exiled Thomas Mann. In addition, recent theories on the paradigm shifts from modernity to postmodernity are destabilizing literary canons; in this process, Thomas Mann, generally more associated with tradition than innovation,

stands a good chance of becoming a prime expositor of the newly
evolving aesthetic and philosophical strategies of postmodernity.

Thomas Mann was born in 1875 in the northern Hanseatic city
of Lübeck into a patrician and once prosperous merchant dynasty. As
a young man Thomas Mann moved to the southern Bavarian city of
Munich and married into a well-established German–Jewish family.
The erstwhile literary bohemian with a guilty bourgeois conscience
soon found himself presiding over an ever-expanding household,
which included wife, maids, and eventually six children. The first of
Mann's published diaries covers the years 1918 to 1921, when he
witnessed the labor pains of Germany's nascent democracy firsthand
in its most violent form, that is, in Munich's short-lived Soviet Republic of 1919. During this period of political turmoil, rampant with
street fights and culminating in the vicious assassination of some of
its political leaders, Mann too repeatedly feared for his own life.

It was in 1918, that the author's *Betrachtungen eines Unpoliti-
schen (Reflections of a Nonpolitical Man)* appeared, a voluminous
work in which he programmatically professed his allegiance to the
cultural and political traditions of a monarchic Germany. The timing
could not have been more ironic for the publication of these ruminat-
ing reflections, a desperate last ditch effort to salvage a thoroughly
lost reality. Within four years, Thomas Mann declared himself in
his public speech "Von deutscher Republik" (On the German Republic) a convinced convert to Weimar's fledgling democracy. "Mann
overboard" was just one of the many cries of distress from former
conservative cohorts and panicking patriots.

In the following years Thomas Mann transformed himself systematically into a politically as well as culturally progressive representative of Weimar Germany. In 1924, his epic and encyclopedic
Bildungsroman, Der Zauberberg (The Magic Mountain), was published. It constituted a veritable summit and summa of European
thought and social decadence on the eve of World War I—resplendent with utopian visions of cultural regeneration. Privately this novel
earned him the affectionate sobriquet "The Magician"; publicly it
won him critical acclaim as one of Germany's and Europe's most
complex and erudite authors. The final years of the republic not
only saw him crowned with the Nobel Prize for literature, but also
strongly engaged as an outspoken critic of rising fascism. The once
aloof author had come down from the Magic Mountain to decry in
unmistakable terms the nationalistic rabble-rousers who were rallying around their rising Führer. In public appearances ranging from

Vienna to Berlin, he warned his countrymen not to regress into the murky realms of a "blood and soil" ideology—a corrupted mother-myth that promised Germany, especially the dregs of its society, a rebirth as a Nietzschean nation of proud "blond beasts." Abroad on a European tour, lecturing on Richard Wagner when Hitler came to power, Mann decided not to return to his native land.

Having been passionately and finally painfully German, the exiled Mann changed his citizenship twice, first becoming a citizen of Czechoslovakia, then of the United States. Throughout his early years of exile in France, Switzerland, and America, he sustained himself mentally as well as financially through the elaborate production of his most voluminous work, *Joseph und seine Brüder* (1933–43, *Joseph and His Brothers*), a tetralogy comprising some 2,500 pages. A revisiting and a revisioning of the Old Testament story of Joseph's exile in Egypt on a Homeric scale, the work is grounded in the then-latest theories of biblical mythography and cultural anthropology, and teems with personal and political allusions to Mann's own life and times. Drawing additional inspiration from Heinrich Zimmer's study on the Indian *Magna Mater,* he wrote the novella "Die Vertauschten Köpfe" (1940, "The Transposed Heads"), suffusing Western metaphysics with Eastern mythology (from Schopenhauer to Vishnu's Great Maya). His next novel was much closer to home, *Lotte in Weimar* (1939, *The Beloved Returns*). It is Mann's first major fictional preoccupation and the beginning of his identification with Goethe, the embodiment of the Other, classical Weimar, and the representation of German culture at its best. In his later life, Mann would increasingly indulge himself in such an ironic *imitatio Goethe,* thereby pursuing and practicing his own theory that great men will invariably follow in the footsteps of former great men of culture and history.

During his years in the United States, Mann became not only the most prominent deputy of German culture but also the most vocal adversary of the Third Reich. In numerous lecture tours crisscrossing the American continent, the self-proclaimed "itinerant preacher of democracy" promised its coming victory while at the same time warning of the growing menace of Nazi Germany. Beyond his American audience, he also attempted to reach his compatriots across the Atlantic through frequent broadcasts on the BBC called *Deutsche Hörer* (Listen, Germany), endeavoring to open their eyes to the true nature of fascism. While the Nazis were revoking Mann's honorary doctorate from Bonn University, the Ivy League universities of Princeton, Harvard, and Columbia were bestowing their highest honors upon him. During these years, the Manns were frequent guests at the White House and Franklin Roosevelt began to consider Thomas Mann as a possible president for a postwar Germany. The author returned the compliment by updating and retooling the economic plans for Egypt of his biblical hero Joseph according to the latest strategies of Roosevelt's New Deal.

In contrast to his unequivocal denunciation of Hitler in his public polemics, he pursued quite a different path in an essay of 1939. In it he delineated several biographical and psychological similarities between himself, the young decadent *littérateur* turned Nobel laureate, and the ex-Austrian *peintre maudit,* now the most powerful politician and mass magician of Germany. Through these uncanny elective affinities, Mann explored and exorcised some of his own youthful national-chauvinistic tendencies. The determined will to power of both made them perfect parodistic antagonists in a topsy-turvy world of art and politics—consummate Nietzschean (nit)wits at their best and worst. Mann called his essayistic fantasy of this satirical sibling rivalry "Ein Bruder" (A brother).

With his magisterial novel *Doktor Faustus: Das Leben des deutschen Tonsetzers Adrian Leverkühn, erzählt von einem Freunde* (1947, *Doctor Faustus: The Life of the German Composer Adrian Leverkühn as Told by a Friend*), Mann wrote the ponderous and even more problematic counterpart to his frivolous fraternizing with the Führer. Leverkühn's life and work are a dauntingly speculative allegory on Germany's creative and destructive genius as it unfolds throughout the centuries, culminating in the disastrous and, according to the Faust fable, demonic events of Nazi Germany. Splitting his emotional loyalties between the protagonist and the narrator of the novel, Mann invents and invests himself twice—and larger than life—in the cultural triumphs and historical traumas of his increasingly schizoid nation. He took his literary labor of love and mourning very personally. "Where I am, there is Germany" became one of Mann's most quoted, celebrated, and criticized statements during these years in exile. In retrospect, he could not have been more correct. Like no other German author he had experienced and personified, analyzed and fictionalized the most momentous developments and events in the history of his country.

Nineteen forty-five brought the end of World War II, but not the end of Mann's involvement in national and international politics. Through numerous committees and public lectures he attempted to moderate and mediate the growing differences between the Soviet Union and the United States. But during the following years he appeared more and more like a crier in the wilderness, his messages drowned out by the rising clamor of the cold war. "Mann overboard" turned into "Mann out of place," and the itinerant preacher's progress took on increasingly quixotic proportions. History finally caught up with him although he had seen it coming a long time ago. On the first of his several sea voyages to the New World, Mann had been reading Cervantes's comic epic and writing a "fictitious diary" entitled *Meerfahrt mit "Don Quijote"* (1934, *Sea Voyage with "Don Quixote"*). This latter-day knight errantry proved to be a telling tale. Now, after the war, the country of freedom and democracy was no longer interested in his dialectical idealism about world politics. Along with other members of his exiled family, the Nobel laureate and possible presidential candidate for a future Germany ended up quite unceremoniously, in the files of the FBI bureaucracy. Such windmills the aging Mann was no longer willing to fight. In 1952 he pulled up stakes one more time and took his immediate family back to the Old World, settling in Zurich, neutral Switzerland, where he died in 1955.

Subsequent scholarship dubbed this last true *Bildungsbürger* of a doomed class and culture "The Ironic German," due to the rich parodistic qualities of his work. However, often overlooked in this context are the pervasive (tragic) ironies in his own life. Two examples beyond Mann's "un-American activities" may suffice. When his son Klaus returned to Munich as an American war correspondent after the collapse of the Third Reich, he found his father's ruined house converted into a makeshift home for unwed German mothers. Sired by racially selected SS soldiers, their offspring were supposed to become Germany's Aryan super race: Tonio Kröger's (young Thomas Mann's) blond beaux, beauties, and would-be beasts had come home—to roost, as it were. On a much larger scale, Mann's own last visit to his homeland also resonates with the tragic irony of its cultural history. To avoid antagonizing either part of Germany, he gave his anniversary speech on Goethe, his beloved alter ego, in both Frankfurt and Weimar. It too was a gesture of double entendres. By now, Goethe's medieval model of Faust and his fateful "two souls" had indeed become a self-fulfilling prophecy for modern divided Germany. His daredevil destiny looms large as a lasting German Gothic (the Germany of Goethe transmogrified). By honoring Goethe on both sides of the political divide, Mann paid his last tribute to the pathetic fallacy of Faustus/Germany. It was to be his final iron(ic) curtain call.

While researching and writing *Doktor Faustus,* Mann also drew on the medieval legends of the *Gesta Romanorum,* which in turn became the source of inspiration for his penultimate novel, *Der Erwählte* (1951, *The Holy Sinner*). It is an imaginative re-creation of the medieval vita of Pope Gregory the Great, a dazzling period piece of courtly love, replete with monstrous sexual aberrations and miraculous spiritual redemption. The novel also exemplifies Mann's most advanced stylistic and linguistic experimentation with hybridized forms of French, English, and Lutheran German (polyglot, onomatopoetic grist for the theory mills of Barthes, Kristeva, et al.). It is no coincidence that this exemplary (im)morality play about a great sinner and saint deploys and displays Mann's most purple prose. In its linguistic brio and stylistic brilliance it is Mann's poetic paean to a world that viewed the history of mankind as primarily determined by the extraordinary (mis)deeds of its "great men."

Mann's last novel, *Bekenntnisse des Hochstaplers Felix Krull. Der Memoiren erster Teil* (1954, *Confessions of Felix Krull, Confidence Man: The Early Years*) spins out the author's lifelong literary quest for ironic imitation and mythic identification into the vagaries and vicissitudes of a modern picaro. Though popular with many readers, the casual sex and con games of the handsome impostor of the novel, half Hermes, half hunk, along with his coy confessions turn out to be—by the measure of Mann—literature lite. However, as such, *Felix Krull* emblematizes the author's own concluding career. On a biographical level Krull's confessions function for Mann as comic, if not erotic, relief from the burden of an exacting life's work. Felix Krull's adventurous pursuit of happiness by courting disaster symbolizes the author's own felicitous though always precarious destiny. Like a baroque picaro in bourgeois disguise, Mann too had experienced the world as a Wheel of Fortune that had extolled and exiled, honored and humiliated him time and again. In his art he had re-created his life and times more and more as a literary *teatrum mundi,* a colorful spectacle of human masks and of humanity's timeless myths. In this light, Felix Krull, the charming trickster, and his amorous confessions stand as Mann's own lighthearted farewell to a world of woes and vanities.

So who is the real Thomas Mann behind all his roles? His cultural and political persona, so poised in public, belies a highly vulnerable and complicated personality. His diaries reveal an often intensely nervous, neurotic, and narcissistic person: a vita as wound. At its core lies—perceptive readers of Thomas Mann have known it for a long time—the author's lifelong agony with his persistently suppressed and sublimated homosexuality. It constitutes the true psychological subtext for Mann's proverbial antagonism between art and life; its conflicts characterize and challenge almost all of his literary protagonists. Mann's diaries contain countless erotic reveries and sexual references, ranging from his enraptured glimpses of handsome young men in various stages of dress—including his own adolescent son—to the melancholy memories of his largely unrequited romances. Even the entries of his last years testify to the undiminished power and passion of his homoerotic fantasies. In their elegiac musings about the unfulfillment of a lifelong yearning, these entries belong to the most moving passages in the work of this last and most eloquent epigone of the romantic *Liebestod,* a tradition which so haunted Germany's late nineteenth century imagination. In this context, Mann's novella *Der Tod in Venedig* (1913, *Death in Venice*) not only stands as a master narrative of literary modernity, but also as "a revolutionary breakthrough in the expression of gay desire."[2]

Certainly the best explanation for Thomas Mann's lasting attraction—and provocation—can be found in his literary accomplishments. Furthermore, if one wants to comprehend the twentieth century, its outstanding achievements, and its even more outrageous failures, be it those of German culture and history, be it those of Western civilization at large, one can arguably find in Mann's literary work its most complex—and controversial—representation and reflection. Certainly no writer of the twentieth century was still so deeply rooted in the cultural traditions of the nineteenth century and at the same time expanded that horizon so systematically as the author of *Buddenbrooks, The Magic Mountain,* the Joseph tetralogy, and *Doctor Faustus.* Seen together, these works constitute a veritable metanarrative of German and Judeo-Christian traditions, as well as a multifaceted montage of archetypal myths and epistemological models, ranging from matriarchal mythography to modern musicology, from Marxism to psychoanalysis, to name but a few. By all accounts, the work of this *poeta doctus redivivus* stands as a formidable bulwark of *Bildung,* representing the quintessence of Germany's modern intellectual history, as if to shore it up one more time against its imminent political catastrophe. In this endeavor, Mann emerges as a central contributor to that Western project that

Adorno and Horkheimer defined and delineated as the "Dialectic of Enlightenment" (an enlightenment at that time doomed to a total eclipse). The frequent illumination of both sides of an issue, and the negotiating of its various contradictions and underlying similarities, became Mann's characteristic trademarks, establishing him as his country's unchallenged literary master of ambivalences.

By the same token, Mann was not only an accomplished architect of serious thoughts and complex (hi)stories, he was also their most skillful and playful underminer. In almost all of his epic works he probed deeper layers of literary traditions and dismantled their cultural conventions, turning them with cunning and loving care into multiple parodies. For it was Mann's conceptual credo that these parodistic strategies would reveal, layer by layer, "Ge-schichte" by "Ge-schichte," at the bottom of all culture the "unity of the human spirit." At one time, such historiographical rhyming and reasoning were regarded with a substantial amount of suspicion in certain intellectual quarters. In view, however, of our recent postmodern shifts and turns—"back to the future"—Mann's literary archaeology gains new meaning and momentum. It anticipates and configurates such seminal paradigms of postmodernity as its ubiquitous retromodes from philosophy to fashion, its programmatic aesthetics of quotes, pastiches, and montages, its cross- and multicultural messages and agendas, and the dialectics of a sexual revolution with its continuing liberation and celebration of (wo)man's polymorphous sexuality—not to mention the once mightiest and most magic word of postmodernity: *deconstruction*.[3]

The present volume aims to offer a representative cross-section of Thomas Mann's literary and essayistic oeuvre.[4] "Tristan" (1903) and "Wälsungenblut" (1921, written 1905, "Blood of the Walsungs") are novellas from Mann's early creative phase, portraying and parodying in literary masks both himself and his in-laws, luxuriating in a sensuous and decadent Wagnerian world of *l'art pour l'art*. "Tonio Kröger" (1903) recaptures with atmospheric accuracy the dreams and aspirations of Thomas Mann's own youthful years. From the young man's memories of a searching and suffering bisexuality to his resolution to dedicate his life to the creation of art, this very German version of *A Portrait of the Artist as a Young Man* has fascinated generations of young readers from Rilke to Kafka to today's college students. *Der Tod in Venedig* (1912, *Death in Venice*), Mann's best-known novella, represents his structurally and stylistically most polished narrative, in which psychosexual fantasies are transformed and sublated into mythopoetic epiphanies—with fatal consequences. "Mario und der Zauberer" (1930, "Mario and the Magician") constitutes one of the very early political allegories on fascism, and represents the first case study of its sadomasochistic pathology, long before Susan Sontag's critical essay "Fascinating Fascism" and the cinematic explorations of Cavani, Visconti, Pasolini, et al. "Das Gesetz" (1944, "The Tables of the Law") belongs to Mann's last creative period. Written in the aftermath of his Joseph tetralogy, "Das Gesetz" also reflects the central exegetical features of this epic, that is, the parodistic dissolution of scriptural authority and the psychosexual reinscription of its human, all-too-human genealogy. Here, God is being revealed (at least partially) as Moses' own mock-heroic projection of himself. Beyond this Mosaic make-believe the great mediator of the Ten Commandments and creator of a chosen people also figures cross-culturally as the ideal counter-model to his future archenemy Adolf Hitler, the ultimate imitator and corruptor of the original Moses–Messiah myth.

The essay "Freud und die Zukunft" (1936, "Freud and the Future"), Mann's public *laudatio* in honor of Freud's eightieth birthday, celebrates the Viennese founding father of psychoanalysis as the legitimate heir to German romanticism and a harbinger of a mankind that will, thanks to his teachings, become more and more enlightened about its darker drives and thus emancipated from its more dangerous desires. In telescoping this Freudian view into the Faustian vision of a truly liberated people, delivered from oppression and ignorance, Mann blends it into the ultimately redemptive history of the conclusion of Goethe's *Faust II*. Unfortunately, Germany had already embarked on a different Faustian finale. The essay "Ein Bruder" (1939, "A Brother") is Mann's personal exposé of how intricately good and evil, *Bildung* and barbarism, can be affiliated. And last but not least, the volume includes "Deutschland und die Deutschen" (1945, "Germany and the Germans"); as one of Mann's final attempts to explicate Germany to a mystified American audience, it was delivered as an address at the Library of Congress in Washington, D.C., on May 29, 1945, barely two weeks after the end of World War II. In essence, it is a reader's guide to *Doctor Faustus*, a hermetic (his)story if there ever was one. In it the author retraces Germany's cultural legacy one more time, from Luther's religious reformation to Bismarck's political romanticism and its ultimate corruption, through Hitler's fascism. Mann concluded his national tour de force: "This story should convince us of one thing:

that there are not two Germanys, a good and a bad one, but one, whose best turned into evil through devilish cunning. . . . Not a word of all that I have just told you about Germany or tried to indicate to you, came out of alien, cool, objective knowledge; it is all within me, I have been through it all."

F. A. L.

Notes

1. Klaus Harpprecht, *Thomas Mann: Eine Biographie.* Reinbek: Rowohlt, 1995, 2,253 pp. Donald Prater, *Thomas Mann: A Life,* New York: Oxford University Press, 1995, 554 pp. Ronald Hayman, *Thomas Mann: A Biography,* New York: Scribner, 1995, 672 pp. Anthony Heilbut, *Thomas Mann: Eros and Literature,* New York: Knopf, 1996, 636 pp. Of the four, Heilbut's biography is unquestionably the most eloquent, erudite, and impassioned account of Mann's life and work.
2. Heilbut, p. 261. This latest biography on Thomas Mann represents the most perceptive and in all likelihood the definitive account on this subject.
3. For an early American tribute to Thomas Mann see Charles Neider, ed., *The Stature of Thomas Mann,* New York: New Directions, 1947. For a late German diatribe against Thomas Mann, see Hanjo Kesting, "Thomas Mann oder der Selbsterwählte: Zehn polemische Thesen über einen Klassiker," in *Der Spiegel,* 22, (1975), reprinted in Hans Schulte and Gerald Chapple, eds., *Thomas Mann. Ein Kolloquium,* Bonn: Bouvier, 1978. In this context see also Marcel Reich-Ranicki, ed., *Was halten Sie von Thomas Mann? Achtzehn Autoren antworten,* Frankfurt: Fischer, 1986. The latter two works are primarily noteworthy for their implied father–son conflict, which is so symptomatic for the relationship between Thomas Mann and the next generation of German writers and intellectuals. Long at the mercy of extremist readers, drawn between panegyrical and parricidal impulses, the literature of Thomas Mann deserves another closer reading and—*pace* Wolfgang Iser—a less "implied reader."
4. For a comprehensive bibliography on Thomas Mann scholarship, see Klaus Jonas's two-volume edition of *Die Thomas Mann-Literatur: Bibliographie der Kritik 1896–1955, 1956–1975,* Berlin 1972, 1979 with a third volume forthcoming covering the period 1976–94.

NOVELLAS

Tonio Kröger

1

The winter sun was no more than a feeble gleam, milky and wan behind layers of cloud above the narrow streets of the town. Down among the gabled houses it was damp and drafty, with occasional showers of a kind of soft hail that was neither ice nor show. School was over. The hosts of liberated pupils streamed across the cobbled yard and out through the wrought-iron gate where they divided and hastened off in opposite directions. The older ones held their bundles of books in a dignified manner, high up against their left shoulders, and with their right arms to windward steered their course toward dinner; the little ones trotted merrily off with their feet splashing in the icy slush and the paraphernalia of learning rattling about in their sealskin satchels. But now and then they would one and all snatch off their caps with an air of pious awe as some senior master with the beard of Jove and the hat of Wotan strode solemnly by . . .

"Are you coming now, Hans?" said Tonio Kröger; he had been waiting in the street for some time. With a smile he approached his friend, who had just emerged from the gate, chattering to some other boys and about to move off with them . . . "What?" he asked, looking at Tonio . . . "Oh yes, of course! All right, let's walk a little."

Tonio did not speak, and his eyes clouded over with sadness. Had Hans forgotten, had he only just remembered that they had arranged to walk home together this afternoon? And he himself, ever since Hans had promised to come, had been almost continuously looking forward to it!

"Well, so long, you fellows," said Hans Hansen to his companions. "I'm just going for a walk now with Kröger." And the two of them turned to the left, while the others sauntered off to the right.

Hans and Tonio had time to take a walk after school, because they both came from families in which dinner was not served until four o'clock. Their fathers were important men of business, who held public office in the town and wielded considerable influence. The Hansens had for many generations owned the big timber yards down by the river, where powerful mechanical saws hissed and spat as they cut up the tree trunks. But Tonio was the son of Consul Kröger, whose sacks of grain could be seen any day being driven through the streets, with his firm's name stamped on them in great black letters; and his spacious old ancestral house was the stateliest in the whole town ... The two friends were constantly having to doff their caps to their numerous acquaintances; indeed, although they were only fourteen, many of those they met were the first to greet them ...

Both had slung their satchels across their shoulders, and both were well and warmly dressed: Hans in a short reefer jacket with the broad blue collar of his sailor's suit hanging out over his back, and Tonio in a gray belted overcoat. Hans wore a Danish sailor's cap with black ribbons, and a shock of his flaxen blond hair stood out from under it. He was extraordinarily good-looking and well built, broad in the shoulders and narrow in the hips, with keen, steely blue eyes set wide apart. But Tonio's complexion, under his round fur cap, was swarthy, his features were sharply cut and quite southern in character, and the look in his dark heavy-lidded eyes, ringed with delicate shadows, was dreamy and a little hesitant ... The outlines of his mouth and chin were unusually soft. His gait was nonchalant and unsteady, whereas Hans's slender black-stockinged legs moved with a springy and rhythmic step ...

Tonio was walking in silence. He was suffering. He had drawn his rather slanting brows together and rounded his lips as if to whistle, and was gazing into vacancy with his head tilted to one side. This attitude and facial expression were characteristic of him.

Suddenly Hans pushed his arm under Tonio's with a sidelong glance at him, for he understood very well what was the matter. And although Tonio still did not speak during the next few steps, he suddenly felt very moved.

"I hadn't forgotten, you know, Tonio," said Hans, gazing down at the sidewalk, "I just thought we probably wouldn't be having our walk after all today, because it's so wet and windy. But I don't mind the weather of course, and I think it's super of you to have waited for me all the same. I'd already decided you must have gone home, and I was feeling cross . . ."

Everything in Tonio began to dance with joy at these words.

"Well, then, let's go round along the promenade!" he said, in a voice full of emotion. "Along the Mühlenwall and the Holstenwall, and that'll take us as far as your house, Hans . . . Oh, of course not, it doesn't matter, I don't mind walking home by myself afterward; you can walk me home next time."

In his heart he was not really convinced by what Hans had said, and sensed very clearly that his friend attached only half as much importance as he did to this tête-à-tête walk. But he perceived nevertheless that Hans was sorry for his forgetfulness and was going out of his way to conciliate him. And Tonio was very far from wishing to resist these consiliatory advances . . .

The fact was that Tonio loved Hans Hansen, and had already suffered a great deal on his account. Whoever loves the more is at a disadvantage and must suffer—life had already imparted this hard and simple truth to his fourteen-year-old soul; and his nature was such that when he learned something in this way he took careful note of it, inwardly writing it down, so to speak, and even taking a certain pleasure in it—though without, of course, modifying his own behavior in the light of it or turning it to any practical account. He had, moreover, the kind of mind that found such lessons much more important and interesting than any of the knowledge that was forced on him at school; indeed, as he sat through the hours of instruction in the vaulted Gothic classrooms, he would chiefly be occupied in savoring these insights to their very depths and thinking out all their implications. And this pastime would give him just the same sort of satisfaction as he felt when he wandered round his own room with his violin (for he played the violin) and drew from it notes of such tenderness as only he could draw, notes which he mingled with the rippling sound of the fountain down in the garden as it leaped and danced under the branches of the old walnut tree . . .

The fountain, the old walnut tree, his violin and the sea in the distance, the Baltic Sea to whose summer reveries he could listen when he visited it in the holidays: these were the things he loved, the things which, so to speak, he arranged around himself and among which his inner life evolved—things with names that may be employed in poetry to good effect, and which did indeed very frequently recur in the poems that Tonio Kröger from time to time composed.

The fact that he possessed a notebook full of poems written by himself had by his own fault become public knowledge, and it very adversely affected his reputation both with his schoolmates and with the masters. Consul Kröger's son on the one hand thought their disapproval stupid and contemptible, and consequently despised his fellow pupils as well as his teachers, whose ill-bred behavior in any case repelled him and whose personal weaknesses had not escaped his uncommonly penetrating eye. But on the other hand he himself felt that there was something extravagant and really improper about writing poetry, and in a certain sense he could not help agreeing with all those who considered it a very odd occupation. Nevertheless this did not prevent him from continuing to write . . .

Since he frittered away his time at home and was lethargic and inattentive in class and out of favor with the masters, he continually brought back absolutely wretched reports, to the great annoyance and distress of his father, a tall carefully dressed man with pensive blue eyes who always wore a wild flower in his buttonhole. To Tonio's mother, however—his beautiful dark-haired mother whose first name was Consuelo and who was in every way so unlike the other ladies of the city, his father having in days gone by fetched her up as his bride-to-be from somewhere right at the bottom of the map—to his mother these school reports did not matter in the least . . .

Tonio loved his dark, fiery mother, who played the piano and the mandolin so enchantingly, and he was glad that his dubious standing in human society did not grieve her. But on the other hand he felt that his father's anger was much more dignified and comme il faut, and though scolded by him he basically agreed with his father's view of the matter and found his mother's blithe unconcern slightly disreputable. Often his thoughts would run rather like this: "It's bad enough that I am as I am, that I won't and can't change and am careless and stubborn and that my mind's full of things no one else thinks about. It's at least only right and proper that I should be seriously scolded and punished for it, instead of having it all passed over with kisses and music. After all, we're not gypsies in a green caravan, but respectable people—the Krögers, Consul Kröger's family . . ." And occasionally he would reflect: "But why am I peculiar, why do I fight against everything, why am I in the masters' bad books and a stranger among the other boys? Just look at them, the good pupils and the solid mediocre ones! They don't find the masters ridiculous, they don't write poetry and they only think the kind of thoughts that one does and should think, the kind that can be spoken aloud. How decent they must feel, how at peace with everything and everyone! It must be good to be like that . . . But what is the matter with me, and what will come of it all?"

This way of thinking, this view of himself and of how he stood to life, was an important factor in Tonio's love for Hans Hansen. He loved him firstly because he was beautiful; but secondly because he saw him as his own counterpart and opposite in all respects. Hans Hansen was an outstanding pupil as well as being a fine fellow, a first-class rider and gymnast and swimmer who enjoyed universal popularity. The masters almost doted on him, called him by his first name and promoted his interests in every way; his schoolmates vied for his favor; ladies and gentlemen stopped him in the street, seized him by the shock of flaxen blond hair that stood out from under his Danish sailor's cap, and said: "Good morning, Hans Hansen, with your nice head of hair! Still top of the class? That's a fine lad! Remember me to your father and mother . . ."

Such was Hans Hansen, and ever since they had first met the very sight of him had filled Tonio Kröger with longing, an envious longing which he could feel as a burning sensation in his chest. "If only one could have blue eyes like yours," he thought, "if only one could live so normally and in such happy harmony with all the world as you do! You are always doing something suitable, something that everyone respects. When you have finished your school tasks you take riding lessons or work at things with your fretsaw, and even when you go down to the sea in the holidays you are busy rowing and sailing and swimming, while I lounge about forlornly on the sand, gazing at the mysterious changing expressions that fleet across the face of the sea. But that is why your eyes are so clear. If I could be like you . . ."

He made no attempt to become like Hans Hansen, indeed his wish to be like him was perhaps even hardly serious. But he did most painfully desire that Hans should love him for what he was; and so he sought his love, wooing him after his fashion—patiently and ardently and devotedly. It was a wooing full of anguish and sadness, and this sadness burned deeper and sharper than any impulsive passion such as might have been expected from someone of Tonio's exotic appearance.

And his wooing was not entirely in vain; for Hans, who in any case respected in Tonio a certain superiority, a certain gift of speech, a talent for expressing complicated things, sensed very clearly that he had aroused in him an unusually strong and tender feeling. He was grateful for this, and responded in a way that gave Tonio much happiness—but also cost him many a pang of jealousy and disappointment in his frustrated efforts to establish intellectual companionship between them. For oddly enough, although Tonio envied Hans Hansen for being the kind of person he was, he constantly strove to entice him into being like Tonio; and the success of such attempts could at best be only momentary and even then only apparent . . .

"I've just been reading something wonderful, something quite splendid . . ." he was saying. They were walking along eating by turns out of a paper bag of fruit lozenges which they had purchased at Iwersen's store in the Mühlenstrasse for ten pfennigs. "You must read it, Hans. It's *Don Carlos* by Schiller, actually . . . I'll lend it to you if you like . . ."

"Oh, no," said Hans Hansen, "don't bother, Tonio, that isn't my kind of thing. I'd rather stick to my horse books, you know. The illustrations in them are really super. Next time you're at my house I'll show you them. They're instantaneous photographs, so you can see the horses trotting and galloping and jumping, in all the positions—you can never see them like that in real life because they move so fast . . ."

"In all the positions?" asked Tonio politely. "Yes, that must be nice. But *Don Carlos,* you know, it's quite unbelievable. There are passages in it, you'll find, they're so beautiful they give you a jolt, it's like a kind of explosion . . ."

"An explosion?" asked Hans Hansen . . . "How do you mean?"

"For example, the passage where the king has wept because the marquis has betrayed him . . . but the marquis, you see, has only betrayed him to help the prince, he's sacrificing himself for the prince's sake. And then word is brought from the king's study into the anteroom that the king has wept. 'Wept?' 'The king wept?' All the courtiers are absolutely amazed, and it pierces you through and through, because he's a frightfully strict and stern king. But you can understand so well why he weeps, and actually I feel sorrier for him than for the prince and the marquis put together. He's always so very alone, and no one loves him, and then he thinks he has found someone, and that's the very man who betrays him . . ."

Hans Hansen glanced sideways at Tonio's face, and something in it must have aroused his interest in the subject, for he suddenly linked arms with him again and asked:

"Why, how does he betray him, Tonio?"

Tonio's heart leapt.

"Well, you see," he began, "all the dispatches for Brabant and Flanders . . ."

"Here comes Erwin Jimmerthal," said Hans.

Tonio fell silent. If only, he thought, the earth would open and swallow that fellow Jimmerthal up! Why does he have to come and interrupt us? If only he doesn't join us and spend the whole walk talking about their riding lessons! For Erwin Jimmerthal took riding lessons too. He was the bank manager's son and lived out here beyond the city wall. He had already got rid of his satchel and was advancing toward them along the avenue with his bandy legs and slitlike eyes.

"Hullo, Jimmerthal," said Hans. "I'm going for a bit of a walk with Kröger . . ."

"I've got to go into town and get something," said Jimmerthal. "But I'll walk along with you for a little way . . . Are those fruit lozenges you've got there? Yes, thanks, I'll have a couple. It's our lesson again tomorrow, Hans." He was referring to the riding lesson.

"Super!" said Hans. "I'm going to be given my leather gaiters now, you know, because I was top in the essay the other day . . ."

"You don't take riding lessons, I suppose, Kröger?" asked Jimmerthal and his eyes were just a pair of glinting slits . . .

"No . . ." replied Tonio in uncertain accents.

Hans Hansen remarked: "You should ask your father to let you have lessons too, Kröger."

"Yes . . ." said Tonio, hastily and without interest, his throat suddenly contracting because Hans had called him by his surname; Hans seemed to sense this and added by way of explanation:

"I call you Kröger because you've got such a crazy first name, you know; you mustn't mind my saying so, but I really can't stand it. Tonio . . . why, it isn't a name at all! Though of course it's not your fault, goodness me!"

"No, I suppose they called you that mainly because it sounds so foreign and special . . ." said Jimmerthal, with an air of trying to say something nice.

Tonio's mouth twitched. He pulled himself together and said:

"Yes, it's a silly name, God knows I'd rather it were Heinrich or Wilhelm, I can assure you. But it's all because I was christened after one of my mother's brothers whose name's Antonio; my mother comes from abroad, you know . . ."

Then he was silent and let the others talk on about horses and leather equipment. Hans had linked arms with Jimmerthal and was speaking with a fluent enthusiasm which *Don Carlos* could never had inspired in him . . . From time to time Tonio felt the tears welling up inside him, his nose tingled, and his chin kept trembling so that he could hardly control it . . .

Hans could not stand his name, and there was nothing to be done about it. His own name was Hans, and Jimmerthal's was Erwin—two good names which everyone recognized, to which no one could object. But "Tonio" was something foreign and special. Yes, he was a special case in every way, whether he liked it or not; he was isolated, he did not belong among decent normal people—notwithstanding the fact that he was no gypsy in a green caravan, but Consul Kröger's son, a member of the Kröger family . . . But why did Hans always call him Tonio when they were alone together, if he felt ashamed of him as soon as anyone else appeared? Sometimes indeed there was a closeness between them, he was temporarily won over. "Why, how does he betray him, Tonio?" he had asked, and had taken his arm. But the moment Jimmerthal had turned up he had breathed a sigh of relief nevertheless, he had dropped him and gratuitously criticized him for his foreign first name. How it hurt to have to understand all this so well! . . . He knew that in fact Hans Hansen did like him a little, when they were by themselves; but when anyone else was there he would feel ashamed and throw him over. And Tonio would be alone again. He thought of King Philip. The king wept . . .

"Oh, God," said Erwin Jimmerthal, "I really must go into town now. Good-bye, you two—thanks for the fruit lozenges!" Whereupon he jumped onto a wooden seat at the side of the avenue, ran along it with his bandy legs and trotted away.

"I like Jimmerthal!" said Hans emphatically. Privileged as he was, he had a self-assured way of declaring his likes and dislikes, of graciously conferring them, so to speak . . . And then, having warmed to the theme, he went on talking about his riding lessons. In any case they were by now quite near the Hansens' house; it did not take long to reach it by the promenade along the old fortifications. They clutched their caps and bent their heads before the wind, the strong damp breeze that moaned and jarred among the leafless branches. And Hans Hansen talked, with Tonio merely interjecting an occasional insincere "Ah!" or "Oh, yes," and getting no pleasure from the fact that Hans, in the excitement of his discourse, had again linked arms with him; for it was merely a superficial and meaningless contact . . .

Presently, not far from the station, they turned off the promenade; they watched a train bustling and puffing past, counted the coaches just for fun, and as the last one went by, waved to the man who sat up there wrapped in his fur overcoat. Then they stopped in the Lindenplatz in front of the villa of Herr Hansen the wholesale timber merchant, and Hans demonstrated in detail what fun it was to stand on the bottom rail of the garden gate and swing oneself to and fro on its creaking hinges. But after that he took his leave.

"Well, I must go in now," he said. "Good-bye, Tonio. Next time I'll walk *you* home, I promise."

"Good-bye, Hans," said Tonio. "It was a nice walk."

Their hands, as they touched, were all wet and rusty from the garden gate. But when Hans glanced into Tonio's eyes he seemed to recollect himself, and a look of contrition came over his handsome face.

"And by the way, I'll read *Don Carlos* sometime soon," he said quickly. "That bit about the king in his study must be super!" Whereupon he hitched his satchel under his arm and ran off through the front garden. Before disappearing into the house he turned round and nodded once more.

And Tonio Kröger sped off homeward, joy lending him wings. The wind was behind him, but it was not only the wind that bore him so lightly along.

Hans was going to read *Don Carlos,* and then they would have something in common, something they could talk about, and neither Jimmerthal nor anyone else would be able to join in! How well they understood each other! Perhaps—who could say?—he would one day even be able to get him to write poetry, like Tonio himself . . . No, no, he didn't want that to happen. Hans must never become like Tonio, but stay as he was, with his strength and his sunlike happiness which made everyone love him, and Tonio most of all! But still, it would do him no harm to read *Don Carlos.* . . . And Tonio walked under the low arch of the old gate, he walked along the quayside and up the steep, drafty, damp little street with its gabled buildings, till he reached his parents' house. His heart was alive in those days; in it there was longing, and sad envy, and just a touch of contempt, and a whole world of innocent delight.

2

Ingeborg Holm, the daughter of Dr. Holm who lived in the market square with its tall pointed complicated Gothic fountain—the fair-haired Inge it was whom Tonio Kröger loved at the age of sixteen. How did it come about? He had seen her hundreds of times; but one evening he saw her in a certain light. As she talked to a friend he saw how she had a certain way of tossing her head to one side with a saucy laugh, and a certain way of raising her hand—a hand by no means particularly tiny or delicately girlish—to smooth her hair at the back, letting her sleeve of fine white gauze slide away from her elbow. He heard her pronounce some word in a certain way, some quite insignificant word, but with a certain warm timbre in her voice. And his heart was seized by a rapture far more intense than the rapture he had sometimes felt at the sight of Hans Hansen, long ago, when he had still been a silly little boy.

That evening her image remained imprinted on his mind: her thick blond tresses, her rather narrowly cut laughing blue eyes, the delicate hint of freckles across the bridge of her nose. The timbre of her voice haunted him and he could not sleep; he tried softly to imitate the particular way she had pronounced that insignificant word, and a tremor ran through him as he did so. He knew from experience that this was love. And he knew only too well that love would cost him much pain, distress and humiliation; he knew also that it destroys the lover's peace of mind, flooding his heart with music and leaving him no time to form and shape his experience, to recollect it in tranquility and forge it into a whole. Nevertheless he accepted this love with joy, abandoning himself to it utterly and nourishing it with all the strength of his spirit; for he knew that it would enrich him and make him more fully alive—and he longed to be enriched and more fully alive, rather than to recollect things in tranquility and forge them into a whole . . .

It was thus that Tonio Kröger had lost his heart to the blithe Inge Holm; and it had happened in Frau Consul Husteede's drawing room, from which the furniture had been removed that evening, because it was the Frau Consul's turn to have the dancing class at her house. It was a private class, attended only by members of the best families, and the parents took turns in inviting all the young people together to receive their instruction in dancing and deportment. The dancing master, Herr Knaak, came once a week specially from Hamburg for this purpose.

François Knaak was his name, and what a character he was! *"J'ai l'honneur de me vous représenter,"* he would say, *"mon nom est Knaak* ... And we say this not during our bow but after it, when we are standing up straight again. Quietly, but distinctly. It does not happen every day that we have to introduce ourselves in French, but if we can do it correctly and faultlessly in that language then we are all the more likely to get it right in German."* How magnificently his silky black tailcoat clung to his plump hips! His trousers fell in soft folds over his patent leather shoes with their wide satin bows, and his brown eyes gazed round with an air of wearily satisfied consciousness of their own beauty ...

His self-assurance and urbanity were absolutely overwhelming. He would walk—and no one but he could walk with so rhythmic, so supple, so resilient, so royal a tread—up to the lady of the house, bow to her and wait for her to extend her hand. When she had done so he would murmur his thanks, step buoyantly back, turn on his left heel, smartly raise his right foot from the ground, pointing it outward and downward, and walk away with his hips swaying to and fro.

When one left a party one stepped backward out of the door, with a bow; when one fetched a chair, one did not seize it by one leg and drag it across the floor, but carried it lightly by the back and set it down noiselessly. One did not stand with one's hands crossed on one's stomach and one's tongue in the corner of one's mouth; if anyone did do so, Herr Knaak had a way of imitating the posture that put one off it for the rest of one's life ...

So much for deportment. As for dancing, Herr Knaak's mastery of that was possibly even more remarkable. The empty drawing room was lit by a gas chandelier and by candles over the fireplace. Talcum powder had been strewn on the floor and the pupils stood round in a silent semicircle; and in the adjacent room, beyond the curtained doorways, their mothers and aunts sat on plush-covered chairs watching Herr Knaak through their lorgnettes, as with a forward inclination of the body, two fingers of each hand grasping his coattails, he capered elastically through a step-by-step demonstration of the mazurka. But when he wished to dumbfound his audience utterly, he would all of a sudden and for no good reason leap vertically off the floor, whirling his legs round each other in the air with bewildering rapidity as though he were executing a trill with them, and then return to terra firma with a discreet but earth-shaking thump ...

"What a preposterous monkey!" thought Tonio Kröger to himself. But he could not fail to notice that Inge, blithe Inge Holm, would often watch Herr Knaak's every movement with rapt and smiling attention; and this was not the only reason why, in the last resort, he could not help feeling a certain grudging admiration for the dancing master's impressively controlled physique. How calm and imperturbable was Herr Knaak's gaze! His eyes did not look deeply into things, they did not penetrate to the point at which life becomes complex and sad; all they knew was that they were beautiful brown eyes. But that was why he had such a proud bearing! Yes, it was necessary to be stupid in order to be able to walk like that; and then one was loved, for then people found one charming. How well he understood why Inge, sweet fair-haired Inge, gazed at Herr Knaak the way she did. But would no girl ever look that way at Tonio?

Oh yes, it did happen. There was the daughter, for instance, of Dr. Vermehren the lawyer—Magdalena Vermehren, with her gentle mouth and her big, dark, glossy eyes so full of solemn enthusiasm. She often fell over when she danced. But when it was the ladies' turn to choose partners she always came to him; for she knew that he wrote poems, she had twice asked him to show them to her and she would often sit with her head drooping and gaze at him from a distance. But what good was that to Tonio? *He* loved Inge Holm, blithe, fair-haired Inge, who certainly despised him for his poetical scribblings . . . He watched her, he watched her narrow blue eyes so full of happiness and mockery; and an envious longing burned in his heart, a bitter insistent pain at the thought that to her he would always be an outsider and a stranger . . .

"First couple *en avant!*" said Herr Knaak, and words cannot describe how exquisitely he enunciated the nasal vowel. They were practicing quadrilles, and to Tonio Kröger's profound alarm he was in the same set as Inge Holm. He avoided her as best he could, and yet constantly found himself near her; he forced his eyes not to look at her, and yet they constantly wandered in her direction . . . And now, hand in hand with the red-haired Ferdinand Matthiessen, she came gliding and running toward him, tossed her head back and stopped opposite him, recovering her breath. Herr Heinzelmann, the pianist, attacked the keyboard with his bony hands, Herr Knaak called out his instructions and the quadrille began.

She moved to and fro in front of him, stepping and turning, forward and backward; often he caught a fragrance from her hair or from the delicate white material of her dress, and his eyes clouded over with ever-increasing pain. "I love you, dear, sweet Inge," he said to himself, and the words contained all the anguish he felt as he saw her so eagerly and happily concentrating on the dance and paying no attention to him. A wonderful poem by Theodor Storm came into his mind: "I long to sleep, to sleep, but you must dance." What a torment, what a humiliating contradiction it was to have to dance when one's heart was heavy with love . . .

"First couple *en avant!*" said Herr Knaak; the next figure was beginning. *"Compliment! Moulinet des dames! Tour de main!"* And no words can do justice to his elegant muting of the *e* in *"de."* "Second couple *en avant!*" Tonio Kröger and his partner were the second couple. *"Compliment!"* And Tonio Kröger bowed. *"Moulinet des dames!"* And Tonio Kröger, with bent head and frowning brows, laid his hand on the hands of the four ladies, on Inge Holm's hand, and danced the moulinet.

All round him people began to titter and laugh. Herr Knaak struck a ballet dancer's pose expressing stylized horror. "Oh dear, oh dear!" he exclaimed. "Stop, stop! Kröger has got mixed up with the ladies! *En arrière,* Miss Kröger, get back, *fi donc!* Everyone but you understands the steps by now. *Allons, vite!* Begone! *Retirez-vous!"* And he drew out his yellow silk handkerchief and flapped it at Tonio Kröger, chasing him back to his place.

Everyone laughed, the boys and the girls and the ladies in the next room, for Herr Knaak had turned the incident to such comical account; it was as entertaining as a play. Only Herr Heinzelmann, with a dry professional air, waited for the signal to go on playing; he was inured against Herr Knaak's devices.

And the quadrille continued. Then there was an interval. The parlormaid entered with a tray of wine jellies in clinking glass cups, closely followed by the cook with a load of plum cake. But Tonio Kröger slipped unobtrusively out of the room into the corridor, and stood with his hands on his back gazing at a window, regardless of the fact that since the venetian blind was down one could see nothing and it was therefore absurd to stand in front of this window pretending to be looking out of it.

But it was inward he was looking, inward at his own grief and longing. Why, why was he here? Why was he not sitting at the window in his own room, reading Storm's *Immensee* and occasionally glancing out into the garden where it lay in the evening light, with the old walnut tree and its heavy creaking branches? That was where he should have been. Let the others dance and enjoy them-

selves and be good at it! . . . But no, no, this was his place nevertheless—here where he knew he was near Inge, even if all he could do
was to stand by himself in the distance, listening to the hum and the
clatter and the laughter and trying to pick out her voice from among
it all, her voice so full of warmth and life. Dear, fair-haired Inge,
with your narrow-cut, laughing blue eyes! Only people who do not
read *Immensee* and never try to write anything like it can be as
beautiful and lighthearted as you; that is the tragedy! . . .

Surely she would come! Surely she would notice that he had left
the room, and feel what he was suffering, and slip out after him—
even if it was only pity that brought her—and put her hand on his
shoulder and say: "Come back and join us, don't be sad, I love
you!" And he listened to the voices behind him, waiting in senseless
excitement for her to come. But she did not come. Such things did
not happen on earth.

Had she laughed at him too, like all the others? Yes, she had,
however much he would have liked to deny it for her sake and his.
And yet he had only joined in the *moulinet des dames* because he
had been so engrossed by her presence. And what did it matter
anyway? One day perhaps they would stop laughing. Had he not
recently had a poem accepted by a periodical—even if the periodical
had gone out of business before the poem could appear? The day
was coming when he would be famous and when everything he
wrote would be printed; and then it would be seen whether that
would not impress Inge Holm . . . No; it would *not* impress her;
that was just the point. Magdalena Vermehren, the girl who was
always falling over—yes, she would be impressed. But not Inge
Holm, not blithe blue-eyed Inge, never. So what was the good of
it all? . . .

Tonio Kröger's heart contracted in anguish at the thought. How
it hurt to feel the upsurge of wonderful sad creative powers within
one, and yet to know that they can mean nothing to those happy
people at whom one gazes in love and longing across a gulf of inac-
cessibility! And yet—alone and excluded though he was, standing
hopelessly with his distress in front of a drawn blind pretending to
be looking through it—he was nevertheless happy. For his heart was
alive in those days. Warmly and sorrowfully it throbbed for you,
Ingeborg Holm, and in blissful self-forgetfulness his whole soul embraced your blond, radiant, exuberantly normal little personality.

More than once he stood thus by himself, with flushed cheeks, in
out-of-the-way corners where the music, the scent of flowers and

the clink of glasses could only faintly be heard, trying to pick out the timbre of your voice from among the other distant festive sounds; he stood there and pined for you, and was nevertheless happy. More than once it mortified him that he should be able to talk to Magdalena Vermehren, the girl who was always falling over—that she should understand him and laugh with him and be serious with him, whereas fair-haired Inge, even when he was sitting beside her, seemed distant and alien and embarrassed by him, for they did not speak the same language. And nevertheless he was happy. For happiness, he told himself, does not consist in being loved; that merely gratifies one's vanity and is mingled with repugnance. Happiness consists in loving—and perhaps snatching a few little moments of illusory nearness to the beloved. And he inwardly noted down this reflection, thought out all its implications and savored it to its very depths.

"*Fidelity!*" thought Tonio Kröger. "I will be faithful and love you, Ingeborg, for the rest of my life." For he had a well-meaning nature. And nevertheless there was a sad whisper of misgiving within him, reminding him that he had, after all, quite forgotten Hans Hansen too, although he saw him daily. And the hateful, pitiable thing was that this soft, slightly mocking voice turned out to be right. Time went by, and the day came when Tonio Kröger was no longer so unreservedly ready as he had once been to lay down his life for the blithe Inge; for he now felt within himself the desire and the power to achieve something of his own in this world, indeed to achieve in his own way much that would be remarkable.

And he hovered watchfully round the sacrificial altar on which his love burned like a pure, chaste flame; he knelt before it and did all he could to fan it and feed it and remain faithful. And he found that after a time, imperceptibly, silently and without fuss, the flame had nevertheless gone out.

But Tonio Kröger stood on for a while before the cold altar, full of astonishment and disillusionment as he realized that in this world fidelity is not possible. Then he shrugged his shoulders and went his way.

3

He went the way he had to go; rather nonchalantly and unsteadily, whistling to himself, gazing into vacancy with his head tilted to one side. And if it was the wrong way, then that was because for certain people no such thing as a right way exists. When he was asked what on earth he intended to do with his life, he would give various answers; for he would often remark (and had already written the observation down) that he carried within himself a thousand possible ways of life, although at the same time privately aware that none of them was possible at all . . .

Even before he left his native city and its narrow streets, the threads and bonds that held him to it had been quietly severed. The old Kröger family had gradually fallen into a state of decay and disintegration, and Tonio Kröger's own existence and nature were with good reason generally regarded as symptomatic of this decline. His father's mother, the family's senior and dominant member, had died; and his father, that tall, pensive, carefully dressed man with the wild flower in his buttonhole, had not been long in following her. The great Kröger mansion with all its venerable history was put up for sale and the firm was liquidated. But Tonio's mother, his beautiful fiery mother who played the piano and the mandolin so enchantingly and to whom nothing really mattered, got married again a year later—to a musician, a virtuoso with an Italian name, with whom she departed to live under far-off blue skies. Tonio Kröger thought this slightly disreputable; but who was he to set himself against it? He wrote poetry and could not even give an answer when asked what on earth he intended to do with his life . . .

So he left his hometown with its gabled houses and the damp wind whistling round them; he left the fountain and the old walnut tree in the garden, those faithful companions of his youth; he left the sea too, his beloved sea, and left it all without a pang. For he was grown up and enlightened now, he understood his situation and was full of contempt for the crude and primitive way of life that had enveloped him for so long.

He surrendered himself utterly to that power which he felt to be the sublimest power on earth, to the service of which he felt called and which promised him honor and renown: the power of intellect and words, a power that sits smilingly enthroned above mere inarticulate, unconscious life. He surrendered to it with youthful passion, and it rewarded him with all that it has to give, while inexorably exacting its full price in return.

It sharpened his perceptions and enabled him to see through the high-sounding phrases that swell the human breast, it unlocked for him the mysteries of the human mind and of his own, it made him clear-sighted, it showed him life from the inside and revealed to him the fundamental motives behind what men say and do. But what did he see? Absurdity and wretchedness—absurdity and wretchedness. And with the torment and the pride of such insight came loneliness; for he could not feel at ease among the innocent, among the light of heart and dark of understanding, and they shrank from the sign on his brow. But at the same time he savored ever more sweetly the delight of words and of form, for he would often remark (and had already written the observation down) that mere knowledge of human psychology would in itself infallibly make us despondent if we were not cheered and kept alert by the satisfaction of expressing it . . .

He lived in large cities in the south, for he felt that his art would ripen more lushly in the southern sun; and perhaps it was heredity on his mother's side that drew him there. But because his heart was dead and had no love in it, he fell into carnal adventures, far into the hot guilty depths of sensuality, although such experiences cost him intense suffering. Perhaps it was because of something inside him inherited from his father—from the tall, pensive, neatly dressed man with the wild flower in his buttonhole—that he suffered so much there: something that often stirred within him the faint nostalgic recollection of a more heartfelt joy he had once known and which now, amid these other pleasures, he could never recapture.

He was seized by revulsion, by a hatred of the senses, by a craving for purity and decency and peace of mind; and yet he was breathing the atmosphere of art, the mild, sweet, heavily fragrant air of a continual spring in which everything sprouts and burgeons and germinates in mysterious procreative delight. And so he could do no more than let himself be cast helplessly to and fro between gross extremes, between icy intellectuality on the one hand and devouring feverish lust on the other. The life he lived was exhausting, tormented by remorse, extravagant, dissipated and monstrous, and one which Tonio Kröger himself in his heart of hearts abhorred. "How far astray I have gone!" he would sometimes think. "How was it possible for me to become involved in all these eccentric adventures? After all, I wasn't born a Gypsy in a green caravan . . ."

But as his health suffered, so his artistry grew more refined: it became fastidious, exquisite, rich, subtle, intolerant of banality and hypersensitive in matters of tact and taste. His first publication was received by the competent critics with considerable acclaim and appreciation, for it was a well-made piece of work, full of humor and the knowledge of suffering. And very soon his name—the same name that had once been shouted at him by angry schoolmasters, the name with which he had signed his first verses addressed to the sea and the walnut tree and the fountain, this mixture of southern and northern sounds, this respectable middle-class name with an exotic flavor—became a formula betokening excellence. For the profound painfulness of his experience of life was allied to a rare capacity for hard, ambitious, unremitting toil; and of this perseverance, joined in anguished combat with his fastidiously sensitive taste, works of quite unusual quality were born.

He worked, not like a man who works in order to live, but like one who has no desire but to work, because he sets no store by himself as a living human being, seeks recognition only as a creative artist, and spends the rest of his time in a gray incognito, like an actor with his makeup off, who has no identity when he is not performing. He worked in silence, in invisible privacy, for he utterly despised those minor hacks who treated their talent as a social ornament—who whether they were poor or rich, whether they affected an unkempt and shabby appearance or sumptuous individualistic neckwear, aimed above all else at living happily, charmingly, and artistically, little suspecting that good work is brought forth only under the pressure of a bad life, that living and working are incompatible and that one must have died if one is to be wholly a creator.

4

"Do I disturb you?" asked Tonio Kröger, pausing at the studio door. He had his hat in his hand and even bowed slightly, although Lisaveta Ivanovna was an intimate friend and he could talk to her about anything.

"For pity's sake, Tonio Kröger, come in and never mind the politeness," she answered in her jerky accent. "We all know that you were well brought up and taught how to behave." So saying, she transferred her brush to the same hand as her palette, held out her right hand to him and gazed at him laughingly, shaking her head.

"Yes, but you're working," he said. "Let me see ... Oh, but you've made progress." And he looked by turns at the color sketches propped against chair backs on either side of the easel, and at the great canvas marked off in squares and covered with a confused schematic charcoal sketch on which the first patches of color were beginning to appear.

They were in Munich, in a rear apartment on the Schellingstrasse, several floors up. Outside the wide north-facing window the sky was blue, the birds twittered and the sun shone; and the young sweet spring air, streaming in through an open pane, mingled in the large studio with the smell of fixative and oil paint. The bright golden afternoon light flooded unhindered all over the bare spacious room, frankly showing up the rather worn floorboards, falling on the rough window table covered with brushes and tubes and little bottles, and on the unframed studies that hung on the unpapered walls; it fell on the torn silk screen that enclosed a tastefully furnished little living corner near the door; it fell on the work that was gradually taking shape on the easel, and on the painter and the writer as they looked at it.

She was about the same age as himself, rather over thirty. In her dark blue paint-stained overall she sat on a low stool, propping her chin in her hand. Her brown hair was firmly set, graying a little at the sides already, and slightly waved over the temples; it framed a dark, very charming face of Slav cut, with a snub nose, prominent cheekbones and little shiny black eyes. Tensely, skeptically, with an air almost of irritation, she scrutinized her work from the side, with her eyes half closed.

He stood beside her with his right hand on his hip and his left hand rapidly twirling his brown moustache. His slanting brows were frowning and working energetically, and he whistled softly to himself as usual. He was very carefully and punctiliously dressed, in a quiet gray suit of reserved cut. But his forehead, under the dark hair with its exceedingly correct and simple parting, twitched nervously, and his southern features were already sharp, clear-cut and traced as if with a hard chisel, although his mouth and chin were so gently and softly outlined . . . Presently he drew his hand across his forehead and eyes and turned away.

"I shouldn't have come," he said.

"Why not, Tonio Kröger?"

"I've just been working, Lisaveta, and inside my head everything looks just as it does on this canvas. A skeleton, a faint sketch, a mess of corrections, and a few patches of color, to be sure; and now I come here and see the same thing. And the same contradiction is here too," he said, sniffing the air, "the same conflict that was bothering me at home. It's odd. Once a thought has got hold of you, you find expressions of it everywhere, you even *smell* it in the wind, don't you? Fixative and the scent of spring! Art and—well, what is the opposite? Don't call it 'nature,' Lisaveta, 'nature' isn't an adequate term. Oh, no, I daresay I ought to have gone for a walk instead, though the question is whether that would have made me feel any better! Five minutes ago, quite near here, I met a colleague— Adalbert, the short-story writer. 'God damn the spring!' he said in his aggressive way. 'It is and always was the most abominable season of the year! Can you think a single thought that makes sense, Krö- ger? Have you peace of mind enough to work out any little thing, anything pointed and effective, with all this indecent itching in your blood and a whole swarm of irrelevant sensations pestering you, which turn out when you examine them to be absolutely trivial, unusable rubbish? As for me, I'm off to a café. It's neutral territory, you know, untouched by change of season; it so to speak symbolizes literature—that remote and sublime sphere in which one is incapable of grosser thoughts . . .' And off he went into the café; and perhaps I should have followed him."

Lisaveta was amused.

"Very good, Tonio Kröger! 'Indecent itching'—that's good. And he's not far wrong, because one really doesn't get much work done in spring. But now listen to me. I am now, in spite of the spring, going to do this little piece here—work out this pointed little effect, as Adalbert would say—and then we shall go into my 'salon' and have some tea, and you shall tell me all; for I can see well enough that you have got a lot on your mind today. Until then please arrange yourself somewhere—on that chest, for example, unless you think your aristocratic garments will be the worse for it . . ."

"Oh, stop going on at me about my clothes, Lisaveta Ivanovna! Would you like me to be running around town in a torn velvet jacket or a red silk waistcoat? As an artist I'm already enough of an adventurer in my inner life. So far as outward appearances are concerned one should dress decently, damn it, and behave like a respectable citizen . . . No, I haven't got a lot on my mind," he went on, watching her mix some colors on her palette. "As I told you, I'm just preoccupied with a certain problem and contradiction, and it's been preventing me from working . . . What were we talking about just now? Yes: Adalbert, the short-story writer—he's a proud man and knows his own mind. 'Spring is the most abominable sea- son,' he said, and went into a café. One must know what one wants, mustn't one? You see, I get nervous in spring too; I get distracted by the sweet trivial memories and feelings it revives in me. The difference is that I can't bring myself to put the blame on the spring and to despise it; for the fact is that the spring makes me feel ashamed. I am put to shame by its pure naturalness, its triumphant youthfulness. And I don't know whether to envy or despise Adalbert for not having any such reaction . . .

"One certainly does work badly in spring: and why? Because one's feelings are being stimulated. And only amateurs think that a creative artist can afford to have feelings. It's a naive amateur illusion; any genuine honest artist will smile at it. Sadly, perhaps, but he will smile. Because, of course, *what* one says must never be one's main concern. It must merely be the raw material, quite indifferent in itself, out of which the work of art is made; and the act of making must be a game, aloof and detached, performed in tranquility. If you attach too much importance to what you have to say, if it means too much to you emotionally, then you may be certain that your work will be a complete fiasco. You will become solemn, you will become sentimental, you will produce something clumsy, ponderous, pompous, ungainly, unironical, insipid, dreary and commonplace; it will be of no interest to anyone, and you yourself will end up disillusioned and miserable . . . For that is how it is, Lisaveta: emotion, warm, heartfelt emotion, is invariably commonplace and unserviceable—only the stimulation of our corrupted nervous system, its cold ecstasies and acrobatics, can bring forth art. One simply has to be something inhuman, something standing outside humanity, strangely remote and detached from its concerns, if one is to have the ability or indeed even the desire to play this game with it, to play with men's lives, to portray them effectively and tastefully. Our stylistic and formal talent, our gift of expression, itself presupposes this cold-blooded, fastidious attitude to mankind, indeed it presupposes a certain human impoverishment and stagnation. For the fact is: all healthy emotion, all strong emotion lacks taste. As soon as an artist becomes human and begins to feel, he is finished as an artist. Adalbert knew this, and that is why he retreated into a café, into the 'remote sphere'—ah yes!"

"Well, God be with him, *batushka,*" said Lisaveta, washing her hands in a tin basin. "After all, there's no need for you to follow him."

"No, Lisaveta, I shall not follow him; and the only reason I shall not is that I am occasionally capable, when confronted with spring, of feeling slightly ashamed of being an artist. You know, I sometimes get letters from complete strangers, from appreciative and grateful readers, expressions of admiration from people whom my work has moved. I read these communications and am touched by the warm, clumsy emotions stirred up by my art—I am overcome by a kind of pity for the enthusiastic naiveté that speaks from every line, and I blush to think what a sobering effect it would have on the honest man who wrote such a letter if he could ever take a look behind the scenes, if his innocent mind could ever grasp the fact that the last thing any proper, healthy, decent human being ever does is to write or act or compose ... Though needless to say all this does not stop me using his admiration for my genius as an enrichment and a stimulus; I still take it uncommonly seriously and ape the solemn airs of a great man ... Oh, don't start contradicting me, Lisaveta! I tell you I am often sick to death of being a portrayer of humanity and having no share in human experience ... Can one even say that an artist *is* a man? Let Woman answer that! I think we artists are all in rather the same situation as those artificial papal sopranos ... Our voices are quite touchingly beautiful. But—"

"Be ashamed of yourself, Tonio Kröger. Come along and have tea. The water will be boiling in a minute, and here are some *papirosi*. Now, you stopped at the soprano singers; so please continue from that point. But you ought to be a little ashamed of what you are saying. If I did not know how passionately devoted to your profession and how proud of it you are ..."

"Don't speak to me of my 'profession,' Lisaveta Ivanovna! Literature isn't a profession at all, I'll have you know—it is a curse. And when do we first discover that this curse has come upon us? At a terribly early age. An age when by rights one should still be living at peace and harmony with God and the world. You begin to feel that you are a marked man, mysteriously different from other people, from ordinary normal folk; a gulf of irony, of skepticism, of antagonism, of awareness, of sensibility, is fixed between you and your fellow men—it gets deeper and deeper, it isolates you from them, and in the end all communication with them becomes impossible. What a fate! Always supposing, of course, that you still have enough feeling, enough *love* left in your heart to know how appalling it is ... You develop an exacerbated self-consciousness, because you are well aware that you are marked out among thousands by a sign on your brow which no one fails to notice. I once knew an actor of genius who, as a man, had to struggle against a morbid instability and lack of confidence. This was how his overstimulated consciousness of himself affected him when he was not actually engaged in performing a part. He was a consummate artist and an impoverished human being ... A real artist is not one who has taken up art as his profession, but a man predestined and foredoomed to it; and such an artist can be picked out from a crowd by anyone with the slightest perspicacity. You can read in his face that he is a man apart, a man who does not belong, who feels that he is recognized and is being watched; there is somehow an air of royalty about him and at the same time an air of embarrassment. A prince walking incognito among the people wears a rather similar expression. But the incognito doesn't work, Lisaveta! Disguise yourself, put on civilian costume, dress up like an attaché or a guards lieutenant on leave—you will hardly have raised your eyes and uttered a word before everyone will know that you are not a human being but something strange, something alien, something different . . .

"But what *is* an artist? I know of no other question to which human complacency and incuriosity has remained so impervious. 'That sort of thing is a gift,' say average decent folk humbly, when a work of art has produced its intended effect upon them; and because in the goodness of their hearts they assume that exhilarating and noble effects must necessarily have exhilarating and noble causes, it never enters their heads that the origins of this so-called 'gift' may well be extremely dubious and extremely disreputable . . . It's well known that artists are easily offended; and it's also well known that this is not usually the case with people who have a good conscience and solidly grounded self-confidence . . . You see, Lisaveta, I harbor in my very soul a rooted suspicion of the artist as a type—I suspect him no less deeply, though in a more intellectual way, than every one of my honorable ancestors up there in that city of narrow streets would have suspected any sort of mountebank or performing adventurer who had strolled into his house. Listen to this. I know a banker, a middle-aged man of business, who has a talent for writing short stories. He exercises this talent in his spare time, and what he writes is often quite first class. Despite—I call it 'despite'—this admirable gift he is a man of not entirely blameless reputation: on the contrary he has already served quite a heavy prison sentence, and for good reason. In fact it was actually in jail that he first became aware of his talents, and his experiences as a prisoner are the basic theme in all his work. One might draw the rather fanciful conclusion from this that it is necessary to have been in some kind of house of correction if one is to become a writer. But can one help suspecting that in its roots and origins his artistic tendency had less to do with his experiences in jail than with *what got him sent there*? A banker who writes short stories: that's an oddity, isn't it? But a banker with no criminal record and no stain

on his character who writes short stories—*there's no such phenome-*
non . . . Yes, you may laugh, but I am half serious nevertheless.
There's no problem on earth so tantalizing as the problem of what
an artist is and what art does to human beings. Take the case of
the most remarkable masterpiece of the most typical and therefore
mightiest of all artists—take a morbid, profoundly equivocal work
like *Tristan and Isolde,* and observe the effects of this work on a
young, healthy listener of entirely normal sensibility. He will be filled
with exaltation, animation, warm, honest enthusiasm, perhaps even
inspired to 'artistic' creative efforts of his own . . . Poor, decent
dilettante! We artists have an inner life very different from what our
'warmhearted' admirers in their 'genuine enthusiasm' imagine. I
have seen artists with women and young men crowding round them,
applauding and idolizing them, artists about whom *I knew the truth*
. . . The sources and side-effects and preconditions of artistic talent
are something about which one constantly makes the most curious
discoveries . . ."

"Discoveries, Tonio Kröger—forgive my asking—about other artists? Or not only about others?"

He did not reply. He contracted his slanting brows in a frown and
whistled to himself.

"Give me your cup, Tonio. The tea's not strong. And have another
cigarette. And in any case you know very well that it is not necessary
to take such a view of things as you are taking . . ."

"That's Horatio's answer, isn't it, my dear Lisaveta. ''Twere to
consider too curiously to consider so.'"

"I mean, Tonio Kröger, that they can be considered just as curiously from another angle. I am only a stupid painting female, and
if I can manage to make any reply to you, and offer some sort of
defense of your own profession against you, I am sure there will be
nothing new to you in what I say; I can only remind you of things
you know very well yourself . . . Of the purifying, sanctifying effect
of literature, for example; of the way our passions dissolve when
they are grasped by insight and expressed in words; of literature as
a path to understanding, to forgiveness and love. Think of the redeeming power of language, of the literary intellect as the sublimest
manifestation of the human spirit, of the writer as supreme humanity, the writer as a saint—to consider things so, is that not to consider them curiously enough?"

"You have a right to talk that way, Lisaveta Ivanovna, and it is
conferred upon you by your national literature, by the sublime writ-

ers of Russia; their work I will willingly worship as the sacred literature of which you speak. But I have not left your objections out of
account, on the contrary they too are part of what I have got on
my mind today . . . Look at me. I don't look exactly bursting with
high spirits, do I? Rather old and sharp-featured and weary, don't
I? Well, to revert to the subject of 'insight': can you not imagine
someone with an innately unskeptical disposition, placid and well
meaning and a bit sentimental, being quite literally worn out and
destroyed by psychological enlightenment? Not to let oneself be
overwhelmed by the sadness of everything; to observe and study it
all, to put even anguish into a category, and to remain in a good
humor into the bargain, if only because of one's proud consciousness
of moral superiority over the abominable invention of existence—
oh, yes, indeed! But there are times, notwithstanding all the delights
of expression, when the whole thing becomes a little too much for
one. *'Tout comprendre c'est tout pardonner?'* I'm not so sure. There
is something that I call the nausea of knowledge, Lisaveta: a state
of mind in which a man has no sooner seen through a thing than so
far from feeling reconciled to it he is immediately sickened to death
by it. This was how Hamlet felt, Hamlet the Dane, that typical
literary artist. He knew what it was like to be called upon to bear
a burden of knowledge for which one was not born. To be clear-
sighted even through the mist of tears—even then to have to understand, to study, to observe and ironically to discard what one has
seen—even at moments when hands clasp and lips touch and eyes
fail, blinded by emotion—it's infamous, Lisaveta, it's contemptible
and outrageous . . . But what's the use of feeling outraged?

"Another equally charming aspect of the matter, of course, is the
way one becomes sophisticated and indifferent to truth, blasé and
weary of it all. It's well known that you'll never find such mute
hopelessness as among a gathering of intellectuals, all of them thoroughly hagridden already. All insights are old and stale to them. Try
telling them about some truth you have discovered, in the acquisition
and possession of which you perhaps feel a certain youthful pride,
and their response to your vulgar knowledgeableness will be a very
brief expulsion of air through the nose . . . Oh yes, Lisaveta, literature wears people out! I assure you that in ordinary human society,
by sheer skepticism and suspension of judgment, one can give the
impression of being stupid, whereas in fact one is merely arrogant
and lacking in courage . . . So much for 'insight.' As for 'words,' I
wonder if they really redeem our passions: is it not rather that they

refrigerate them and put them in cold storage? Don't you seriously
think that there is a chilling, outrageous effrontery in the instant
facile process by which literary language eliminates emotion? What
does one do when one's heart is too full, when some sweet or sublime experience has moved one too deeply? The answer is simple!
Apply to a writer: the whole thing will be settled in a trice. He will
analyze it all for you, formulate it, name it, express it and make it
articulate, and so far as you are concerned the entire affair will be
eliminated once and for all: he will have turned it for you into a
matter of total indifference, and will not even expect you to thank
him for doing so. But you will go home with your heart lightened,
all warmth and all mystery dispelled, wondering why on earth you
were distraught with such delicious excitement only a moment ago.
Can we seriously defend this vain coldhearted charlatan? Anything
that has been expressed has thereby been eliminated—that is his
creed. When the whole world has been expressed, it too will have
been eliminated, redeemed, abolished . . . *Très bien!* But I am not a
nihilist . . ."

"You are not a—" said Lisaveta . . . She was just about to take a
sip of tea and stopped dead with the spoon near her mouth.

"Well, of course not . . . What's the matter with you, Lisaveta! I
tell you I am not a nihilist inasmuch as I affirm the value of living
emotion. Don't you see, what the literary artist basically fails to
grasp is that life goes on, that it is not ashamed to go on living,
even after it has been expressed and 'eliminated.' Lo and behold!
Literature may redeem it as much as it pleases, it just carries on in
its same old sinful way; for to the intellectual eye all activity is
sinful . . .

"I'm nearly finished, Lisaveta. Listen to me. I love life—that is a
confession. I present it to you for safekeeping; you are the first
person to whom I have made it. It has been said, it has even been
written and printed, that I hate or fear or despise or abominate life.
I enjoy this suggestion, I have always felt flattered by it; but it is
nonetheless false. I love life . . . You smile, Lisaveta, and I know
why. But I implore you not to mistake what I am saying for mere
literature! Do not think of Cesare Borgia or of any drunken philosophy that makes him its hero! This Cesare Borgia is nothing to me,
I feel not a particle of respect for him, and I shall never be able to
understand this idealization and cult of the extraordinary and the
demonic. No: 'life' confronts intellect and art as their eternal opposite—but not as a vision of bloodstained greatness and savage

beauty. We who are exceptions do not see life as something exceptional; on the contrary! normality, respectability, decency—these are our heart's desire, this to us is life, life in its seductive banality! No one, my dear, has a right to call himself an artist if his profoundest craving is for the refined, the eccentric and the satanic—if his heart knows no longing for innocence, simplicity and living warmth, for a little friendship and self-surrender and familiarity and human happiness—if he is not secretly devoured, Lisaveta, by this longing for the bliss of the commonplace! ...

"A human friend! Will you believe me when I say that it would make me proud and happy to win the friendship of a human being? But until now all my friends have been demons, hobgoblins, phantoms struck dumb by the ghoulish profundity of their insight—in other words, men of letters.

"Sometimes I find myself on some public platform, facing a roomful of people who have come to listen to me. Do you know, it can happen on such occasions that I find myself surveying the audience, I catch myself secretly peering round the hall, and in my heart there is a question: Who are these who have come to me, whose is this grateful applause I hear, with whom have I achieved this spiritual union through my art? ... I don't find what I am looking for, Lisaveta. I find my own flock, my familiar congregation, a sort of gathering of early Christians: people with clumsy bodies and refined souls, the kind of people, so to speak, who are always falling over when they dance, if you see what I mean; people to whom literature is a quiet way of taking their revenge on life—all of them sufferers, all repining and impoverished: never once is there one of the others among them, Lisaveta, one of the blue-eyed innocents who don't need intellect! ...

"And after all it would be deplorably inconsistent, wouldn't it, to be glad if things were otherwise! It is absurd to love life and nevertheless to be trying with all the skill at one's command to entice it from its proper course, to interest it in our melancholy subtleties, in this whole sick aristocracy of literature. The kingdom of art is enlarging its frontiers in this world, and the realm of health and innocence is dwindling. What is left of it should be most carefully preserved: we have no right to try to seduce people into reading poetry when they would much rather be looking at books full of snapshots of horses!

"For when all's said and done, can you imagine a more pitiable spectacle than that of life attempting to be artistic! There is no one whom we artists so utterly despise as the dilettante, the living human being who thinks he can occasionally try his hand at being an artist as well. I assure you this particular kind of contempt is very familiar to me from personal experience. I am a guest, let us say, at a party, among members of the best society; we are eating and drinking and talking, and all getting on famously, and I am feeling glad and grateful to have escaped for a while into the company of simple, conventionally decent people who are treating me as an equal. And suddenly (this actually happened to me once) an officer rises to his feet, a lieutenant, a good-looking, fine upstanding man whom I should never have believed capable of any conduct unbecoming his uniform, and asks in so many words for permission to recite to us a few lines of verse which he has composed. The permission is granted, with some smiling and raising of eyebrows, and he carries out his intention: he produces a piece of paper which he has hitherto been concealing in his coattail pocket, and he reads us his work. It was something or other about music and love, deeply felt and totally inept. I ask you: a lieutenant! A man of the world! What need was there for him to do it, good heavens above! . . . Well, there was the predictable result: long faces, silence, a little polite applause and everyone feeling thoroughly uncomfortable. The first psychological effect upon myself of which I became aware was a feeling that I too, and not only this rash young man, was to blame for spoiling the party; and sure enough there were some mocking and unfriendly glances in my direction as well, for it was my trade he had bungled. But my second reaction was that this man, for whose character and way of life I had only a moment ago felt the sincerest respect, suddenly began to sink and sink and sink in my esteem . . . I felt sorry for him, I was filled with benevolent indulgence toward him. I and one or two other good-natured guests plucked up heart to approach him with a few encouraging words. 'Congratulations, lieutenant!' I said. 'What a charming talent you have! That was really very pretty!' And I very nearly patted him on the shoulder. But is indulgence a proper thing to feel toward a lieutenant? . . . It was his own fault! There he stood, in utter embarrassment, suffering the penalty of having supposed that one may pluck even a single leaf from the laurel-tree of art and not pay for it with one's life. Oh, no! Give me my colleague, the banker with the criminal record . . . But don't you think, Lisaveta, that my eloquence today is worthy of Hamlet?"

"Have you finished now, Tonio Kröger?"

"No. But I shall say no more."

"Well, you have certainly said enough. Are you expecting an answer?"

"Have you got one for me?"

"I certainly have. I have listened to you carefully, Tonio, from beginning to end, and I will now tell you what the answer is to everything you have said this afternoon, and what the solution is to the problem that has been worrying you so much. So! The solution is quite simply that you are, and always will be, a bourgeois."

"Am I?" he asked, with a somewhat crestfallen air . . .

"That's a hard home truth for you, isn't it. And I don't wonder. So I don't mind modifying it a little, for it so happens that I can. You are a bourgeois who has taken the wrong turning, Tonio Kröger—a bourgeois manqué."

There was silence. Then he got up resolutely and seized his hat and walking stick.

"Thank you, Lisaveta Ivanovna; now I can go home with a good conscience. *I have been eliminated.*"

5

Near the end of the summer Tonio Kröger said to Lisaveta Ivanovna:

"Well, I'm leaving now, Lisaveta; I must have a change of air, a change of scene, I must get away from it all."

"So, *batushka*, I suppose you will honor Italy with another visit?"

"Oh God, Lisaveta, don't talk to me of Italy! I am bored with Italy to the point of despising it! It's a long time since I thought I felt at home there. The land of art! Velvet blue skies, heady wine and sweet sensuality . . . No thank you, that's not for me. I renounce it. All that *bellezza* gets on my nerves. And I can't stand all that dreadful southern vivacity, all those people with their black animal eyes. They've no conscience in their eyes, those Latin races . . . No, this time I'm going for a little trip to Denmark."

"Denmark?"

"Yes. And I think I shall benefit from it. It so happens that I've never yet got round to going there, although I was so near the frontier during the whole of my youth, and yet it's a country I've always known about and loved. I suppose I must get this northern predilection from my father, for my mother really preferred the *bellezza*, you know, that is insofar as anything mattered to her at all. But think of the books they write up there in the north, Lisaveta, books of such depth and purity and humor—there's nothing like them, I love them. Think of the Scandinavian meals, those incomparable meals, only digestible in a strong salty air—in fact, I doubt if I shall be able to digest them at all now; I know them too from my childhood, the food's just like that even where I come from. And just think of the names, the names they christen people by up there—you'll find a lot of them in my part of the world as well: names like 'Ingeborg,' for instance—three syllables plucked on a harp of purest poetry. And then there's the sea—one is on the Baltic Sea up there! . . . Anyway, that's where I'm going, Lisaveta. I want to see the Baltic again, to hear those names again, to read those books in the country where they were written; and I want to stand on the battlements at Kronborg, where the 'spirit'* descended upon Hamlet and brought anguish and death to the poor noble youth . . ."

"How shall you travel, Tonio, if I may ask? What route will you be taking?"

"The usual route," he said, shrugging his shoulders and blushing visibly. "Yes, I shall be passing through my—my point of departure, Lisaveta, after these thirteen years, and I daresay it may be a rather odd experience."

She smiled.

"That's what I wanted to hear, Tonio Kröger. Well, be off with you, in God's name. And be sure you write to me, won't you? I'm looking forward to an eventful description of your journey to—Denmark . . ."

6

And Tonio Kröger traveled north. He traveled first class (for he would often say that a man whose psychological problems are so much more difficult than those of other people has a right to a little external comfort) and he continued without a halt until the towers of his native town, that town of narrow streets, rose before him into the gray sky. There he made a brief and singular sojourn . . .

It was a dreary afternoon, already almost evening, when the train steamed into the little smoke-stained terminus which he remembered with such strange vividness; under its dirty glass roof the smoke was still rolling up into clouds or drifting to and fro in straggling wisps, just as it had done long ago when Tonio Kröger had left this place

---

*Mann here untranslatably plays upon two different meanings of the word *Geist* ("intellect" and "ghost").—Tr.

with nothing but mockery in his heart. He saw to his luggage, gave instructions that it was to be sent to his hotel and left the station.

There stood the cabs, black and absurdly tall and wide, each drawn by a pair of horses, the cabs that had always been used in this town, waiting in a row outside the station! He did not take one; he merely looked at them, and he looked at everything else as well: the narrow gables and the pointed towers that looked back at him over the nearby roofs, the fair-haired, easygoing, unsophisticated people with their broad yet rapid way of talking—there they were, all round him, and laughter welled up within him, strangely hysterical laughter that was not far from tears. He went on foot, walking slowly, feeling the steady pressure of the damp wind on his face; he crossed the bridge, with its parapets decorated by mythological statues, and walked a little way along the quayside.

Great heavens, what a tiny, nookshotten place it all seemed! Had it been like this all these years, with these narrow gabled streets climbing so steeply and quaintly up into the town? The ships' funnels and masts swayed gently in the dusk as the wind swept across the dull gray river. Should he walk up that street now, that street that led to the house he remembered so well? No, he would go tomorrow. He was feeling so sleepy now. The journey had made him drowsy, and his head was full of drifting nebulous thoughts.

Occasionally during these thirteen years, when suffering from indigestion, he had dreamed he was at home again in the old, echoing house on the slanting street, and that his father was there again too, indignantly upbraiding him for his degenerate way of life; and he had always felt that this was entirely as it should be. And he could in no way distinguish his present impressions from one of these delusive and compelling fabrications of the dreaming mind during which one asks oneself whether this is fantasy or reality and is driven firmly to the latter conclusion, only to end by waking up after all . . . He advanced through the half empty, drafty streets, bending his head before the breeze, moving like a sleepwalker toward the hotel where he had decided to spend the night, the best hotel in the town. Ahead of him, a bowlegged man with rolling nautical gait was carrying a pole with a little flame at the top, and lighting the gas lamps with it.

What was he really feeling? Under the ashes of his weariness something was glowing, obscurely and painfully, not flickering up into a clear flame: what was it? Hush, he must not say it! He must not put it into words! He would have liked to stroll on indefinitely, in the wind and the dusk, along these familiar streets of his dreams. But it was all so close, so near together. One reached one's destination at once.

In the upper part of the town there were arc-lamps, and they were just coming alight. There was the hotel, and there were the two black lions couched in front of it; as a child he had always been afraid of them. They were still staring at each other, looking as if they were just about to sneeze; but they seemed to have grown much smaller now. Tonio Kröger walked between them into the hotel.

As a guest arriving on foot he was received without much ceremony. He encountered the inquiring gaze of the porter and of a very smartly dressed gentleman in black who was doing the honors, and who had a habit of constantly pushing his shirt cuffs back into his coat sleeves with his little fingers. They both looked him carefully up and down from head to foot, obviously trying hard to place him, to assign him an approximate position in the social hierarchy which would determine the degree of respect that was his due; they were unable, however, to reach a satisfying conclusion on this point, and therefore decided in favor of a moderate show of politeness. A mild-mannered waiter with sandy side-whiskers, a frock coat shiny with age, and rosettes on his noiseless shoes, conducted him two floors up to a neatly furnished old-fashioned room. From its window, in the twilight, there was a picturesque medieval view of courtyards, gables and the bizarre massive outlines of the church near which the hotel was situated. Tonio Kröger stood for a while looking out of this window; then he sat with folded arms on the commodious sofa, frowning and whistling to himself.

Lights were brought, and his luggage arrived. At the same time the mild-mannered waiter laid the registration form on the table, and Tonio Kröger, with his head tilted to one side, scrawled something on it that would pass for his name and status and place of origin. He then ordered some supper and continued to stare into vacancy from the corner of his sofa. When the food had been placed before him he left it untouched for a long time, then finally ate a morsel or two and walked up and down in the room for another hour, occasionally stopping and closing his eyes. Then he slowly undressed and went to bed. He slept for a long time and had confused, strangely nostalgic dreams.

When he woke up his room was full of broad daylight. In some haste and confusion he recalled where he was, and got up to draw the curtains. The blue of the late summer sky was already rather pale, and covered with wind-reft wisps of cloud; but the sun was shining over his native town.

He devoted more care than usual to his toilet, washed and shaved meticulously until he was as fresh and immaculate as if he were about to pay a call on a conventional well-bred family with whom he would have to look his best and be on his best behavior; and as he went through the processes of dressing he listened to the anxious beating of his heart.

How bright it was outside! He would have felt better if the streets had been dusky like yesterday; but now he would have to walk through clear sunlight exposed to the public gaze. Would he meet people he knew, would they stop him and call him to account by asking him how he had spent the last thirteen years? No, thank God, no one knew him now, and anyone who remembered him would not recognize him, for he had indeed somewhat changed in the meantime. He inspected himself attentively in the mirror, and suddenly felt safer behind his mask, behind his face on which experience had laid its mark early, his face that was older than his years . . . He sent for breakfast, and then he went out, passing through the front hall under the calculating gaze of the porter and the elegant gentleman in black, and passing out into the street between the two lions.

Where was he going? He scarcely knew. He had the same sensation as yesterday. No sooner was he surrounded again by this strangely dignified and long-familiar complex of gables, turrets, arcades and fountains—no sooner did he feel again on his face the pressure of the wind, this strong fresh wind full of the delicate sharp flavor of distant dreams—than a misty veil of fantasy benumbed his senses . . . The muscles of his face relaxed; and his eyes as he gazed at people and things had grown calm. Perhaps, at the next corner, just over there, he would wake up after all . . .

Where was he going? He had an impression that the route he chose was not unconnected with last night's sad and strangely rueful dreams . . . He walked to the market square, under the arcades of the town hall; here were the butchers, weighing their wares with bloodstained hands, and here on the square was the tall pointed complicated Gothic fountain. Here he paused in front of a certain house, a simple narrow house much like any of the others, with an ornamental pierced gable. He stood gazing at it, read the name on the plate by the door, and let his eyes rest for a little on each of the windows in turn. Then he turned slowly away.

Where was he going? He was going home. But he made a detour, he took a walk outside the old city walls, for he had plenty of time. He walked along the Mühlenwall and the Holstenwall, clutching his hat before the wind that rustled and jarred among the trees. Presently, not far from the station, he turned off the promenade, watched a train bustling and puffing past, counted the coaches just for fun and gazed after the man who sat up there on the last one as it went by. But in the Lindenplatz he stopped in front of one of its handsome villas, stared for a long time into the garden and up at the windows, and finally took to swinging the iron gate to and fro on its creaking hinges. He gazed for a few moments at his hands, cold now and stained with rust; then he went on his way, he walked under the low arch of the old gate, along the harbor and up the steep drafty little street to his parents' house.

There it stood, surrounded by the neighboring buildings, its gable rising above them: it was as gray and solemn as it had been for the last three hundred years, and Tonio Kröger read the pious motto engraved over the doorway in letters now half obliterated. Then he took a deep breath and went in.

His heart was beating anxiously, for it would not have surprised him if his father had thrown open one of the doors on the ground floor as he passed them, emerging in his office coat and with his pen behind his ear to confront him and take him severely to task for his dissolute life; and Tonio would have felt that this was just as it should be. But he got past without being interfered with by anyone. The inner door of the porch was not closed, only left ajar, a fact which he noted with disapproval, although at the same time he had the sensation of being in one of those elated dreams in which obstacles dissolve before one of their own accord and one advances unimpeded, favored by some miraculous good fortune. . . . The wide entrance hall, paved with great square flagstones, reechoed with the sound of his footsteps. Opposite the kitchen, which was silent now, the strange, clumsy but neatly painted wooden cubicles still projected from high up in the wall as they had always done: these had been the maids' rooms, only accessible from the hall by a kind of open flight of stairs. But the great cupboards and the carved chest that had once stood here were gone . . . The son of the house began to climb the imposing main stairway, resting his hand on the white-painted openwork balustrade; with every step he took he raised it and gently let it fall again, as if he were diffidently trying to discover whether his former familiarity with this solid old handrail could be reestablished . . . But on the landing he stopped. At the entrance to the intermediate floor was a white board with black lettering which said: "Public Library."

Public library? thought Tonio Kröger, for in his opinion this was no place either for the public or for literature. He knocked on the door . . . He was bidden to enter, and did so. Tense and frowning, he beheld before him a most unseemly transformation.

There were three rooms on this intermediate floor, and their communicating doors stood open. The walls were covered almost up to the ceiling with uniformly bound books, standing in long rows on dark shelves. In each of the rooms a seedy-looking man was sitting writing at a sort of counter. Two of them merely turned their heads toward Tonio Kröger, but the first rose hastily to his feet, placed both hands on the desk to support himself, thrust his head forward, pursed his lips, raised his eyebrows and surveyed the visitor with rapidly blinking eyes . . .

"Excuse me," said Tonio Kröger, still staring at the multitude of books. "I am a stranger here, I am making a tour of the town. So this is the public library? Would you allow me to take a short look at your collection?"

"Certainly!" said the official, blinking more vigorously than ever . . . "Certainly, anyone may do so. Please take a look round . . . Would you like a catalogue?"

"No, thank you," answered Tonio Kröger. "I shall find my way about quite easily." And he began to walk slowly along the walls, pretending to be studying the titles of the books. Finally he took down a volume, opened it, and stationed himself with it at the window.

This had been the morning room. They had always had breakfast here, not upstairs in the big dining room, with its blue wallpaper boldly decorated with the white figures of Greek gods . . . The adjoining room had been used as a bedroom. His father's mother had died there, and her death struggle had been terrible, old as she was, for she had been a woman of the world who enjoyed life and clung to it. And later in this same room his father too had breathed his last, the tall, correct, rather sad and pensive gentleman with the wild flower in his buttonhole . . . Tonio had sat at the foot of his deathbed, his eyes hot with tears, in sincere and utter surrender to an inarticulate intense emotion of love and grief. And his mother too had knelt by the bed, his beautiful fiery mother, weeping her heart out; whereupon she had departed with that artist from the south to live under far-off blue skies . . . But the third room, the little one at the back, now fully stocked with books like the other two, with a seedy-looking attendant to supervise them—this for many years had been his own room. This was the room to which he had returned from school, perhaps after just such a walk as he had taken just now; there was the wall where his desk had stood, with its drawer where he had kept his first heartfelt clumsy efforts at verse composition . . . The walnut tree . . . He felt a sharp pang of grief. He glanced sideways through the window. The garden was neglected and over-grown, but the old walnut tree was still there, heavily creaking and rustling in the wind. And Tonio Kröger let his eyes wander back to the book he was holding in his hand, an outstanding work of litera-ture which he knew well. He looked down at the black lines of print and groups of sentences, followed the elegant flow of the text for a little, observing its passionate stylization, noting how effectively it rose to a climax and fell away from it again . . .

Yes, that's well done, he said to himself; he replaced the work on the shelf and turned away. And he noticed that the official was still on his feet, still blinking hard, with a mingled expression of eager servility and puzzled suspicion.

"I see you have an excellent collection," said Tonio Kröger. "I have already formed a general impression of it. I am most grateful to you. Good day." Whereupon he left the room; but it was not a very successful exit, and he had the strong impression that the library attendant was so disconcerted by his visit that he would still be standing there blinking several minutes later.

He felt disinclined to explore further. He had visited his home. The large rooms upstairs, beyond the pillared hall, were now obvi-ously occupied by strangers; for the staircase ended in a glass door which had not previously been there, and there was some kind of nameplate beside it. He turned away, walked downstairs and across the echoing entrance hall and left the house of his fathers. He went to a restaurant and sat at a corner table, deep in thought, eating a rich heavy meal; then he returned to his hotel.

"I have finished my business," he said to the elegant gentleman in black. "I shall leave this afternoon." And he asked for his bill, at the same time ordering a cab which would take him down to the harbor to board the steamer for Copenhagen. Then he went to his room and sat upright and in silence, resting his cheek on his hand and gazing down at the desk with unseeing eyes. Later he settled his bill and packed his luggage. At the appointed time the cab was announced and Tonio Kröger went downstairs, ready for his journey. At the foot of the staircase the elegant gentleman in black was waiting for him.

"Excuse me!" he said, pushing his cuffs back into his sleeves with his little fingers . . . "I beg your pardon, sir, but we must just detain you for one moment. Herr Seehaase—the proprietor of the hotel—would like to have a word with you. A mere formality . . . He's just over there . . . Would you be so kind as to come with me . . . It's *only* Herr Seehaase, the proprietor."

And with polite gestures he ushered Tonio Kröger to the back of the hall. There, to be sure, stood Herr Seehaase. Tonio Kröger knew him by sight, from days gone by. He was short, plump, and bow-legged. His clipped side-whiskers were white now; but he still wore a low-cut frock coat and a little velvet cap embroidered with green. He was, moreover, not alone. Beside him, at a small high desk which was fixed to the wall, stood a policeman with his helmet on and his gloved right hand resting on a complicated-looking document which lay before him on the desk. He was looking straight at Tonio Kröger with his honest soldierly eyes as if he expected him to sink right into the ground at the sight of him.

Tonio Kröger looked from one to the other and decided to await developments.

"Have you come here from Munich?" asked the policeman eventually in a slow, good-natured voice.

Tonio Kröger answered this question in the affirmative.

"You are traveling to Copenhagen?"

"Yes, I am on my way to a Danish seaside resort."

"Seaside resort? Well, you must let me see your papers," said the policeman, uttering the last word with an air of special satisfaction.

"Papers . . . ?" He had no papers. He took out his pocketbook and glanced at its contents; but apart from some money it contained only the proofs of a short story, which he intended to correct at his destination. He did not like dealing with officials, and had never yet had a passport issued to him . . .

"I am sorry," he said, "but I have no papers with me."

"Indeed!" said the policeman . . . "None at all? What is your name?"

Tonio Kröger answered him.

"Is that the truth?" asked the policeman, drawing himself up to his full height and suddenly opening his nostrils as wide as he could.

"Certainly," replied Tonio Kröger.

"And what's your occupation, may I ask?"

Tonio Kröger swallowed and in a firm voice named his profession. Herr Seehaase raised his head and looked up at him with curiosity.

"Hm!" said the policeman. "And you allege that you are not identical with an individial of the name of—" He said "individial," and proceeded to spell out from the complicated document a highly intricate and romantic name which seemed to have been bizarrely compounded from the languages of various races; Tonio Kröger had no sooner heard it than he had forgotten it. "An individial," the policeman continued, "of unknown parentage and doubtful provenance, who is wanted by the Munich police in connection with various frauds and other offenses and is probably trying to escape to Denmark?"

"I do not merely 'allege' this," said Tonio Kröger, with a nervous movement of his shoulders. That made a certain impression.

"What? Oh, quite, yes, of course!" said the policeman. "But you can't identify yourself in any way, can you!"

Herr Seehaase attempted a conciliatory intervention.

"The whole thing is a formality," he said, "nothing more! You must realize that the officer is merely doing his duty. If you could show some kind of identification . . . some document . . ."

They all fell silent. Should he make an end of the matter by disclosing who he was, by informing Herr Seehaase that he was not an adventurer of uncertain provenance, not born a gypsy in a green caravan, but the son of Consul Kröger, a member of the Kröger family? No, he had no wish to say anything of the sort. And were they not right, in a way, these representatives of bourgeois society? In a certain sense he entirely agreed with them . . . He shrugged his shoulders and said nothing.

"What have you got there?" asked the policeman. "There, in your pocketbook?"

"Here? Nothing. Only a proof," answered Tonio Kröger.

"Proof? Proof of what? Let's have a look."

And Tonio Kröger handed him his work. The policeman spread it out on the desk and began to read it. Herr Seehaase, stepping closer, did the same. Tonio Kröger glanced over their shoulders to see what part of the text they had reached. It was a good passage, pointed and effective; he had taken pains with it and got it exactly right. He was satisfied with his work.

"You see!" he said. "There is my name. I wrote this, and now it is being published, you understand."

"Well, that's good enough!" said Herr Seehaase decisively. He put the sheets together, folded them and returned them to their author. "It must be good enough, Petersen," he repeated curtly, surreptitiously closing his eyes and shaking his head to forestall any objections. "We must not delay the gentleman any longer. His cab is waiting. I hope, sir, you will excuse this slight inconvenience. The officer was of course only doing his duty, though I told him at once that he was on the wrong track . . ."

"Did you, now?" thought Tonio Kröger.

The policeman did not seem entirely satisfied; he raised some further query about "individial" and "identification." But Herr Seehaase conducted his guest back through the foyer, with repeated expressions of regret; he accompanied him out between the two lions to his cab and saw him into it, closing the door himself with a great display of respect. Whereupon the absurdly tall, broad vehicle, rumbling and stumbling, noisily and clumsily rolled down the steep narrow streets to the harbor . . .

And that was Tonio Kröger's curious visit to the city of his fathers.

7

Night was falling, and the moon was rising, its silver radiance floating up the sky, as Tonio Kröger's ship moved out into the open sea. He stood in the bows, warmly wrapped against the mounting wind, and gazed down at the dark restless wandering of the great smooth waves beneath him, watching them slithering round each other, dashing against each other, darting away from each other in unexpected directions with a sudden glitter of foam . . .

His heart was dancing with silent elation. The experience of being nearly arrested in his native town as a criminal adventurer had somewhat damped his spirits, to be sure—even although in a certain sense he had felt that this was just as it should be. But then he had come on board and stood, as he had sometimes done with his father as a boy, watching the freight being loaded onto the boat: its capacious hold had been stuffed with bales and crates, amid shouts in a mixture of Danish and Plattdeutsch, and even a polar bear and a Bengal tiger had been lowered into it in cages with strong iron bars; evidently they had been sent from Hamburg for delivery to some Danish menagerie. And all this had cheered him up. Later, as the steamer had slipped downstream between the flat embankments, he had completely forgotten his interrogation by Constable Petersen, and all his previous impressions had revived again in his mind: his sweet, sad, rueful dreams, his walk, the sight of the walnut tree. And now, as they passed out of the estuary, he saw in the distance the shore where as a boy he had listened to the sea's summer reveries, he saw the flash of the lighthouse and the lighted windows of the resort's principal hotel at which he and his parents had stayed . . . The Baltic Sea! He bent his head before the strong salt wind which was blowing now with full unimpeded force; it enveloped him, drowning all other sounds, making him feel slightly giddy, half numbed with a blissful lethargy which swallowed up all his unpleasant memories, all his sufferings and errors and efforts and struggles. And in the clashing, foaming, moaning uproar all round him he thought he heard the rustle and jarring of the old walnut tree, the creaking of a garden gate . . . The darkness was thickening.

"The sstars, my God, just look at the sstars!" said a voice suddenly. It spoke in a plaintively singsong northern accent and seemed to come from the interior of a large barrel. He had heard it already; it belonged to a sandy-haired, plainly dressed man with reddened eyelids and a chilled, damp look, as if he had just been bathing. He had sat next to Tonio Kröger at dinner in the saloon and had consumed, in a modest and hesitant manner, astonishing quantities of lobster omelet. He was now standing beside him leaning against the rail, staring up at the sky and holding his chin between his thumb and forefinger. He was obviously in one of those exceptional, festive and contemplative moods in which the barriers between oneself and one's fellow men are lowered, one's heart is laid bare to strangers and one's tongue speaks of matters on which it would normally preserve an embarrassed silence . . .

"Look, sir, just look at the sstars! Twinkling away up there; by God, the whole sky's full of them. And when you look up at it all and consider that a lot of them are supposed to be a hundred times the size of the earth, well, I ask you, how does it make one feel! We men have invented the telegraph and the telephone and so many wonders of modern times, yes, so we have. But when we look up there we have to realize nevertheless that when all's said and done we are just worms, just miserable little worms and nothing more— am I right or am I wrong, sir? Yes," he concluded, answering his own question, "that's what we are: worms!" And he nodded toward the firmament in abject contrition.

Oh, Lord, thought Tonio Kröger. No, he's got no literature in his system. And at once he recalled something he had recently read by a famous French writer, an essay on the cosmological and the psychological world view; it had been quite a clever piece of verbiage.

He made some kind of reply to the young man's heartfelt observation, and they then continued to converse, leaning over the rail and gazing into the flickering, stormy dusk. It turned out that Tonio Kröger's traveling companion was a young businessman from Hamburg who was devoting his holiday to this excursion . . .

"I thought: why not take the ssteamer and pop up to Copenhagen?" he explained. "So here I am, and so far so good, I must say. But those lobster omelets were a mistake, sir, I can tell you, because there's going to be a gale tonight, the captain said so himself, and that's no joke with indigestible food like that in your sstomach . . ."

Tonio Kröger listened with a certain secret sympathy to these foolish familiar overtures.

"Yes," he said, "the food's generally too heavy up in these parts. It makes one sluggish and melancholy."

"Melancholy?" repeated the young man, looking at him in some puzzlement, then suddenly added: "You're a sstranger here, sir, I suppose?"

"Oh yes, I'm from a long way away!" answered Tonio Kröger with a vague and evasive gesture.

"But you're right," said the young man. "God knows, you're right about feeling melancholy! I'm nearly always melancholy, but esspecially on evenings like this when there are sstars in the sky." And he rested his chin again on his thumb and forefinger.

He probably writes poetry, thought Tonio Kröger; deeply felt, honest, businessman's poetry . . .

It was getting late, and the wind was so high now that it made conversation impossible. So they decided to retire, and bade each other good-night.

Tonio Kröger lay down on the narrow bunk in his cabin, but could not sleep. The strong gale with its sharp tang had strangely excited him, and his heart beat anxiously, as if troubled by the expectation of some sweet experience. He also felt extremely seasick, for the ship was in violent motion, sliding down one steep wave after another with its screw lifting right out of the water and whirring convulsively. He put on all his clothes again and returned to the deck.

Clouds were racing across the moon. The sea was dancing. The waves were not rounded and rolling in ordered succession, they were being lashed and torn and churned into frenzy as far as the eye could reach. In the pallid, flickering light they licked and leaped upward like gigantic pointed tongues of flame: between foam-filled gulfs, jagged and incredible shapes were hurled on high: the sea seemed to be lifting mighty arms, tossing its spume into the air in wild, monstrous exhilaration. The ship was having a hard passage: pitching and rolling, thudding and groaning, it struggled on through the tumult, and from time to time the polar bear and the tiger could be heard roaring miserably from below decks. A man in an oilskin, with the hood over his head and a lantern strapped round his waist, was pacing the deck with straddled legs, keeping his balance with difficulty. But there in the stern, leaning far overboard, stood the young man from Hamburg, woefully afflicted.

"My God," he remarked in hollow, unsteady tones when he caught sight of Tonio Kröger, "just look at the uproar of the elements, sir!" But at this point he was interrupted and turned away hastily.

Tonio Kröger clutched the first taut piece of rope he could find and stood gazing out into all this mad, exuberant chaos. His spirits soared in an exultation that felt mighty enough to outshout the storm and the waves. Inwardly he began to sing a song of love, a paean of praise to the sea. Friend of my youth, ah wild sea weather, once more we meet, once more together . . . But there the poem ended. It was not a finished product, not an experience formed and shaped, recollected in tranquility and forged into a whole. His heart was alive . . .

Thus he stood for a long time; then he lay down on a bench beside the deckhouse and looked up at the sky with its glittering array of stars. He even dozed off for a while. And when the cold foam sprayed his face as he lay there half asleep, he felt it as a caress.

Vertical chalk cliffs loomed ghostly in the moonlight and drew nearer; it was the island of Møn. And again he dozed off, wakened from time to time by salt showers of spray which bit into his face and numbed his features . . . By the time he was fully awake it was already broad daylight, a fresh pale gray morning, and the green sea was calmer. At breakfast he again encountered the young businessman, who blushed scarlet, obviously ashamed of having said such discreditably poetical things under cover of darkness. He readjusted his small reddish moustache, stroking it upward with all five fingers, barked out a brisk military "Good morning!" to Tonio Kröger and then carefully steered clear of him.

And Tonio Kröger landed in Denmark. He arrived in Copenhagen, gave a tip to everyone who showed signs of expecting him to do so and then spent three days exploring the city from his hotel, holding his guidebook open in front of him and in general behaving like a well-bred foreigner intent on improving his mind. He inspected Kongens Nytorv and the "Horse" in its midst, glanced up respectfully at the columns of the Fruekirke, paused long before Thorwaldsen's noble and charming sculptures, climbed the Round Tower, visited various palaces and passed two colorful evenings at Tivoli. Yet all this was not really what he saw.

He saw houses which often exactly resembled those of his native town, houses with ornamental pierced gables, and the names by their front doors were names familiar to him from long ago, names symbolizing for him something tender and precious, and containing at the same time a kind of reproach, the sorrowful nostalgic reminder of something lost. And everywhere he went, slowly and pensively breathing in the damp sea air, he saw eyes just as blue, hair just as blond, faces just like those that had filled the strange sad rueful dreams of that night in his native town. As he walked these streets he would suddenly encounter a look, a vocal inflection, a peal of laughter, that pierced him to the heart . . .

The lively city did not hold him for long. He felt driven from it by a certain restlessness, by mingled memory and expectancy, and because he longed to be able to lie quietly somewhere on the seashore and not have to play the part of a busily circulating tourist. And so he embarked once more and sailed northward, on a dull day, over an inky sea, up the coast of Zealand to Elsinore. From there he at once continued his journey for another few miles by coach along the main road, which also ran close to the sea, until he reached his final and true destination. It was a little white seaside hotel with green shutters, surrounded by a cluster of low-lying houses and looking out with its wooden-shingled tower across the sound toward the Swedish coast. Here he alighted, took possession of the bright sunny room they had reserved for him, filled its shelves and cupboards with his belongings and settled down to live here for a while.

8

It was late September already; there were not many visitors left in Aalsgaard. Meals were served in the big dining room on the ground floor, which had a beamed ceiling and tall windows overlooking the glazed veranda and the sea; they were presided over by the proprietress, an elderly spinster with white hair, colorless eyes, faintly pink cheeks and a vague twittering voice, who always tried to arrange her reddened hands on the tablecloth in a manner that would display them to their best advantage. One of the guests was a short-necked old gentleman with a hoary sailor's beard and a dark bluish complexion; he was a fish dealer from the capital and could speak German. He seemed to be completely congested and inclined to apoplexy, for he breathed in short gasps and occasionally lifted a ringed index finger to his nose, pressed it against one nostril and blew hard enough through the other as if to clear it a little. Notwithstanding this he addressed himself continually to a bottle of aquavit which stood before him at breakfast, lunch and dinner. The only other members of the company were three tall American boys with their tutor or director of studies, who played football with them day in and day out and otherwise merely fidgeted with his spectacles and said nothing. The three youths had reddish fair hair parted in the middle, and elongated expressionless faces. "Will you pass me some of that *Wurst*, please," one of them would say in English. "It's not *Wurst*, it's *Schinken*," the other would reply; and that was the extent of their contribution to the conversation; for the rest of the time they and their tutor sat in silence drinking hot water.

Such were Tonio Kröger's neighbors at table, and they could not have been more to his liking. He was left in peace, and sat listening to the Danish glottal stops and front and back vowels in the speeches which the fish dealer and the proprietress now and then addressed to each other; with the former he would exchange an occasional simple remark about the state of the weather; he would then take his leave, pass through the veranda and walk down again to the beach, where he had already spent most of the morning.

Sometimes it was all summer stillness there. The sea lay idle and smooth, streaked with blue and bottle green and pale red, and the light played over it in glittering silvery reflections. The seaweed withered like hay in the sun, and the stranded jellyfish shriveled. There was a slight smell of decay, and a whiff of tar from the fishing boat against which Tonio Kröger leaned as he sat on the sand, facing away from the Swedish coast and toward the open horizon; but over it all swept the pure, fresh, gentle breath of the sea.

And then there would be gray, stormy days. The waves curved downward like bulls lowering their horns for a charge, and dashed themselves furiously against the shore, which was strewn with shining wet sea grass, mussel shells and pieces of driftwood, for the water rushed far inland. Under the overcast sky the wave troughs were foaming green, like long valleys between ranges of watery hills; but where the sun shone down from beyond the clouds, the sea's surface shimmered like white velvet.

Tonio Kröger would stand there enveloped in the noise of the wind and the surf, immersed in this perpetual, ponderous, deafening roar he loved so much. When he turned and moved away, everything all round him suddenly seemed calm and warm. But he always knew that the sea was behind him, calling, luring, beckoning. And he would smile.

He would walk far inland, along solitary paths across meadows, and would soon find himself surrounded by the beech-trees which covered most of the low undulating coastland. He would sit on the mossy ground, leaning against a tree trunk, at a point from which a strip of the sea was still visible through the wood. Sometimes the clash of the surf, like wooden boards falling against each other in the distance, would be carried to him by the breeze. Crows cawed above the treetops, hoarse and desolate and forlorn . . . He would sit with a book on his knees, but reading not a word of it. He was experiencing a profound forgetfulness, floating as if disembodied above space and time, and only at certain moments did he feel his heart stricken by a pang of sorrow, a brief, piercing, nostalgic or remorseful emotion which in his lethargic trance he made no attempt to define or analyze.

Thus many days passed; he could not have told how many, and had no desire to know. But then came one on which something happened; it happened when the sun was shining and many people were there, and Tonio Kröger did not even find it particularly surprising.

There was something festive and delightful about that day from its very beginning. Tonio Kröger woke unusually early and quite suddenly; he was gently and vaguely startled out of his sleep and at once confronted with an apparently magical spectacle, an elfin miracle of morning radiance. His room had a glass door and balcony facing out over the sound; it was divided into a sleeping and a living area by a white gauze curtain, and papered and furnished lightly in delicate pale shades, so that it always looked bright and cheerful. But now, before his sleep-dazed eyes, it had undergone an unearthly transfiguration and illumination, it was completely drenched in an indescribably lovely and fragrant rose-colored light: the walls and furniture shone golden and the gauze curtain was a glowing pink ... For some time Tonio Kröger could not understand what was happening. But when he stood by the glass door and looked out, he saw that the sun was rising.

It had been dull and rainy for several days on end, but now, over land and sea, the sky was like tight-stretched pale blue silk, bright and glistening; and the sun's disk, traversed and surrounded by resplendent red and gold clouds, was mounting in triumph above the shimmering, wrinkled water, which seemed to quiver and catch fire beneath it ... Thus the day opened, and in joy and confusion Tonio Kröger threw on his clothes; he had breakfast down in the veranda before anyone else, then swam some way out into the sound from the little wooden bathing hut, then walked for an hour along the beach. When he got back to the hotel there were several horse-drawn omnibuses standing in front of it, and from the dining room he could see that a large number of visitors had arrived: both in the adjoining parlor where the piano stood, and on the veranda and on the terrace in front of it, they were sitting at round tables consuming beer and sandwiches and talking excitedly. They were visitors in simple middle-class attire, whole families, young people and older people, even a few children.

At midmorning lunch—the table was heavily laden with cold food, smoked and salted delicacies and pastries—Tonio Kröger inquired what was afoot.

"Day visitors!" declared the fish dealer. "A party from Elsinore; they're having a dance here. Yes, God help us, we'll not sleep a wink tonight. There'll be dancing and music, and you can depend on it, they'll go on till all hours. It's some sort of subscription affair with various families taking part, an excursion in the country with a ball afterward, to make the most of the fine day. They came by boat and by road and now they're having lunch. Afterward they'll go for another drive, but they'll be back in the evening, and then it'll be dancing and fun and games here in the dining room. Yes, damn and confound it, we'll not shut an eye this night ..."

"It makes an agreeable change," said Tonio Kröger.

Whereupon silence was resumed. The proprietress sorted out her red fingers, the fish dealer snorted through his right nostril to clear it a little and the Americans drank hot water and made long faces.

Then suddenly it happened: *Hans Hansen and Ingeborg Holm walked through the dining room.*

Tonio Kröger, pleasantly weary after his swim and his rapid walk, was leaning back in his chair eating smoked salmon on toast; he was facing the veranda and the sea. And suddenly the door opened and the two of them sauntered in, unhurried, hand-in-hand. Ingeborg, the fair-haired Inge, was wearing a light-colored frock, just as she had done at Herr Knaak's dancing lessons. It was made of thin material with a floral pattern, and reached down only to her ankles; round her shoulders was a broad white tulle collar cut well down in front and exposing her soft, supple neck. She had tied the ribbons of her hat together and slung it over one arm. She had perhaps grown up a little since he had last seen her, and her wonderful blond tresses were wound round her head now; but Hans Hansen was just as he had always been. He was wearing his reefer jacket with the gold buttons and with the broad blue collar hanging out over his back; in his free hand he held his sailor's cap with its short ribbons, carelessly dangling it to and fro. Ingeborg kept her narrow-cut eyes averted, feeling perhaps a little shy under the gaze of the people sitting over their lunch. But Hans Hansen, as if in defiance of all and sundry, turned his head straight toward the table, and his steely blue eyes inspected each member of the company in turn, with a challenging and slightly contemptuous air; he even let go of Ingeborg's hand and swung his cap more vigorously to and fro, to show what a fine fellow he was. Thus the pair of them passed by before Tonio Kröger's eyes, against the background of the calm blue sea; they walked the length of the dining room and disappeared through the door at the far end, into the parlor.

This happened at half-past eleven, and while the residents were still eating, the visiting party next door and on the veranda set out on their excursion; no one else came into the dining room, they left the hotel by the side entrance. Outside, they could be heard getting into their omnibuses, amid much laughter and joking, and then there was the sound of one vehicle after another rumbling away . . .

"So they're coming back?" asked Tonio Kröger.

"They are indeed!" said the fish dealer. "And God damn the whole thing, I say. They've engaged a band, and I sleep right over this room."

"It makes an agreeable change," said Tonio Kröger again. Then he got up and left.

He spent that day as he had spent the others, on the beach and in the woods, holding a book on his knee and blinking in the sunlight. There was only one thought in his mind: that they would be coming back and holding a dance in the dining room, as the fish dealer had predicted; and he did nothing all day but look forward to this, with a sweet apprehensive excitement such as he had not felt throughout all these long, dead years. Once, by some associative trick of thought, he fleetingly remembered a far-off acquaintance: Adalbert, the short-story writer, the man who knew what he wanted and had retreated into a café to escape the spring air. And he shrugged his shoulders at the thought of him . . .

Dinner was earlier than usual; supper was also served in advance of the normal time and in the parlor, because preparations for the dance were already being made in the dining room: the whole normal program was delightfully disarranged for so festive an occasion. Then, when it was already dark and Tonio Kröger was sitting in his room, there were signs of life again on the road and in the hotel. The party was returning; there were even new guests arriving from Elsinore by bicycle or by carriage, and already he could hear, down below, a violin being tuned and the nasal tones of a clarinet practicing scales . . . There was every indication that it would be a magnificent ball.

And now the little orchestra began playing: a march in strict time, muted but clearly audible upstairs. The dancing began with a polonaise. Tonio Kröger sat on quietly for a while and listened. But when the march tempo changed to a waltz rhythm, he rose and slipped quietly out of his room.

From his corridor there was a subsidiary flight of stairs leading down to the side entrance of the hotel, and from there one could reach the glazed veranda without passing through any of the rooms. He went this way, walking softly and stealthily as if he had no business to be there, groping cautiously through the darkness, irresistibly drawn toward the foolish, happily lilting music; he could hear it now quite loudly and distinctly.

The veranda was empty and unlit, but in the dining room the two large paraffin lamps with their polished reflectors were shining brightly, and the glass door stood open. He crept noiselessly up to it; here he could stand in the dark unobserved, watching the dancers in the lighted room, and this furtive pleasure made his skin tingle. Quickly and eagerly he glanced round for the pair he sought . . .

The festivity was already in full swing, although the dancing had begun less than half an hour ago; but the participants had of course been already warmed up and excited by the time they had got back here, having spent the whole day together in happy and carefree companionship. In the parlor, into which Tonio Kröger could see if he ventured forward a little, several older men had settled down to smoke and drink and play cards; others again were sitting with their wives on the plush-upholstered chairs in the foreground or along the walls of the dining room, watching the dance. They sat resting their hands on their outspread knees, with prosperous puffed-out faces; the mothers, wearing bonnets high up on their parted hair, looked on at the whirl of young people, with their hands folded in their laps and their heads tilted sideways. A platform had been erected against one of the longer walls, and on it the musicians were doing their best. There was even a trumpeter among them, blowing on his instrument rather diffidently and cautiously—it seemed to be afraid of its own voice, which despite all efforts kept breaking and tripping over itself . . . The dancing couples circled round each other, swaying and gyrating, while others walked about the room hand in hand. The company was not properly dressed for a ball, merely for a summer Sunday outing in the country: the young beaux wore suits of provincial cut which they obviously used only at weekends, and the girls were in light pale frocks with bunches of wild flowers on their bosoms. There were even some children present, dancing with each other after their fashion, even when the band was not playing. The master of ceremonies appeared to be a long-legged man in a swallow-tailed coat, some kind of small-town dandy with a monocle and artificially curled hair, an assistant postmaster perhaps—a comic character straight out of a Danish novel. He devoted himself heart and soul to his task, positively perspiring with officiousness; he was everywhere at once, curvetting busily round the room with a mincing gait, setting his toes down first and artfully crisscrossing his feet, which were clad in shining pointed half-boots of military cut. He waved his arms, issued instructions, called for music and clapped his hands; as he moved, the ribbons of the gaily colored bow which had been pinned to his shoulder in token of his office fluttered behind him, and from time to time he glanced lovingly round at it.

Yes, there they were, the pair who had walked past Tonio Kröger that morning in the sunlight: he saw them again, his heart suddenly leaping with joy as he caught sight of them almost simultaneously. There stood Hans Hansen, quite near him, not far from the door; with outspread legs and leaning forward slightly, he was slowly and carefully devouring a large slice of sponge cake, holding one hand cupped under his chin to catch the crumbs. And there by the wall sat Ingeborg Holm, the fair-haired Inge; at that very moment the assistant postmaster minced up to her and invited her to dance with a stilted bow, placing one hand on the small of his back and gracefully inserting the other into his bosom, but she shook her head and indicated that she was too much out of breath and must rest for a little, whereupon the assistant postmaster sat down beside her.

Tonio Kröger looked at them both, those two for whom long ago he had suffered love: Hans and Ingeborg. For that was who they were—not so much by virtue of particular details of their appearance or similarities of dress, but by affinity of race and type: they too had that radiant blondness, those steely blue eyes, that air of untroubled purity and lightness of heart, of proud simplicity and unapproachable reserve . . . He watched them, watched Hans Hansen standing there in his sailor suit, bold and handsome as ever, broad in the shoulders and narrow in the hips; he watched Ingeborg's way of tossing her head to one side with a saucy laugh, her way of raising her hand—a hand by no means particularly tiny or delicately girlish—to smooth her hair at the back, letting her light sleeve slide away from the elbow; and suddenly his heart was pierced by such an agony of homesickness that he instinctively shrank further back into the shadows to hide the twitching of his face.

"Had I forgotten you?" he asked. "No, never! I never forgot you, Hans, nor you, sweet fair-haired Inge! It was for you I wrote my works, and when I heard applause I secretly looked round the room to see if you had joined in it . . . Have you read *Don Carlos* yet, Hans Hansen, as you promised me at your garden gate? Don't read it! I no longer want you to. What has that lonely weeping king to do with you? You must not make your bright eyes cloudy and dreamy and dim by peering into poetry and sadness . . . If I could be like you! If only I could begin all over again and grow up like you, decent and happy and simple, normal and *comme il faut,* at peace with God and the world, loved by the innocent and light of heart—and marry you, Ingeborg Holm, and have a son like you, Hans Hansen! If only I could be freed from the curse of insight and the creative torment, and live and love and be thankful and blissfully commonplace! . . . Begin all over again? It would be no good. It would all turn out the same—all happen again just as it has happened. For certain people are bound to go astray because for them no such thing as a right way exists."

The music had stopped; there was an interval, and refreshments were being handed round. The assistant postmaster in person was tripping about with a trayful of herring salad, offering it to the ladies; but before Ingeborg Holm he even went down on one knee as he handed her the dish, and this made her blush with pleasure.

The spectator by the glass door of the dining room was now beginning to attract attention after all, and from handsome flushed faces uncordial and inquiring looks were cast in his direction; but he stood his ground. Ingeborg and Hans glanced at him too, almost simultaneously, with that air of utter indifference so very like contempt. But suddenly he became conscious that a gaze from some other quarter had sought him out and was resting on him . . . He turned his head, and his eyes at once met those whose scrutiny he had sensed. Not far from him a girl was standing, a girl with a pale, slender delicate face whom he had noticed before. She had not been dancing much, the gentlemen had paid scant attention to her, and he had seen her sitting alone by the wall with tightly pursed lips. She was standing by herself now too. She wore a light-colored frock like the other girls, but through its transparent gossamerlike material one could glimpse bare shoulders which were thin and pointed, and between these meager shoulders her thin neck sat so low that this quiet girl almost gave the impression of being slightly deformed. She had thin short gloves on, and held her hands against her flat breasts with their fingers just touching. She had lowered her head and was gazing up at Tonio Kröger with dark, melting eyes. He turned away . . .

Here, quite near him, sat Hans and Ingeborg. Possibly they were brother and sister; Hans had sat down next to her, and surrounded by other young people with healthy pink complexions they were eating and drinking, chattering and enjoying themselves and exchanging pleasantries, and their bright clear voices and laughter rang through the air. Could he not perhaps approach them for a moment? Could he not speak to one or other of them, make whatever humorous remark occurred to him, and would they not at least have to answer with a smile? It would give him such pleasure; he longed for it to happen; he would go back to his room contented, in the knowledge of having established some slight contact with them both. He thought out something he might say to them; but he could not nerve himself to go forward and say it. After all, the situation was as it had always been: they would not understand, they would listen to his words in puzzled embarrassment. For they did not speak the same language.

The dancing, apparently, was on the point of beginning again. The assistant postmaster burst into ubiquitous activity. He hurried to and fro, urged everyone to choose a partner, helped the waiter to clear chairs and glasses out of the way, issued instructions to the musicians and pushed a few awkward uncomprehending dancers into place, steering them by the shoulders. What was about to happen? Squares were being formed, of four couples each . . . A dreadful memory made Tonio Kröger blush. They were going to dance quadrilles.

The music began; the couples bowed and advanced and interchanged. The assistant postmaster directed the dance; great heavens, he was actually directing it in French, and pronouncing the nasal vowels with incomparable distinction! Ingeborg Holm was dancing just in front of Tonio Kröger, in the set nearest to the glass door. She moved to and fro in front of him, stepping and turning, forward and backward; often he caught a fragrance from her hair or from the delicate white material of her dress, and he closed his eyes, filled with an emotion so long familiar to him: during all these last days he had been faintly aware of its sharp enchanting flavor, and now it was welling up once more inside him in all its sweet urgency. What was it? Desire, tenderness? envy? self-contempt? . . . *Moulinet des dames!* Did you laugh, fair-haired Inge, did you laugh at me on that occasion, when I danced the *moulinet* and made such a miserable fool of myself? And would you still laugh today, even now when I have become, in my own way, a famous man? Yes, you would—and you would be a thousand times right to do so, and even if I, singlehanded, had composed the Nine Symphonies and written *The World as Will and Idea* and painted the *Last Judgment*—you would still be right to laugh, eternally right . . . He looked at her, and remembered a line of poetry, a line he had long forgotten and that was nevertheless so close to his mind and heart: "I long to sleep, to sleep, but you must dance." He knew so well the melancholy northern mood it expressed, awkward and half-articulate and heartfelt. To sleep . . . To long to be able to live simply for one's feelings alone, to rest idly in sweet self-sufficient emotion, uncompelled to translate it into activity, unconstrained to dance—and to have to dance nevertheless, to have to be alert and nimble and perform the difficult, difficult and perilous sword-dance of art, and never to be able quite to forget the humiliating paradox of having to dance when one's heart is heavy with love . . .

Suddenly, all round him, a wild extravagant whirl of movement developed. The sets had broken up, and everyone was leaping and gliding about in all directions: the quadrille was finishing with a

gallopade. The couples, keeping time to the music's frantic prestis-
simo, were darting past Tonio Kröger, chasséing, racing, overtaking
each other with little gasps of laughter. One of them, caught up and
swept forward by the general rush, came spinning toward him. The
girl had a delicate pale face and thin, hunched shoulders. And all at
once, directly in front of him, there was a slipping and tripping and
stumbling . . . The pale girl had fallen over. She fell so hard and
heavily that it looked quite dangerous, and her partner collapsed
with her. He had evidently hurt himself so badly that he completely
forgot the lady and began in a half-upright posture to grimace with
pain and rub his knee; the girl seemed quite dazed by her fall and
was still lying on the floor. Whereupon Tonio Kröger stepped forward, took her gently by both arms and lifted her to her feet. She
looked up at him, exhausted, bewildered and wretched, and suddenly a pink flush spread over her delicate face.

"Thank you! Oh, thank you so much!" she said in Danish, and
looked up at him with dark melting eyes.

"You had better not dance again, Fräulein," he said gently. Then
he glanced round until once more he saw *them,* Hans and Ingeborg;
and turned away. He left the veranda and the ball and went back
up to his room.

He was elated by these festivities in which he had not shared, and
wearied by jealousy. It had all been the same as before, so exactly
the same! With flushed face he had stood in the darkness, his heart
aching for you all, you the fair-haired, the happy, the truly alive;
and then he had gone away, alone. Surely someone would come
now! Surely Ingeborg would come now, surely she would notice that
he had left, and slip out after him, put her hand on his shoulder
and say: "Come back and join us! Don't be sad! I love you!" But
she did not come. Such things do not happen. Yes, it was all as it
had been long ago, and he was happy as he had been long ago. For
his heart was alive. But what of all these years he had spent in
becoming what he now was? Paralysis; barrenness; ice; and intellect!
and art! . . .

He undressed and got into bed and put out the light. He whispered
two names into his pillow, whispered those few chaste northern
syllables which symbolized his true and native way of loving and
suffering and being happy—which to him meant life and simple
heartfelt emotion and home. He looked back over the years that
had passed between then and now. He remembered the dissolute
adventures in which his senses, his nervous system and his mind had

indulged; he saw himself corroded by irony and intellect, laid waste and paralyzed by insight, almost exhausted by the fevers and chills of creation, helplessly and contritely tossed to and fro between gross extremes, between saintly austerity and lust—oversophisticated and impoverished, worn out by cold, rare, artificial ecstasies, lost, ravaged, racked and sick—and he sobbed with remorse and nostalgia.

Round about him there was silence and darkness. But lilting up to him from below came the faint music, the sweet trivial waltz rhythm of life.

<h1 style="text-align:center">9</h1>

Tonio Kröger sat in the north writing to his friend Lisaveta Ivanovna, as he had promised he would do.

"My dear Lisaveta down there in Arcadia," he wrote, "to which I hope soon to return: here is a letter of sorts, but I am afraid it may disappoint you, for I propose to write in rather general terms. Not that I have nothing to tell you, or have not, after my fashion, undergone one or two experiences. At home, in my native town, I was even nearly arrested . . . but of that you shall hear by word of mouth. I sometimes now have days on which I prefer to attempt a well-formulated general statement, rather than narrate particular events.

"I wonder if you still remember, Lisaveta, once calling me a bourgeois manqué? You called me that on an occasion on which I had allowed myself to be enticed by various indiscreet confessions I had already let slip into avowing to you my love for what I call 'life'; and I wonder if you realized how very right you were, and how truly my bourgeois nature and my love for 'life' are one and the same. My journey here has made me think about this point . . .

"My father, as you know, was of a Northern temperament: contemplative, thorough, puritanically correct, and inclined to melancholy. My mother was of a vaguely exotic extraction, beautiful, sensuous, naive, both reckless and passionate, and given to impulsive, rather disreputable behavior. There is no doubt that this mixed heredity contained extraordinary possibilities—and extraordinary dangers. Its result was a bourgeois who went astray into art, a bohemian homesick for his decent background, an artist with a bad conscience. For after all it is my bourgeois conscience that makes me see the whole business of being an artist, of being any kind of exception or genius, as something profoundly equivocal, profoundly dubi-

Tristan

1

Here we are at *Einfried,* the well-known sanatorium! It is white and rectilinear, a long low-lying main building with a side wing, standing in a spacious garden delightfully adorned with grottoes, leafy arcades and little bark pavilions; and behind its slate roofs the massive pine-green mountains rear their softly outlined peaks and clefts into the sky.

The director of the establishment, as always, is Dr. Leander. With his double-pointed black beard, curled as crisply as horse-hair stuffing, his thick flashing spectacles and his general air of one into whom science has instilled a certain coldness and hardness and silent tolerant pessimism, he holds sway in his abrupt and reserved manner over his patients—over all these people who are too weak to impose laws upon themselves and obey them, and who therefore lavish their fortunes on Dr. Leander in return for the protection of his rigorous regime.

As for Fräulein von Osterloh, she manages all domestic matters here, and does so with tireless devotion. Dear me, what a whirl of activity! She hurries upstairs and downstairs and from one end of the institution to the other. She is mistress of the kitchen and storerooms, she climbs about in the linen cupboards, she has the servants at her beck and call, she plans the clients' daily fare on principles of economy, hygiene, taste and elegance. She keeps house with fanatical thoroughness; and in her extreme efficiency there lies concealed a standing reproach to the entire male sex, not one member of which has ever taken it into his head to make her his wife. But in two round crimson spots on her cheeks there burns the inextinguishable hope that one day she will become Frau Dr. Leander. . . .

Ozone, and still, unstirring air . . . Einfried, whatever Dr. Leander's envious detractors and rivals may say, is most warmly to be

ous, profoundly suspect; and it too has made me fall so foolisl
love with simplicity and naiveté, with the delightfully norma
respectable and mediocre.

"I stand between two worlds, I am at home in neither, an
makes things a little difficult for me. You artists call me a bour
and the bourgeois feel they ought to arrest me . . . I don't
which of the two hurts me more bitterly. The bourgeois are
but you worshipers of beauty, you who say I am phlegmat
have no longing in my soul, you should remember that the
kind of artist so profoundly, so primordially fated to be an
that no longing seems sweeter and more precious to him th
longing for the bliss of the commonplace.

"I admire those proud, cold spirits who venture out alc
paths of grandiose, demonic beauty and despise 'humanity'
do not envy them. For if there is anything that can turn a *litt*
into a true writer, then it is this bourgeois love of mine
human and the living and the ordinary. It is the source of all v
of all kindheartedness and of all humor, and I am almost pe
it is that very love without which, as we are told, one ma
with the tongues of men and of angels and yet be a soundi
and a tinkling cymbal.

"What I have achieved so far is nothing, not much, as
nothing. I shall improve on it, Lisaveta—this I promise y
write this, I can hear below me the roar of the sea, and I
eyes. I gaze into an unborn, unembodied world that dema
ordered and shaped, I see before me a host of shadowy h
ures whose gestures implore me to cast upon them the
shall be their deliverance: tragic and comic figures, and
are both at once—and to those I am strongly drawn. But n
and most secret love belongs to the fair-haired and the
the bright children of life, the happy, the charming and th

"Do not disparage this love, Lisaveta; it is good and
it there is longing, and sad envy, and just a touch of con
a whole world of innocent delight."

Translated by I

recommended for all tubercular cases. But not only consumptives reside here: there are patients of all kinds—ladies, gentlemen and even children; Dr. Leander can boast of successes in the most varied fields. There are people with gastric disorders, such as Magistratsrätin Spatz, who is also hard of hearing; there are heart cases, paralytics, rheumatics and nervous sufferers of all sorts and conditions. There is a diabetic general, who grumbles continually as he consumes his pension. There are several gentlemen with lean, shriveled faces, walking with that unruly dancing gait which is always a bad sign. There is a lady of fifty, Pastorin Höhlenrauch, who has had nineteen children and is now totally incapable of thought, despite which her mind is still not at peace: for a whole year now, driven by some restless nervous impulse, she has been wandering aimlessly all over the house—a staring, speechless, uncanny figure, leaning on the arm of her private attendant.

Occasionally a death occurs among the "serious cases," those who are confined to their beds and do not appear at meals or in the drawing room; and no one is ever aware of it, not even the patient next door. In the silence of night the waxen guest is removed, and Einfried pursues the even tenor of its way: the massage, the electrical treatment, the injections, douches, medicinal baths, gymnastics, exsudations and inhalations all continue, in premises equipped with every wonder of modern science . . .

Ah yes, this is a lively place. The establishment is flourishing. The porter at the entrance in the side wing sounds the great bell when new guests arrive, and all who leave are shown to the carriage with due formality by Dr. Leander and Fräulein von Osterloh in person. Many an odd figure has lived under Einfried's hospitable roof. There is even a writer here, idling away his time—an eccentric fellow with a name reminiscent of some sort of mineral or precious stone. . . .

Apart from Dr. Leander there is, moreover, a second resident physician, who deals with those cases which are not serious at all and those which are hopeless. But his name is Müller and we need waste no time discussing him.

2

At the beginning of January Herr Klöterjahn the wholesale merchant, of the firm of A. C. Klöterjahn & Co., brought his wife to Einfried. The porter sounded the bell, and Fräulein von Osterloh came to greet the new arrivals after their long journey; she met them in the reception room, which like almost all the rest of this elegant old house was furnished in remarkably pure *Empire* style: In a moment or two Dr. Leander also appeared; he bowed, and an introductory, mutually informative conversation ensued.

Outside lay the wintry garden, its flower beds covered with matting, its grottoes blocked with snow, its little temples isolated; and two porters were dragging in the new guests' luggage from the carriage which had stopped at the wrought iron gate, for there was no drive up to the house.

"Take your time, Gabriele, take care, darling, and keep your mouth closed," Herr Klöterjahn had said as he conducted his wife across the garden; and the moment one saw her one's heart trembled with such tender solicitude that one could not help inwardly echoing his words—though it must be admitted that Herr Klöterjahn's "take care," which he had said in English, could equally well have been said in German.

The coachman who had driven the lady and gentleman from the station to the sanatorium was a plain, unsophisticated and unsentimental fellow; but he had positively bitten his tongue in an agony of helpless caution as the wholesale merchant assisted his wife down from the carriage. Indeed, even the two bay horses, as they stood steaming in the silent frosty air, had seemed to be rolling back their eyes and intently watching this anxious operation, full of concern for so much fragile grace and delicate charm.

The young lady had an ailment affecting her trachea, as was expressly stated in the letter which Herr Klöterjahn had dispatched from the shores of the Baltic to the medical director of Einfried, announcing their intended arrival; the trachea, and not, thank God, the lungs! And yet—even if it had been the lungs, this new patient could scarcely have looked more enchantingly remote, ethereal and insubstantial than she did now, as she sat by her burly husband, leaning softly and wearily back in her straight, white-lacquered armchair, listening to his conversation with the doctor.

Her beautiful pale hands, bare of jewelry except for a simple wedding ring, were resting in her lap among the folds of a dark, heavy cloth skirt, above which she wore a close-fitting silver gray bodice with a stand up-collar and a pattern of cut velvet arabesques. But these warm and weighty materials made her ineffably delicate, sweet, languid little head look all the more touching, unearthly and lovely. Her light brown hair was brushed smoothly back and gathered in a knot low down on her neck; only one stray curl drooped toward her right temple, not far from the spot where a strange, sickly little pale blue vein branched out above one of her well-marked eyebrows and across the clear, unblemished, almost transparent surface of her forehead. This little blue vein over one eye rather disturbingly dominated the whole of her delicate oval face. It stood out more strongly as soon as she began to speak, indeed as soon as she even smiled; and when this happened it gave her a strained look, an expression almost of anxiety, which filled the onlooker with obscure foreboding. And nevertheless she spoke, and she smiled. She spoke with candor and charm in her slightly husky voice, and she smiled with her eyes, although she seemed to find it a little difficult to focus them, indeed they sometimes showed a slight uncontrollable unsteadiness. At their corners, on each side of her slender nose, there were deep shadows. She smiled with her mouth as well, which was wide and beautiful and seemed to shine despite its pallor, perhaps because the lips were so very sharply and clearly outlined. Often she would clear her throat a little. When she did so, she would put her handkerchief to her mouth and then look at it.

"Now, Gabriele darling, don't clear your throat," said Herr Klöterjahn. "You know Dr. Hinzpeter at home particularly told you not to do that, my dear, and it's merely a matter of pulling oneself together. As I said, it's the trachea," he repeated. "I really did think it was the lungs when it began; bless my soul, what a fright I got! But it's not the lungs—good God, no, we're not standing for any of that sort of thing, are we, Gabriele, what? Oh-ho, no!"

"Indubitably not," said Dr. Leander, flashing his spectacles at them.

Whereupon Herr Klöterjahn asked for coffee—coffee and buttered rolls; and the gutteral northern way he pronounced "coffee" and "butter" was expressive enough to give anyone an appetite.

He was served with the desired refreshments, rooms were provided for him and his wife and they made themselves at home.

We should add that Dr. Leander personally took charge of the case, without availing himself of the services of Dr. Müller.

3

The personality of the new patient caused a considerable stir in Einfried; and Herr Klöterjahn, accustomed to such successes, accepted with satisfaction all the homage that was paid to her. The diabetic general stopped grumbling for a moment when he first caught sight of her; the gentlemen with the shriveled faces, when they came anywhere near her, smiled and made a great effort to keep their legs under control; and Magistratsrätin Spatz immediately appointed herself her friend and chaperone. Ah yes, this lady who bore Herr Klöterjahn's name most certainly made an impression! A writer who had for a few weeks been passing his time in Einfried— an odd fish with a name reminiscent of some kind of precious stone—positively changed color when she passed him in the corridor: he stopped short and was still standing as if rooted to the spot long after she had disappeared.

Not two days had passed before her story was known to every inmate of the sanatorium. She had been born in Bremen, a fact in any case attested by certain charming little peculiarities of her speech; and there, some two years since, she had consented to become the wedded wife of Herr Klöterjahn the wholesale merchant. She had gone with him to his native town up there on the Baltic coast, and about ten months ago she had borne him a child—an admirably lively and robust son and heir, born under quite extraordinarily difficult and dangerous circumstances. But since these terrible days she had never really recovered her strength, if indeed she had ever had any strength to recover. She had scarcely risen from her confinement, utterly exhausted, her vital powers utterly impoverished, when in a fit of coughing she had brought up a little blood— oh, not much, just an insignificant little drop; but it would of course have been better if there had been none at all. And the disturbing thing was that before long the same unpleasant little incident recurred. Well, this was a matter that could be death with, and Dr. Hinzpeter, the family physician, took the appropriate measures. Complete rest was ordered, little pieces of ice were swallowed, morphine was prescribed to check the coughing and all possible steps were taken to tranquilize the heart. Nevertheless the patient's condition failed to improve; and whereas the child, the magnificent infant Anton Klöterjahn, Jr., won and held his place in life with colossal energy and ruthlessness, his young mother seemed to be gently fading away, quietly burning herself out ... It was, as we have mentioned, the trachea; and this word, when Dr. Hinzpeter used it, had a remarkably soothing, reassuring, almost cheering effect upon all concerned. But even though it was not the lungs, the doctor had in the end strongly recommended a milder climate, and a period of residence in a sanatorium, to hasten the patient's recovery; and the reputation of Einfried and of its director had done the rest.

Thus matters stood; and Herr Klöterjahn himself would tell the whole story to anyone sufficiently interested to listen. He had a loud, slovenly, good-humored way of talking, like a man whose digestion is as thoroughly sound as his finances. He spoke with extravagant movements of the lips, broadly yet fluently, as people from the north coast do; many of his words were spluttered out with a minor explosion in every syllable, and he would laugh at this as if at a successful joke.

He was of medium height, broad, strongly built, with short legs, a round red face, watery blue eyes, pale blond eyelashes, wide nostrils and moist lips. He wore English side-whiskers and a complete outfit of English clothes, and was delighted to encounter an English family at Einfried—father, mother and three attractive children with their nurse, who were here simply and solely because they could not think of anywhere else to live. Herr Klöterjahn ate an English breakfast with them every morning. He had a general predilection for eating and drinking plentifully and well; he displayed a real conoisseur's knowledge of food and wine, and would entertain the inmates of the sanatorium with highly stimulating accounts of dinners given by his friends at home, describing in particular certain choice dishes unknown in these southern parts. As he did so his eyes would narrow benevolently, while his speech became increasingly palatal and nasal and was accompanied by slight munching sounds at the back of his throat. He was also not altogether averse to certain other worldly pleasures, as was made evident one evening when one of the patients at Einfried, a writer by profession, saw him flirting rather disgracefully with a chambermaid in the corridor—a trifling, humorous incident to which the writer in question reacted with a quite ludicrous grimace of disapproval.

As for Herr Klöterjahn's wife, it was plain for all to see that she was deeply attached to him. She watched his every movement and smiled at all he said. Her manner showed no trace of that patronizing indulgence with which many sick people treat those who are well; on the contrary, she behaved as kindly as good-natured patients do, taking genuine pleasure in the hearty self-assurance of persons blessed with good health.

Herr Klöterjahn did not remain at Einfried for long. He had escorted his wife here; but after a week, having assured himself that she was well provided for and in good hands, he saw no reason to prolong his stay. Equally pressing duties—his flourishing child and his no less flourishing business—recalled him to his native town;

they obliged him to depart, leaving his wife behind to enjoy the best of care.

4

The name of the writer who had been living in Einfried for several weeks was Spinell—Detlev Spinell; and his appearance was rather extraordinary.

Let us imagine a tall well-built man in his early thirties, with dark hair already beginning to turn distinctly gray about the temples, and a round, white, rather puffy face on which there was not the slightest sign of any growth of beard. It had not been shaved—that would have been noticeable; it was soft, indistinctly outlined and boyish, with nothing on it but an occasional little downy hair. And this really did look very odd. He had gentle, glistening, chestnut brown eyes and a thick, rather too fleshy nose. He also had an arched, porous, Roman-looking upper lip, large carious teeth and feet of remarkable dimensions. One of the gentlemen with the unruly legs, a cynic and would-be wit, had christened him behind his back "the putrefied infant"; but this was malicious and wide of the mark. He dressed well and fashionably, in a long dark coat and a waistcoat with colored spots.

He was unsociable and kept company with no one. Only occasionally was he seized by a mood of affability and exuberant friendliness, and this always happened when his aesthetic sensibilities were aroused—when the sight of something beautiful, a harmonious combination of colors, a vase of noble shape or the light of the setting sun on the mountains, transported him to articulate expressions of admiration. "What beauty!" he would then exclaim, tilting his head to one side, raising his shoulders, spreading out his hands and curling back his nose and lips. "Ah, dear me, pray observe, how beautiful that is!" And in the emotion of such moments Herr Spinell was capable of falling blindly upon the neck of no matter who might be at hand, whatever their status or sex . . .

On his desk, permanently on view to anyone who entered his room, lay the book he had written. It was a novel of moderate length with a completely baffling cover design, printed on the kind of paper one might use for filtering coffee, in elaborate typography with every letter looking like a Gothic cathedral. Fräulein von Oster-loh had read it in an idle quarter of an hour and had declared it to be "refined," which was her polite circumlocution for "unconscionably tedious." Its scenes were set in fashionable drawing rooms and luxurious boudoirs full of exquisite objets d'art, full of Gobelin tapestries, very old furniture, priceless porcelain, rare materials and artistic treasures of every sort. They were all described at length and with loving devotion, and as one read one constantly seemed to see Herr Spinell curling back his nose and exclaiming: "What beauty! Ah, dear me, pray observe, how beautiful that is!" It was, to be sure, rather surprising that he had not written any other books but this one, since his passion for writing was evidently extreme. He spent most of the time in his room doing so, and sent an extraordinary number of letters to the post, one or two almost every day— though the odd and amusing thing was that he himself very rarely received any . . .

5

Herr Spinell sat opposite Herr Klöterjahn's wife at table. On the occasion of the new guests' first appearance in the great dining room on the ground floor of the side wing, he arrived a minute or two late, murmured a greeting to the company generally and took his seat, whereupon Dr. Leander, without much ceremony, introduced him to the new arrivals. He bowed and began to eat, evidently a trifle embarrassed, and maneuvering his knife and fork in a rather affected manner with his large white well-formed hands which emerged from very narrow coat sleeves. Later he seemed less ill at ease and looked calmly by turns at Herr Klöterjahn and at his wife. Herr Klöterjahn too, in the course of the meal, addressed one or two questions and remarks to him about the topography and climate of Einfried; his wife also interspersed a few charming words, and Herr Spinell answered politely. His voice was soft and really quite agreeable, though he had a slightly impeded, dragging way of speaking, as if his teeth were getting in the way of his tongue.

After the meal, when the company had moved over into the drawing room and Dr. Leander was uttering the usual courtesies to the new guests in particular, Herr Klöterjahn's wife inquired about the gentlemen who had sat opposite.

"What is his name?" she asked . . . "Spinelli? I didn't quite catch it."

"Spinell—not Spinelli, madam. No, he's not an Italian, merely a native of Lemberg, so far as I know . . ."

"Did you say he was a writer, or something like that?" asked Herr Klöterjahn. His hands were in the pockets of his easy-fitting English trousers; he tilted one ear toward the doctor, and opened his mouth to listen, as some people do.

"Yes, I don't know—he writes . . ." answered Dr. Leander. "He has published a book, I believe, some kind of novel; I really don't know . . ."

These repeated declarations of ignorance indicated that Dr. Leander had no very high opinion of the writer and declined all responsibility for him.

"But that is extremely interesting!" said Herr Klöterjahn's wife. She had never yet met a writer face to face.

"Oh, yes," replied Dr. Leander obligingly. "I am told he has a certain reputation . . ." After that no more was said about him.

But a little later, when the new guests had withdrawn and Dr. Leander too was just about to leave the drawing room, Herr Spinell detained him and made inquiries in his turn.

"What is the name of the couple?" he asked . . . "I didn't catch it, of course."

"Klöterjahn," answered Dr. Leander, already turning to go.

"*What* is his name?" asked Herr Spinell . . .

"Their name is *Klöterjahn*," said Dr. Leander, and walked away. He really had no very high opinion of the writer.

6

I think we had reached the point at which Herr Klöterjahn had returned home. Yes—he was back on the shores of the Baltic with his business and his baby, that ruthless vigorous little creature who had cost his mother so much suffering and a slight defect of the trachea. She herself, the young wife, remained behind at Einfried, and Magistratsrätin Spatz appointed herself as her friend and chaperone. This however did not prevent Herr Klöterjahn's wife from being on friendly terms with the other inmates of the sanatorium—for example, with Herr Spinell, who to everyone's astonishment (for hitherto he had kept company with no one) treated her from the outset in an extraordinarily devoted and courteous manner; and she for her part, during the few leisure hours permitted by her rigorous daily regime, seemed by no means averse to his conversation.

He would approach her with extreme circumspection and deference, and always talked to her in a carefully muted voice, so that

Rätin Spatz, who was hard of hearing, usually did not catch a word of what he said. He would tiptoe on his great feet up to the armchair on which Herr Klöterjahn's wife reclined, fragile and smiling; at a distance of two paces he would stop, with one leg poised a little way behind the other and bowing from the waist; and in this posture he would talk to her in his rather impeded, dragging way, softly and intensely, but ready at any moment to withdraw and disappear as soon as her face should show the slightest sign of fatigue or annoyance. But she was not annoyed; she would invite him to sit down beside her and Frau Spatz; she would ask him some question or other and then listen to him with smiling curiosity, for often he said amusing and strange things such as no one had ever said to her before.

"Why actually are you at Einfried?" she asked. "What treatment are you taking, Herr Spinell?"

"Treatment? . . . Oh, I am having a little electrical treatment. It's really nothing worth mentioning. I will tell you, dear madam, why I am here: it is on account of the style."

"Ah?" said Herr Klöterjahn's wife, resting her chin on her hand and turning toward him with an exaggerated show of interest, as one does to children when they want to tell one something.

"Yes. Einfried is pure *Empire;* I am told it used to be a palace, a summer residence. This side wing of course is a later addition, but the main building is old and genuine. Now, there are times when I simply cannot do without *Empire,* times when it is absolutely necessary to me if I am to achieve even a modest degree of well-being. You will appreciate that one's state of mind when one is surrounded by voluptuously soft and luxurious furniture differs entirely from the mood inspired by the straight lines of these tables and chairs and draperies . . . This brightness and hardness, this cold, austere simplicity, this rigorous reserve imparts its composure and dignity to the beholder: prolonged contact with it has an inwardly purifying and restoring effect on me—there is no doubt that it raises my moral tone."

"Really, how remarkable," she said. "And I think I can understand what you mean, if I make an effort."

Whereupon he replied that what he meant was certainly not worth making an effort to understand, and they both laughed. Rätin Spatz also laughed and thought it remarkable; but she did not say that she understood what he meant.

The drawing room was large and beautiful. A tall white double door, standing wide open, led to the adjacent billiard room in which the gentlemen with the unruly legs and some others were playing. On the other side was a glass door giving onto the wide terrace and the garden. Near it stood a piano. There was a card table with a green top at which the diabetic general and a few other gentlemen were playing whist. Ladies sat reading or doing needlework. The room was heated by an iron stove, but in front of the elegant fireplace with its pieces of imitation coal pasted over with glowing red paper, there were comfortable places to sit and talk.

"You are an early riser, Herr Spinell. I have already quite by chance seen you two or three times leaving the house at half-past seven in the morning."

"An early riser? ... Ah, only in a rather special sense, dear madam. The fact is that I rise early because I am really a late sleeper."

"Now, that you must explain, Herr Spinell!"—Rätin Spatz also desired an explanation.

"Well ... if one is an early riser, then it seems to me that one does not really need to get up so early. Conscience, dear lady— conscience is a terrible thing! I and my kind spend all our lives battling with it, and we have our hands full trying from time to time to deceive it and to satisfy it in cunning little ways. We are useless creatures, I and my kind, and apart from our few good hours we do nothing but chafe ourselves sore and sick against the knowledge of our own uselessness. We hate everything that is useful, we know that it is vulgar and ugly, and we defend this truth fanatically, as one only defends truths that are absolutely necessary to one's existence. And nevertheless our bad conscience so gnaws at us that it leaves not one spot on us unscathed. In addition, matters are made worse by the whole character of our inner life, by our outlook, our way of working—they are terribly unwholesome, they undermine us, they exhaust us. And so one has recourse to certain little palliatives, without which it would all be quite unendurable. For example, some of us feel the need for a well-conducted outward existence, for a certain hygienic austerity in our habits. To get up early, cruelly early; to take a cold bath and a walk out into the snow ... That makes us feel moderately satisfied with ourselves for perhaps an hour or so. If I were to act in accordance with my true nature, I should lie in bed until well into the afternoon, believe me. My early rising is really hypocrisy."

"Why, not at all, Herr Spinell! I call it self-discipline . . . Don't you, Frau Rätin?" Rätin Spatz also called it self-discipline.

"Hypocrisy or self-discipline—whichever word you prefer! I have a melancholically honest disposition, and consequently . . ."

"That's just it. I am sure you are much too melancholic."

"Yes, dear madam, I am melancholic."

The fine weather continued. Everything was bright, hard and clean, windless and frosty; the house and garden, the surrounding countryside and the mountains, lay mantled in dazzling whiteness and pale blue shadows; and over it all stood a vaulted sky of delicate azure and utter purity, in which a myriad of shimmering light particles and dazzling crystals seemed to be dancing. At this period Herr Klöterjahn's wife seemed to be in tolerably good health; she had no fever, scarcely coughed at all, and had not too bad an appetite. Often she would sit out on the terrace for hours in the frost and the sun, as her doctor had prescribed. She sat in the snow, warmly wrapped in blankets and furs, hopefully breathing in the pure icy air for the benefit of her trachea. Sometimes she would see Herr Spinell walking in the garden; he too was warmly dressed and wore fur boots which made his feet look absolutely enormous. He walked through the snow with a tentative gait and a careful, prim posture of the arms; when he reached the terrace he would greet her very respectfully and mount the steps to engage her in a little conversation.

"I saw a beautiful woman on my morning walk today . . . Ah, dear me, how beautiful she was!" he said, leaning his head to one side and spreading out his hands.

"Really, Herr Spinell? Do describe her to me!"

"No, that I cannot do. Or if I did, I should be giving you an incorrect picture of her. I only glanced fleetingly at the lady as I passed, I did not really see her. But that uncertain glimpse was sufficient to stir my imagination, and I received and took away with me a vision of beauty . . . ah, of what beauty!"

She laughed. "Is that your way of looking at beautiful women, Herr Spinell?"

"Yes, dear madam; and it is a better way than if I were to stare them in the face with a crude appetite for reality, and imprint their actual imperfections on my mind . . ."

"'Appetite for reality' . . . what a strange phrase! That really is a phrase only a writer could have used, Herr Spinell! But I must confess that it impresses me. It suggests something to me that I partly understand, a certain feeling of independence and freedom, even a certain disrespect for reality—although I know that reality is more deserving of respect than anything else, indeed that it is the only truly respectable thing . . . And then I realize that there is something beyond what we can see and touch, something more delicate . . ."

"I know only one face," he said suddenly, speaking with a strange exaltation, raising his clenched hands to his shoulders and showing his carious teeth in an ecstatic smile . . . "I know only one face which even in reality is so noble and spiritual that any attempt by my imagination to improve upon it would be blasphemy—a face at which I could gaze, which I long to contemplate, not for minutes, not for hours, but for the whole of my life, for in it I should lose myself utterly and forget all earthly things . . ."

"Yes, quite, Herr Spinell. But Fräulein von Osterloh's ears stick out rather far, don't you think?"

He made no reply and bowed deeply. When he raised his eyes again, they rested with an expression of embarrassment and sadness on the strange, sickly little pale blue vein that branched out across the clear, almost transparent surface of her forehead.

7

A strange fellow, a really very odd fellow! Herr Klöterjahn's wife sometimes thought about him, for she had plenty of time for thinking. Perhaps the beneficial effect of the change of air had begun to wear off, or perhaps some positively harmful influence was at work upon her: at all events her state of health had deteriorated, the condition of her trachea seemed to leave much to be desired, she felt weak and weary, she had lost her appetite and was often feverish. Dr. Leander had most emphatically urged her to rest, not to talk too much, to exercise the utmost care. And so, when she was allowed up at all, she would sit with Rätin Spatz, not talking too much, holding her needlework idly in her lap and thinking her thoughts as they came and went.

Yes, this curious Herr Spinell made her think and wonder; and the remarkable thing was that he made her think not so much about him as about herself; somehow he awakened in her a strange curiosity about her own nature, a kind of interest in it she had never felt before. One day, in the course of conversation, he had remarked:

"Yes, women are certainly very mysterious . . . the facts are nothing new, and yet they are a perpetual source of astonishment. One is confronted, let us say, with some wonderful creature—a sylph, a figure from a dream, a faery's child. And what does she do? She goes off and marries some fairground Hercules, some butcher's apprentice. And there she comes, leaning on his arm, perhaps even with her head on his shoulder, and looking about her with a subtle smile as if to say: 'Well, here's a phenomenon to make you all rack your brains!' And we rack them, we do indeed."

This was a speech which Herr Klöterjahn's wife had repeatedly pondered.

On another occasion, to the astonishment of Rätin Spatz, the following dialogue took place between them:

"I am sure, dear madam, that it is very impertinent of me, but may I ask you what your name is—what it really is?"

"But my name is Klöterjahn, Herr Spinell, as you know!"

"H'm. Yes, that I know. Or rather: that I deny. I mean of course your own name, your maiden name. You must in all fairness concede, dear madam, that if anyone were to address you as 'Frau Klöterjahn' he would deserve to be horsewhipped."

She laughed so heartily that the little blue vein over her eyebrow stood out alarmingly clearly and gave her sweet delicate face a strained, anxious expression which was deeply disturbing.

"Why, good gracious, Herr Spinell! Horsewhipped? Do you find 'Klöterjahn' so appalling?"

"Yes, dear madam, I have most profoundly detested that name ever since I first heard it. It is grotesque, it is unspeakably ugly; and to insist on social convention to the point of calling you by your husband's name is barbaric and outrageous."

"Well, what about 'Eckhof'? Is Eckhof any better? My father's name is Eckhof."

"Ah, there now, you see! 'Eckhof' is quite another matter! There was once even a great actor called Eckhof. Eckhof is appropriate. You only mentioned your father. Is your mother . . ."

"Yes; my mother died when I was little."

"I see. Please tell me a little more about yourself; do you mind my asking? If it tires you, then do not do it. Just rest, and I will go on describing Paris to you, as I did the other day. But you could talk very softly, you know; you could even whisper, and it would make what you tell me all the more beautiful. . . . You were born in Bremen?" He uttered this question almost voicelessly, with an expression of reverent awe, as if he were asking something momentous, as if Bremen were some city beyond compare, full of ineffable excitements and hidden beauties, and as if to have been born there conferred some kind of mysterious distinction.

"Yes, just fancy!" she said involuntarily. "I was born in Bremen."

"I was there once," he remarked meditatively.

"Good gracious, you've been there, too? Why, Herr Spinell, I do believe you've seen everything there is to see between Tunis and Spitzbergen!"

"Yes, I was there once," he repeated. "For a few short hours, one evening. I remember an old, narrow street with gabled houses and the moon slanting strangely down on them. And then I was in a vaulted basement room that smelt of wine and decay. How vividly I recall it . . ."

"Really? I wonder where that was? Yes, I was born in a gray gabled house like that, an old patrician merchant's house with an echoing front hall and a white-painted gallery."

"Then your father is a man of business?" he asked a little hesitantly.

"Yes. But in addition, or perhaps I should really say in the first place, he is an artist."

"Ah! Ah! What kind of artist?"

"He plays the violin. But that is not saying much. It is *how* he plays it that matters. Herr Spinell! I have never been able to listen to certain notes without tears coming to my eyes—such strange, hot tears! No other experience has ever moved me like that. I daresay you will scarcely believe me . . ."

"I believe you! Oh, I believe you indeed! . . . Tell me, dear lady: surely your family is an old one? Surely, in that gray gabled house, many generations have already lived and labored and been gathered to their forefathers?"

"Yes. Buy why do you ask?"

"Because it often happens that an old family, with traditions that are entirely practical, sober and bourgeois, undergoes in its declining days a kind of artistic transfiguration."

"Is that so? Well, so far as my father is concerned he is certainly more of an artist than many a man who calls himself one and is famous for it. I only play the piano a little. Of course, now they have forbidden me to play; but I still did in those days, when I was at home. Father and I used to play together . . . Yes, all those years are a precious memory to me; especially the garden, our garden behind the house. It was terribly wild and overgrown, and the walls round it were crumbling and covered with moss; but that was just what gave it its great charm. It had a fountain in the middle, surrounded by a dense border of flag irises. In summer I used to sit there for hours with my friends. We would all sit on little garden chairs round the fountain ..."

"What beauty!" said Herr Spinell, raising his shoulders. "You sat round it singing?"

"No, we were usually crocheting."

"Ah, nevertheless ... nevertheless ..."

"Yes, we crocheted and gossiped, my six friends and I ..."

"What beauty! Ah, dear me, how beautiful that is!" cried Herr Spinell, with his face quite contorted.

"But what is so particularly beautiful about that, Herr Spinell?"

"Oh, the fact that there were six young ladies besides yourself, the fact that you were not one of their number, but stood out amongst them like a queen ... You were singled out from your six friends. A little golden crown, quite inconspicuous yet full of significance, gleamed in your hair ..."

"Oh, what nonsense, there was no such crown ..."

"Ah, but there was: it gleamed there in secret. I should have seen it, I should have seen it in your hair quite plainly, if I had been standing unnoticed among the bushes on one of those occasions ..."

"Heaven knows what you would have seen. But you were not standing there, on the contrary it was my husband, as he now is, who one day stepped out of the bushes with my father beside him. I'm afraid they had even been listening to a lot of our chatter ..."

"So that, dear madam, was where you first met your husband?"

"Yes, that was where I met him!" Her voice was firm and happy, and as she smiled the little delicate blue vein stood out strangely and strenuously above her brow. "He was visiting my father on business, you see. He came to dinner the following evening, and only three days later he asked for my hand."

"Really! Did it all happen so very fast?"

"Yes ... Or rather, from then on it went a little more slowly. You see, my father was not at all keen on the marriage, and insisted on our postponing it for quite a long time to think it over properly. It was partly that he would have preferred me to go on living with him, and he had other reservations about it as well. But ..."

"But?"

"But *I* was quite determined," she said with a smile, and once more the little pale blue vein overshadowed her sweet face with an anxious, sickly expression.

"Ah, you were determined."

"Yes, and I made my wishes quite clear and stood my ground, as you see . . ."

"As I see. Yes."

". . . so that my father had to give his consent in the end."

"And so you forsook him and his violin, you forsook the old house and the overgrown garden and the fountain and your six friends, and followed after Herr Klöterjahn."

"'And followed after. . . .' How strangely you put things, Herr Spinell! It sounds almost biblical! Yes, I left all that behind me, for after all, that is the law of nature."

"Of nature, yes, I daresay it is."

"And after all, my future happiness was at stake."

"Of course. And you came to know that happiness . . ."

"I came to know it, Herr Spinell, when they first brought little Anton to me, our little Anton, and when I heard him crying so noisily with his healthy little lungs, the strong, healthy little creature . . ."

"I have heard you mention the good health of your little Anton before, dear lady. He must be a quite exceptionally healthy child?"

"Yes, he is. And he looks so absurdly like my husband!"

"Ah! I see. So that was how it happened. And now your name is no longer Eckhof, but something else, and you have your healthy little Anton and a slight defect of the trachea."

"Yes. And as for *you*, Herr Spinell, you are a most mysterious person, I do assure you . . ."

"Yes, God bless my soul, so you are!" said Rätin Spatz, who was, after all, still there.

But this conversation too was one to which Herr Klöterjahn's wife afterward frequently reverted in her thoughts. Insignificant though it had been, there had nevertheless been several things latent in it which gave her food for reflection about herself. Could *this* be the harmful influence that was affecting her? Her weakness increased, and her temperature often rose: she would lie in a quiet feverish glow, in a state of mild euphoria to which she surrendered herself pensively, fastidiously, complacently, with a faintly injured air. When she was not confined to her bed, Herr Spinell would approach her, tiptoeing up to her on his great feet with extreme circumspection, stopping at a distance of two paces with one leg poised a little way behind the other, and bowing from the waist; he would talk to her in a deferentially muted voice, as if he were raising her gently aloft with reverent awe, and laying her down on soft cushioning clouds where no strident noise nor earthly contact should reach her. At such moments she would remember Herr Klöterjahn's way of saying "Careful, Gabriele, take care, darling, and keep your mouth closed!" in a voice as hard as a well-meant slap on the back. But then she would at once put this memory aside and lie back weakly and euphorically on the cloudy cushions which Herr Spinell so assiduously spread out beneath her.

One day, apropos of nothing at all, she suddenly reverted to the little conversation they had had about her background and earlier life.

"So it is really true, Herr Spinell," she asked, "that you would have seen the crown?"

And although it was already a fortnight since they had talked of this, he at once knew what she meant and ardently assured her that if he had been there then, as she sat with her six friends by the fountain, he would have seen the little golden crown gleaming— would have seen it secretly gleaming in her hair.

A few days later one of the patients politely inquired whether her little Anton at home was in good health. She exchanged a fleeting glance with Herr Spinell who was nearby, and answered with a slightly bored expression:

"Thank you, he is quite well; why should he not be? And so is my husband."

8

One frosty day at the end of February, a day purer and more brilliant than any that had preceded it, high spirits prevailed at Einfried. The heart cases chattered away to each other with flushed cheeks, the diabetic general hummed and chirruped like a boy, and the gentlemen with the unruly legs were quite beside themselves with excitement. What was it all about? A communal outing had been planned, nothing less: an excursion into the mountains in several sleighs, with jingling bells and cracking whips. Dr. Leander had decided upon this diversion for his patients.

Of course, the "serious cases" would have to stay at home, poor things! With much meaningful nodding it was tacitly agreed that the entire project must be concealed from them, and the opportunity to exercise this degree of compassion and consideration filled everyone with a glow of self-righteousness. But even a few of those who might very well have taken part in the treat declined to do so. Fräulein von Osterloh was of course excused in any case. No one so overburdened with duties as herself could seriously contemplate going on sleigh excursions. The tasks of the household imperatively required her presence—and in short, at Einfried she remained. But there was general disappointment when Herr Klöterjahn's wife also declared her intention of staying at home. In vain Dr. Leander urged upon her the benefits of the refreshing trip; she insisted that she was not in the mood, that she had a headache, that she felt tired; and so there was no more to be said. But the cynical would-be wit took occasion to observe:

"Mark my words, now the Putrefied Infant won't come either."

And he was right, for Herr Spinell let it be known that he intended to spend the afternoon working—he was very fond of describing his dubious activity as "work." The prospect of his absence was in any case regretted by no one, and equally little dismay was caused by Rätin Spatz's decision to remain behind and keep her young friend company, since (as she said) sleigh riding made her feel seasick.

There was an early lunch that day, at about noon, and immediately after it the sleighs drew up in front of Einfried. The patients, warmly wrapped up, made their way across the garden in animated groups, full of excitement and curiosity. The scene was watched by Herr Klöterjahn's wife and Rätin Spatz from the glass door leading out onto the terrace, and by Herr Spinell from the window of his room. There was a certain amount of playful and hilarious fighting about who should sit where; Fräulein von Osterloh, with a fur boa round her neck, darted from sleigh to sleigh pushing hampers of food under the seats; finally Dr. Leander, wearing a fur cap above his flashing spectacles, sat down himself after a last look round, and gave the signal for departure . . . The horses drew away, a few ladies shrieked and fell over backward, the bells jangled, the short-shafted whips cracked and their long lashes trailed across the snow beside the runners; and Fräulein von Osterloh stood at the garden gate waving her handkerchief until the vehicles slid out of sight round a bend in the road and the merry noise died away. Then she hurried back through the garden to set about her tasks again; the two ladies left the glass door, and almost simultaneously Herr Spinell retired from his vantage point.

Silence prevailed in Einfried. The expedition was not expected back before evening. The "serious cases" lay in their rooms and suffered. Herr Klöterjahn's wife and her companion took a short walk and then withdrew to their rooms. Herr Spinell, too, was in his room, occupied after his fashion. At about four o'clock half a litre of milk was brought to each of the ladies, and Herr Spinell was served with his usual weak tea. Shortly after this Herr Klöterjahn's wife tapped on the wall between her room and that of Magistratsrätin Spatz and said:

"Shall we go down into the drawing room, Frau Rätin? I really can't think of anything else to do here."

"Certainly, my dear, I'll come at once," answered Frau Spatz. "I'll just put on my boots, if you don't mind, because I've just been taking a bit of a rest, as a matter of fact."

As might have been expected, the drawing room was empty. The ladies sat down by the fireplace. Rätin Spatz was embroidering flowers on a piece of canvas; Herr Klöterjahn's wife, too, began a little needlework, but presently let it drop into her lap and gazed dreamily over the arm of her chair at nothing in particular. Finally she made a remark which was really not worth opening one's mouth to reply to. Rätin Spatz, however, nevertheless asked: "What did you say, my dear?" so that to her humiliation she had to repeat the whole sentence. Rätin Spatz again asked: "What?" But just at this moment they heard steps in the lobby, the door opened and Herr Spinell came into the room.

"Do I disturb you?" he asked softly, pausing on the threshold, looking only at Herr Klöterjahn's wife, and executing a kind of delicately hovering half-bow from the waist . . . She replied:

"Why, not at all, Herr Spinell! In the first place this room is supposed to be open to all comers, as you know, and in any case what is there to disturb? I have a very strong suspicion that I am boring Frau Spatz . . ."

He could think of no answer to this, but merely smiled, showing his carious teeth. The eyes of the two ladies followed him as with a certain air of embarrassment he walked to the glass door, where he stopped and stood looking out, rather ill-manneredly turning his back on them. Then he half turned toward them, but continued to gaze out into the garden as he said:

"The sun has disappeared. The sky has imperceptibly clouded over. It's beginning to get dark already."

"Yes, indeed, there are shadows everywhere," replied Herr Klöterjahn's wife. "I should think it may well be snowing before our sleighing party gets back. Yesterday at this time it was still broad daylight, and now dusk is falling."

"Oh," he said, "what a relief it is to the eyes! There has been too much brightness these last few weeks—too much of this sun which glares with such obtrusive clarity on everything, whether beautiful or vulgar . . . I am really thankful that it is hiding its face for a little at last."

"Do you not like the sun, Herr Spinell?"

"Well, I am no painter, you know . . . When there is no sun one feels more spiritual. There is a thick, pale gray layer of cloud all over the sky. Perhaps it means there will be a thaw tomorrow. Incidentally I would not advise you, dear madam, to go on gazing at your needlework over there."

"Oh, you need not worry, I've stopped it in any case. But what else is there to do?"

He had sat down on the revolving stool in front of the piano, leaning on the lid of the instrument with one arm.

"Music . . ." he said. "If only there were a chance to hear a little music nowadays! Sometimes the English children sing little negro songs, and that is all."

"And yesterday afternoon Fräulein von Osterloh gave a high-speed rendering of 'The Monastery Bells,'" remarked Herr Klöterjahn's wife.

"But dear lady, you play, do you not?" he said pleadingly, and rose to his feet . . . "There was a time when you used to make music every day with your father."

"Yes, Herr Spinell, that was in the old days! The days of the fountain in the garden, you know . . ."

"Do it today!" he begged. "Play a few bars just this once! If you knew how I craved to hear them . . ."

"Our family doctor and Dr. Leander have both expressly forbidden me to play, Herr Spinell."

"They are not here; neither of them here! We are free . . . you are free, dear lady! A few trifling little chords . . ."

"No, Herr Spinell, it's no use your trying to persuade me. Heaven knows what sort of marvels you expect of me! And I have forgotten everything, I assure you. I can play scarcely a note by heart."

"Oh, then play that! Play scarcely a note! Besides, there is some music here too—here it is, on the top of the piano. No, this is nothing. But here is some Chopin . . ."

"Chopin?"

"Yes, the nocturnes. And now all that remains is for us to light the candles . . ."

"Don't imagine that I am going to play, Herr Spinell! I must not play! What if it were to do me harm?"

He was silent. With his great feet, his long black coat, his gray hair and his beardless face with its indistinctly outlined features, he stood there in the light of the two piano candles, letting his hands hang down by his sides.

Finally he said in a soft voice: "In that case I cannot ask it of you. If you are afraid it will do you harm, dear madam, then let the beauty that might come to life under your fingers remain dead and mute. You were not always so very prudent; at least you were not so when you were asked to make the opposite decision and renounce beauty. You were not concerned about your bodily welfare then, you showed less hesitation and a stronger will when you left the fountain and took off the little golden crown . . . Listen!" he said after a pause, dropping his voice still lower. "If you sit here now and play as you once did, when your father was still standing beside you and drawing those notes out of his violin that brought tears to your eyes—then perhaps it will be seen again, gleaming secretly in your hair, the little golden crown . . ."

"Really?" she said, with a smile. It somehow happened that her voice failed her on this word, which came out huskily and half in a whisper. She cleared her throat and asked:

"Are those really Chopin's nocturnes you have there?"

"Indeed they are. They are open and everything is ready."

"Well, then, in God's name, I will play one of them," she said. "But only one, do you understand? In any case, after one you certainly won't want to hear any more."

So saying she rose, put down her needlework and came across to the piano. She sat down on the revolving stool, on which two or three bound volumes of music lay; she adjusted the lights, and began turning over the pages of the Chopin album. Herr Spinell had drawn up a chair, and sat beside her like a music master.

She played the Nocturne in E-flat major, opus 9, no. 2. If it was really true that she had forgotten anything of what she had once learned, then she must in those days have been a consummate artist. The piano was only a mediocre one, but after the very first notes she was able to handle it with perfect taste and control. She showed a fastidious ear for differences of timbre, and her enthusiastic command of rhythmic mobility verged on the fantastic. Her touch was both firm and gentle. Under her hands the melody sang forth its uttermost sweetness, and the figurations entwined themselves round it with diffident grace.

She was wearing the dress she had worn the day of her arrival, the one with the dark heavy bodice and the thick cut-velvet arabesques, which gave to her head and her hands a look of such unearthly delicacy. The expression of her face did not change as she played, but her lips seemed to grow more clear-cut than ever and the shadows seemed to deepen in the corners of her eyes. When she had finished she lowered her hands to her lap and went on gazing at the music. Herr Spinell sat on motionless, without saying a word.

She played another nocturne, she played a second and a third. Then she rose, but only to look for some more music on the top of the piano.

It occurred to Herr Spinell to examine the black bound albums on the piano stool. Suddenly he uttered an unintelligible sound, and his great white hands passionately fingered one of the neglected volumes.

"It's not possible! ... It can't be true! ... And yet there is no doubt of it! ... Do you know what this is? ... Do you realize what has been lying here—what I have in my hands? ..."

"What is it?" she asked.

Speechlessly he pointed to the title page. He had turned quite pale; he lowered the volume and looked at her with trembling lips.

"Indeed? I wonder how that got here? Well, give it to me," she said simply. She put it on the music stand, sat down, and after a moment's silence began to play the first page.

He sat beside her, leaning forward, with his hands between his knees and his head bowed. She played the opening at an extravagantly, tormentingly slow tempo, with a disturbingly long pause between each of the phrases. The *Sehnsucht* motif, a lonely wandering voice in the night, softly uttered its tremulous question. Silence followed, a silence of waiting. And then the answer: the same hesitant, lonely strain, but higher in pitch, more radiant and tender. Silence again. And then, with that wonderful muted sforzando which is like an upsurging, uprearing impulse of joy and passion, the love motif began: it rose, it climbed ecstatically to a mingling sweetness, reached its climax and fell away, while the deep song of the cellos came into prominence and continued the melody in grave, sorrowful rapture . . .

Despite the inferiority of her instrument the performer tried with some success to suggest the appropriate orchestral effects. She rendered with brilliant precision the violin scales in the great crescendo. She played with fastidious reverence, lingering faithfully over every significant detail of the structure, humbly and ceremoniously exhibiting it, like a priest elevating the sacred host. What story did the music tell? It told of two forces, two enraptured lovers reaching out toward each other in suffering and ecstasy and embracing in a convulsive mad desire for eternity, for the absolute . . . The prelude blazed to its consummation and died down. She stopped at the point where the curtain parts and continued to gaze silently at the music.

The boredom of Rätin Spatz had by this time reached that degree of intensity at which it causes protrusion of the eyes and a terrifying, corpselike disfigurement of the human countenance. In addition this kind of music affected her stomach nerves, it threw her dyspeptic organism into a turmoil of anxiety, and Frau Spatz began to fear that she was about to have a fit.

"I'm afraid I must go to my room," she said in a faint voice. "Good-bye, I shall be back presently."

And she departed. The evening dusk was already far advanced. Outside on the terrace, thick snow was silently falling. The two candles gave a close and flickering light.

"The second act," he whispered; and she turned the pages and began playing the second act.

The sound of horns dying away in the distance . . . or was it the wind in the leaves? The soft murmuring of the stream? Already the night had flooded the grove with its stillness and hushed the castle halls, and no warning entreaty availed now to stem the tide of overmastering desire. The sacred mystery was enacted. The torch was extinguished; the descending notes of the death motif spoke with a strange, suddenly clouded sonority; and in tumultuous impatience the white veil was passionately waved, signaling to the beloved as he approached with outspread arms through the darkness.

Oh boundless, oh unending exultation of this meeting in an eternal place beyond all visible things! Delivered from the tormenting illusion, set free from the bondage of space and time, self and notself blissfully mingling, "thine" and "mine" mystically made one! The mocking falsehoods of day could divide them, but its pomp and show no longer had power to deceive them, for the magic potion had opened their eyes: it had made them initiates and visionaries of night. He who has gazed with love into the darkness of death and

beheld its sweet mystery can long for one thing only while daylight
still holds him in its delusive thrall: all his desire and yearning is for
the sacred night which is eternal and true, and which unifies all that
has been separated.

O sink down, night of love, upon them; give them that forgetfulness they long for, enfold them utterly in your joy and free them
from the world of deception and division! "See, the last lamp has
been extinguished! Thought and the vanity of thinking have vanished in the holy twilight, the world-redeeming dusk outspread over
all illusion and all woe. And then, as the shining phantasms fade
and my eyes fail with passion: then this, from which delusive day
debarred me, with which it falsely and tormentingly confronted my
endless desire—then I myself, oh wonder of wishes granted! then *I
myself* am the world . . ." And there followed Brangäne's warning
call, with those rising violin phrases that pass all understanding.

"I am not always sure what it means, Herr Spinell; I can only
guess at some of it. What is 'then—I myself am the world'?"

He explained it to her, softly and briefly.

"Yes, I see. But how can you understand it all so well, and yet
not be able to play it?"

Strangely enough, this simple question quite overwhelmed him.
He colored, wrung his hands and seemed to sink into the floor, chair
and all. Finally he answered in stricken tones:

"The two seldom go together. No, I cannot play. But please
continue."

And the drunken paeans of the mystery drama continued. "Can
love ever die? Tristan's love? The love of thy Isolde, of my Isolde?
Oh, it is everlasting, death cannot assail it! What could perish by
death but the powers that interfere, the pretenses that part us, we
who are two and one?" By the sweet word "and" love bound them
together—and if death should sunder that bond, how could death
come to either of them and not bring with it the other's own life?
. . . And thus they sang their mysterious duo, sang of their nameless
hope, their death-in-love, their union unending, lost for ever in the
embrace of night's magic kingdom. O sweet night, everlasting night
of love! Land of blessedness whose frontiers are infinite! What visionary once has dreamed of you and does not dread to wake again
into desolate day? O grace of death, cast out that dread! Set free
these lovers utterly from the anguish of waking! Ah, this miraculous
tempest of rhythms, this chromatic uprushing ecstasy, this meta-
physical revelation! "A rapture beyond knowing, beyond foregoing,

far from the pangs of the light that parts us, a tender longing with no fear or feigning, a ceasing in beauty with no pain, an enchanted dreaming in immensity! Thou art Isolde, I am Isolde no longer; I am Tristan no longer, thou art Tristan—"

At this point there was a startling interruption. The pianist suddenly stopped playing and shaded her eyes with her hand to peer into the darkness; and Herr Spinell swung round on his chair. At the far side of the room the door that led into the passage had opened, and a shadowy figure entered, leaning on the arm of a second figure. It was one of the Einfried patients, one who had also been unable to join in the sleigh ride, but had chosen this evening hour for one of her pathetic instinctive tours round the institution: it was the lady who had had nineteen children and was no longer capable of thought—it was Pastorin Höhlenrauch on the arm of her attendant. She did not raise her eyes, but wandered with groping steps across the background of the room and disappeared through the opposite door, like a sleepwalker, dumb and staring and conscious of nothing. All was silent.

"That was Pastorin Höhlenrauch," he said.

"Yes, that was poor Frau Höhlenrauch," she replied. Then she turned the pages and played the closing passage of the whole work, the *Liebestod,* Isolde's death song.

How pale and clear her lips were, and how the shadows deepened in the corners of her eyes! The little pale blue vein over one eyebrow, which gave her face such a disturbingly strained look, stood out more and more prominently on her transparent forehead. Under her rapidly moving hands the fantastic crescendo mounted to its climax, broken by that almost shameless, sudden pianissimo in which the ground seems to slide away under our feet and a sublime lust to engulf us in its depths. The triumph of a vast release, a tremendous fulfillment, a roaring tumult of immense delight, was heard and heard again, insatiably repeated, flooding back and reshaping itself; when it seemed on the point of ebbing away it once more wove the *Sehnsucht* motif into its harmony, then breathed out its uttermost breath and died, faded into silence, floated into nothingness. A profound stillness reigned.

They both sat listening, tilting their heads to one side and listening.

"That's the sound of bells," she said.

"It's the sleighs," he said. "I shall go."

He rose and walked across the room. When he came to the door at the far end he stopped, turned round and stood for a moment, uneasily shifting his weight from one foot to the other. And then, fifteen or twenty paces from her, he suddenly sank down on his knees—down on both knees, without a word. His long black frock coat spread out around him on the floor. His hands were clasped across his mouth and his shoulders twitched convulsively.

She sat with her hands in her lap, leaning forward away from the piano, and looked at him. She was smiling with a strained, uncertain smile, and her eyes gazed pensively into the half-darkness, focusing themselves with difficulty, with a slight uncontrollable unsteadiness.

From some way off the jangle of sleigh bells, the crack of whips and a babel of human voices could be heard approaching.

9

The sleigh excursion, which remained the chief topic of conversation for a considerable time, had taken place on the twenty-sixth of February. On the twenty-seventh a thaw set in, everything turned soft and slushy and dripped and dribbled, and on that day Herr Klöterjahn's wife was in excellent health. On the twenty-eighth she coughed up a little blood—oh, hardly any to speak of; but it was blood. At the same time she began to feel weaker than she had ever felt before, and took to her bed.

Dr. Leander examined her, and his face as he did so was cold and hard. He then prescribed the remedies indicated by medical science: little pieces of ice, morphine, complete rest. It also happened that on the following day he declared himself unable to continue the treatment personally owing to pressure of work, and handed it over to Dr. Müller, who meekly undertook it, as his contract required. He was a quiet, pale, insignificant, sad-looking man, whose modest and unapplauded function it was to care for those patients who were scarcely ill at all and for those whose cases were hopeless.

The opinion expressed by Dr. Müller, first and foremost, was that the separation between Herr Klöterjahn and his wedded wife had now lasted rather a long time. It was, in his view, extremely desirable that Herr Klöterjahn—if, of course, his prosperous business could possibly spare him—should pay another visit to Einfried. One might write to him, one might even send him a little telegram . . . And it would, Dr. Müller thought, undoubtedly cheer and strengthen the young mother if he were to bring little Anton with him—quite apart from the fact that it would be of considerable interest to the doctors to make the acquaintance of this very healthy little child.

And lo and behold, Herr Klöterjahn came. He had received Dr. Müller's little telegram and had arrived from the Baltic coast. He dismounted from the carriage, ordered coffee and buttered rolls and looked extremely put out.

"Sir," he said, "what is the matter? Why have I been summoned to her?"

"Because it is desirable," answered Dr. Müller, "that you should be near your wife at the present time."

"Desirable . . . desirable . . . ! But is it *necessary?* I have to consider my money, sir—times are bad and railway fares are high. Was this lengthy journey really indispensable? I'd say nothing if for example it were her lungs; but since, thank God, it's only her trachea . . ."

"Herr Klöterjahn," said Dr. Müller gently, "in the first place the trachea is an important organ . . ." He said "in the first place," although this was incorrect, since he did not then mention any second place.

But simultaneously with Herr Klöterjahn a buxom young woman appeared in Einfried, clad entirely in red and tartan and gold, and it was she who on one arm carried Anton Klöterjahn, Jr., little healthy Anton. Yes—he was here, and no one could deny that he was in fact a prodigy of good health. Pink and white, cleanly and freshly clothed, fat and fragrant, he reposed heavily upon the bare red arm of his gold-braided nurse, devoured enormous quantities of milk and chopped meat, screamed and abandoned himself in all respects to his instincts.

From the window of his room, the writer Spinell had observed the arrival of the Klöterjahn child. Through half-closed eyes, with a strange yet penetrating scrutiny, he had watched him being lifted out of the carriage and conveyed into the house; and he had then stood on motionless for some time with his expression unchanged.

Thereafter, so far as was feasible, he avoided all contact with Anton Klöterjahn, Jr.

10

Herr Spinell was sitting in his room "working."

It was a room like all the others in Einfried, furnished in a simple and elegant period style. The massive chest of drawers had metal lion's-head mountings; the tall pier glass was not one smooth sheet, but composed of numerous small panes framed in lead; the gleaming floor was uncarpeted and the stiff legs of the furniture seemed to extend as light shadows into its bluish, varnished surface. A large writing table stood near the window, across which the novelist had drawn a yellow curtain, presumably to make himself feel more spiritual.

In a yellowish twilight he was sitting bowed over the desk and writing—he was writing one of those numerous letters which he sent to the post every week and to which, comically enough, he usually received no reply. A large thick sheet of writing paper lay before him, and in its top left-hand corner, under an intricately vignetted landscape, the name "Detlev Spinell" was printed in letters of an entirely novel design. He was covering this sheet with tiny handwriting, with a neat and most carefully executed calligraphy.

"Sir!" he had written, "I am addressing the following lines to you because I simply cannot help it—because my heart is so full of what I have to say to you that it aches and trembles, and the words come to me in such a rush that they would choke me if I could not unburden myself of them in this letter . . ."

To be strictly correct, this statement about the words coming to him in a rush was quite simply untrue, and God knows what foolish vanity induced Herr Spinell to make such an assertion. Rushing was the very last thing his words seemed to be doing; indeed, for one whose profession and social status it was to be a writer, he was making miserably slow progress, and no one could have watched him without reaching the conclusion that a writer is a man to whom writing comes harder than to anyone else.

Between two fingertips he held one of the strange little downy hairs that grew on his face and went on twirling it for periods of a quarter of an hour or more, at the same time staring into vacancy and adding not a line to his composition; he would then daintily pen a few words and come to a halt once more. On the other hand it must be admitted that what he finally produced did give the impression of smooth spontaneity and vigor, notwithstanding its odd and dubious and often scarcely intelligible content.

"I am," the letter continued, "under an inescapable compulsion to make you see what I see, to make you share the inextinguishable vision that has haunted me for weeks, to make you see it with my eyes, illuminated by the language in which I myself would express what I inwardly behold. An imperative instinct bids me communicate my experiences to the world, to communicate them in unforgettable words each chosen and placed with burning accuracy; and this is an instinct which it is my habit to obey. I ask you, therefore, to hear me.

"I merely wish to tell you about something as it was and as it now is. It is a quite short and unspeakably outrageous story, and I shall tell it without comment, accusation or judgment, but in my own words. It is the story of Gabriele Eckhof, sir, the lady whom you call your wife . . . and please note: although the experience was yours, it is nevertheless I whose words will for the first time raise it for you to the level of a significant event.

"Do you remember the garden, sir, the old neglected garden behind the gray patrician house? Green moss grew in the crevices of the weather-beaten walls that surrounded this wild and dreaming place. And do you remember the fountain in the center? Lilac-colored sword lilies drooped over its crumbling edge, and its silvery jet murmured mysteriously as it played upon the riven stonework. The summer day was drawing to its close.

"Seven maidens were sitting in a circle round the fountain; but in the hair of the seventh, the one and chiefest among them all, the sunset's rays seemed secretly to be weaving a glittering emblem of royal rank. Her eyes were like troubled dreams, and yet her bright lips were parted in a smile . . .

"They were singing. Lifting their slender faces they watched the leaping jet, they gazed up at the point where it wearily and nobly curved into its fall, and their soft clear voices hovered around its graceful dance. Their delicate hands, perhaps, were clasped about their knees as they sang . . .

"Do you remember this scene, sir? Did you even see it? No, you did not. It was not for your eyes, and yours were not the ears to hear the chaste sweetness of that melody. Had you seen it, you would not have dared to draw breath, and your heart would have checked its beat. You would have had to withdraw, go back into life, back to your own life, and preserve what you had beheld as something untouchable and inviolable, as a sacred treasure within your soul, to the end of your earthly days. But what did you do?

"That scene, sir, was the end of a tale. Why did you have to come and destroy it, why give the story so vulgar and ugly and painful a sequel? It had been a moving, tranquil apotheosis, immersed in the transfiguring sunset glow of decline and decay and extinction. An old family, already grown too weary and too noble for life and action, had reached the end of its history, and its last utterances were sounds of music: a few violin notes, full of the sad insight which is ripeness for death . . . Did you look into the eyes that were filled with tears by those notes? It may be that the souls of her six companions belonged to life—but not hers, the soul of their sister and queen: for on it beauty and death had set their mark.

"You saw it, that death-doomed beauty: you looked upon it to lust after it. No reverence, no awe touched your heart at the sight of something so moving and holy. You were not content to look upon it: you had to possess it, to exploit it, to desecrate it. . . . What a subtle choice you made! You are a gourmet, sir, a plebeian gourmet, a peasant with taste.

"Please note that I have no wish whatever to offend you. What I have said is not abuse: I am merely stating the formula, the simple psychological formula of your simple, aesthetically quite uninteresting personality; and I am stating it solely because I feel the need to shed a little light for you on your own nature and behavior—because it is my ineluctable vocation on this earth to call things by their names, to make them articulate, and to illuminate whatever is unconscious. The world is full of what I call 'the unconscious type,' and all these unconscious types are what I cannot bear! I cannot bear all this primitive, ignorant life, all this naive activity, this world of infuriating intellectual blindness all round me! I am possessed by a tormenting irresistible impulse to analyze all these human lives in my vicinity, to do my utmost to give to each its correct definition and bring it to consciousness of itself—and I am unrestrained by consideration of the consequences of doing so, I care not whether my words help or hinder, whether they carry comfort and solace or inflict pain.

"You, sir, as I have said, are a plebeian gourmet, a peasant with taste. Although in fact your natural constitution is coarse and your position on the evolutionary scale extremely low, your wealth and your sedentary habits have enabled you to achieve a certain barbarian corruption of the nervous system, sudden and historically quite inappropriate, but lending a certain lascivious refinement to your appetites. I dare say your throat muscles began to contract automatically, as if stimulated by the prospect of swallowing some delicious soup or masticating some rare dish, when you decided to take possession of Gabriele Eckhof . . .

"And so indeed you did: interrupting her dream and imposing your misguided will upon hers; leading her out of the neglected garden into life and ugliness; giving her your vulgar name and mak-

ing her a married woman, a housewife, a mother. You degraded that
weary diffident beauty, which belonged to death and was blossoming
in sublime uselessness, by harnessing it to the service of everyday
triviality and of that mindless, gross and contemptible idol which is
called 'nature'; and your peasant conscience has never stirred with
the slightest inkling of how profound an outrage you committed.

"Once again: what in fact has happened? She, with those eyes
that are like troubled dreams, has borne you a child; to that creature,
that mere continuation of its begetter's crude existence, she at the
same time gave every particle of vitality and viability she possessed—and now she dies. She is dying, sir! And if nevertheless her
departure is not vulgar and trivial, if at the very end she has risen
from her degradation and perishes proudly and joyfully under the
deadly kiss of beauty, then it is *I* who have made it my business to
bring that about. You, I dare say, were in the meantime diverting
yourself in quiet corridors with chambermaids.

"But her son, Gabriele Eckhof's son, is living and thriving and
triumphant. Perhaps he will continue his father's career and become
an active trading citizen, paying his taxes and eating well; perhaps
he will be a soldier or an official, an unenlightened and efficient
pillar of society; in any case he will be a normally functioning philistine type, unscrupulous and self-assured, strong and stupid.

"Let me confess to you, sir, that I hate you, you and your child,
as I hate life itself—the vulgar, absurd and nevertheless triumphant
life which you represent, and which is the eternal antithesis and
archenemy of beauty. I cannot say that I despise you. I am unable
to despise you. I honestly admit this. You are the stronger man. In
our struggle I have only one thing to turn against you, the sublime
avenging weapon of the weak: intellect and the power of words.
Today I have used this weapon. For this letter—here too let me make
an honest admission—is nothing but an act of revenge; and if it
contains even a single phrase that is biting and brilliant and beautiful
enough to strike home, to make you aware of an alien force, to
shake your robust equanimity even for one moment, then I shall
exult in that discomfiture.—DETLEV SPINELL."

And Herr Spinell put this piece of writing into an envelope, added
a stamp, daintily penned an address, and delivered it to the post.

11

Herr Klöterjahn knocked at the door of Herr Spinell's room; he
held a large, neatly written sheet of paper in one hand, and wore

the air of a man determined upon energetic measures. The post had done its duty, the letter had completed its curious journey from Einfried to Einfried and had duly reached its intended recipient. The time was four o'clock in the afternoon.

When Herr Klöterjahn entered, Herr Spinell was sitting on the sofa reading his own novel, the book with the baffling cover design. He rose to his feet with a surprised and interrogative glance at his visitor, while at the same time coloring perceptibly.

"Good afternoon," said Herr Klöterjahn. "Pardon my intrusion upon your occupations. But may I ask whether you wrote this?" So saying he held up the large, neatly written sheet in his left hand and struck it with the back of his right, making it crackle sharply. He then pushed his right hand into the pocket of his wide, easy-fitting trousers, tilted his head to one side and opened his mouth to listen, as some people do.

Oddly enough Herr Spinell smiled; with an obliging, rather confused and half apologetic smile he raised one hand to his forehead as if he were trying to recollect what he had done, and said:

"Ah yes . . . that is so . . . I took the liberty . . ."

The fact was that on this particular day he had acted in accordance with his true nature and slept until noon. Consequently he was suffering from a bad conscience, his head was not clear, he felt nervous and his resistance was low. In addition there was now a touch of spring in the air, which he found fatiguing and deeply depressing. This must all be mentioned in extenuation of the pitifully silly figure he cut throughout the following scene.

"Did you indeed? Ah-ha! Very well!" Herr Klöterjahn, having got this opening formality out of the way, thrust his chin down against his chest, raised his eyebrows, flexed his arms and gave various other indications that he was about to come mercilessly to the point. His exuberant self-satisfaction was such that he slightly overdid these preparatory antics, so that what eventually followed did not quite live up to the elaborate menace of the preliminary pantomime. But Herr Spinell had turned several shades paler.

"Very well, my dear sir!" repeated Herr Klöterjahn. "Then I shall answer it by word of mouth, if you don't mind, having regard to the fact that I consider it idiotic to write letters several pages long to a person to whom one can speak at any hour of the day . . ."

"Well . . . idiotic perhaps . . ." said Herr Spinell with an apologetic, almost humble smile.

"Idiotic!" repeated Herr Klöterjahn, energetically shaking his head in token of the utter unassailability of his position. "And I'd not be wasting words now on this scribbled piece of trash, frankly I'd not even have kept it to use for wrapping up sandwiches, but for the fact that it has opened my eyes and clarified certain matters which I had not understood, certain changes . . . however, that's no concern of yours and it's beside the point. I am a busy man, I have more important things to think about than your indistinguishable visions . . ."

"I wrote 'inextinguishable vision,'" said Herr Spinell, drawing himself up to his full height. During this whole scene it was the one moment in which he displayed a minimum of dignity.

"Inextinguishable . . . indistinguishable . . .!" retorted Herr Klöterjahn, glancing at the manuscript. "Your handwriting's wretched, my dear sir; you'd not get a job in my office. At first sight it seems decent enough, but when you look at it closely it's full of gaps and all of a quiver. However, that's your affair and not mine. I came here to tell you that in the first place you are a fool and a clown— well, let's hope you're aware of that already. But in addition you are a damned coward, and I dare say I don't need to prove that to you in detail either. My wife once wrote to me that when you meet women you don't look them square in the face but just give them a sort of squint from the side, because you're afraid of reality and want to carry away a beautiful impression in your mind's eye. Later on unfortunately she stopped mentioning you in her letters, or I'd have heard some more fine stories about you. But that's the sort of man you are. It's 'beauty' and 'beauty' in every sentence you speak, but the basis of it all is cringing cowardice and envy, and I suppose that also explains your impudent allusion to 'quiet corridors.' I dare say that remark was intended to knock me absolutely flat, and all it did was to give me a good laugh. A damned good laugh! Well, now have I told you a few home truths? Have I—let me see—'shed a little light for you on your nature and behavior,' you miserable specimen? Not of course that it's my 'indestructible vocation' to do so, heh, heh! . . ."

"I wrote 'ineluctable vocation,'" said Herr Spinell; but he let the point go. He stood there crestfallen and helpless, like a great pathetic gray-haired scolded schoolboy.

"Indestructible . . . ineluctable . . . I tell you you are a contempt-ible cowardly cur. Every day you see me at table. You bow to me and smile, you pass me dishes and smile, you say the polite things and smile. And one fine day you fling this screed of abusive drivel into my face. Ho, yes, you're bold enough on paper! And this ridiculous letter's not the whole story. You've been plotting against me behind my back, I see that now quite clearly ... Although you needn't imagine you've had any success. If you flatter yourself that you've put any fancy notions into my wife's head, then you're barking up the wrong tree, my fine friend! My wife has too much common sense! Or if you should even be thinking that when I got here with the child her behavior toward us was in any way different from what it used to be, then you're even more of a half-wit than I supposed! It's true she didn't kiss the little fellow, but that was a precaution, because just lately the suggestion's been made that the trouble isn't with her trachea but with her lungs, and if that's so one can't be too ... but anyhow they're still a long way from proving their lung theory, and as for you and your 'she is dying, sir'—why, you crazy ninny, you ...!"

Here Herr Klöterjahn struggled a little to recover his breath. By now he had worked himself up into a passionate rage; he kept stabbing the air with his right forefinger and crumpling the manuscript with his left hand till it was scarcely fit to be seen. His face, between its blond English side-whiskers, had turned terribly red, and swollen veins ran like streaks of wrathful lightning across his clouded brow.

"You hate me," he went on, "and you would despise me if I were not the stronger man ... Yes, and so I am, by God! My heart's in the right place; and where's yours? In your boots most of the time I suppose, and if it were not forbidden by law I'd knock you to pieces, with your 'intellect and power of words' and all, you blithering snake in the grass! But that does not mean, my fine fellow, that I intend to put up with your insults lying down, and when I get back and show my lawyer that bit about my 'vulgar name'—then we'll see whether you don't get the shock of your life. My name is good, sir, and it's my own hard work that made it good. Just you ask yourself whether anyone will lend you a brass farthing on yours, you idle tramp from God knows where! The law of the land is for dealing with people like you! You're a public danger! You drive people crazy! ... But I'll have you know that you've not got away with your little tricks this time, my very smart friend! I'm not the man to let your sort get the better of me, oh no! My heart's in the right place ..."

Herr Klöterjahn was now in a real fury. He was positively bellowing, and kept on repeating that his heart was in the right place.

"'They were singing.' Full stop. They were doing nothing of the sort! They were knitting. What's more, from what I overheard, they were discussing a recipe for potato pancakes; and when I show this passage about 'decline and decay' to my father-in-law, he'll take you to court too, you may be sure of that! ... 'Do you remember that scene, did you see it?' Of course I saw it, but what I don't see is why I should have held my breath at the sight and run away. I don't squint and leer at women from the side, I look them in the face, and if I like the look of them and they like me, I go ahead and get them. My heart's in the right pl ..."

Someone was knocking. Knocking at the door of the room, nine or ten times in rapid succession, in an urgent, frantic little tattoo which stopped Herr Klöterjahn in mid-sentence; and a voice exclaimed, panic-stricken and stumbling with distress and haste:

"Herr Klöterjahn, Herr Klöterjahn—oh, is Herr Klöterjahn there?"

"Keep out!" said Herr Klöterjahn rudely. "What's the matter? I'm busy here talking."

"Herr Klöterjahn," said the tremulous, gasping voice, "you must come ... the doctors are there too ... oh, it's so dreadfully sad ..."

He was at the door with one stride and snatched it open. Rätin Spatz was standing outside. She was holding her handkerchief to her mouth, and great long tears were rolling down into it from both her eyes.

"Herr Klöterjahn," she managed to say, "... it's so terribly sad ... She brought up so much blood, such a dreadful lot ... She was sitting up quite quietly in her bed humming a little snatch of music to herself, and then it came—oh, God, there was such a lot, you never saw such a lot ..."

"Is she dead?" shrieked Herr Klöterjahn, seizing Frau Spatz by the arm and dragging her to and fro on the threshold ... "No, not quite, what? Not quite dead yet, she can still see me, can't she? Brought up a little blood again, has she? From the lungs, was it? Maybe it does come from the lungs, I admit that it may ... Gabriele!" he cried suddenly, tears starting to his eyes, and the warm, kindly, honest, human emotion that welled up from within him was plain to see. "Yes, I'm coming!" he said, and with long strides he dragged Frau Spatz out of the room and away along the corridor. From far in the distance his rapidly receding voice could still be heard: "Not quite, what? ... From her lungs, you say?"

12

Herr Spinell went on standing exactly where he had stood throughout Herr Klöterjahn's so abruptly terminated visit. He stared at the open door; finally he advanced a few steps into the passage and listened. But in the distance all was silent; and so he returned to his room, closing the door behind him.

He looked at himself in the mirror for several minutes, then went to his desk, took a small flask and a glass from somewhere inside it and swallowed a brandy—for which in the circumstances he could scarcely be blamed. Then he lay down on the sofa and closed his eyes.

The window was open at the top. Outside in the garden of Einfried the birds were twittering; and somehow the whole of spring was expressed in those subtle, tender, penetrating, insolent little notes. At one point Herr Spinell muttered the phrase "indestructible vocation . . .!" to himself, and shook his head from side to side, sucking the breath in between his teeth as if afflicted by acute nervous discomfort.

To regain calm and composure was out of the question. One's constitution is really quite unsuited to these coarse experiences! By a psychological process the analysis of which would carry us too far afield, Herr Spinell reached the decision to get up and take a little exercise, a short walk in the open air. Accordingly he picked up his hat and left his room.

As he stepped out of the house into the balmy, fragrant air he turned his head back toward the building and slowly raised his eyes until they reached a certain window, a window across which the curtains had been drawn: he gazed fixedly at it for a while, and his expression was grave and somber. Then, with his hands on his back, he went on his way along the gravel path. He was deep in thought as he walked.

The flower beds were still covered with matting, the trees and bushes were still bare; but the snow had gone, and there were only a few damp patches here and there on the paths. The spacious garden with its grottoes, leafy arcades and little pavilions was bathed in the splendid intense colors of late afternoon, full of strong shadows and a rich golden glow, and intricate patterns of dark branches and twigs stood sharply and finely silhouetted against the bright sky.

It was the time of day at which the sun's outline becomes clear, when it is no longer a shapeless brilliant mass but a visibly sinking disk whose richer, milder glow the eye can bear to behold. Herr Spinell did not see the sun; he walked with his head bowed, humming a little snatch of music to himself, a brief phrase, a few anguished, plaintively rising notes: the *Sehnsucht* motif . . . But suddenly, with a start, with a quick convulsive intake of breath, he stood still as if rooted to the spot and stared straight ahead of him, wide-eyed, with sharply contracted brows and an expression of horrified repugnance . . .

The path had turned; it now led straight toward the setting sun, which stood large and low in the sky, its surface intersected by two narrow wisps of gleaming cloud with gilded edges, its warm yellow radiance flooding the garden and setting the treetops on fire. And in the very midst of this golden transfiguration, erect on the path with the sun's disk surrounding her head like a mighty halo, stood a buxom young woman clad entirely in red and gold and tartan. She was resting her right hand on her well-rounded hip, while with her left she lightly rocked a graceful little perambulator to and fro. But in front of her, in this perambulator, sat the child—sat Anton Klöterjahn, Jr., Gabriele Eckhof's fat son!

There he sat among his cushions, in a white wooly jacket and a big white hat—chubby, magnificent and robust; and his eyes, unabashed and alive with merriment, looked straight into Herr Spinell's. The novelist was just on the point of pulling himself together; after all, he was a grown man, he would have had the strength to step right past this unexpected sight, this resplendent phenomenon, and continue his walk. But at the very moment the appalling thing happened: Anton Klöterjahn began to laugh—he screamed with laughter, he squealed, he crowed: it was inexplicable. It was positively uncanny.

God knows what had come over him, what had set him off into this wild hilarity: the sight of the black-clad figure in front of him perhaps, or some sudden spasm of sheer animal high spirits. He had a bone teething ring in one hand and a tin rattle in the other, and he held up these two objects triumphantly into the sunshine, brandishing them and banging them together, as if he were mockingly trying to scare someone off. His eyes were almost screwed shut with pleasure, and his mouth gaped open so wide that his entire pink palate was exposed. He even wagged his head to and fro in his exultation.

And Herr Spinell turned on his heel and walked back the way he had come. Pursued by the infant Klöterjahn's jubilant shrieks, he walked along the gravel path, holding his arms in a careful, prim posture; and something in his gait suggested that it cost him an effort to walk slowly—the effort of a man intent upon concealing the fact that he is inwardly running away.

Translated by David Luke

Death in Venice

1

On a spring afternoon in 19—, the year in which for months on end so grave a threat seemed to hang over the peace of Europe, Gustav Aschenbach, or von Aschenbach as he had been officially known since his fiftieth birthday, had set out from his apartment on the Prinzregentenstrasse in Munich to take a walk of some length by himself. The morning's writing had overstimulated him: his work had now reached a difficult and dangerous point which demanded the utmost care and circumspection, the most insistent and precise effort of will, and the productive mechanism in his mind—that *motus animi continuus* which according to Cicero is the essence of eloquence—had so pursued its reverberating rhythm that he had been unable to halt it even after lunch, and had missed the refreshing daily siesta which was now so necessary to him as he became increasingly subject to fatigue. And so, soon after taking tea, he had left the house hoping that fresh air and movement would set him to rights and enable him to spend a profitable evening.

It was the beginning of May, and after a succession of cold, wet weeks a premature high summer had set in. The Englischer Garten, although still only in its first delicate leaf, had been as sultry as in August, and at its city end full of traffic and pedestrians. Having made his way to the Aumeister along less and less frequented paths, Aschenbach had briefly surveyed the lively scene at the popular open-air restaurant, around which a few cabs and private carriages were standing; then, as the sun sank, he had started homeward across the open meadow beyond the park, and since he was now tired and a storm seemed to be brewing over Föhring, he had stopped by the Northern Cemetery to wait for the tram that would take him straight back to the city.

As it happened, there was not a soul to be seen at or near the tram-stop. Not one vehicle passed along the Föhringer Chaussee or the paved Ungererstrasse on which solitary gleaming tramrails pointed toward Schwabing; nothing stirred behind the fencing of the stonemasons' yards, where crosses and memorial tablets and monuments, ready for sale, composed a second and untenanted burial ground; across the street, the mortuary chapel with its Byzantine styling stood silent in the glow of the westering day. Its facade, adorned with Greek crosses and brightly painted hieratic motifs, is also inscribed with symmetrically arranged texts in gilt lettering, selected scriptural passages about the life to come, such as: "They shall go in unto the dwelling-place of the Lord," or "May light perpetual shine upon them." The waiting Aschenbach had already been engaged for some minutes in the solemn pastime of deciphering the words and letting his mind wander in contemplation of the mystic meaning that suffused them, when he noticed something that brought him back to reality: in the portico of the chapel, above the two apocalyptic beasts that guard the steps leading up to it, a man was standing, a man whose slightly unusual appearance gave his thoughts an altogether different turn.

It was not entirely clear whether he had emerged through the bronze doors from inside the chapel or had suddenly appeared and mounted the steps from outside. Aschenbach, without unduly pondering the question, inclined to the former hypothesis. The man was moderately tall, thin, beardless and remarkably snub-nosed; he belonged to the red-haired type and had its characteristic milky, freckled complexion. He was quite evidently not of Bavarian origin; at all events he wore a straw hat with a broad straight brim which gave him an exotic air, as of someone who had come from distant parts. It is true that he also had the typical Bavarian rucksack strapped to his shoulders and wore a yellowish belted outfit of what looked like frieze, as well as carrying a gray rain-cape over his left forearm which was propped against his waist, and in his right hand an iron-pointed walking stick which he had thrust slantwise into the ground, crossing his feet and leaning his hip against its handle. His head was held high, so that the Adam's apple stood out stark and bare on his lean neck where it rose from the open shirt; and there were two pronounced vertical furrows, rather strangely ill-matched to his turned-up nose, between the colorless red-lashed eyes with which he peered sharply into the distance. There was thus—and perhaps the raised point of vantage on which he stood contributed to this impression—an air of imperious survey, something bold or even wild about his posture; for whether it was because he was dazzled into a grimace by the setting sun or by reason of some permanent facial deformity, the fact was that his lips seemed to be too short and were completely retracted from his teeth, so that the latter showed white and long between them, bared to the gums.

Aschenbach's half absentminded, half inquisitive scrutiny of the stranger had no doubt been a little less than polite, for he suddenly became aware that his gaze was being returned: the man was in fact staring at him so aggressively, so straight in the eye, with so evident an intention to make an issue of the matter and outstare him, that Aschenbach turned away in disagreeable embarrassment and began to stroll along the fence, casually resolving to take no further notice of the fellow. A minute later he had put him out of his mind. But whether his imagination had been stirred by the stranger's itinerant appearance, or whether some other physical or psychological influence was at work, he now became conscious, to his complete surprise, of an extraordinary expansion of his inner self, a kind of roving restlessness, a youthful craving for far-off places, a feeling so new or at least so long unaccustomed and forgotten that he stood as if rooted, with his hands clasped behind his back and his eyes to the ground, trying to ascertain the nature and purport of his emotion.

It was simply a desire to travel; but it had presented itself as nothing less than a seizure, with intensely passionate and indeed hallucinatory force, turning his craving into vision. His imagination, still not at rest from the morning's hours of work, shaped for itself a paradigm of all the wonders and terrors of the manifold earth, of all that it was now suddenly striving to encompass: he saw it, saw a landscape, a tropical swampland under a cloud-swollen sky, moist and lush and monstrous, a kind of primeval wilderness of islands, morasses and muddy alluvial channels; far and wide around him he saw hairy palm-trunks thrusting upward from rank jungles of fern, from among thick fleshy plants in exuberant flower; saw strangely misshapen trees with roots that arched through the air before sinking into the ground or into stagnant shadowy-green glassy waters where milk-white blossoms floated as big as plates, and among them exotic birds with grotesque beaks stood hunched in the shallows, their heads tilted motionlessly sideways; saw between the knotted stems of the bamboo thicket the glinting eyes of a crouching tiger; and his heart throbbed with terror and mysterious longing. Then the vision

faded; and with a shake of his head Aschenbach resumed his peram-
bulation along the fencing of the gravestone yards.

His attitude to foreign travel, at least since he had had the means
at his disposal to enjoy its advantages as often as he pleased, had
always been that it was nothing more than a necessary health precaution, to be taken from time to time however disinclined to it one
might be. Too preoccupied with the tasks imposed upon him by his
own sensibility and by the collective European psyche, too heavily
burdened with the compulsion to produce, too shy of distraction to
have learned how to take leisure and pleasure in the colorful external
world, he had been perfectly well satisfied to have no more detailed
a view of the earth's surface than anyone can acquire without stirring far from home, and he had never even been tempted to venture
outside Europe. This had been more especially the case since his life
had begun its gradual decline and his artist's fear of not finishing
his task—the apprehension that his time might run out before he
had given the whole of himself by doing what he had it in him to
do—was no longer something he could simply dismiss as an idle
fancy; and during this time his outward existence had been almost
entirely divided between the beautiful city which had become his
home and the rustic mountain retreat he had set up for himself and
where he passed his rainy summers.

And sure enough, the sudden and belated impulse that had just
overwhelmed him very soon came under the moderating and corrective influence of common sense and of the self-discipline he had
practiced since his youth. It had been his intention that the book to
which his life was at present dedicated should be advanced to a
certain point before he moved to the country, and the idea of a jaunt
in the wide world that would take him away from his work for
months now seemed too casual, too upsetting to his plans to be
considered seriously. Nevertheless, he knew the reason for the unexpected temptation only too well. This longing for the distant and
the new, this craving for liberation, relaxation and forgetfulness—it
had been, he was bound to admit, an urge to escape, to run away
from his writing, away from the humdrum scene of his cold, inflex-
ible, passionate duty. True, it was a duty he loved, and by now he
had almost even learned to love the enervating daily struggle between his proud, tenacious, tried and tested will and that growing
weariness which no one must be allowed to suspect nor his finished
work betray by any telltale sign of debility or lassitude. Nevertheless,
it would be sensible, he decided, not to span the bow too far and

willfully stifle a desire that had erupted in him with such vivid force. He thought of his work, thought of the passage at which he had again, today as yesterday, been forced to interrupt it—that stubborn problem which neither patient care could solve nor a decisive *tour de main* dispel. He reconsidered it, tried to break or dissolve the inhibition, and, with a shudder of repugnance, abandoned the attempt. It was not a case of very unusual difficulty, he was simply paralyzed by a scruple of distaste, manifesting itself as a perfectionistic fastidiousness which nothing could satisfy. Perfectionism, of course, was something which even as a young man he had come to see as the innermost essence of talent, and for its sake he had curbed and cooled his feelings; for he knew that feeling is apt to be content with high-spirited approximations and with work that falls short of supreme excellence. Could it be that the enslaved emotion was now avenging itself by deserting him, by refusing from now on to bear up his art on its wings, by taking with it all his joy in words, all his appetite for the beauty of form? Not that he was writing badly: it was at least the advantage of his years to be master of his trade, a mastery of which at any moment he could feel calmly confident. But even as it brought him national honor he took no pleasure in it himself, and it seemed to him that his work lacked that element of sparkling and joyful improvisation, that quality which surpasses any intellectual substance in its power to delight the receptive world. He dreaded spending the summer in the country, alone in that little house with the maid who prepared his meals and the servant who brought them to him; dreaded the familiar profile of the mountain summits and mountain walls which would once again surround his slow discontented toil. So what did he need? An interlude, some impromptu living, some *dolce far niente,* the invigoration of a distant climate, to make his summer bearable and fruitful. Very well then— he would travel. Not all that far, not quite to where the tigers were. A night in the wagon-lit and a siesta of three or four weeks at some popular holiday resort in the charming south . . .

Such were his thoughts as the tram clattered toward him along the Ungererstrasse, and as he stepped into it he decided to devote that evening to the study of maps and timetables. On the platform it occurred to him to look round and see what had become of the man in the straw hat, his companion for the duration of this not inconsequential wait at a tram-stop. But the man's whereabouts remained a mystery, for he was no longer standing where he had stood, nor was he to be seen anywhere else at the stop or in the tramcar itself.

2

The author of the lucid and massive prose-epic about the life of Frederick of Prussia; the patient artist who with long toil had woven the great tapestry of the novel called *Maya,* so rich in characters, gathering so many human destinies together under the shadow of one idea; the creator of that powerful tale entitled *A Study in Abjection,* which earned the gratitude of a whole younger generation by pointing to the possibility of moral resolution even for those who have plumbed the depths of knowledge; the author (lastly but not least in this summary enumeration of his maturer works) of that passionate treatise *Intellect and Art* which in its ordering energy and antithetical eloquence has led serious critics to place it immediately alongside Schiller's disquisition *On Naive and Sentimental Poetry:** in a word, Gustav Aschenbach, was born in L . . . , an important city in the province of Silesia, as the son of a highly-placed legal official. His ancestors had been military officers, judges, government administrators; men who had spent their disciplined, decently austere life in the service of the king and the state. A more inward spirituality had shown itself in one of them who had been a preacher; a strain of livelier, more sensuous blood had entered the family in the previous generation with the writer's mother, the daughter of a director of music from Bohemia. Certain exotic racial characteristics in his external appearance had come to him from her. It was from this marriage between hard-working, sober conscientiousness and darker, more fiery impulses that an artist, and indeed this particular kind of artist, had come into being.

With his whole nature intent from the start upon fame, he had displayed not exactly precocity, but a certain decisiveness and personal trenchancy in his style of utterance, which at an early age made him ripe for a life in the public eye and well suited to it. He had made a name for himself when he had scarcely left school. Ten years later he had learned to perform, at his writing desk, the social and administrative duties entailed by his reputation; he had learned to write letters which, however brief they had to be (for many claims beset the successful man who enjoys the confidence of the public), would always contain something kindly and pointed. By the age of forty he was obliged, wearied though he might be by the toils and vicissitudes of his real work, to deal with a daily correspondence that bore postage-stamps from every part of the globe.

His talent, equally remote from the commonplace and from the excentric, had a native capacity both to inspire confidence in the general public and to win admiration and encouragement from the discriminating connoisseur. Ever since his boyhood the duty to achieve—and to achieve exceptional things—had been imposed on him from all sides, and thus he had never known youth's idleness, its carefree negligent ways. When in his thirty-fifth year he fell ill in Vienna, a subtle observer remarked of him on a social occasion: "You see, Aschenbach has always only lived like *this*"—and the speaker closed the fingers of his left hand tightly into a fist—"and never like *this*"—and he let his open hand hang comfortably down along the back of the chair. It was a correct observation; and the morally courageous aspect of the matter was that Aschenbach's native constitution was by no means robust, and that the constant harnessing of his energies was something to which he had been called, but not really born.

As a young boy, medical advice and care had made school attendance impossible and obliged him to have his education at home. He had grown up by himself, without companions, and had nevertheless had to recognize in good time that he belonged to a breed not seldom talented, yet seldom endowed with the physical basis which talent needs if it is to fulfill itself—a breed that usually gives of its best in youth, and in which the creative gift rarely survives into mature years. But he would "stay the course"—it was his favorite motto, he saw his historical novel about Frederick the Great as nothing if not the apotheosis of this, the king's word of command, *"durchhalten!"* which to Aschenbach epitomized a manly ethos of suffering action. And he dearly longed to grow old, for it had always been his view that an artist's gift can only be called truly great and wide-ranging, or indeed truly admirable, if it has been fortunate enough to bear characteristic fruit at all the stages of human life.

They were not broad, the shoulders on which he thus carried the tasks laid upon him by his talent; and since his aims were high, he stood in great need of discipline—and discipline, after all, was fortunately his inborn heritage on his father's side. At the age of forty or fifty, and indeed during those younger years in which other men live prodigally and dilettantishly, happily procrastinating the execution of great plans, Aschenbach would begin his day early by dashing cold water over his chest and back, and then, with two tall wax candles in silver candlesticks placed at the head of his manuscript, he would offer up to art, for two or three ardently conscientious morning hours, the strength he had gathered during sleep. It was a pardonable error, indeed it was one that betokened as nothing else could the triumph of his moral will, that uninformed critics should mistake the great world of *Maya*, or the massive epic unfolding of Frederick's life, for the product of solid strength and long stamina, whereas in fact they had been built up to their impressive size from layer upon layer of daily opuscula, from a hundred or a thousand separate inspirations; and if they were indeed so excellent, both absolutely and in every detail, it was only because their creator, showing that same constancy of will and tenacity of purpose as had once conquered his native Silesia, had held out for years under the pressure of one and the same work, and had devoted to actual composition only his best and worthiest hours.

For a significant intellectual product to make a broad and deep immediate appeal, there must be a hidden affinity, indeed a congruence, between the personal destiny of the author and the wider destiny of his generation. The public does not know why it grants the accolade of fame to a work of art. Being in no sense connoisseurs, readers imagine they perceive a hundred good qualities in it which justify their admiration; but the real reason for their applause is something imponderable, a sense of sympathy. Hidden away among Aschenbach's writings was a passage directly asserting that nearly all the great things that exist owe their existence to a defiant despite: it is despite grief and anguish, despite poverty, loneliness, bodily weakness, vice and passion and a thousand inhibitions, that they have come into being at all. But this was more than an observation, it was an experience, it was positively the formula of his life and his fame, the key to his work; is it surprising then that it was also the moral formula, the outward gesture, of his work's most characteristic figures?

The new hero-type favored by Aschenbach, and recurring in his books in a multiplicity of individual variants, had already been remarked upon at an early stage by a shrewd commentator, who had described his conception as that of "an intellectual and boyish manly virtue, that of a youth who clenches his teeth in proud shame and stands calmly on as the swords and spears pass through his body." That was well put, perceptive and precisely true, for all its seemingly rather too passive emphasis. For composure under the blows of fate, grace in the midst of torment—this is not only endurance: it is an active achievement, a positive triumph, and the figure of Saint Sebastian is the most perfect symbol if not of art in general, then certainly of the kind of art here in question. What did one see if one looked in any depth into the world of this writer's fiction? Elegant self-control concealing from the world's eyes until the very last moment a state of inner disintegration and biological decay; sallow ugliness, sensuously marred and worsted, which nevertheless is able to fan its smouldering concupiscence to a pure flame, and even to exalt itself to mastery in the realm of beauty; pallid impotence, which from the glowing depths of the spirit draws strength to cast down a whole proud people at the foot of the Cross and set its own foot upon them as well; gracious poise and composure in the empty austere service of form; the false, dangerous life of the born deceiver, his ambition and his art which lead so soon to exhaustion—to contemplate all these destinies, and many others like them, was to doubt if there is any other heroism at all but the heroism of weakness. In any case, what other heroism could be more in keeping with the times? Gustav Aschenbach was the writer who spoke for all those who work on the brink of exhaustion, who labor and are heavy-laden, who are worn out already but still stand upright, all those moralists of achievement who are slight of stature and scanty of resources, but who yet, by some ecstasy of the will and by wise husbandry, manage at least for a time to force their work into a semblance of greatness. There are many such, they are the heroes of our age. And they all recognized themselves in his work, they found that it confirmed them and raised them on high and celebrated them; they were grateful for this, and they spread his name far and wide.

He had been young and raw with the times: ill advised by fashion, he had publicly stumbled, blundered, made himself look foolish, offended in speech and writing against tact and balanced civility. But he had achieved dignity, that goal toward which, as he declared, every great talent is innately driven and spurred; indeed it can be said that the conscious and defiant purpose of his entire development had been to leave all the inhibitions of skepticism and irony behind him and to ascend to dignity.

Lively, clear-outlined, intellectually undemanding presentation is the delight of the great mass of the middle-class public, but passionate radical youth is interested only in problems: and Aschenbach had been as problematic and as radical as any young man ever was.

He had been in thrall to intellect, had exhausted the soil by excessive analysis and ground up the seed corn of growth; he had uncovered what is better kept hidden, made talent seem suspect, betrayed the truth about art—indeed, even as the sculptural vividness of his descriptions was giving pleasure to his more naive devotees and lifting their minds and hearts, he, this same youthful artist, had fascinated twenty-year-olds with his breathtaking cynicisms about the questionable nature of art and of the artist himself.

But it seems that there is nothing to which a noble and active mind more quickly becomes inured than that pungent and bitter stimulus, the acquisition of knowledge; and it is very sure that even the most gloomily conscientious and radical sophistication of youth is shallow by comparison with Aschenbach's profound decision as a mature master to repudiate knowledge as such, to reject it, to step over it with head held high—in the recognition that knowledge can paralyze the will, paralyze and discourage action and emotion and even passion, and rob all these of their dignity. How else is the famous short story *A Study in Abjection* to be understood but as an outbreak of disgust against an age indecently undermined by psychology and represented by the figure of that spiritless, witless semiscoundrel who cheats his way into a destiny of sorts when, motivated by his own ineptitude and depravity and ethical whimsicality, he drives his wife into the arms of a callow youth—convinced that his intellectual depths entitle him to behave with contemptible baseness? The forthright words of condemnation which here weighed vileness in the balance and found it wanting—they proclaimed their writer's renunciation of all moral skepticism, of every kind of sympathy with the abyss; they declared his repudiation of the laxity of that compassionate principle which holds that to understand all is to forgive all. And the development that was here being anticipated, indeed already taking place, was that "miracle of reborn naiveté" to which, in a dialogue, written a little later, the author himself had referred with a certain mysterious emphasis. How strange these associations! Was it an intellectual consequence of this "rebirth," of this new dignity and rigor, that, at about the same time, his sense of beauty was observed to undergo an almost excessive resurgence, that his style took on the noble purity, simplicity and symmetry that were to set upon all his subsequent works that so evident and evidently intentional stamp of the classical master? And yet: moral resoluteness at the far side of knowledge, achieved in despite of all corrosive and inhibiting insight—does this not in its turn signify a simplification, a morally simplistic view of the world and of human psychology, and thus also a resurgence of energies that are evil, forbidden, morally impossible? And is form not two-faced? Is it not at one and the same time moral and immoral—moral as the product and expression of discipline, but immoral and even antimoral inasmuch as it houses within itself an innate moral indifference, and indeed essentially strives for nothing less than to bend morality under its proud and absolute scepter?

Be that as it may! A development is a destiny; and one that is accompanied by the admiration and mass confidence of a wide public must inevitably differ in its course from one that takes place far from the limelight and from the commitments of fame. Only the eternal intellectual vagrant is bored and prompted to mockery when a great talent grows out of its libertinistic chrysalis-stage, becomes an expressive representative of the dignity of mind, takes on the courtly bearing of that solitude which has been full of hard, uncounseled, self-reliant sufferings and struggles, and has achieved power and honor among men. And what a game it is too, how much defiance there is in it and how much satisfaction, this self-formation of a talent! As time passed, Gustav Aschenbach's presentations took on something of an official air, of an educator's stance; his style in later years came to eschew direct audacities, new and subtle nuances, it developed toward the exemplary and definitive, the fastidiously conventional, the conservative and formal and even formulaic; and as tradition has it of Louis XIV, so Aschenbach as he grew older banned from his utterance every unrefined word. It was at this time that the education authority adopted selected pages from his works for inclusion in the prescribed school readers. And when a German prince who had just come to the throne granted personal nobilitation to the author of *Frederick of Prussia* on his fiftieth birthday, he sensed the inner appropriateness of this honor and did not decline it.

After a few restless years of experimental living in different places, he soon chose Munich as his permanent home and lived there in the kind of upper-bourgeois status which is occasionally the lot of certain intellectuals. The marriage which he had contracted while still young with the daughter of an academic family had been ended by his wife's death after a short period of happiness. She had left him a daughter, now already married. He had never had a son.

Gustav von Aschenbach was of rather less than average height, dark and clean-shaven. His head seemed a little too large in proportion to his almost delicate stature. His brushed-back hair, thinning at the top, very thick and distinctly gray over the temples, framed a high, deeply lined, scarred-looking forehead. The bow of a pair of gold spectacles with rimless lenses cut into the base of his strong, nobly curved nose. His mouth was large, often relaxed, often suddenly narrow and tense; the cheeks were lean and furrowed, the well-formed chin slightly cleft. Grave visitations of fate seemed to have passed over this head, which usually inclined to one side with an air of suffering. And yet it was art that had here performed that fashioning of the physiognomy which is usually the work of a life full of action and stress. The flashing exchanges of the dialogue between Voltaire and the king on the subject of war had been born behind that brow; these eyes that looked so wearily and deeply through their glasses had seen the bloody inferno of the Seven Years War sick bays. Even in a personal sense, after all, art is an intensified life. By art one is more deeply satisfied and more rapidly used up. It engraves on the countenance of its servant the traces of imaginary and intellectual adventures, and even if he has outwardly existed in cloistral tranquility, it leads in the long term to overfastidiousness, overrefinement, nervous fatigue and overstimulation, such as can seldom result from a life full of the most extravagant passions and pleasures.

3

Mundane and literary business of various kinds delayed Aschenbach's eagerly awaited departure until about a fortnight after that walk in Munich. Finally he gave instructions that his country house was to be made ready for occupation in four weeks' time, and then, one day between the middle and end of May, he took the night train to Trieste, where he stayed only twenty-four hours, embarking on the following morning for Pola.

What he sought was something strange and random, but in a place easily reached, and accordingly he took up his abode on an Adriatic island which had been highly spoken of for some years: a little way off the Istrian coast, with colorful ragged inhabitants speaking a wild unintelligible dialect, and picturesque fragmented cliffs overlooking the open sea. But rain and sultry air, a self-enclosed petit-bourgeois Austrian hotel clientele, the lack of that restful intimate contact with the sea which can only be had on a gentle, sandy coast, filled him with vexation and with a feeling that he had not yet come to his journey's end. He was haunted by an inner impulse that still had no clear direction; he studied shipping timetables, looked up one place after another—and suddenly his surprising yet at the same time self-evident destination stared him in the face. If one wanted to travel overnight to somewhere incomparable, to a fantastic mutation of normal reality, where did one go? Why, the answer was obvious. What was he doing here? He had gone completely astray. *That* was where he had wanted to travel. He at once gave notice of departure from his present, mischosen stopping place. Ten days after his arrival on the island, in the early morning mist, a rapid motor-launch carried him and his luggage back over the water to the naval base, and here he landed only to re-embark immediately, crossing the gangway onto the damp deck of a ship that was waiting under steam to leave for Venice.

It was an ancient Italian boat, out of date and dingy and black with soot. Aschenbach was no sooner aboard than a grubby hunch-backed seaman, grinning obsequiously, conducted him to an artificially lit cavelike cabin in the ship's interior. Here, behind a table, with his cap askew and a cigarette end in the corner of his mouth, sat a goat-bearded man with the air of an old-fashioned circus director and a slick caricatured business manner, taking passengers' particulars and issuing their tickets. "To Venice!" he exclaimed, echoing Aschenbach's request, and extending his arm he pushed his pen into some coagulated leftover ink in a tilted inkstand. "One first class to Venice. Certainly, sir!" He scribbled elaborately, shook some blue sand from a box over the writing and ran it off into an earthenware dish, then folded the paper with his yellow bony fingers and wrote on it again. "A very happily chosen destination!" he chattered as he did so. "Ah, Venice! A splendid city! A city irresistibly attractive to the man of culture, by its history no less than by its present charms!" There was something hypnotic and distracting about the smooth facility of his movements and the glib empty talk with which he accompanied them, almost as if he were anxious that the traveler might have second thoughts about his decision to go to Venice. He hastily took Aschenbach's money and with the dexterity of a croupier dropped the change on the stained tablecloth. *"Buon divertimento, signore,"* he said, bowing histrionically. "It is an honor to serve you . . . Next, please, gentlemen!" he exclaimed with a wave of the arm, as if he were doing a lively trade, although in fact there was no one else there to be dealt with. Aschenbach returned on deck.

Resting one elbow on the handrail, he watched the idle crowd hanging about the quayside to see the ship's departure, and watched the passengers who had come aboard. Those with second-class tickets were squatting, men and women together, on the forward deck, using boxes and bundles as seats. The company on the upper deck consisted of a group of young men, probably shop or office workers from Pola, a high-spirited party about to set off on an excursion to Italy. They were making a considerable exhibition of themselves and their enterprise, chattering, laughing, fatuously enjoying their own gesticulations, leaning overboard and shouting glibly derisive ribaldries at their friends on the harbor-side street, who were hurrying about their business with briefcases under their arms and waved their sticks peevishly at the holiday-makers. One of the party, who wore a light yellow summer suit of extravagant cut, a scarlet necktie and a rakishly tilted Panama hat, was the most conspicuous of them all in his shrill hilarity. But as soon as Aschenbach took a slightly closer look at him, he realized with a kind of horror that the man's youth was false. He was old, there was no mistaking it. There were wrinkles round his eyes and mouth. His cheeks' faint carmine was rouge, the brown hair under his straw hat with its colored ribbon was a wig, his neck was flaccid and scrawny, his small stuck-on moustache and the little imperial on his chin were dyed, his yellowish full complement of teeth, displayed when he laughed, were a cheap artificial set, and his hands, with signet rings on both index fingers, were those of an old man. With a spasm of distaste Aschenbach watched him as he kept company with his young friends. Did they not know, did they not notice that he was old, that he had no right to be wearing foppish and garish clothes like theirs, no right to be acting as if he were one of them? They seemed to be tolerating his presence among them as something habitual and to be taken for granted, they treated him as an equal, reciprocated without embarrassment when he teasingly poked them in the ribs. How was this possible? Aschenbach put his hand over his forehead and closed his eyes, which were hot from too little sleep. He had a feeling that something not quite usual was beginning to happen, that the world was undergoing a dreamlike alienation, becoming increasingly deranged and bizarre, and that perhaps this process might be arrested if he were to cover his face for a little and then take a fresh look at things. But at that moment he had the sensation of being afloat, and starting up in irrational alarm, he noticed that the dark heavy hulk of the steamer was slowly parting company with the stone quayside. Inch by inch, as the engine pounded and reversed, the width of the dirty glinting water between the hull and the quay increased, and after clumsy maneuverings the ship turned its bows toward the open sea. Aschenbach crossed to the starboard side, where the hunchback had set up a deck chair for him and a steward in a grease-stained frock coat offered his services.

The sky was gray, the wind damp. The port and the islands had been left behind, and soon all land was lost to view in the misty panorama. Flecks of sodden soot drifted down on the washed deck, which never seemed to get dry. After only an hour an awning was set up, as it was beginning to rain.

Wrapped in his overcoat, a book lying on his lap, the traveler rested, scarcely noticing the hours as they passed him by. It had stopped raining; the canvas shelter was removed. The horizon was complete. Under the turbid dome of the sky the desolate sea surrounded him in an enormous circle. But in empty, unarticulated space our mind loses its sense of time as well, and we enter the twilight of the immeasurable. As Aschenbach lay there, strange and shadowy figures, the foppish old man, the goat-bearded purser from the ship's interior, passed with uncertain gestures and confused dream-words through his mind, and he fell asleep.

At midday he was requested to come below for luncheon in the long, narrow dining saloon, which ended in the doors to the sleeping berths; here he ate at the head of the long table, at the other end of which the group of apprentices, with the old man among them, had been quaffing since ten o'clock with the good-humored ship's captain. The meal was wretched and he finished it quickly. He needed to be back in the open air, to look at the sky; perhaps it would clear over Venice.

It had never occurred to him that this would not happen, for the city had always received him in its full glory. But the sky and the sea remained dull and leaden, from time to time misty rain fell, and he resigned himself to arriving by water in a different Venice, one he had never encountered on the landward approach. He stood by the foremast, gazing into the distance, waiting for the sight of land. He recalled that poet of plangent inspiration who long ago had seen the cupolas and bell-towers of his dream rise before him out of these same waters; inwardly he recited a few lines of the measured music that had been made from that reverence and joy and sadness, and effortlessly moved by a passion already shaped into language, he questioned his grave and weary heart, wondering whether some new inspiration and distraction, some late adventure of the emotions, might yet be in store for him on his leisured journey.

And now, on his right, the flat coastline rose above the horizon, the sea came alive with fishing vessels, the island resort appeared: the steamer left it on its port side, glided at half speed through the narrow channel named after it, entered the lagoon, and presently, near some shabby miscellaneous buildings, came to a complete halt, as this was where the launch carrying the public health inspector must be awaited.

An hour passed before it appeared. One had arrived and yet not arrived; there was no hurry, and yet one was impelled by impatience. The young men from Pola had come on deck, no doubt also patriotically attracted by the military sound of bugle calls across the water from the direction of the Public Gardens; and elated by the Asti they had drunk, they began cheering the *bersaglieri* as they drilled there in the park. But the dandified old man, thanks to his spurious fraternization with the young, was now in a condition repugnant to behold. His old head could not carry the wine as his sturdy youthful companions had done, and he was lamentably drunk. Eyes glazed, a cigarette between his trembling fingers, he stood swaying, tilted to and fro by inebriation and barely keeping his balance. Since he would have fallen at his first step he did not dare move from the spot, and was nevertheless full of wretched exuberance, clutching at everyone who approached him, babbling, winking, sniggering, lifting his ringed and wrinkled forefinger as he uttered some bantering inanity, and licking the corners of his mouth with the tip of his tongue in a repellently suggestive way. Aschenbach watched him with frowning disapproval, and once more a sense of numbness came over him, a feeling that the world was somehow, slightly yet uncontrollably, sliding into some kind of bizarre and grotesque derangement. It was a feeling on which, to be sure, he was unable to brood further in present circumstances, for at this moment the thudding motion of the engine began again, and the ship, having stopped short so close to its destination, resumed its passage along the San Marco Canal.

Thus it was that he saw it once more, that most astonishing of all landing places, that dazzling composition of fantastic architecture which the Republic presented to the admiring gaze of approaching seafarers: the unburdened splendor of the Ducal Palace, the Bridge of Sighs, the lion and the saint on their two columns at the water's edge, the magnificently projecting side wing of the fabulous basilica, the vista beyond it of the gate tower and the Giants' Clock; and as he contemplated it all he reflected that to arrive in Venice by land, at the station, was like entering a palace by a back door: that only as he was now doing, only by ship, over the high sea, should one come to this most extraordinary of cities.

The engine stopped, gondolas pressed alongside, the gangway was let down, customs officers came on board and perfunctorily discharged their duties; disembarkation could begin. Aschenbach indicated that he would like a gondola to take him and his luggage to the stopping place of the small steamboats that ply between the city and the Lido, since he intended to stay in a hotel by the sea. His wishes were approved, his orders shouted down to water level, where the gondoliers were quarreling in Venetian dialect. He was still prevented from leaving the ship, held up by his trunk which at that moment was being laboriously dragged and maneuvered down the ladderlike gangway; and thus, for a full minute or two, he could not avoid the importunate attentions of the dreadful old man, who on some obscure drunken impulse felt obliged to do this stranger the parting honors. "We wish the signore a most enjoyable stay!" he bleated, bowing and scraping. "We hope the signore will not forget us! *Au revoir, excusez* and *bon jour,* your Excellency!" He drooled, he screwed up his eyes, licked the corners of his mouth, and the dyed imperial on his senile underlip reared itself upward. "Our compliments," he driveled, touching his lips with two fingers, "our compliments to your sweetheart, to your most charming, beautiful sweetheart . . ." And suddenly the upper set of his false teeth dropped half out of his jaw. Aschenbach was able to escape. "Your sweetheart, your pretty sweetheart!" he heard from behind his back, in gurgling, cavernous, encumbered tones, as he clung to the rope railing and descended the gangway.

Can there be anyone who has not had to overcome a fleeting sense of dread, a secret shudder of uneasiness, on stepping for the first time or after a long interval of years into a Venetian gondola? How strange a vehicle it is, coming down unchanged from times of old romance, and so characteristically black, the way no other thing is black except a coffin—a vehicle evoking lawless adventures in the plashing stillness of night, and still more strongly evoking death itself, the bier, the dark obsequies, the last silent journey! And has it been observed that the seat of such a boat, that armchair with its coffin-black lacquer and dull black upholstery, is the softest, the most voluptuous, most enervating seat in the world? Aschenbach became aware of this when he had settled down at the gondolier's feet, sitting opposite his luggage, which was neatly assembled at the prow. The oarsmen were still quarreling; raucously, unintelligibly, with threatening gestures. But in the peculiar silence of this city of water their voices seemed to be softly absorbed, to become bodiless, dissipated above the sea. It was sultry here in the harbor. As the warm breath of the sirocco touched him, as he leaned back in cushions on the yielding element, the traveler closed his eyes in the enjoyment of this lassitude as sweet as it was unaccustomed. It will be a short ride, he thought; if only it could last forever! In a gently swaying motion he felt himself gliding away from the crowd and the confusion of voices.

How still it was growing all round him! There was nothing to be heard except the splashing of the oar, the dull slap of the wave against the boat's prow where it rose up steep and black and armed at its tip like a halberd, and a third sound also: that of a voice speaking and murmuring—it was the gondolier, whispering and muttering to himself between his teeth, in intermittent grunts pressed out of him by the labor of his arms. Aschenbach looked up and noticed with some consternation that the lagoon was widening round him and that his gondola was heading out to sea. It was thus evident that he must not relax too completely, but give some attention to the proper execution of his instructions.

"Well! To the *vaporetto* stop!" he said, half turning round. The muttering ceased, but no answer came.

"I said to the *vaporetto* stop!" he repeated, turning round completely and looking up into the face of the gondolier, who was standing behind him on his raised deck, towering between him and the pale sky. He was a man of displeasing, indeed brutal appearance, wearing blue seaman's clothes, with a yellow scarf round his waist and a shapeless, already fraying straw hat tilted rakishly on his head. To judge by the cast of his face and the blond curling moustache under his snub nose, he was quite evidently not of Italian origin. Although rather slightly built, so that one would not have thought him particularly well suited to his job, he plied his oar with great energy, putting his whole body into every stroke. Occasionally the effort made him retract his lips and bare his white teeth. With his reddish eyebrows knitted, he stared right over his passenger's head as he answered peremptorily, almost insolently:

"You are going to the Lido."

Aschenbach replied:

"Of course. But I only engaged this gondola to row me across to San Marco. I wish to take the *vaporetto*."

"You cannot take the *vaporetto,* signore."

"And why not?"

"Because the *vaporetto* does not carry luggage."

That was correct, as Aschenbach now remembered. He was silent. But the man's abrupt, presumptuous manner, so uncharacteristic of the way foreigners were usually treated in this country, struck him as unacceptable. He said:

"That is my business. I may wish to deposit my luggage. Will you kindly turn round."

There was silence. The oar splashed, the dull slap of the water against the bow continued, and the talking and muttering began again: the gondolier was talking to himself between his teeth.

What was to be done? Alone on the sea with this strangely contumacious, uncannily resolute fellow, the traveler could see no way of compelling him to obey his instructions. And in any case, how luxurious a rest he might have here if he simply accepted the situation! Had he not wished the trip were longer, wished it to last forever? It was wisest to let things take their course, and above all it was very agreeable to do so. A magic spell of indolence seemed to emanate from his seat, from this low black-upholstered armchair, so softly rocked by the oarstrokes of the high-handed gondolier behind him. The thought that he had perhaps fallen into the hands of a criminal floated dreamily across Aschenbach's mind—powerless to stir him to any active plan of self-defence. There was the more annoying possibility that the whole thing was simply a device for extorting money from him. A kind of pride or sense of duty, a recollection, so to speak, that there are precautions to be taken against such things, impelled him to make one further effort. He asked:

"What is your charge for the trip?"

And looking straight over his head, the gondolier answered:

"You will pay, signore."

The prescribed retort to this was clear enough. Aschenbach answered mechanically:

"I shall pay nothing, absolutely nothing, if you take me where I do not want to go."

"The signore wants to go to the Lido."

"But not with you."

"I can row you well."

True enough, thought Aschenbach, relaxing. True enough, you will row me well. Even if you are after my cash and dispatch me to the house of Hades with a blow of your oar from behind, you will have rowed me well.

But nothing of the sort happened. He was even provided with company: a boat full of piratical musicians, men and women singing to the guitar or mandolin, importunately traveling hard alongside the gondola and for the foreigner's benefit filling the silence of the waters with mercenary song. Aschenbach threw some money into the outheld hat, whereupon they fell silent and moved off. And the gondolier's muttering became audible again, as in fits and starts he continued his self-colloquy.

And so in due course one arrived, bobbing about in the wake of a *vaporetto* bound for the city. Two police officers, with their hands on their backs, were pacing up and down the embankment and looking out over the lagoon. Aschenbach stepped from the gondola onto the gangway, assisted by the old man with a boat hook who turns up for this purpose at every landing stage in Venice; and having run out of small change, he walked across to the hotel opposite the pier, intending to change money and pay off the oarsman with some suitable gratuity. He was served at the hall desk, and returned to the landing stage to find his luggage loaded onto a trolley on the embankment: the gondola and the gondolier had vanished.

"He left in a hurry," said the old man with the boat hook. "A bad man, a man without a licence, signore. He is the only gondolier who has no licence. The others telephoned across to us. He saw that he was expected. So he left in a hurry."

Aschenbach shrugged his shoulders.

"The signore has had a free trip," said the old man, holding out his hat. Aschenbach threw coins into it. He directed that his luggage should be taken to the Hotel des Bains, and followed the trolley along the avenue, that white-blossoming avenue, bordered on either side by taverns and bazaars and guesthouses, which runs straight across the island to the beach.

He entered the spacious hotel from the garden terrace at the back, passing through the main hall and the vestibule to the reception office. As his arrival had been notified in advance, he was received with obsequious obligingness. A manager, a soft-spoken, flatteringly courteous little man with a black moustache and a frock coat of French cut, accompanied him in the lift to the second floor and showed him to his room, an agreeable apartment with cherry-wood furniture, strongly scented flowers put out to greet him, and a view through tall windows to the open sea. He went and stood by one of them when the manager had withdrawn, and as his luggage was brought in behind him and installed in the room, he gazed out over the beach, uncrowded at this time of the afternoon, and over the sunless sea which was at high tide, its long low waves beating with a quiet regular rhythm on the shore.

The observations and encounters of a devotee of solitude and silence are at once less distinct and more penetrating than those of the sociable man; his thoughts are weightier, stranger, and never without a tinge of sadness. Images and perceptions which might otherwise be easily dispelled by a glance, a laugh, an exchange of comments, concern him unduly, they sink into mute depths, take on significance, become experiences, adventures, emotions. The fruit of solitude is originality, something daringly and disconcertingly beautiful, the poetic creation. But the fruit of solitude can also be the perverse, the disproportionate, the absurd and the forbidden. And thus the phenomena of his journey to this place, the horrible old made-up man with his maudlin babble about a sweetheart, the illicit gondolier who had been done out of his money, were still weighing on the traveler's mind. Without in any way being rationally inexplicable, without even really offering food for thought, they were nevertheless, as it seemed to him, essentially strange, and indeed it was no doubt this very paradox that made them disturbing. In the meantime he saluted the sea with his gaze and rejoiced in the knowledge that Venice was now so near and accessible. Finally he turned round, bathed his face, gave the room maid certain instructions for the enhancement of his comfort, and then had himself conveyed by the green-uniformed Swiss lift attendant to the ground floor.

He took tea on the front terrace, then went down to the beach and walked some way along the esplanade in the direction of the Hotel Excelsior. When he returned, it was already nearly time to be changing for dinner. He did so in his usual leisurely and precise manner, for it was his custom to work while performing his toilet; despite this, he arrived a little early in the hall, where he found a considerable number of the hotel guests assembled, unacquainted with each other and affecting a studied mutual indifference, yet all united in expectancy by the prospect of their evening meal. He picked up a newspaper from the table, settled down in a leather armchair and took stock of the company, which differed very agreeably from what he had encountered at his previous hotel.

A large horizon opened up before him, tolerantly embracing many elements. Discreetly muted, the sounds of the major world languages mingled. Evening dress, that internationally accepted uniform of civilization, imparted a decent outward semblance of unity to the wide variations of mankind here represented. One saw the dry elongated visages of Americans, many-membered Russian families, English ladies, German children with French nurses. The Slav component seemed to predominate. In his immediate vicinity he could hear Polish being spoken.

It was a group of adolescent and barely adult young people, sitting round a cane table under the supervision of a governess or companion: three young girls, of fifteen to seventeen as it seemed, and a long-haired boy of about fourteen. With astonishment Aschenbach noticed that the boy was entirely beautiful. His countenance, pale and gracefully reserved, was surrounded by ringlets of honey-colored hair, and with its straight nose, its enchanting mouth, its expression of sweet and divine gravity, it recalled Greek sculpture of the noblest period; yet despite the purest formal perfection, it had such unique personal charm that he who now contemplated it felt he had never beheld, in nature or in art, anything so consummately successful. What also struck him was an obvious contrast of educational principles in the way the boy and his sisters were dressed and generally treated. The system adopted for the three girls, the eldest of whom could be considered to be grown-up, was austere and chaste to the point of disfigurement. They all wore exactly the same slate-colored half-length dresses, sober and of a deliberately unbecoming cut, with white turnover collars as the only relieving feature, and any charm of figure they might have had was suppressed and negated from the outset by this cloistral uniform. Their hair, smoothed and stuck back firmly to their heads, gave their faces a nunlike emptiness and expressionlessness. A mother was clearly in charge here; and it had not even occurred to her to apply to the boy the same pedagogic strictness as she thought proper for the girls. In his life, softness and tenderness were evidently the rule. No one had ever dared to cut short his beautiful hair; like that of the *Boy Extracting a Thorn* it fell in curls over his forehead, over his ears, and still lower over his neck. The English sailor's suit, with its full sleeves tapering down to fit the fine wrists of his still childlike yet slender hands, and with its lanyards and bows and embroideries, enhanced his delicate shape with an air of richness and indulgence. He was sitting, in semiprofile to Aschenbach's gaze, with one foot in its patent leather shoe advanced in front of the other, with one elbow propped on the arm of his basket chair, with his cheek nestling against the closed hand, in a posture of relaxed dignity, without a trace of the almost servile stiffness to which his sisters seemed to have accustomed themselves. Was he in poor health? For his complexion was white as ivory against the dark gold of the surrounding curls. Or was he simply a pampered favorite child, borne up by the partiality of a capricious love? Aschenbach was inclined to think so. Inborn in almost every artistic nature is a luxuriant, treacherous bias in favor of the injustice that creates beauty, a tendency to sympathize with aristocratic preference and pay it homage.

A waiter circulated and announced in English that dinner was served. Gradually the company disappeared through the glass door into the dining room. Latecomers passed, coming from the vestibule or the lifts. The service of dinner had already begun, but the young Poles were still waiting round their cane table, and Aschenbach, comfortably ensconced in his deep armchair, and additionally having the spectacle of beauty before his eyes, waited with them.

The governess, a corpulent and rather unladylike, red-faced little woman, finally gave the signal for them to rise. With arched brows she pushed back her chair and bowed as a tall lady, dressed in silvery gray and very richly adorned with pearls, entered the hall. This lady's attitude was cool and poised, her lightly powdered coiffure and the style of her dress both had that simplicity which is the governing principle of taste in circles where piety is regarded as one of the aristocratic values. In Germany she might have been the wife of a high official. The only thing that did give her appearance a fantastic and luxurious touch was her jewels, which were indeed beyond price, consisting of earrings as well as a very long three-stranded necklace of gently shimmering pearls as big as cherries.

The brother and sisters had quickly risen to their feet. They bowed over their mother's hand to kiss it, while she, with a restrained smile on her well-maintained but slightly weary and angular face, looked over their heads and addressed a few words in French to the governess. Then she walked toward the glass door. Her children followed her: the girls in order of age, after them the governess, finally the boy. For some reason or other he turned round before crossing the threshold, and as there was now no one else in the hall, his strangely twilight-gray eyes met those of Aschenbach, who with his paper in his lap, lost in contemplation, had been watching the group leave.

What he had seen had certainly not been remarkable in any particular. One does not go in to table before one's mother, they had waited for her, greeted her respectfully, and observed normal polite precedence in entering the dining room. But this had all been carried out with such explicitness, with such a strongly accented air of discipline, obligation and self-respect, that Aschenbach felt strangely moved. He lingered for another few moments, then he too crossed into the dining room and had himself shown to his table—which, as he noticed with a brief stirring of regret, was at some distance from that of the Polish family.

Tired and yet intellectually stimulated, he beguiled the long and tedious meal with abstract and indeed transcendental reflections. He meditated on the mysterious combination into which the canonical and the individual must enter for human beauty to come into being, proceeded from this point to general problems of form and art, and concluded in the end that his thoughts and findings resembled certain seemingly happy inspirations that come to us in dreams, only to be recognized by the sober senses as completely shallow and worthless. After dinner he lingered for a while, smoking and sitting and walking about, in the evening fragrance of the hotel garden, then retired early and passed the night in sleep which was sound and long, though dream images enlivened it from time to time.

Next day the weather did not seem to be improving. The wind was from landward. Under a pallid overcast sky the sea lay sluggishly still and shrunken-looking, with the horizon in prosaic proximity and the tide so far out that several rows of long sandbars lay exposed. When Aschenbach opened his window, he thought he could smell the stagnant air of the lagoon.

Vexation overcame him. The thought of leaving occurred to him then and there. Once before, years ago, after fine spring weeks, this same weather had come on him here like a visitation, and so adversely affected his health that his departure from Venice had been like a precipitate escape. Were not the same symptoms now presenting themselves again, that unpleasant feverish sensation, the pressure in the temples, the heaviness in the eyelids? To move elsewhere yet again would be tiresome; but if the wind did not change, then there was no question of his staying here. As a precaution he did not unpack completely. At nine he breakfasted in the buffet between the hall and the main restaurant which was used for serving breakfast.

The kind of ceremonious silence prevailed here which a large hotel always aims to achieve. The serving waiters moved about noiselessly. A clink of crockery, a half-whispered word, were the only sounds audible. In one corner, obliquely opposite the door and two tables away from his own, Aschenbach noticed the Polish girls with their governess. Perched very upright, their ash-blond hair newly brushed and with reddened eyes, in stiff blue linen dresses with little white turnover collars and cuffs, they sat there passing each other a jar of preserves. They had almost finished their breakfast. The boy was missing.

Aschenbach smiled. Well, my little Phaeacian! he thought. You seem, unlike these young ladies, to enjoy the privilege of sleeping your fill. And with his spirits suddenly rising, he recited to himself the line: "Varied garments to wear, warm baths and restful reposing."

He breakfasted unhurriedly, received some forwarded mail from the porter who came into the breakfast room with his braided cap in hand, and opened a few letters as he smoked a cigarette. Thus it happened that he was still present to witness the entry of the lie-abed they were waiting for across the room.

He came through the glass door and walked in the silence obliquely across the room to his sisters' table. His walk was extraordinarily graceful, in the carriage of his upper body, the motion of his knees, the placing of his white-shod foot; it was very light, both delicate and proud, and made still more beautiful by the childlike modesty with which he twice, turning his head toward the room, raised and lowered his eyes as he passed. With a smile and a murmured word in his soft liquescent language, he took his seat; and now especially, as his profile was exactly turned to the watching Aschenbach, the latter was again amazed, indeed startled, by the truly godlike beauty of this human creature. Today the boy was wearing a light casual suit of blue and white striped linen material with a red silk breast-knot, closing at the neck in a simple white stand-up collar. But on this collar—which did not even match the rest of the suit very elegantly—there, like a flower in bloom, his head was gracefully resting. It was the head of Eros, with the creamy luster of Parian marble, the brows fine-drawn and serious, the temples and ear darkly and softly covered by the neat right-angled growth of the curling hair.

Good, good! thought Aschenbach, with that cool professional approval in which artists confronted by a masterpiece sometimes cloak their ecstasy, their rapture. And mentally he added: Truly, if the sea and the shore did not await me, I should stay here as long as you do! But as it was, he went, went through the hall accompanied by the courteous attentions of the hotel staff, went down over the great terrace and straight along the wooden passageway to the enclosed beach reserved for hotel guests. Down there, a barefooted old man with linen trousers, sailor's jacket and straw hat functioned as bathing attendant: Aschenbach had himself conducted by him to his reserved beach cabin, had his table and chair set up on the sandy wooden platform in front of it, and made himself comfortable in the deck chair which he had drawn further out toward the sea across the wax-yellow sand.

The scene on the beach, the spectacle of civilization taking its carefree sensuous ease at the brink of the element, entertained and delighted him as much as ever. Already the gray shallow sea was alive with children wading, with swimmers, with assorted figures lying on the sandbars, their crossed arms under their heads. Others were rowing little keelless boats painted red and blue, and capsizing with shrieks of laughter. In front of the long row of *capanne,* with their platforms like little verandahs to sit on, there was animated play and leisurely sprawling repose, there was visiting and chattering, there was punctilious morning elegance as well as unabashed nakedness contentedly enjoying the liberal local conventions. Further out, on the moist firm sand, persons in white bathing robes, in loose-fitting colorful shirtwear wandered to and fro. On the right, a complicated sand castle built by children was bedecked by flags in all the national colors. Vendors of mussels, cakes and fruit knelt to display their wares. On the left, in front of one of the huts in the row that was set at right angles to the others and to the sea, forming a boundary to the beach at this end, a Russian family was encamped: men with beards and big teeth, overripe indolent women, a Baltic spinster sitting at an easel and with exclamations of despair painting the sea, two good-natured hideous children, an old nanny in a headcloth who behaved in the caressingly deferential manner of the born serf. There they all were, gratefully enjoying their lives, tirelessly shouting the names of their disobediently romping children, mustering a few Italian words to joke at length with the amusing old man who sold them sweets, kissing each other on the cheeks and caring not a jot whether anyone was watching their scene of human solidarity.

Well, I shall stay, thought Aschenbach. What better place could I find? And with his hands folded in his lap, he let his eyes wander in the wide expanse of the sea, let his gaze glide away, dissolve and die in the monotonous haze of this desolate emptiness. There were profound reasons for his attachment to the sea: he loved it because as a hard-working artist he needed rest, needed to escape from the demanding complexity of phenomena and lie hidden on the bosom of the simple and tremendous; because of a forbidden longing deep within him that ran quite contrary to his life's task and was for that very reason seductive, a longing for the unarticulated and immeasurable, for eternity, for nothingness. To rest in the arms of perfection is the desire of any man intent upon creating excellence; and is not nothingness a form of perfection? But now, as he mused idly on such profound matters, the horizontal line of the sea's shore was suddenly intersected by a human figure, and when he had retrieved his gaze from limitless immensity and concentrated it again, he beheld the beautiful boy, coming from the left and walking past him across the sand. He walked barefoot, ready for wading, his slender legs naked to above the knees; his pace was leisured, but as light and proud as if he had long been used to going about without shoes. As he walked he looked round at the projecting row of huts: but scarcely had he noticed the Russian family, as it sat there in contented concord and going about its natural business, than a storm of angry contempt gathered over his face. He frowned darkly, his lips pouted, a bitter grimace pulled them to one side and distorted his cheek; his brows were contracted in so deep a scowl that his eyes seemed to have sunk right in under their pressure, glaring forth a black message of hatred. He looked down, looked back again menacingly, then made with one shoulder an emphatic gesture of rejection as he turned his back and left his enemies behind him.

A kind of delicacy or alarm, something like respect and embarrassment, moved Aschenbach to turn away as if he had seen nothing; for no serious person who witnesses a moment of passion by chance will wish to make any use, even privately, of what he has observed. But he was at one and the same time entertained and moved, that is to say he was filled with happiness. Such childish fanaticism, directed against so harmless a piece of good-natured living—it gave a human dimension to mute divinity, it made a statuesque masterpiece of nature, which had hitherto merely delighted the eyes, seem worthy of a profounder appreciation as well; and it placed the figure of this adolescent, remarkable already by his beauty, in a context which enabled one to take him seriously beyond his years.

With his head still averted, Aschenbach listened to the boy's voice, his high, not very strong voice, as he called out greetings to his playmates working at the sand castle, announcing his arrival when he was still some way from them. They answered, repeatedly shouting his name or a diminutive of his name, and Aschenbach listened for this with a certain curiosity, unable to pick up anything more precise than two melodious syllables that sounded something like "Adgio" or still oftener "Adgiu," called out with a long *u* at the end. The sound pleased him, he found its euphony befitting to its object, repeated it quietly to himself and turned again with satisfaction to his letters and papers.

With his traveling writing-case on his knees, he took out his fountain pen and began to deal with this and that item of correspondence. But after no more than a quarter of an hour he felt that it was a great pity to turn his mind away like this from the present situation, this most enjoyable of all situations known to him, and to miss the experience of it for the sake of an insignificant activity. He threw his writing materials aside, he returned to the sea; and before long, his attention attracted by the youthful voices of the sand castle builders, he turned his head comfortably to the right against the back of his chair, to investigate once more the whereabouts and doings of the excellent Adgio.

His first glance found him; the red breast-knot was unmistakable. He and some others were busy laying an old plank as a bridge across the damp moat of the sand castle, and he was supervising this work, calling out instructions and motioning with his head. With him were about ten companions, both boys and girls, of his age and some of them younger, all chattering together in tongues, in Polish, in French and even in Balkan idioms. But it was his name that was most often heard. It was obvious that he was sought after, wooed, admired. One boy in particular, a Pole like him, a sturdy young fellow whom they called something like "Jashu," with glossy black hair and wearing a linen belted suit, seemed to be his particular vassal and friend. When the work on the sand castle ended for the time being, they walked along the beach with their arms round each other, and the boy they called "Jashu" kissed his beautiful companion.

Aschenbach was tempted to shake his finger at him. "But I counsel you, Critoboulos," he thought with a smile, "to go traveling for a year! You will need that much time at least before you are cured." And he then breakfasted on some large, fully ripe strawberries which he bought from a vendor. It had grown very warm, although the sun was unable to break through the sky's layer of cloud. Even as one's senses enjoyed the tremendous and dizzying spectacle of the sea's stillness, lassitude paralyzed the mind. To the mature and serious Aschenbach it seemed an appropriate, fully satisfying task and occupation for him to guess or otherwise ascertain what name this could be that sounded approximately like "Adgio." And with the help of a few Polish recollections he established that what was meant must be "Tadzio," the abbreviation of "Tadeusz" and changing in the vocative to "Tadziu."

Tadzio was bathing. Aschenbach, who had lost sight of him, identified his head and his flailing arm far out to sea; for the water was evidently still shallow a long way out. But already he seemed to be giving cause for alarm, already women's voices were calling out to him from the bathing huts, again shrieking this name which ruled the beach almost like a war cry, and which with its soft consonants, its long-drawn-out *u*-sound at the end, had both a sweetness and a wildness about it: "Tadziu! Tadziu!" He returned, he came running, beating the resisting water to foam with his feet, his head thrown back, running through the waves. And to behold this living figure, lovely and austere in its early masculinity, with dripping locks and beautiful as a young god, approaching out of the depths of the sky and the sea, rising and escaping from the elements—this sight filled the mind with mythical images, it was like a poet's tale from a primitive age, a tale of the origins of form and of the birth of the gods. Aschenbach listened with closed eyes to this song as it began its music deep within him, and once again he reflected that it was good to be here and that here he would stay.

Later on, Tadzio lay in the sand resting from his bathe, wrapped in his white bathing robe which he had drawn through under his right shoulder, and cradling his head on his naked arm; and even when Aschenbach was not watching him but reading a few pages in his book, he almost never forgot that the boy was lying there, and that he need only turn his head slightly to the right to have the admired vision again in view. It almost seemed to him that he was sitting here for the purpose of protecting the half-sleeping boy— busy with doings of his own and yet nevertheless constantly keeping watch over this noble human creature there on his right, only a little way from him. And his heart was filled and moved by a paternal fondness, the tender concern by which he who sacrifices himself to beget beauty in the spirit is drawn to him who possesses beauty.

After midday he left the beach, returned to the hotel and took the lift up to his room. Here he spent some time in front of the looking glass studying his gray hair, his weary sharp-featured face. At that moment he thought of his fame, reflected that many people recognized him on the streets and would gaze at him respectfully, saluting the unerring and graceful power of his language—he recalled all the external successes he could think of that his talent had brought him, even calling to mind his elevation to the nobility. Then he went down to the restaurant and took lunch at his table. When he had finished and was entering the lift again, a group of young people who had also just been lunching crowded after him into the hovering cubicle, and Tadzio came with them. He stood quite near Aschenbach, so near that for the first time the latter was not seeing him as a distant image, but perceiving and taking precise cognizance of the details of his humanity. The boy was addressed by someone, and as he replied, with an indescribably charming smile, he was already leaving the lift again as it reached the first floor, stepping out backward with downcast eyes. The beautiful are modest, thought Aschenbach, and began to reflect very intensively on why this should be so. Nevertheless, he had noticed that Tadzio's teeth were not as attractive as they might have been: rather jagged and pale, lacking the luster of health and having that peculiar brittle transparency that is sometimes found in cases of anemia. "He's very delicate, he's sickly," thought Aschenbach, "he'll probably not live to grow old." And he made no attempt to explain to himself a certain feeling of satisfaction or relief that accompanied this thought.

He spent two hours in his room, and in mid-afternoon took the *vaporetto* across the stale-smelling lagoon to Venice. He got out at San Marco, took tea on the Piazza, and then, in accordance with the daily program he had adopted for his stay here, set off on a walk through the streets. But it was this walk that brought about a complete change in his mood and intentions.

An unpleasant sultriness pervaded the narrow streets; the air was so thick that the exhalations from houses and shops and hot food stalls, the reek of oil, the smell of perfume and many other odors hung about in clouds instead of dispersing. Cigarette smoke lingered and was slow to dissipate. The throng of people in the alleyways annoyed him as he walked instead of giving him pleasure. The further he went, the more overwhelmingly he was afflicted by that appalling condition sometimes caused by a combination of the sea air with the sirocco, a condition of simultaneous excitement and exhaustion. He began to sweat disagreeably. His eyes faltered, his chest felt constricted, he was feverish, the blood throbbed in his head. He fled from the crowded commercial thoroughfares, over bridges, into the poor quarters. There he was besieged by beggars, and the sickening stench from the canals made it difficult to breathe. In a silent square, one of those places in the depths of Venice that seem to have been forgotten and put under a spell, he rested on the edge of a fountain, wiped the sweat from his forehead and realized that he would have to leave.

For the second time, and this time definitively, it had become evident that this city, in this state of the weather, was extremely injurious to him. To stay on willfully would be contrary to good sense, the prospect of a change in the wind seemed quite uncertain. He must make up his mind at once. To return straight home was out of the question. Neither his summer nor his winter quarters were ready to receive him. But this was not the only place with the sea and a beach, and elsewhere they were to be had without the harmful additional ingredient of this lagoon with its mephitic vapors. He remembered a little coastal resort not far from Trieste which had been recommended to him. Why not go there? And he must do so without delay, if it was to be worthwhile changing to a different place yet again. He declared himself resolved and rose to his feet. At the next gondola stop he took a boat and had himself conveyed back to San Marco through the murky labyrinth of canals, under delicate marble balconies flanked with carved lions, round the slimy stone corners of buildings, past the mournful facades of *palazzi* on which boards bearing the names of commercial enterprises were mirrored in water where refuse bobbed up and down. He had some trouble getting to his destination, as the gondolier was in league with lace factories and glassworks and tried to land him at every place where he might view the wares and make a purchase; and whenever this bizarre journey through Venice might have cast its spell on him, he was effectively and irksomely disenchanted by the cutpurse mercantile spirit of the sunken queen of the Adriatic.

Back in the hotel, before he had even dined, he notified the office that unforeseen circumstances obliged him to leave on the following morning. Regret was expressed, his bill was settled. He took dinner and spent the warm evening reading newspapers in a rocking chair on the back terrace. Before going to bed he packed completely for departure.

He slept fitfully, troubled by his impending further journey. When he opened his windows in the morning, the sky was still overcast, but the air seemed fresher, and—he began even now to regret his decision. Had he not given notice too impulsively, had it not been a mistake, an action prompted by a mere temporary indisposition? If only he had deferred it for a little, if only, without giving up so soon, he had taken a chance on acclimatizing himself to Venice or waiting for the wind to change, then he would now have before him not the hurry and flurry of a journey, but a morning on the beach like that of the previous day. Too late. What he had wanted yesterday he must go on wanting now. He got dressed and took the lift down to breakfast at eight o'clock.

When he entered the breakfast room it was still empty of guests. A few came in as he was sitting waiting for what he had ordered. As he sipped his tea he saw the Polish girls arrive with their companion: strict and matutinal, with reddened eyes, they proceeded to their table in the window corner. Shortly after this the porter approached with cap in hand and reminded him that it was time to leave. The motor coach was standing ready to take him and other passengers to the Hotel Excelsior, from which point the motor launch would convey the ladies and gentlemen through the company's private canal and across to the station. Time is pressing, signore.—In Aschenbach's opinion time was doing nothing of the sort. There was more than an hour till his train left. He found it extremely annoying that hotels should make a practice of getting their departing clients off the premises unnecessarily early, and indicated to the porter that he wished to have his breakfast in peace. The man hesitantly withdrew, only to reappear five minutes later. It was impossible, he said, for the automobile to wait any longer. Aschenbach retorted angrily that in that case it should leave, and take his trunk with it. He himself would take the public steamboat when it was time, and would they kindly leave it to him to deal with the problem of his own departure. The hotel servant bowed. Aschenbach, glad to have fended off these tiresome admonitions, finished his breakfast unhurriedly, and even got the waiter to hand him a newspaper. It was indeed getting very late by the time he rose. It so happened that at that same moment Tadzio entered through the glass door.

As he walked to his family's table his path crossed that of the departing guest. Meeting this gray-haired gentleman with the lofty brow, he modestly lowered his eyes, only to raise them again at once in his enchanting way, in a soft and full glance; and then he had passed. Good-bye, Tadzio! thought Aschenbach. How short our meeting was. And he added, actually shaping the thought with his lips and uttering it aloud to himself, as he normally never did: "May God bless you!"—He then went through the routine of departure, distributed gratuities, received the parting courtesies of the soft-spoken little manager in the French frock coat, and left the hotel on foot as he had come, walking along the white-blossoming avenue with the hotel servant behind him carrying his hand luggage, straight across the island to the *vaporetto* landing stage. He reached it, he took his seat on board—and what followed was a voyage of sorrow, a grievous passage that plumbed all the depths of regret.

It was the familiar trip across the lagoon, past San Marco, up the Grand Canal. Aschenbach sat on the semicircular bench in the bows, one arm on the railing, shading his eyes with his hand. The Public Gardens fell away astern, the Piazzetta revealed itself once more in its princely elegance and was left behind, then came the great flight of the *palazzi*, with the splendid marble arch of the Rialto appearing as the waterway turned. The traveler contemplated it all, and his heart was rent with sorrow. The atmosphere of the city, this slightly moldy smell of sea and swamp from which he had been so anxious to escape—he breathed it in now in deep, tenderly painful drafts. Was it possible that he had not known, had not considered how deeply his feelings were involved in all these things? What had been a mere qualm of compunction this morning, a slight stirring of doubt as to the wisdom of his behavior, now became grief, became real suffering, an anguish of the soul, so bitter that several times it brought tears to his eyes, and which as he told himself he could not possibly have foreseen. What he found so hard to bear, what was indeed at times quite unendurable, was evidently the thought that he would never see Venice again, that this was a parting forever. For since it had become clear for a second time that this city made him ill, since he had been forced a second time to leave it precipitately, he must of course from now on regard it as an impossible and forbidden place to which he was not suited, and which it would be senseless to attempt to revisit. Indeed, he felt that if he left now, shame and pride must prevent him from ever setting eyes again on this beloved city which had twice physically defeated him; and this contention between his soul's desire and his physical capacities suddenly seemed to the aging Aschenbach so grave and important, the bodily inadequacy so shameful, so necessary to overcome at all costs, that he could not understand the facile resignation with which he had decided yesterday, without any serious struggle, to tolerate that inadequacy and to acknowledge it.

In the meantime the *vaporetto* was approaching the station, and Aschenbach's distress and sense of helplessness increased to the point of distraction. In this torment he felt it to be impossible to leave and no less impossible to turn back. He entered the station torn by this acute inner conflict. It was very late, he had not a moment to lose if he was to catch his train. He both wanted to catch it and wanted to miss it. But time was pressing, lashing him on; he hurried to get his ticket, looking round in the crowded concourse for the hotel company's employee who would be on duty here. The man appeared and informed him that his large trunk had been sent off as registered baggage. Sent off already? Certainly—to Como. To Como? And from hasty comings and goings, from angry questions and embarrassed replies, it came to light that the trunk, before even leaving the luggage room in the Hotel Excelsior, had been put with some quite different baggage and dispatched to a totally incorrect address.

Aschenbach had some difficulty preserving the facial expression that would be the only comprehensible one in these circumstances. A wild joy, an unbelievable feeling of hilarity, shook him almost convulsively from the depths of his heart. The hotel employee rushed to see if it was still possible to stop the trunk, and needless to say returned without having had any success. Aschenbach accordingly declared that he was not prepared to travel without his luggage, that he had decided to go back and wait at the Hotel des Bains for the missing article to turn up again. Was the company's motor launch still at the station? The man assured him that it was waiting immediately outside. With Italian eloquence he prevailed upon the official at the ticket office to take back Aschenbach's already purchased ticket. He swore that telegrams would be sent, that nothing would be left undone and no effort spared to get the trunk back in no time at all—and thus it most strangely came about that the traveler, twenty minutes after arriving at the station, found himself back on the Grand Canal and on his way back to the Lido.

How unbelievably strange an experience it was, how shaming, how like a dream in its bizarre comedy: to be returning, by a quirk of fate, to places from which one has just taken leave forever with the deepest sorrow—to be sent back and to be seeing them again within the hour! With spray tossing before its bows, deftly and entertainingly tacking to and fro between gondolas and *vaporetti*, the rapid little boat darted toward its destination, while its only passenger sat concealing under a mask of resigned annoyance the anxiously exuberant excitement of a truant schoolboy. From time to time he still inwardly shook with laughter at this mishap, telling himself that even a man born under a lucky star could not have had a more welcome piece of ill luck. There would be explanations to be given, surprised faces to be confronted—and then, as he told himself, everything would be well again, a disaster would have been averted, a grievous mistake corrected, and everything he thought he had turned his back on for good would lie open again for him to enjoy, would be his for as long as he liked ... And what was more, did the rapid movement of the motor launch deceive him, or was there really now, to crown all else, a breeze blowing from the sea?

The bow waves dashed against the concrete walls of the narrow canal that cuts across the island to the Hotel Excelsior. There a motor omnibus was waiting for the returning guest and conveyed him along the road above the rippling sea straight to the Hotel des Bains. The little manager with the moustache and the fancily-cut frock coat came down the flight of steps to welcome him.

In softly flattering tones he expressed regret for the incident, described it as highly embarrassing for himself and for the company, but emphatically endorsed Aschenbach's decision to wait here for his luggage. His room, to be sure, had been relet, but another, no less comfortable, was immediately at his disposal. *"Pas de chance, monsieur!"* said the Swiss lift-attendant as they glided up. And thus the fugitive was once more installed in a room situated and furnished almost exactly like the first.

Exhausted and numbed by the confusion of this strange morning, he had no sooner distributed the contents of his hand luggage about the room than he collapsed into a reclining chair at the open window. The sea had turned pale green, the air seemed clearer and purer, the beach with its bathing cabins and boats more colorful, although the sky was still gray. Aschenbach gazed out, his hands folded in his lap, pleased to be here again but shaking his head with displeasure at his irresolution, his ignorance of his own wishes. Thus he sat for about an hour, resting and idly daydreaming. At midday he caught sight of Tadzio in his striped linen suit with the red breast-knot, coming from the sea, through the beach barrier and along the boarded walks back to the hotel. From up here at his window Aschenbach recognized him at once, before he had even looked at him properly, and some such thought came to him as: Why, Tadzio, there you are again too! But at the same instant he felt that casual greeting die on his lips, stricken dumb by the truth in his heart—he felt the rapturous kindling of his blood, the joy and the anguish of his soul, and realized that it was because of Tadzio that it had been so hard for him to leave.

He sat quite still, quite unseen at his high vantage point, and began to search his feelings. His features were alert, his eyebrows rose, an attentive, intelligently inquisitive smile parted his lips. Then he raised his head, and with his arms hanging limply down along the back of his chair, described with both of them a slowly rotating and lifting motion, the palms of his hands turning forward, as if to sketch an opening and outspreading of the arms. It was a gesture that gladly bade welcome, a gesture of calm acceptance.

4

Now day after day the god with the burning cheeks soared naked, driving his four fire-breathing steeds through the spaces of heaven, and now, too, his yellow-gold locks fluttered wide in the outstorming east wind. Silk-white radiance gleamed on the slow-swelling deep's vast waters. The sand glowed. Under the silvery quivering blue of the ether, rust-colored awnings were spread out in front of the beach cabins, and one spent the morning hours on the sharply defined patch of shadow they provided. But exquisite, too, was the evening, when the plants in the park gave off a balmy fragrance, and the stars on high moved through their dance, and the softly audible murmur of the night-surrounded sea worked its magic on the soul. Such an evening carried with it the delightful promise of a new sunlit day of leisure easily ordered, and adorned with countless close-knit possibilities of charming chance encounter.

The guest whom so convenient a mishap had detained here was very far from seeing the recovery of his property as a reason for yet another departure. For a couple of days he had had to put up with some privations and appear in the main dining room in his traveling clothes. Then, when finally the errant load was once more set down in his room, he unpacked completely and filled the cupboards and drawers with his possessions, resolving for the present to set no time limit on his stay; he was glad now to be able to pass his hours on the beach in a tussore suit and to present himself again in seemly evening attire at the dinner table.

The lulling rhythm of this existence had already cast its spell on him; he had been quickly enchanted by the indulgent softness and splendor of this way of life. What a place this was indeed, combining the charms of a cultivated seaside resort in the south with the familiar ever-ready proximity of the strange and wonderful city! Aschenbach did not enjoy enjoying himself. Whenever and wherever he had to stop work, have a breathing space, take things easily, he would soon find himself driven by restlessness and dissatisfaction—and this had been so in his youth above all—back to his lofty travail, to his stern and sacred daily routine. Only this place bewitched him, re-laxed his will, gave him happiness. Often in the forenoon, under the awning of his hut, gazing dreamily at the blue of the southern sea, or on a mild night perhaps, reclining under a star-strewn sky on the cushions of a gondola that carried him back to the Lido from the Piazza where he had long lingered—and as the bright lights, the melting sounds of the serenade dropped away behind him—often he recalled his country house in the mountains, the scene of his summer labors, where the low clouds would drift through his gar-den, violent evening thunderstorms would put out all the lights, and the ravens he fed would take refuge in the tops of the pine trees. Then indeed he would feel he had been snatched away now to the Elysian land, to the ends of the earth, where lightest of living is granted to mortals, where no snow is nor winter, no storms and no rain downstreaming, but where Oceanus ever causes a gentle cooling breeze to ascend, and the days flow past in blessed idleness, with no labor or strife, for to the sun alone and its feasts they are all given over.

Aschenbach saw much of the boy Tadzio, he saw him almost constantly; in a confined environment, with a common daily pro-gram, it was natural for the beautiful creature to be near him all day, with only brief interruptions. He saw him and met him every-where: in the ground floor rooms of the hotel, on their cooling journeys by water to the city and back, in the sumptuous Piazza itself, and often elsewhere from time to time, in alleys and byways, when chance had played a part. But it was during the mornings on the beach above all, and with the happiest regularity, that he could devote hours at a time to the contemplation and study of this exqui-site phenomenon. Indeed, it was precisely this ordered routine of happiness, this equal daily repetition of favorable circumstances, that so filled him with contentment and zest for life, that made this place so precious to him, that allowed one sunlit day to follow an-other in such obligingly endless succession.

He rose early, as he would normally have done under the insistent compulsion of work, and was down at the beach before most of the other guests, when the sun's heat was still gentle and the sea lay dazzling white in its morning dreams. He greeted the barrier attend-ant affably, exchange familiar greetings also with the barefooted, white-bearded old man who had prepared his place for him, spread the brown awning and shifted the cabin furniture out to the platform where Aschenbach would settle down. Three hours or four were then his, hours in which the sun would rise to its zenith and to terrible power, hours in which the sea would turn a deeper and deeper blue, hours in which he would be able to watch Tadzio.

He saw him coming, walking along from the left by the water's edge, saw him from behind as he emerged between the cabins, or indeed would sometimes look up and discover, gladdened and startled, that he had missed his arrival and that the boy was already there, already in the blue and white bathing costume which now on the beach was his sole attire. There he would be, already busy with his customary activities in the sun and the sand—this charmingly trivial, idle yet ever-active life that was both play and repose, a life of sauntering, wading, digging, snatching, lying about and swimming, under the watchful eyes and at the constant call of the women on their platform, who with their high-pitched voices would cry out his name: "Tadziu! Tadziu!" and to whom he would come running with eager gesticulation, to tell them what he had experienced, to show them what he had found, what he had caught: jellyfish, little seahorses, and mussels, and crabs that go sideways. Aschenbach understood not a word of what he said, and commonplace though it might be, it was liquid melody in his ears. Thus the foreign sound of the boy's speech exalted it to music, the sun in its triumph shed lavish brightness all over him, and the sublime perspective of the sea was the constant contrasting background against which he appeared.

Soon the contemplative beholder knew every line and pose of that noble, so freely displayed body, he saluted again with joy each already familiar perfection, and there was no end to his wonder, to the delicate delight of his senses. The boy would be summoned to greet a guest who was making a polite call on the ladies in their cabin; he would run up, still wet perhaps from the sea, throw back his curls, and as he held out his hand, poised on one leg with the other on tiptoe, he had an enchanting way of turning and twisting his body, gracefully expectant, charmingly shamefaced, seeking to please because good breeding required him to do so. Or he would be lying full-length, his bathing robe wrapped round his chest, his finely chiseled arm propped on the sand, his hand cupping his chin; the boy addressed as "Jashu" would squat beside him caressing him, and nothing could be more bewitching than the way the favored Tadzio, smiling with his eyes and lips, would look up at this lesser and servile mortal. Or he would be standing at the edge of the sea, alone, some way from his family, quite near Aschenbach, standing upright with his hands clasped behind his neck, slowly rocking to and fro on the balls of his feet and dreamily gazing into the blue distance, while little waves ran up and bathed his toes. His honey-colored hair nestled in ringlets at his temples and at the back of his neck, the sun gleamed in the down on his upper spine, the subtle outlining of his ribs and the symmetry of his breast stood out through the scanty covering of his torso, his armpits were still as smooth as those of a statue, the hollows of his knees glistened and their bluish veins made his body seem composed of some more trans-lucent material. What discipline, what precision of thought was ex-pressed in that outstretched, youthfully perfect physique! And yet the austere pure will that had here been darkly active, that had succeeded in bringing this divine sculptured shape to light—was it not well known and familiar to Aschenbach as an artist? Was it not also active in him, in the sober passion that filled him as he set free from the marble mass of language that slender form which he had beheld in the spirit, and which he was presenting to mankind as a model and mirror of intellectual beauty?

A model and mirror! His eyes embraced that noble figure at the blue water's edge, and in rising ecstasy he felt he was gazing on Beauty itself, on Form as a thought of God, on the one and pure perfection which dwells in the spirit and of which a human image and likeness had here been lightly and graciously set up for him to worship. Such was his emotional intoxication; and the aging artist welcomed it unhesitatingly, even greedily. His mind was in labor, its store of culture was in ferment, his memory threw up thoughts from ancient tradition which he had been taught as a boy, but which had never yet come alive in his own fire. Had he not read that the sun turns our attention from spiritual things to the things of the senses? He had read that it so numbs and bewitches our intelligence and memory that the soul, in its joy, quite forgets its proper state and clings with astonished admiration to that most beautiful of all the things the sun shines upon: yes, that only with the help of a bodily form is the soul then still able to exalt itself to a higher vision. That Cupid, indeed, does as mathematicians do, when they show dull-witted children tangible images of the pure Forms: so too the love god, in order to make spiritual things visible, loves to use the shapes and colors of young men, turning them into instruments of recollec-tion by adorning them with all the reflected splendor of Beauty, so that the sight of them will truly set us on fire with pain and hope.

Such were the thoughts the god inspired in his enthusiast, such were the emotions of which he grew capable. And a delightful vision came to him, spun from the sea's murmur and the glittering sunlight. It was the old plane tree not far from the walls of Athens—that place of sacred shade, fragrant with chaste-tree blossoms, adorned with sacred statues and pious gifts in honor of the nymphs and of Acheloüs. The stream trickled crystal clear over smooth pebbles at the foot of the great spreading tree; the crickets made their music. But on the grass, which sloped down gently so that one could hold up one's head as one lay, there reclined two men, sheltered here from the heat of the noonday: one elderly and one young, one ugly and one beautiful, the wise beside the desirable. And Socrates, wooing him with witty compliments and jests, was instructing Phaedrus on desire and virtue. He spoke to him of the burning tremor of fear which the lover will suffer when his eye perceives a likeness of eternal Beauty; spoke to him of the lusts of the profane and base who cannot turn their eyes to Beauty when they behold its image and are not capable of reverence; spoke of the sacred terror that visits the noble soul when a godlike countenance, a perfect body appears to him—of how he trembles then and is beside himself and hardly dares look at the possessor of beauty, and reveres him and would even sacrifice to him as to a graven image, if he did not fear to seem foolish in the eyes of men. For Beauty, dear Phaedrus, only Beauty is at one and the same time divinely desirable and visible: it is, mark well, the only form of the spiritual that we can receive with our senses and endure with our senses. For what would become of us if other divine things, if Reason and Virtue and Truth were to appear to us sensuously? Should we not perish in a conflagration of love, as once upon a time Semele did before Zeus? Thus Beauty is the lover's path to the spirit—only the path, only a means, little Phaedrus . . . And then he uttered the subtlest thing of all, that sly wooer: he who loves, he said, is more divine than the beloved, because the god is in the former, but not in the latter—this, the tenderest perhaps and the most mocking thought ever formulated, a thought alive with all the mischievousness and most secret voluptuousness of the heart.

The writer's joy is the thought that can become emotion, the emotion that can wholly become a thought. At that time the solitary Aschenbach took possession and control of just such a pulsating thought, just such a precise emotion: namely, that Nature trembles with rapture when the spirit bows in homage before Beauty. He suddenly desired to write. Eros indeed, we are told, loves idleness and is born only for the idle. But at this point of Aschenbach's crisis and visitation his excitement was driving him to produce. The occasion was almost a matter of indifference. An inquiry, an invitation to express a personal opinion on a certain important cultural problem, a burning question of taste, had been circulated to the intellectual world and had been forwarded to him on his travels. The theme was familiar to him, it was close to his experience; the desire to illuminate it in his own words was suddenly irresistible. And what he craved, indeed, was to work on it in Tadzio's presence, to take the boy's physique for a model as he wrote, to let his style follow the lineaments of this body which he saw as divine, and to carry its beauty on high into the spiritual world, as the eagle once carried the Trojan shepherd boy up into the ether. Never had he felt the joy of the word more sweetly, never had he known so clearly that Eros dwells in language, as during those perilously precious hours in which, seated at his rough table under the awning, in full view of his idol and with the music of his voice in his ears, he used Tadzio's beauty as a model for his brief essay—that page and a half of exquisite prose which with its limpid nobility and vibrant controlled passion was soon to win the admiration of many. It is as well that the world knows only a fine piece of work and not also its origins, the conditions under which it came into being; for knowledge of the sources of an artist's inspiration would often confuse readers and shock them, and the excellence of the writing would be of no avail. How strange those hours were! How strangely exhausting that labor! How mysterious this act of intercourse and begetting between a mind and a body! When Aschenbach put away his work and left the beach, he felt worn out, even broken, and his conscience seemed to be reproaching him as if after some kind of debauch.

On the following morning, just as he was leaving the hotel, he noticed from the steps that Tadzio, already on his way to the sea—and alone—was just approaching the beach barrier. The wish to use this opportunity, the mere thought of doing so, and thereby lightly, lightheartedly, making the acquaintance of one who had unknowingly so exalted and moved him: the thought of speaking to him, of enjoying his answer and his glance—all this seemed natural, it was the irresistibly obvious thing to do. The beautiful boy was walking in a leisurely fashion, he could be overtaken, and Aschenbach quickened his pace. He reached him on the boarded way behind the bathing cabins, he was just about to lay his hand on his head or his shoulder, and some phrase or other, some friendly words in French were on the tip of his tongue—when he felt his heart, perhaps partly because he had been walking fast, hammering wildly inside him, felt so breathless that he would only have been able to speak in a strangled and trembling voice. He hesitated, struggled to control himself, then was suddenly afraid that he had already been walking too long close behind the beautiful boy, afraid that Tadzio would notice this, that he would turn and look at him questioningly; he made one more attempt, failed, gave up, and hurried past with his head bowed.

Too late! he thought at that moment. Too late! But was it too late? This step he had failed to take would very possibly have been all to the good, it might have had a lightening and gladdening effect, led perhaps to a wholesome disenchantment. But the fact now seemed to be that the aging lover no longer wished to be disenchanted, that the intoxication was too precious to him. Who shall unravel the mystery of an artist's nature and character! Who shall explain the profound instinctual fusion of discipline and dissoluteness on which it rests! For not to be able to desire wholesome disenchantment is to be dissolute. Aschenbach was no longer disposed to self-criticism; taste, the intellectual mold of his years, self-respect, maturity and late simplicity all disinclined him to analyze his motives and decide whether what had prevented him from carrying out his intention had been a prompting of conscience or a disreputable weakness. He was confused, he was afraid that someone, even if only the bathing attendant, might have witnessed his haste and his defeat; he was very much afraid of exposure to ridicule. For the rest, he could not help inwardly smiling at his comic-sacred terror. "Crestfallen," he thought, "spirits dashed, like a frightened cock hanging its wings in a fight! Truly this is the god who at the sight of the desired beauty so breaks our courage and dashes our pride so utterly to the ground . . ." He toyed with the theme, gave rein to his enthusiasm, plunged into emotions he was too proud to fear.

He was no longer keeping any tally of the leisure time he had allowed himself; the thought of returning home did not even occur to him. He had arranged for ample funds to be made available to him here. His one anxiety was that the Polish family might leave; but he had surreptitiously learned, by a casual question to the hotel barber, that these guests had arrived at the hotel only very shortly before he had arrived himself. The sun was browning his face and hands, the stimulating salty breeze heightened his capacity for feeling, and whereas formerly, when sleep or food or contact with nature had given him any refreshment, he would always have expended it completely on his writing, he now, with high-hearted prodigality, allowed all the daily revitalization he was receiving from the sun and leisure and sea air to burn itself up in intoxicating emotion.

He slept fleetingly; the days of precious monotony were punctuated by brief, happily restless nights. To be sure, he would retire early, for at nine o'clock, when Tadzio had disappeared from the scene, he judged his day to be over. But at the first glint of dawn a pang of tenderness would startle him awake, his heart would remember its adventure, he could bear his pillows no longer, he would get up, and lightly wrapped against the early morning chill he would sit down at the open window to wait for the sunrise. His soul, still fresh with the solemnity of sleep, was filled with awe by this wonderful event. The sky, the earth and the sea still wore the glassy paleness of ghostly twilight; a dying star still floated in the void. But a murmur came, a winged message from dwelling places no mortal may approach, that Eos was rising from her husband's side; and now it appeared, that first sweet blush at the farthest horizon of the sky and sea, which heralds the sensuous disclosure of creation. The goddess approached, that ravisher of youth, who carried off Cleitus and Cephalus and defied the envy of all the Olympians to enjoy the love of the beautiful Orion. A scattering of roses began, there at the edge of the world, an ineffably lovely shining and blossoming: childlike clouds, transfigured and transparent with light, hovered like serving *amoretti* in the vermilion and violet haze; crimson light fell across the waves, which seemed to be washing it landward; golden spears darted from below into the heights of heaven, the gleam became a conflagration, noiselessly and with overwhelming divine power the glow and the fire and the blazing flames reared upward, and the sacred steeds of the goddess's brother Helios, tucking their hooves, leapt above the earth's round surface. With the splendor of the god irradiating him, the lone watcher sat; he closed his eyes and let the glory kiss his eyelids. Feelings he had had long ago, early and precious dolors of the heart, which had died out in his life's austere service and were now, so strangely transformed, returning to him— he recognized them with a confused and astonished smile. He meditated, he dreamed, slowly a name shaped itself on his lips, and still smiling, with upturned face, his hands folded in his lap, he fell asleep in his chair once more.

With such fiery ceremony the day began, but the rest of it, too, was strangely exalted and mythically transformed. Where did it come from, what was its origin, this sudden breeze that played so gently and speakingly around his temples and ears, like some higher insufflation? Innumerable white fleecy clouds covered the sky, like the grazing flocks of the gods. A stronger wind rose, and the horses of Poseidon reared and ran; his bulls too, the bulls of the blue-haired sea god, roared and charged with lowered horns. But among the rocks and stones of the more distant beach the waves danced like leaping goats. A sacred, deranged world, full of Panic life, enclosed the enchanted watcher, and his heart dreamed tender tales. Sometimes, as the sun was sinking behind Venice, he would sit on a bench in the hotel park to watch Tadzio, dressed in white with a colorful sash, at play on the rolled gravel tennis court; and in his mind's eye he was watching Hyacinthus, doomed to perish because two gods loved him. He could even feel Zephyr's grievous envy of his rival, who had forgotten his oracle and his bow and his zither to be forever playing with the beautiful youth; he saw the discus, steered by cruel jealousy, strike the lovely head; he himself, turning pale too, caught the broken body in his arms, and the flower that sprang from that sweet blood bore the inscription of his undying lament.

Nothing is stranger, more delicate, than the relationship between people who know each other only by sight—who encounter and observe each other daily, even hourly, and yet are compelled by the constraint of convention or by their own temperament to keep up the pretense of being indifferent strangers, neither greeting nor speaking to each other. Between them is uneasiness and overstimulated curiosity, the nervous excitement of an unsatisfied, unnaturally suppressed need to know and to communicate; and above all, too, a kind of strained respect. For man loves and respects his fellow man for as long as he is not yet in a position to evaluate him, and desire is born of defective knowledge.

It was inevitable that some kind of relationship and acquaintance should develop between Aschenbach and the young Tadzio, and with a surge of joy the older man became aware that his interest and attention were not wholly unreciprocated. Why, for example, when the beautiful creature appeared in the morning on the beach, did he now never use the boarded walk behind the bathing cabins, but always take the front way, through the sand, passing Aschenbach's abode and often passing unnecessarily close to him, almost touching his table or his chair, as he sauntered toward the cabin where his family sat? Was this the attraction, the fascination exercised by a superior feeling on its tender and thoughtless object? Aschenbach waited daily for Tadzio to make his appearance and sometimes pretended to be busy when he did so, letting the boy pass him seemingly unnoticed. But sometimes, too, he would look up, and their eyes would meet. They would both be deeply serious when this happened. In the cultured and dignified countenance of the older man, nothing betrayed an inner emotion; but in Tadzio's eyes there was an inquiry, a thoughtful questioning, his walk became hesitant, he looked at the ground, looked sweetly up again, and when he had passed, something in his bearing seemed to suggest that only good breeding restrained him from turning to look back.

But once, one evening, it was different. The Poles and their governess had been absent from dinner in the main restaurant—Aschenbach had noticed this with concern. After dinner, very uneasy about where they might be, he was walking in evening dress and a straw hat in front of the hotel, at the foot of the terrace, when suddenly he saw the nunlike sisters appearing with their companion, in the light of the arc lamps, and four paces behind them was Tadzio. Obviously they had come from the *vaporetto* pier, having for some reason dined in the city. The crossing had been chilly perhaps; Tadzio was wearing a dark blue reefer jacket with gold buttons and a naval cap to match. The sun and sea air never burned his skin, it was marble-pale as always; but today he seemed paler than usual, either because of the cool weather or in the blanching moonlight of the lamps. His symmetrical eyebrows stood out more sharply, his eyes seemed much darker. He was more beautiful than words can express, and Aschenbach felt, as so often already, the painful awareness that language can only praise sensuous beauty, but not reproduce it.

He had not been prepared for the beloved encounter, it came unexpectedly, he had not had time to put on an expression of calm and dignity. Joy no doubt, surprise, admiration, were openly displayed on his face when his eyes met those of the returning absentee—and in that instant it happened that Tadzio smiled: smiled at him, speakingly, familiarly, enchantingly and quite unabashed, with his lips parting slowly as the smile was formed. It was the smile of Narcissus as he bows his head over the mirroring water, that profound, fascinated, protracted smile with which he reaches out his arms toward the reflection of his own beauty—a very slightly contorted smile, contorted by the hopelessness of his attempt to kiss the sweet lips of his shadow; a smile that was provocative, curious and imperceptibly troubled, bewitched and bewitching.

He who had received this smile carried it quickly away with him like a fateful gift. He was so deeply shaken that he was forced to flee the lighted terrace and the front garden and hurry into the darkness of the park at the rear. Words struggled from his lips, strangely indignant and tender reproaches: "You mustn't smile like that! One mustn't, do you hear, mustn't smile like that at anyone!" He sank down on one of the seats, deliriously breathing the nocturnal fragrance of the flowers and trees. And leaning back, his arms hanging down, overwhelmed, trembling, shuddering all over, he whispered the standing formula of the heart's desire—impossible here, absurd, depraved, ludicrous and sacred nevertheless, still worthy of honor even here: "I love you!"

5

During the fourth week of his stay at the Lido Gustav von Aschenbach began to notice certain uncanny developments in the outside world. In the first place it struck him that as the height of the season approached, the number of guests at his hotel was diminishing rather than increasing, and in particular that the German language seemed to be dying away into silence all round him, so that in the end only foreign sounds fell on his ear at table and on the beach. Then one day the hotel barber, whom he visited frequently now, let slip in conversation a remark that aroused his suspicions. The man had mentioned a German family who had just left after only a brief stay, and in his chattering, flattering manner he added: "But you are staying on, signore; you are not afraid of the sickness." Aschenbach looked at him. "The sickness?" he repeated. The fellow stopped his talk, pretended to be busy, had not heard the question. And when it was put to him again more sharply, he declared that he knew nothing and tried with embarrassed loquacity to change the subject.

That was at midday. In the afternoon, with the sea dead calm and the sun burning, Aschenbach crossed to Venice, for he was now driven by a mad compulsion to follow the Polish boy and his sisters, having seen them set off toward the pier with their companion. He did not find his idol at San Marco. But at tea, sitting at his round wrought-iron table on the shady side of the Piazza, he suddenly scented in the air a peculiar aroma, one which it now seemed to him he had been noticing for days without really being conscious of it— a sweetish, medicinal smell that suggested squalor and wounds and suspect cleanliness. He scrutinized it, pondered and identified it, finished his tea and left the Piazza at the far end opposite the basilica. In the narrow streets the smell was stronger. At corners, printed notices had been pasted up in which the civic authorities, with fatherly concern, gave warning to the local population that since certain ailments of the gastric system were normal in this weather, they should refrain from eating oysters and mussels and indeed from using water from the canals. The euphemistic character of the announcement was obvious. Groups of people were standing about silently on bridges or in squares, and the stranger stood among them, brooding and scenting the truth.

He found a shopkeeper leaning against his vaulted doorway, surrounded by coral necklaces and trinkets made of imitation amethyst, and asked him about the unpleasant smell. The man looked him over with heavy eyes, and hastily gathered his wits. "A precautionary measure, signore," he answered, gesticulating. "The police have laid down regulations, and quite right too, it must be said. This weather is oppressive, the sirocco is not very wholesome. In short, the signore will understand—an exaggerated precaution no doubt . . ." Aschenbach thanked him and walked on. Even on the *vaporetto* taking him back to the Lido he now noticed the smell of the bactericide.

Back at the hotel, he went at once to the table in the hall where the newspapers were kept, and carried out some research. In the foreign papers he found nothing. Those in his own language mentioned rumors, quoted contradictory statistics, reported official denials and questioned their veracity. This explained the withdrawal of the German and Austrian clientele. Visitors of other nationalities evidently knew nothing, suspected nothing, still had no apprehensions. "They want it kept quiet!" thought Aschenbach in some agitation, throwing the newspapers back on the table. "They're hushing this up!" But at the same time his heart filled with elation at the thought of the adventure in which the outside world was about to be involved. For to passion, as to crime, the assured everyday order and stability of things is not opportune, and any weakening of the civil structure, any chaos and disaster afflicting the world, must be welcome to it, as offering a vague hope of turning such circumstances to its advantage. Thus Aschenbach felt an obscure sense of satisfaction at what was going on in the dirty alleyways of Venice, cloaked in official secrecy—this guilty secret of the city, which merged with his own innermost secret and which it was also so much in his own interests to protect. For in his enamored state his one anxiety was that Tadzio might leave, and he realized with a kind of horror that he would not be able to go on living if that were to happen.

Lately he had not been content to owe the sight and proximity of the beautiful boy merely to daily routine and chance: he had begun pursuing him, following him obtrusively. On Sunday, for example, the Poles never appeared on the beach; he rightly guessed that they were attending mass in San Marco, and hastened to the church himself. There, stepping from the fiery heat of the Piazza into the golden twilight of the sanctuary, he would find him whom he had missed, bowed over a prie-dieu and performing his devotions. Then he would stand in the background, on the cracked mosaic floor, amid a throng of people kneeling, murmuring and crossing themselves, and the massive magnificence of the oriental temple would weigh sumptuously on his senses. At the front, the ornately vested priest walked to and fro, doing his business and chanting. Incense billowed up, clouding the feeble flames of the altar candles, and with its heavy, sweet sacrificial odor another seemed to mingle: the smell of the sick city. But through the vaporous dimness and the flickering lights Aschenbach saw the boy, up there at the front, turn his head and seek him with his eyes until he found him.

Then, when the great doors were opened and the crowd streamed out into the shining Piazza swarming with pigeons, the beguiled lover would hide in the antebasilica, he would lurk and lie in wait. He would see the Poles leave the church, see the brother and sisters take ceremonious leave of their mother, who would then set off home, turning toward the Piazzetta; he would observe the boy, the cloistral sisters and the governess turn right and walk through the clock tower gateway into the Merceria, and after letting them get a little way ahead he would follow them—follow them furtively on their walk through Venice. He had to stop when they lingered, had to take refuge in hot food stalls and courtyards to let them pass when they turned round; he would lose them, search for them frantically and exhaustingly, rushing over bridges and along filthy culs-de-sac, and would then have to endure minutes of mortal embarrassment when he suddenly saw them coming toward him in a narrow passageway where no escape was possible. And yet one cannot say that he suffered. His head and his heart were drunk, and his steps followed the dictates of that dark god whose pleasure it is to trample man's reason and dignity underfoot.

Presently, somewhere or other, Tadzio and his family would take a gondola, and while they were getting into it Aschenbach, hiding behind a fountain or the projecting part of a building, would wait till they were a little way from the shore and then do the same.

Speaking hurriedly and in an undertone, he would instruct the oarsman, promising him a large tip, to follow that gondola ahead of them that was just turning the corner, to follow it at a discreet distance; and a shiver would run down his spine when the fellow, with the roguish compliance of a pander, would answer him in the same tone, assuring him that he was at his service, entirely at his service.

Thus he glided and swayed gently along, reclining on soft black cushions, shadowing that other black, beaked craft, chained to its pursuit by its infatuation. Sometimes he would lose sight of it and become distressed and anxious, but his steersman, who seemed to be well practiced in commissions of this kind, would always know some cunning maneuver, some side-canal or short cut that would again bring Aschenbach in sight of what he craved. The air was stagnant and malodorous, the sun burned oppressively through the haze that had turned the sky to the color of slate. Water lapped against wood and stone. The gondolier's call, half warning and half greeting, was answered from a distance out of the silent labyrinth, in accordance with some strange convention. Out of little overhead gardens umbelliferous blossoms spilled over and hung down the crumbling masonry, white and purple and almond scented. Moorish windows were mirrored in the murky water. The marble steps of a church dipped below the surface; a beggar squatted on them, protesting his misery, holding out his hat and showing the whites of his eyes as if he were blind; an antiques dealer beckoned to them with crawling obsequiousness as they passed his den, inviting them to stop and be swindled. This was Venice, the flattering and suspect beauty—this city, half fairy tale and half tourist trap, in whose insalubrious air the arts once rankly and voluptuously blossomed, where composers have been inspired to lulling tones of somniferous eroticism. Gripped by his adventure, the traveler felt his eyes drinking in this sumptuousness, his ears wooed by these melodies; he remembered, too, that the city was stricken with sickness and concealing it for reasons of cupidity, and he peered around still more wildly in search of the gondola that hovered ahead.

So it was that in his state of distraction he could no longer think of anything or want anything except this ceaseless pursuit of the object that so inflamed him: nothing but to follow him, to dream of him when he was not there, and after the fashion of lovers to address tender words to his mere shadow. Solitariness, the foreign environment, and the joy of an intoxication of feeling that had come to him so late and affected him so profoundly—all this encouraged and persuaded him to indulge himself in the most astonishing ways: as when it had happened that late one evening, returning from Venice and reaching the first floor of the hotel, he had paused outside the boy's bedroom door, leaning his head against the doorframe in a complete drunken ecstasy, and had for a long time been unable to move from the spot, at the risk of being surprised and discovered in this insane situation.

Nevertheless, there were moments at which he paused and half came to his senses. Where is this leading me! he would reflect in consternation at such moments. Where was it leading him! Like any man whose natural merits move him to take an aristocratic interest in his origins. Aschenbach habitually let the achievements and successes of his life remind him of his ancestors, for in imagination he could then feel sure of their approval, of their satisfaction, of the respect they could not have withheld. And he thought of them even here and now, entangled as he was in so impermissible an experience, involved in such exotic extravagances of feeling; he thought, with a sad smile, of their dignified austerity, their decent manliness of character. What would they say? But for that matter, what would they have said about his entire life, a life that had deviated from theirs to the point of degeneracy, this life of his in the compulsive service of art, this life about which he himself, adopting the civic values of his forefathers, had once let fall such mocking observations—and which nevertheless had essentially been so much like theirs! He too had served, he too had been a soldier and a warrior, like many of them: for art was a war, an exhausting struggle, it was hard these days to remain fit for it for long. A life of self-conquest and of defiant resolve, an astringent, steadfast and frugal life which he had turned into the symbol of that heroism for delicate constitutions, that heroism so much in keeping with the times—surely he might call this manly, might call it courageous? And it seemed to him that the kind of love that had taken possession of him did, in a certain way, suit and befit such a life. Had it not been highly honored by the most valiant of peoples, indeed had he not read that in their cities it had flourished by inspiring valorous deeds? Numerous warrior-heroes of olden times had willingly borne its yoke, for there was no kind of abasement that could be reckoned as such if the god had imposed it; and actions that would have been castigated as signs of cowardice had their motives been different, such as falling to the ground in supplication, desperate pleas and slavish demeanor—these were accounted no disgrace to a lover, but rather won him still greater praise.

Such were the thoughts with which love beguiled him, and thus he sought to sustain himself, to preserve his dignity. But at the same time he kept turning his attention, inquisitively and persistently, to the disreputable events that were evolving in the depths of Venice, to that adventure of the outside world which darkly mingled with the adventure of his heart, and which nourished his passion with vague and lawless hopes. Obstinately determined to obtain new and reliable information about the status and progress of the malady, he would sit in the city's coffee houses searching through the German newspapers, which several days ago had disappeared from the reading table in the hotel foyer. They carried assertions and retractions by turns. The number of cases, the number of deaths, was said to be twenty, or forty, or a hundred and more, such reports being immediately followed by statements flatly denying the outbreak of an epidemic, or at least reducing it to a few quite isolated cases brought in from outside the city. Scattered here and there were warning admonitions, or protests against the dangerous policy being pursued by the Italian authorities. There was no certainty to be had.

The solitary traveler was nevertheless conscious of having a special claim to participation in this secret, and although excluded from it, he took a perverse pleasure in putting embarrassing questions to those in possession of the facts, and thus, since they were pledged to silence, forcing them to lie to him directly. One day, at luncheon in the main dining room, he interrogated the hotel manager in this fashion, the soft-footed little man in the French frock coat who was moving around among the tables supervising the meal and greeting the clients, and who also stopped at Aschenbach's table for a few words of conversation. Why, in fact, asked his guest in a casual and nonchalant way, why on earth had they begun recently to disinfect Venice?—"It is merely a police measure, sir," answered the trickster, "taken in good time, as a safeguard against various disagreeable public health problems that might otherwise arise from this sultry and exceptionally warm weather—a precautionary measure which it is their duty to take."—"Very praiseworthy of the police," replied Aschenbach; and after exchanging a few meteorological observations with him the manager took his leave.

On the very same day, in the evening after dinner, it happened that a small group of street singers from the city gave a performance in the front garden of the hotel. They stood by one of the iron arc

lamp standards, two men and two women, their faces glinting white
in the glare, looking up at the great terrace where the hotel guests
sat over their coffee and cooling drinks, resigned to watching this
exhibition of folk culture. The hotel staff, the lift boys, waiters,
office employees, had come out to listen in the hall doorways. The
Russian family, eager to savor every pleasure, had had cane chairs
put out for them down in the garden in order to be nearer the
performers and were contentedly sitting there in a semicircle. Behind
her master and mistress, in a turbanlike headcloth, stood their
aged serf.

The beggar virtuosi were playing a mandolin, a guitar, a harmon-
ica and a squeaking fiddle. Instrumental developments alternated
with vocal numbers, as when the younger of the women, shrill and
squawky of voice, joined the tenor with his sweet falsetto notes in
an ardent love duet. But the real talent and leader of the ensemble
was quite evidently the other man, the one who had the guitar and
was a kind of buffo-baritone character, with hardly any voice but
with a mimic gift and remarkable comic verve. Often he would
detach himself from the rest of the group and come forward, playing
his large instrument and gesticulating, toward the terrace, where his
pranks were rewarded with encouraging laughter. The Russians in
their parterre seats took special delight in all this southern vivacity,
and their plaudits and admiring shouts led him on to ever further
and bolder extravagances.

Aschenbach sat by the balustrade, cooling his lips from time to
time with the mixture of pomegranate juice and soda water that
sparkled ruby-red in the glass before him. His nervous system greedily drank in the jangling tones, for passion paralyzes discrimination
and responds in all seriousness to stimuli which the sober senses
would either treat with humorous tolerance or impatiently reject.
The antics of the mountebank had distorted his features into a
rictuslike smile which he was already finding painful. He sat on with
a casual air, but inwardly he was utterly engrossed; for six paces
from him Tadzio was leaning against the stone parapet.

There he stood, in the white belted suit he occasionally put on
for dinner, in a posture of innate and inevitable grace, his left forearm on the parapet, his feet crossed, his right hand on the supporting
hip; and he was looking down at the entertainers with an expression
that was scarcely a smile, merely one of remote curiosity, a polite
observation of the spectacle. Sometimes he straightened himself,
stretching his chest, and with an elegant movement of both arms

drew his white tunic down through his leather belt. But sometimes, too, and the older man noticed it with a mind-dizzying sense of triumph as well as with terror, he would turn his head hesitantly and cautiously, or even quickly and suddenly as if to gain the advantage of surprise, and look over his left shoulder to where his lover was sitting. Their eyes did not meet, for an ignominious apprehension was forcing the stricken man to keep his looks anxiously in check. Behind them on the terrace sat the woman who watched over Tadzio, and at the point things had now reached, the enamored Aschenbach had reason to fear that he had attracted attention and aroused suspicion. Indeed, he had several times, on the beach, in the hotel foyer, and on the Piazza San Marco, been frozen with alarm to notice that Tadzio was being called away if he was near him, that they were taking care to keep them apart—and although his pride writhed in torments it had never known under the appalling insult that this implied, he could not in conscience deny its justice.

In the meantime the guitarist had begun a solo to his own accompaniment, a song in many stanzas which was then a popular hit all over Italy, and which he managed to perform in a graphic and dramatic manner, with the rest of his troupe joining regularly in the refrain. He was a lean fellow, thin and cadaverous in the face as well, standing there on the gravel detached from his companions, with a shabby felt hat on the back of his head and a quiff of his red hair bulging out under the brim, in a posture of insolent bravado; strumming and thrumming on his instrument, he tossed his pleasantries up to the terrace in a vivid *parlando,* enacting it all so strenuously that the veins swelled on his forehead. He was quite evidently not of Venetian origin, but rather of the Neapolitan comic type, half pimp, half actor, brutal and bold-faced, dangerous and entertaining. The actual words of his song were merely foolish, but in his presentation, with his grimaces and bodily movements, his way of winking suggestively and lasciviously licking the corner of his mouth, it had something indecent and vaguely offensive about it. Though otherwise dressed in urban fashion he wore a sports shirt, out of the soft collar of which his skinny neck projected, displaying a remarkably large and naked Adam's apple. His pallid snub-nosed face, the features of which gave little clue to his age, seemed to be lined with contortions and vice, and the grinning of his mobile mouth was rather strangely ill-matched to the two deep furrows that stood defiantly, imperiously, almost savagely, between his reddish brows. But what really fixed the solitary Aschenbach's deep attention on him was his observation that this suspect figure seemed to be carrying his own suspect atmosphere about with him as well. For every time the refrain was repeated the singer would perform, with much face-pulling and shaking of his hand as if in greeting, a grotesque march round the scene, which brought him immediately below where Aschenbach sat; and every time this happened a stench of carbolic from his clothes or his body drifted up to the terrace.

Having completed his ballad he began to collect money. He started with the Russians, who were seen to give generously, and then came up the steps. Saucy as his performance had been, up here he was humility itself. Bowing and scraping, he crept from table to table, and a sly obsequious grin bared his prominent teeth, although the two furrows still stood threateningly between his red eyebrows. The spectacle of this alien being gathering in his livelihood was received with curiosity and not a little distaste; one threw coins with the tips of one's fingers into the hat, which one took care not to touch. Removal of the physical distance between the entertainer and decent folk always causes, however great one's pleasure has been, a certain embarrassment. He sensed this, and sought to make amends by cringing. He approached Aschenbach, and with him came the smell, which no one else in the company appeared to have noticed.

"Listen to me!" said the solitary traveler in an undertone and almost mechanically. "Venice is being disinfected. Why?"—The co-median answered hoarsely: "Because of the police! It's the regula-tions, signore, when it's so hot and when there's sirocco. The sirocco is oppressive. It is not good for the health . . ." He spoke in a tone of surprise that such a question could be asked, and demonstrated with his outspread hand how oppressive the sirocco was.—"So there is no sickness in Venice?" asked Aschenbach very softly and between his teeth.—The clown's muscular features collapsed into a grimace of comic helplessness. "A sickness? But what sickness? Is the sirocco a sickness? Is our police a sickness perhaps? The signore is having his little joke! A sickness! Certainly not, signore! A preventive meas-ure, you must understand, a police precaution against the effects of the oppressive weather . . ." He gesticulated. "Very well," said Aschenbach briefly, still without raising his voice, and quickly dropped an unduly large coin into the fellow's hat. Then he mo-tioned him with his eyes to clear off. The man obeyed, grinning and bowing low. But he had not even reached the steps when two hotel servants bore down on him, and with their faces close to his sub-jected him to a whispered cross examination. He shrugged, gave assurances, swore that he had been discreet; it was obvious. Released, he returned to the garden, and after a brief consultation with his colleagues under the arc lamp he came forward once more, to express his thanks in a parting number.

It was a song that Aschenbach could not remember ever having heard before; a bold hit in an unintelligible dialect, and having a laughing refrain in which the rest of the band regularly and loudly joined. At this point both the words and the instrumental accompaniment stopped, and nothing remained except a burst of laughter, to some extent rhythmically ordered but treated with a high degree of naturalism, the soloist in particular showing great talent in his lifelike rendering of it. With artistic distance restored between himself and the spectators, he had recovered all his impudence, and the simulated laughter which he shamelessly directed at the terrace was a laughter of mockery. Even before the end of the articulated part of each stanza he would pretend to be struggling with an irresistible impulse of hilarity. He would sob, his voice would waver, he would press his hand against his mouth and hunch his shoulders, till at the proper moment the laughter would burst out of him, exploding in a wild howl, with such authenticity that it was infectious and communicated itself to the audience, so that a wave of objectless and merely self-propagating merriment swept over the terrace as well. And precisely this seemed to redouble the singer's exuberance. He bent his knees, slapped his thighs, held his sides, he nearly burst with what was now no longer laughing but shrieking; he pointed his finger up at the guests, as if that laughing company above him were itself the most comical thing in the world, and in the end they were all laughing, everyone in the garden and on the verandah, the waiters and the lift boys and the house servants in the doorways.

Aschenbach reclined in his chair no longer, he was sitting bolt upright as if trying to fend off an attack or flee from it. But the laughter, the hospital smell drifting toward him, and the nearness of the beautiful boy, all mingled for him into an immobilizing nightmare, an unbreakable and inescapable spell that held his mind and senses captive. In the general commotion and distraction he ventured to steal a glance at Tadzio, and as he did so he became aware that the boy, returning his glance, had remained no less serious than himself, just as if he were regulating his attitude and expression by those of the older man, and as if the general mood had no power over him while Aschenbach kept aloof from it. There was something so disarming and overwhelmingly moving about this childlike submissiveness, so rich in meaning, that the gray-haired lover could only with difficulty restrain himself from burying his face in his hands. He had also had the impression that the way Tadzio from time to time drew himself up with an intake of breath was like a kind of sighing, as if from a constriction of the chest. "He's sickly, he'll probably not live long," he thought again, with that sober objectivity into which the drunken ecstasy of desire sometimes strangely escapes; and his heart was filled at one and the same time with pure concern on the boy's behalf and with a certain wild satisfaction.

In the meantime the troupe of Venetians had finished their performance and were leaving. Applause accompanied them, and their leader took care to embellish even his exit with comical pranks. His bowing and scraping and hand-kissing amused the company, and so he redoubled them. When his companions were already outside, he put on yet another act of running backward and painfully colliding with a lamppost, then hobbling to the gate apparently doubled up in agony. When he got there however, he suddenly discarded the mask of comic underdog, uncoiled like a spring to his full height, insolently stuck out his tongue at the hotel guests on the terrace and slipped away into the darkness. The company was dispersing; Tadzio had left the balustrade some time ago. But the solitary Aschenbach, to the annoyance of the waiters, sat on and on at his little table over his unfinished pomegranate drink. The night was advancing, time was ebbing away. In his parents' house, many years ago, there had been an hourglass—he suddenly saw that fragile symbolic little instrument as clearly as if it were standing before him. Silently, subtly, the rust-red sand trickled through the narrow glass aperture, dwindling away out of the upper vessel, in which a little whirling vortex had formed.

On the very next day, in the afternoon, Aschenbach took a further step in his persistent probing of the outside world, and this time his success was complete. What he did was to enter the British travel agency just off the Piazza San Marco, and after changing some money at the cash desk, he put on the look of a suspicious foreigner and addressed his embarrassing question to the clerk who had served him. The clerk was a tweed-clad Englishman, still young, with his hair parted in the middle, his eyes close set, and having that sober, honest demeanor which makes so unusual and striking an impression amid the glib knaveries of the south. "No cause for concern, sir," he began. "An administrative measure, nothing serious. They often issue directives of this kind, as a precaution against the unhealthy effects of the heat and the sirocco . . ." But raising his blue eyes he met those of the stranger, which were looking wearily and rather sadly at his lips, with an expression of slight contempt. At this the Englishman colored. "That is," he continued in an undertone and with some feeling, "the official explanation, which the authorities here see fit to stick to. I can tell you that there is rather more to it than that." And then, in his straightforward comfortable language, he told Aschenbach the truth.

For several years now, Asiatic cholera had been showing an increased tendency to spread and migrate. Originating in the sultry morasses of the Ganges delta, rising with the mephitic exhalations of that wilderness of rank useless luxuriance, that primitive island jungle shunned by man, where tigers crouch in the bamboo thickets, the pestilence had raged with unusual and prolonged virulence all over northern India; it had struck eastward into China, westward into Afghanistan and Persia, and following the main caravan routes, it had borne its terrors to Astrakhan and even to Moscow. But while Europe trembled with apprehension that from there the specter might advance and arrive by land, it had been brought by Syrian traders over the sea; it had appeared almost simultaneously in several Mediterranean ports, raising its head in Toulon and Malaga, showing its face repeatedly in Palermo and Naples, and taking a seemingly permanent hold all over Calabria and Apulia. The northern half of the peninsula had still been spared. But in the middle of May this year, in Venice, the dreadful comma-bacilli had been found on one and the same day in the emaciated and blackened corpses of a ship's hand and of a woman who sold greengroceries. The two cases were hushed up. But a week later there were ten, there were twenty and then thirty, and they occurred in different quarters of the city. A man from a small provincial town in Austria who had ben taking a few days' holiday in Venice died with unmistakable symptoms after returning home, and that was why the first rumors of a Venetian outbreak had appeared in German newspapers. The city authorities replied with a statement that the public health situation in Venice had never been better, and at the same time adopted the most necessary preventive measures. But the taint had probably now passed into foodstuffs, into vegetables or meat or milk; for despite every denial and concealment, the mortal sickness went on eating its way through the narrow little streets, and with the premature summer heat warming the water in the canals, conditions for the spread of infection were particularly favorable. It even seemed as if the pestilence had undergone a renewal of its energy, as if the tenacity and fertility of its pathogens had redoubled. Cases of recovery were rare; eighty percent of the victims died, and they died in a horrible manner, for the sickness presented itself in an extremely acute form and was frequently of the so-called "dry" type, which is the most dangerous of all. In this condition the body could not even evacuate the massive fluid lost from the blood-vessels. Within a few hours the patient would become dehydrated, his blood would thicken like pitch and he would suffocate with convulsions and hoarse cries. He was lucky if, as sometimes happened, the disease took the form of a slight malaise followed by a deep coma from which one never, or scarcely at all, regained consciousness. By the beginning of June the isolation wards in the Ospedale Civile were quietly filling, the two orphanages were running out of accommodation, and there was a gruesomely brisk traffic between the quayside of the Fondamente Nuove and the cemetery island of San Michele. But fear of general detriment to the city, concern for the recently opened art exhibition in the Public Gardens, consideration of the appalling losses which panic and disrepute would inflict on the hotels, on the shops, on the whole nexus of the tourist trade, proved stronger in Venice than respect for the truth and for international agreements; it was for this reason that the city authorities obstinately adhered to their policy of concealment and denial. The city's chief medical officer, a man of high repute, had resigned from his post in indignation and had been quietly replaced by a more pliable personality. This had become public knowledge; and such corruption in high places, combined with the prevailing insecurity, the state of crisis into which the city had been plunged by the death that walked its streets, led at the lower social levels to a certain breakdown of moral standards, to an activation of the dark and antisocial forces, which manifested itself in intemperance, shameless license and growing criminality. Drunkenness in the evenings became noticeably more frequent; thieves and ruffians, it was said, were making the streets unsafe at night; there were repeated robberies and even murders, for it had already twice come to light that persons alleged to have died of the plague had in fact been poisoned by their own relatives; and commercial vice now took on obtrusive and extravagant forms which had hitherto been unknown in this area and indigenous only to southern Italy or eastern countries.

The Englishman's narrative conveyed the substance of all this to Aschenbach. "You would be well advised, sir," he concluded, "to leave today rather than tomorrow. The imposition of quarantine can be expected any day now."—"Thank you," said Aschenbach, and left the office.

The Piazza was sunless and sultry. Unsuspecting foreigners were sitting at the cafés, or standing in front of the church with pigeons completely enveloping them, watching the birds swarm and beat their wings and push each other out of the way as they snatched with their beaks at the hollow hands offering them grains of maize. Feverish with excitement, triumphant in his possession of the truth, yet with a taste of disgust on his tongue and a fantastic horror in his heart, the solitary traveler paced up and down the flagstones of the magnificent precinct. He was considering a decent action which would cleanse his conscience. Tonight, after dinner, he might approach the lady in the pearls and address her with words which he now mentally rehearsed: "Madam, allow me as a complete stranger to do you a service, to warn you of something which is being concealed from you for reasons of self-interest. Leave here at once with Tadzio and your daughters! Venice is plague-stricken." He might then lay his hand in farewell on the head of a mocking deity's instrument, turn away and flee from this quagmire. But at the same time he sensed an infinite distance between himself and any serious resolve to take such a step. It would lead him back to where he had been, give him back to himself again; but to one who is beside himself, no prospect is so distasteful as that of self-recovery. He remembered a white building adorned with inscriptions that glinted in the evening light, suffused with mystic meaning in which his mind had wandered; remembered then that strange itinerant figure who had wakened in him, in his middle age, a young man's longing to rove to far-off and strange places; and the thought of returning home, of levelheadedness and sobriety, of toil and mastery, filled him with such repugnance that his face twisted into an expression of physical nausea. "They want it kept quiet!" he whispered vehemently. And: "I shall say nothing!" The consciousness of his complicity in the secret, of his share in the guilt, intoxicated him as small quantities of wine intoxicate a weary brain. The image of the stricken and disordered city, hovering wildly before his mind's eye, inflamed him with hopes that were beyond comprehension, beyond reason and full of monstrous sweetness. What, compared with such expectations, was that tender happiness of which he had briefly dreamed a few moments ago? What could art and virtue mean to him now, when he might reap the advantages of chaos? He said nothing, and stayed on.

That night he had a terrible dream, if dream is the right word for a bodily and mental experience which did indeed overtake him during deepest sleep, in complete independence of his will and with complete sensuous vividness, but with no perception of himself as present and moving about in any space external to the events themselves; rather, the scene of the events was his own soul, and they irrupted into it from outside, violently defeating his resistance—a profound, intellectual resistance—as they passed through him, and leaving his whole being, the culture of a lifetime, devastated and destroyed.

It began with fear, fear and joy and a horrified curiosity about what was to come. It was night, and his senses were alert; for from far off a hubbub was approaching, an uproar, a compendium of noise, a clangor and blare and dull thundering, yells of exultation and a particular howl with a long-drawn-out *ooo* at the end—all of it permeated and dominated by a terrible sweet sound of flute music; by deep-warbling, infamously persistent, shamelessly clinging tones that bewitched the innermost heart. Yet he was aware of a word, an obscure word, but one that gave a name to what was coming: *"the stranger-god!"* There was a glow of smoky fire: in it he could see a mountain landscape, like the mountains round his summer home. And in fragmented light, from wooded heights, between tree trunks and mossy boulders, it came tumbling and whirling down: a human and animal swarm, a raging rout, flooding the slope with bodies, with flames, with tumult and frenzied dancing. Women, stumbling on the hide garments that fell too far about them from the waist, held up tambourines and moaned as they shook them above their thrownback heads; they swung blazing torches, scattering the sparks, and brandished naked daggers; they carried snakes with flickering tongues which they had seized in the middle of the body, or they bore up their own breasts in both hands, shrieking as they did so. Men with horns over their brows, hairy-skinned and girdled with pelts, bowed their necks and threw up their arms and thighs, clanging brazen cymbals and beating a furious tattoo on drums, while smooth-skinned boys prodded goats with leafy staves, clinging to their horns and yelling with delight as the leaping beasts dragged them along. And the god's enthusiasts howled out the cry with the soft consonants and long-drawn-out final *u*, sweet and wild both at once, like no cry that was ever heard: here it was raised, belled out into the air as by rutting stags, and there they threw it back with many voices, in ribald triumph, urging each other on with it to dancing and tossing of limbs, and never did it cease. But the deep, enticing flute music mingled irresistibly with everything. Was it not also enticing him, the dreamer who experienced all this while struggling not to, enticing him with shameless insistence to the feast and frenzy of the uttermost surrender? Great was his loathing, great his fear, honorable his effort of will to defend to the last what was his and protect it against the Stranger, against the enemy of the composed and dignified intellect. But the noise, the howling grew louder, with the echoing cliffs reiterating it: it increased beyond measure, swelled up to an enrapturing madness. Odors besieged the mind, the pungent reek of the goats, the scent of panting bodies and an exhalation as of staling waters, with another smell, too, that was familiar: that of wounds and wandering disease. His heart throbbed to the drumbeats, his brain whirled, a fury seized him, a blindness, a dizzying lust, and his soul craved to join the round-dance of the god. The obscene symbol, wooden and gigantic, was uncovered and raised on high: and still more unbridled grew the howling of the watchword. With foaming mouths they raged, they roused each other with lewd gestures and licentious hands, laughing and moaning they thrust the prods into each other's flesh and licked the blood from each other's limbs. But the dreamer now was with them and in them, he belonged to the Stranger-God. Yes, they were himself as they flung themselves, tearing and slaying, on the animals and devoured steaming gobbets of flesh, they were himself as an orgy of limitless coupling, in homage to the god, began on the trampled, mossy ground. And his very soul savored the lascivious delirium of annihilation.

Out of this dream the stricken man woke unnerved, shattered and powerlessly enslaved to the daemon-god. He no longer feared the observant eyes of other people; whether he was exposing himself to their suspicions he no longer cared. In any case they were running away, leaving Venice; many of the bathing cabins were empty now, there were great gaps in the clientele at dinner, and in the city one scarcely saw any foreigners. The truth seemed to have leaked out, and however tightly the interested parties closed ranks, panic could no longer be stemmed. But the lady in the pearls stayed on with her family, either because the rumors were not reaching her or because she was too proud and fearless to heed them. Tadzio stayed on; and to Aschenbach, in his beleaguered state, it sometimes seemed that all these unwanted people all round him might flee from the place or die, that every living being might disappear and leave him alone on this island with the beautiful boy—indeed, as he sat every morning by the sea with his gaze resting heavily, recklessly, incessantly on the object of his desire, or as he continued his undignified pursuit of him in the evenings along streets in which the disgusting mortal malady wound its underground way, then indeed monstrous things seemed full of promise to him, and the moral law no longer valid.

Like any other lover, he desired to please and bitterly dreaded that he might fail to do so. He added brightening and rejuvenating touches to his clothes, he wore jewelry and used scent, he devoted long sessions to his toilet several times a day, arriving at table elaborately attired and full of excited expectation. As he beheld the sweet youthful creature who had so entranced him he felt disgust at his own aging body, the sight of his gray hair and sharp features filled him with a sense of shame and hopelessness. He felt a compulsive need to refresh and restore himself physically; he paid frequent visits to the hotel barber.

Cloaked in a hairdressing gown, leaning back in the chair as the chatterer's hands tended him, he stared in dismay at his reflection in the looking glass.

"Gray," he remarked with a wry grimace.

"A little," the man replied. "And the reason? A slight neglect, a slight lack of interest in outward appearances, very understandable in persons of distinction, but not altogether to be commended, especially as one would expect those very persons to be free from prejudice about such matters as the natural and the artificial. If certain people who profess moral disapproval of cosmetics were to be logical enough to extend such rigorous principles to their teeth, the result would be rather disgusting. After all, we are only as old as we feel in our minds and hearts, and sometimes gray hair is actually further from the truth than the despised corrective would be. In your case, signore, one has a right to the natural color of one's hair. Will you permit me simply to give your color back to you?"

"How so?" asked Aschenbach.

Whereupon the eloquent tempter washed his client's hair in two kinds of water, one clear and one dark; and his hair was as black as when he had been young. Then he folded it into soft waves with the curling tongs, stepped back and surveyed his handiwork.

"Now the only other thing," he said, "would be just to freshen up the signore's complexion a little."

And like a craftsman unable to finish, unable to satisfy himself, he passed busily and indefatigably from one procedure to another. Aschenbach, reclining comfortably, incapable of resistance, filled rather with exciting hopes by what was happening, gazed at the glass and saw his eyebrows arched more clearly and evenly, the shape of his eyes lengthened, their brightness enhanced by a slight underlining of the lids: saw below them a delicate carmine come to life as it was softly applied to skin that had been brown and leathery; saw his lips that had just been so pallid now burgeoning cherry-red; saw the furrows on his cheeks, round his mouth, the wrinkles by his eyes, all vanishing under face cream and an aura of youth—with beating heart he saw himself as a young man in his earliest bloom. The cosmetician finally declared himself satisfied, with the groveling politeness usual in such people, by profusely thanking the client he had served. "An insignificant adjustment, signore," he said as he gave a final helping hand to Aschenbach's outward appearance. "Now the signore càn fall in love as soon as he pleases." And the spellbound lover departed, confused and timorous but happy as in a dream. His necktie was scarlet, his broad-brimmed straw hat encircled with a many-colored ribbon.

A warm gale had blown up; it rained little and lightly, but the air was humid and thick and filled with smells of decay. The ear was beset with fluttering, flapping and whistling noises, and to the fevered devotee, sweating under his makeup, it seemed that a vile race of wind demons was disporting itself in the sky, malignant sea birds that churn up and gnaw and befoul a condemned man's food. For the sultry weather was taking away his appetite, and he could not put aside the thought that what he ate might be tainted with infection.

One afternoon, dogging Tadzio's footsteps, Aschenbach had plunged into the confused network of streets in the depths of the sick city. Quite losing his bearings in this labyrinth of alleys, narrow waterways, bridges and little squares that all looked so much like each other, not sure now even of the points of the compass, he was intent above all on not losing sight of the vision he so passionately pursued. Ignominious caution forced him to flatten himself against walls and hide behind the backs of people walking in front of him; and for a long time he was not conscious of the weariness, the exhaustion that emotion and constant tension had inflicted on his body and mind. Tadzio walked behind his family; he usually gave precedence in narrow passages to his attendant and his nunlike sisters, and as he strolled along by himself he sometimes turned his head and glanced over his shoulder with his strange twilight-gray eyes, to ascertain that his lover was still following him. He saw him, and did not give him away. Drunk with excitement as he realized this, lured onward by those eyes, helpless in the leading strings of his mad desire, the infatuated Aschenbach stole upon the trail of his unseemly hope—only to find it vanish from his sight in the end. The Poles had crossed a little humpbacked bridge; the height of the arch hid them from their pursuer, and when in his turn he reached the top of it, they were no longer to be seen. He looked frantically for them in three directions, straight ahead and to left and right along the narrow, dirty canal-side, but in vain. Unnerved and weakened, he was compelled to abandon his search.

His head was burning, his body was covered with sticky sweat, his neck quivered, a no longer endurable thirst tormented him; he looked round for something, no matter what, that would instantly relieve it. At a little greengrocer's shop he bought some fruit, some overripe soft strawberries, and ate some of them as he walked. A little square, one that seemed to have been abandoned, to have been put under a spell, opened up in front of him: he recognized it, he had been here, it was where he had made that vain decision weeks ago to leave Venice. On the steps of the well in its center he sank down and leaned his head against the stone rim. The place was silent, grass grew between the cobblestones, garbage was lying about. Among the dilapidated houses of uneven height all round him there was one that looked like a *palazzo*, with Gothic windows that now had nothing behind them, and little lion balconies. On the ground floor of another there was a chemist's shop. From time to time warm gusts of wind blew the stench of carbolic across to him.

There he sat, the master, the artist who had achieved dignity, the author of A *Study in Abjection,* he who in such paradigmatically pure form had repudiated intellectual vagrancy and the murky depths, who had proclaimed his renunciation of all sympathy with the abyss, who had weighed vileness in the balance and found it wanting; he who had risen so high, who had set his face against his own sophistication, grown out of all his irony, and taken on the commitments of one whom the public trusted; he, whose fame was official, whose name had been ennobled, and on whose style young boys were taught to model themselves—there he sat, with his eyelids closed, with only an occasional mocking and rueful sideways glance from under them which he hid again at once; and his drooping, cosmetically brightened lips shaped the occasional word of the discourse his brain was delivering, his half-asleep brain with its tissue of strange dream-logic.

"For Beauty, Phaedrus, mark well! only Beauty is at one and the same time divine and visible, and so it is indeed the sensuous lover's path, little Phaedrus, it is the artist's path to the spirit. But do you believe, dear boy, that the man whose path to the spiritual passes through the senses can ever achieve wisdom and true manly dignity? Or do you think rather (I leave it to you to decide) that this is a path of dangerous charm, very much an errant and sinful path which must of necessity lead us astray? For I must tell you that we artists cannot tread the path of Beauty without Eros keeping company with us and appointing himself as our guide; yes, though we may be heroes in our fashion and disciplined warriors, yet we are like women, for it is passion that exalts us, and the longing of our soul must remain the longing of a lover—that is our joy and our shame. Do you see now perhaps why we writers can be neither wise nor dignified? That we necessarily go astray, necessarily remain dissolute emotional adventurers? The magisterial poise of our style is a lie and a farce, our fame and social position are an absurdity, the public's faith in us is altogether ridiculous, the use of art to educate the nation and its youth is a reprehensible undertaking which should be forbidden by law. For how can one be fit to be an educator when one has been born with an incorrigible and natural tendency toward the abyss? We try to achieve dignity by repudiating that abyss, but whichever way we turn we are subject to its allurement. We renounce, let us say, the corrosive process of knowledge—for knowledge, Phaedrus, has neither dignity nor rigor: it is all insight and understanding and tolerance, uncontrolled and formless; it sympathizes with the abyss, it *is* the abyss. And so we reject it resolutely, and henceforth our pursuit is of Beauty alone, of Beauty which is simplicity, which is grandeur and a new kind of rigor and a second naiveté, of Beauty which is Form. But form and naiveté, Phaedrus, lead to intoxication and lust; they may lead a noble mind into terrible criminal emotions, which his own fine rigor condemns as infamous; they lead, they too lead, to the abyss. I tell you, that is where they lead us writers; for we are not capable of self-exaltation, we are capable only of self-debauchery. And now I shall go, Phaedrus, and you shall stay here; and leave this place only when you no longer see me."

A few days later Gustav von Aschenbach, who had been feeling unwell, left the Hotel des Bains at a later morning hour than usual. He was being attacked by waves of dizziness, only half physical, and with them went an increasing sense of dread, a feeling of hopelessness and pointlessness, though he could not decide whether this referred to the external world or to his personal existence. In the foyer he saw a large quantity of luggage standing ready for dispatch, asked one of the doormen which guests were leaving, and was given in reply the aristocratic Polish name which he had inwardly been expecting to hear. As he received the information there was no change in his ravaged features, only that slight lift of the head with which one casually notes something one did not need to know. He merely added the question: "When?" and was told: "After lunch." He nodded and went down to the sea.

It was a bleak spectacle there. Tremors gusted outward across the water between the beach and the first long sandbar, wrinkling its wide flat surface. An autumnal, out-of-season air seemed to hang over the once so colorful and populous resort, now almost deserted, with litter left lying about on the sand. An apparently abandoned camera stood on its tripod at the edge of the sea, and the black cloth over it fluttered and flapped in the freshening breeze.

Tadzio, with the three or four playmates he still had, was walking about on the right in front of his family's bathing cabin; and reclining in his deck chair with a rug over his knees, about midway between the sea and the row of cabins, Aschenbach once more sat watching him. The boys' play was unsupervised, as the women were probably busy with travel preparations; it seemed to be unruly and degenerating into roughness. The sturdy boy he had noticed before, the one in the belted suit with glossy black hair who was addressed as "Jashu," had been angered and blinded by some sand thrown into his face: he forced Tadzio to a wrestling match, which soon ended in the downfall of the less muscular beauty. But as if in this hour of leave-taking the submissiveness of the lesser partner had been transformed into cruel brutality, as if he were now bent on revenge for his long servitude, the victor did not release his defeated friend even then, but knelt on his back and pressed his face into the sand so hard and so long that Tadzio, breathless from the fight in any case, seemed to be on the point of suffocation. His attempts to shake off the weight of his tormentor were convulsive; they stopped altogether for moments on end and became a mere repeated twitching. Appalled, Aschenbach was about to spring to the rescue when the bully finally released his victim. Tadzio, very pale, sat up and went on sitting motionless for some minutes, propped on one arm, his hair tousled and his eyes darkening. Then he stood right up and walked slowly away. His friends called to him, laughingly at first, then anxiously and pleadingly; he took no notice. The dark-haired boy, who had no doubt been seized at once by remorse at having gone so far, ran after him and tried to make up the quarrel. A jerk of Tadzio's shoulder rejected him. Tadzio walked on at an angle down to the water. He was barefooted and wearing his striped linen costume with the red bow.

At the edge of the sea he lingered, head bowed, drawing figures in the wet sand with the point of one foot, then walked into the shallow high water, which at its deepest point did not even wet his knees; he waded through it, advancing easily, and reached the sand-bar. There he stood for a moment looking out into the distance and then, moving left, began slowly to pace the length of this narrow strip of unsubmerged land. Divided from the shore by a width of water, divided from his companions by proud caprice, he walked, a quite isolated and unrelated apparition, walked with floating hair out there in the sea, in the wind, in front of the nebulous vastness. Once more he stopped to survey the scene. And suddenly, as if prompted by a memory, by an impulse, he turned at the waist, one hand on his hip, with an enchanting twist of the body, and looked back over his shoulder at the beach. There the watcher sat, as he had sat once before when those twilight-gray eyes, looking back at him then from that other threshold, had for the first time met his. Resting his head on the back of his chair, he had slowly turned it to follow the movements of the walking figure in the distance; now he lifted it toward this last look; then it sank down on his breast, so that his eyes stared up from below, while his face wore the inert, deep-sunken expression of profound slumber. But to him it was as if the pale and lovely soul-summoner out there were smiling to him, beckoning to him; as if he loosed his hand from his hip and pointed outward, hovering ahead and onward, into an immensity rich with unutterable expectation. And as so often, he set out to follow him.

Minutes passed, after he had collapsed sideways in his chair, before anyone hurried to his assistance. He was carried to his room. And later that same day the world was respectfully shocked to receive the news of his death.

Translated by David Luke

The Blood
of the Walsungs

It was seven minutes to twelve. Wendelin came into the first-floor entrance hall and sounded the gong. He straddled in his violet knee-breeches on a prayer-rug pale with age and belabored with his drumstick the metal disk. The brazen din, savage and primitive out of all proportion to its purport, resounded through the drawing-rooms to left and right, the billiard-room, the library, the winter-garden, up and down through the house; it vibrated through the warm and even atmosphere, heavy with exotic perfume. At last the sound ceased, and for another seven minutes Wendelin went about his business while Florian in the dining-room gave the last touches to the table. But on the stroke of twelve the cannibalistic summons sounded a second time. And the family appeared.

Herr Aarenhold came in his little toddle out of the library where he had been busy with his old editions. He was continually acquiring old books, first editions, in many languages, costly and crumbling trifles. Gently rubbing his hands he asked in his slightly plaintive way:

"Beckerath not here yet?"

"No, but he will be. Why shouldn't he? He will be saving a meal in a restaurant," answered Frau Aarenhold, coming noiselessly up the thick-carpeted stairs, on the landing of which stood a small, very ancient church organ.

Herr Aarenhold blinked. His wife was impossible. She was small, ugly, prematurely aged, and shriveled as though by tropic suns. A necklace of brilliants rested upon her shrunken breast. She wore her hair in complicated twists and knots to form a lofty pile, in which, somewhere on one side, sat a great jeweled brooch, adorned in its turn with a bunch of white aigrettes. Herr Aarenhold and the children had more than once, as diplomatically as possible, advised against this style of coiffure. But Frau Aarenhold clung stoutly to her own taste.

The children came: Kunz and Märit, Siegmund and Sieglinde. Kunz was in a braided uniform, a stunning tanned creature with curling lips and a killing scar. He was doing six weeks' service with his regiment of hussars. Märit made her appearance in an uncorseted garment. She was an ashen, austere blond of twenty-eight, with a hooked nose, gray eyes like a falcon's, and a bitter, contemptuous mouth. She was studying law and went entirely her own way in life.

Siegmund and Sieglinde came last, hand in hand, from the second floor. They were twins, graceful as young fawns, and with immature figures despite their nineteen years. She wore a Florentine cinque-cento frock of claret-colored velvet, too heavy for her slight body. Siegmund had on a green jacket suit with a tie of raspberry shantung, patent-leather shoes on his narrow feet, and cuff-buttons set with small diamonds. He had a strong growth of black beard but kept it so close-shaven that his sallow face with the heavy gathered brows looked no less boyish than his figure. His head was covered with thick black locks parted far down on one side and growing low on his temples. Her dark brown hair was waved in long, smooth undulations over her ears, confined by a gold circlet. A large pearl—his gift—hung down upon her brow. Round one of his boyish wrists was a heavy gold chain—a gift from her. They were very like each other, with the same slightly drooping nose, the same full lips lying softly together, the same prominent cheek-bones and black, bright eyes. Likest of all were their long slim hands, his no more masculine than hers, save that they were slightly redder. And they went always hand in hand, heedless that the hands of both inclined to moisture.

The family stood about awhile in the lobby, scarcely speaking. Then Beckerath appeared. He was engaged to Sieglinde. Wendelin opened the door to him and as he entered in his black frock coat he excused himself for his tardiness. He was a government official and came of a good family. He was short of stature, with a pointed beard and a very yellow complexion, like a canary. His manners were punctilious. He began every sentence by drawing his breath in quickly through his mouth and pressing his chin on his chest.

He kissed Sieglinde's hand and said:

"And you must excuse me too, Sieglinde—it is so far from the Ministry to the Zoo—"

He was not allowed to say thou to her—she did not like it. She answered briskly:

"Very far. Supposing that, in consideration of the fact, you left your office a bit earlier."

Kunz seconded her, his black eyes narrowing to glittering cracks:

"It would no doubt have a most beneficial effect upon our household economy."

"Oh, well—business, you know what it is," von Beckerath said dully. He was thirty-five years old.

The brother and sister had spoken glibly and with point. They may have attacked out of a habitual inward posture of self-defense; perhaps they deliberately meant to wound—perhaps again their words were due to the sheer pleasure of turning a phrase. It would have been unreasonable to feel annoyed. They let his feeble answer pass, as though they found it in character; as though cleverness in him would have been out of place. They went to table; Herr Aarenhold led the way, eager to let von Beckerath see that he was hungry.

They sat down, they unfolded their stiff table napkins. The immense room was carpeted, the walls were covered with eighteenth-century paneling, and three electric lustres hung from the ceiling. The family table, with its seven places, was lost in the void. It was drawn up close to the large French window, beneath which a dainty little fountain spread its silver spray behind a low lattice. Outside was an extended view of the still wintry garden. Tapestries with pastoral scenes covered the upper part of the walls; they, like the paneling, had been part of the furnishings of a French château. The dining-chairs were low and soft and cushioned with tapestry. A tapering glass vase holding two orchids stood at each place, on the glistening, spotless, faultlessly ironed damask cloth. With careful, skinny hands Herr Aarenhold settled the pince-nez half-way down his nose and with a mistrustful air read the menu, three copies of which lay on the table. He suffered from a weakness of the solar plexus, that nerve center which lies at the pit of the stomach and may give rise to serious distress. He was obliged to be very careful what he ate.

There was bouillon with beef marrow, sole *au vin blanc,* pheasant, and pineapple.

Nothing else. It was a simple family meal. But it satisfied Herr Aarenhold. It was good, light, nourishing food. The soup was served: a dumb-waiter above the sideboard brought it noiselessly down from the kitchen and the servants handed it round, bending over assiduously, in a very passion of service. The tiny cups were of translucent porcelain, whitish morsels of marrow floated in the hot golden liquid.

Herr Aarenhold felt himself moved to expand a little in the comfortable warmth thus purveyed. He carried his napkin cautiously to his mouth and cast after a means of clothing his thought in words.

"Have another cup, Beckerath," said he. "A working man has a right to his comforts and his pleasures. Do you really like to eat—really enjoy it, I mean? If not, so much the worse for you. To me every meal is a little celebration. Somebody said that life is pretty nice after all—being arranged so that we can eat four times a day. He's my man! But to do justice to the arrangement one has to preserve one's youthful receptivity—and not everybody can do that. We get old—well, we can't help it. But the thing is to keep things fresh and not get used to them. For instance," he went on, putting a bit of marrow on a piece of roll and sprinkling salt on it, "you are about to change your estate, the plane on which you live is going to be a good deal elevated" (von Beckerath smiled), "and if you want to enjoy your new life, really enjoy it, consciously and artistically, you must take care never to get used to your new situation. Getting used to things is death. It is ennui. Don't give in to it, don't let anything become a matter of course, preserve a childlike taste for the sweets of life. You see . . . for some years now I have been able to command some of the amenities of life" (von Beckerath smiled), "and yet I assure you, every morning that God lets me wake up I have a little thrill because my bed-cover is made of silk. That is what it is to be young. I know perfectly well how I did it; and yet I can look round me and feel like an enchanted prince."

The children exchanged looks, so openly that Herr Aarenhold could not help seeing it; he became visibly embarrassed. He knew that they were united against him, that they despised him: for his origins, for the blood which flowed in his veins and through him in theirs; for the way he had earned his money; for his fads, which in their eyes were unbecoming: for his valetudinarianism, which they found equally annoying; for his weak and whimsical loquacity, which in their eyes traversed the bounds of good taste. He knew all this—and in a way conceded that they were right. But after all he had to assert his personality, he had to lead his own life; and above all he had to be able to talk about it. That was only fair—he had proved that it was worth talking about. He had been a worm, a louse if you like. But just his capacity to realize it so fully, with such vivid self-contempt, had become the ground of that persistent, painful, never-satisfied striving which had made him great. Herr Aarenhold had been born in a remote village in East Prussia, had married the daughter of a well-to-do tradesman, and by means of a bold and shrewd enterprise, of large-scale schemings which had as their object a new and productive coal-bed, he had diverted a large and inexhaustible stream of gold into his coffers.

The fish course came on. The servants hurried with it from the sideboard through the length of the room. They handed round with it a creamy sauce and poured out a Rhine wine that prickled on the tongue. The conversation turned to the approaching wedding.

It was very near, it was to take place in the following week. They talked about the dowry, about plans for the wedding journey to Spain. Actually, it was only Herr Aarenhold who talked about them, supported by von Beckerath's polite acquiescence. Frau Aarenhold ate greedily, and as usual contributed nothing to the conversation save some rather pointless questions. Her speech was interlarded with guttural words and phrases from the dialect of her childhood days. Märit was full of silent opposition to the church ceremony which they planned to have; it affronted her highly enlightened convictions. Herr Aarenhold also was privately opposed to the ceremony. Von Beckerath was a Protestant and in Herr Aarenhold's view a Protestant ceremonial was without any aesthetic value. It would be different if von Beckerath belonged to the Roman confession. Kunz said nothing, because when von Beckerath was present he always felt annoyed with his mother. And neither Siegmund nor Sieglinde displayed any interest. They held each other's narrow hands between their chairs. Sometimes their gaze sought each other's, melting together in an understanding from which everybody else was shut out. Von Beckerath sat next to Sieglinde on the other side.

"Fifty hours," said Herr Aarenhold, "and you are in Madrid, if you like. That is progress. It took me sixty by the shortest way. I assume that you prefer the train to the sea route via Rotterdam?"

Von Beckerath hastily expressed his preference for the overland route.

"But you won't leave Paris out. Of course, you could go direct to Lyons. And Sieglinde knows Paris. But you should not neglect the opportunity . . . I leave it to you whether or not to stop before that. The choice of the place where the honeymoon begins should certainly be left to you."

Sieglinde turned her head, turned it for the first time toward her betrothed, quite openly and unembarrassed, careless of the lookers-on. For quite three seconds she bent upon the courteous face beside her the wide-eyed, questioning, expectant gaze of her sparkling black eyes—a gaze as vacant of thoughts as any animal's. Between their chairs she was holding the slender hand of her twin; and Siegmund drew his brows together till they formed two black folds at the base of his nose.

The conversation veered and tacked to and fro. They talked of a consignment of cigars that had just come by Herr Aarenhold's order from Havana, packed in zinc. Then it circled round a point of purely abstract interest, brought up by Kunz: namely, whether, if *a* were the necessary and sufficient condition for *b*, *b* must also be the necessary and sufficient condition for *a*. They argued the matter, they analysed it with great ingenuity, they gave examples; they talked nineteen to the dozen, attacked each other with steely and abstract dialectic, and got no little heated. Märit had introduced a philosophical distinction, that between the actual and the causal principle. Kunz told her, with his nose in the air, that "causal principle" was a pleonasm. Märit, in some annoyance, insisted upon her terminology. Herr Aarenhold straightened himself, with a bit of bread between thumb and forefinger, and prepared to elucidate the whole matter. He suffered a complete rout, the children joined forces to laugh him down. Even his wife jeered at him. "What are you talking about?" she said. "Where did you learn that—you didn't learn much!" Von Beckerath pressed his chin on his breast, opened his mouth, and drew in breath to speak—but they had already passed on, leaving him hanging.

Siegmund began, in a tone of ironic amusement, to speak of an acquaintance of his, a child of nature whose simplicity was such that he abode in ignorance of the difference between dress clothes and dinner jacket. This Parsifal actually talked about a checked dinner jacket. Kunz knew an even more pathetic case—a man who went out to tea in dinner clothes.

"Dinner clothes in the afternoon!" Sieglinde said, making a face. "It isn't even human!"

Von Beckerath laughed sedulously. But inwardly he was remembering that once he himself had worn a dinner coat before six o'clock. And with the game course they passed on to matters of more general cultural interest: to the plastic arts, of which von Beckerath was an amateur, to literature and the theatre, which in the Aarenhold house had the preference—though Siegmund did devote some of his leisure to painting.

The conversation was lively and general and the young people set the key. They talked well, their gestures were nervous and self-assured. They marched in the van of taste, the best was none too good for them. For the vision, the intention, the laboring will, they had no use at all; they ruthlessly insisted upon power achievement, success in the cruel trial of strength. The triumphant work of art they recognized—but they paid it no homage. Herr Aarenhold himself said to von Beckerath:

"You are very indulgent, my dear fellow; you speak up for intentions—but results, *results* are what we are after! You say: 'Of course his work is not much good—but he was only a peasant before he took it up, so his performance is after all astonishing.' Nothing in it. Accomplishment is absolute, not relative. There are no mitigating circumstances. Let a man do first-class work or let him shovel coals. How far should I have got with a good-natured attitude like that? I might have said to myself: 'You're only a poor fish, originally—it's wonderful if you get to be the head of your office.' Well, I'd not be sitting here! I've had to force the world to recognize me, so now I won't recognize anything unless I am forced to!"

The children laughed. At that moment they did not look down on him. They sat there at table, in their low, luxuriously cushioned chairs, with their spoiled, dissatisfied faces. They sat in splendor and security, but their words rang as sharp as though sharpness, hardness, alertness, and pitiless clarity were demanded of them as survival values. Their highest praise was a grudging acceptance, their criticism deft and ruthless; it snatched the weapons from one's hand, it paralysed enthusiasm, made it a laughing-stock. "Very good," they would say of some masterpiece whose lofty intellectual plane would seem to have put it beyond the reach of critique. Passion was a blunder—it made them laugh. Von Beckerath, who tended to be disarmed by his enthusiasms, had hard work holding his own—also his age put him in the wrong. He got smaller and smaller in his chair, pressed his chin on his breast, and in his excitement breathed through his mouth—quite unhorsed by the brisk arrogance of youth. They contradicted everything—as though they found it impossible, discreditable, lamentable, not to contradict. They contradicted most efficiently, their eyes narrowing to gleaming cracks. They fell upon a single word of his, they worried it, they tore it to bits and replaced it by another so telling and deadly that it went straight to the mark and sat in the wound with quivering shaft. Toward the end of luncheon, von Beckerath's eyes were red and he looked slightly deranged.

Suddenly—they were sprinkling sugar on their slices of pine-apple—Siegmund said, wrinkling up his face in the way he had, as though the sun were making him blink:

"Oh, by the bye, von Beckerath, something else, before we forget it. Sieglinde and I approach you with a request—metaphorically speaking, you see us on our knees. They are giving the *Walküre* tonight. We should like, Sieglinde and I, to hear it once more together—may we? We are of course aware that everything depends upon your gracious favor—"

"How thoughtful!" said Herr Aarenhold.

Kunz drummed the Hunding motif on the cloth.

Von Beckerath was overcome at anybody asking his permission about anything. He answered eagerly:

"But by all means, Siegmund—and you too, Sieglinde; I find your request very reasonable—do go, of course; in fact, I shall be able to go with you. There is an excellent cast tonight."

All the Aarenholds bowed over their plates to hide their laughter. Von Beckerath blinked with his effort to be one of them, to understand and share their mirth.

Siegmund hastened to say:

"Oh, well, actually, it's a rather poor cast, you know. Of course, we are just as grateful to you as though it were good. But I am afraid there is a slight misunderstanding. Sieglinde and I were asking you to permit us to hear the *Walküre* once more *alone* together before the wedding. I don't know if you feel now that—"

"Oh certainly. I quite understand. How charming! Of course you *must* go!"

"Thanks, we are most grateful indeed. Then I will have Percy and Leiermann put in for us. . . . "

"Perhaps I may venture to remark," said Herr Aarenhold, "that your mother and I are driving to dinner with the Erlangers and using Percy and Leiermann. You will have to condescend to the brown coupé and Baal and Lampa."

"And your box?" asked Kunz.

"I took it long ago," said Siegmund, tossing back his head.

They all laughed, all staring at the bridegroom.

Herr Aarenhold unfolded with his fingertips the paper of a bella-donna powder and shook it carefully into his mouth. Then he lighted a fat cigarette, which presently spread abroad a priceless fragrance. The servants sprang forward to draw away his and Frau Aarenhold's chairs. The order was given to serve coffee in the winter-garden.

Kunz in a sharp voice ordered his dogcart brought round; he would drive to the barracks.

Siegmund was dressing for the opera; he had been dressing for an hour. He had so abnormal and constant a need for purification that actually he spent a considerable part of his time before the wash-basin. He stood now in front of his large Empire mirror with the white-enameled frame; dipped a powder-puff in its embossed box and powdered his freshly shaven chin and cheeks. His beard was so heavy that when he went out in the evening he was obliged to shave a second time.

He presented a colorful picture as he stood there, in rose-tinted silk drawers and socks, red morocco slippers, and a wadded house-jacket in a dark pattern with revers of gray fur. For background he had his large sleeping-chamber, full of all sorts of elegant and practical white-enameled devices. Beyond the windows was a misty view over the tree-tops of the Tiergarten.

It was growing dark. He turned on the circular arrangement of electric bulbs in the white ceiling—they filled the room with soft milky light. Then he drew the velvet curtains across the darkening panes. The light was reflected from the liquid depths of the mirrors in wardrobe, washing-stand, and toilet-table, it flashed from the polished bottles on the tile-inlaid shelves. And Siegmund continued to work on himself. Now and then some thought in his mind would draw his brows together till they formed two black folds over the base of the nose.

His day had passed as his days usually did, vacantly and swiftly. The opera began at half past six and he had begun to change at half past five, so there had not been much afternoon. He had rested on his chaise-longue from two to three, then drunk tea and employed the remaining hour sprawled in a deep leather arm-chair in the study which he shared with Kunz, reading a few pages in each of several new novels. He had found them pitiably weak on the whole; but he had sent a few of them to the binder's to be artistically bound in choice bindings, for his library.

But in the forenoon he had worked. He had spent the hour from ten to eleven in the atelier of his professor, an artist of European repute, who was developing Siegmund's talent for drawing and painting, and receiving from Herr Aarenhold two thousand marks a month for his services. But what Siegmund painted was absurd. He knew it himself; he was far from having any glowing expectations on the score of his talent in this line. He was too shrewd not to know that the conditions of his existence were not the most favorable in the world for the development of a creative gift. The accoutrements of life were so rich and varied, so elaborated, that almost no place at all was left for life itself. Each and every single accessory was so costly and beautiful that it had an existence above and beyond the purpose it was meant to serve—until one's attention was first confused and then exhausted. Siegmund had been born into superfluity, he was perfectly adjusted to it. And yet it was the fact that this superfluity never ceased to thrill and occupy him, to give him constant pleasure. Whether consciously or not, it was with him as with his father, who practiced the art of never getting used to anything.

Siegmund loved to read, he strove after the word and the spirit as after a tool which a profound instinct urged him to grasp. But never had he lost himself in a book as one does when that single work seems the most important in the world; unique, a little, all-embracing universe, into which one plunges and submerges oneself in order to draw nourishment out of every syllable. The books and magazines streamed in, he could buy them all, they heaped up about him and even while he read, the number of those still to be read disturbed him. But he had the books bound in stamped leather and labeled with Siegmund Aarenhold's beautiful book-plate; they stood in rows, weighing down his life like a possession which he did not succeed in subordinating to his personality.

The day was his, it was given to him as a gift with all its hours from sunrise to sunset; and yet Siegmund found in his heart that he had no time for a resolve, how much less then for a deed. He was no hero, he commanded no giant powers. The preparation, the lavish equipment for what should have been the serious business of life used up all his energy. How much mental effort had to be expended simply in making a proper toilette! How much time and attention went to his supplies of cigarettes, soaps, and perfumes; how much occasion for making up his mind lay in that moment, recurring two or three times daily, when he had to select his cravat! And it was worth the effort. It was important. The blond-haired citizenry of the land might go about in elastic-sided boots and turn-over collars, heedless of the effect. But he—and most explicitly he—must be unassailable and blameless of exterior from head to foot.

And in the end no one expected more of him. Sometimes there came moments when he had a feeble misgiving about the nature of the "actual"; sometimes he felt that this lack of expectation lamed and dislodged his sense of it. . . . The household arrangements were all made to the end that the day might pass quickly and no empty hour be perceived. The next mealtime always came promptly on. They dined before seven; the evening, when one can idle with a good conscience, was long. The days disappeared, swiftly the seasons came and went. The family spent two summer months at their little castle on the lake, with its large and splendid grounds and many tennis courts, its cool paths through the parks, and shaven lawns adorned by bronze statuettes. A third month was spent in the mountains, in hotels where life was even more expensive than at home. Of late, during the winter, he had had himself driven to school to listen to a course of lectures in the history of art which came at a convenient time. But he had had to leave off because his sense of smell indicated that the rest of the class did not wash often enough.

He spent the hour walking with Sieglinde instead. Always she had been at his side since the very first; she had clung to him since they lisped their first syllables, taken their first steps. He had no friends, never had had one but this, his exquisitely groomed, darkly beautiful counterpart, whose moist and slender hand he held while the richly gilded, empty-eyed hours slipped past. They took fresh flowers with them on their walks, a bunch of violets or lilies of the valley, smelling them in turn or sometimes both together, with languid yet voluptuous abandon. They were like self-centered invalids who absorb themselves in trifles, as narcotics to console them for the loss of hope. With an inward gesture of renunciation they doffed aside the evil-smelling world and loved each other alone, for the priceless sake of their own rare uselessness. But all that they uttered was pointed, neat, and brilliant; it hit off the people they met, the things they saw, everything done by somebody else to the end that it might be exposed to the unerring eye, the sharp tongue, the witty condemnation.

Then von Beckerath had appeared. He had a post in the government and came of a good family. He had proposed for Sieglinde. Frau Aarenhold had supported him, Herr Aarenhold had displayed a benevolent neutrality, Kunz the hussar was his zealous partisan. He had been patient, assiduous, endlessly good-mannered and tactful. And in the end, after she had told him often enough that she did not love him, Sieglinde had begun to look at him searchingly, expectantly, mutely, with her sparkling black eyes—a gaze as speaking and as vacant of thought as an animal's—and had said yes. And Siegmund, whose will was her law, had taken up a position too; slightly to his own disgust he had not opposed the match; was not von Beckerath in the government and a man of good family too? Sometimes he wrinkled his brows over his toilette until they made two heavy black folds at the base of his nose.

He stood on the white bearskin which stretched out its claws beside the bed; his feet were lost in the long soft hair. He sprinkled himself lavishly with toilet water and took up his dress shirt. The starched and shining linen glided over his yellowish torso, which was as lean as a young boy's and yet shaggy with black hair. He arrayed himself further in black silk drawers, black silk socks, and heavy black silk garters with silver buckles, put on the well-pressed trousers of silky black cloth, fastened the white silk braces over his narrow shoulders, and with one foot on a stool began to button his shoes. There was a knock on the door.

"May I come in, Gigi?" asked Sieglinde.

"Yes, come in," he answered.

She was already dressed, in a frock of shimmering sea-green silk, with a square neck outlined by a wide band of beige embroidery. Two embroidered peacocks facing each other above the girdle held a garland in their beaks. Her dark brown hair was unadorned; but a large egg-shaped precious stone hung on a thin pearl-chain against her bare skin, the color of smoked meerschaum. Over her arm she carried a scarf heavily worked with silver.

"I am unable to conceal from you," she said, "that the carriage is waiting." He parried at once:

"And I have no hesitation in replying that it will have to wait patiently two minutes more." It was at least ten. She sat down on the white velvet chaise-longue and watched him at his labors.

Out of a rich chaos of ties he selected a white piqué band and began to tie it before the glass.

"Beckerath," said she, "wears colored cravats, crossed over the way they wore them last year."

"Beckerath," said he, "is the most trivial existence I have ever had under my personal observation." Turning to her quickly he added: "Moreover, you will do me the favor of not mentioning that German's name to me again this evening."

She gave a short laugh and replied: "You may be sure it will not be a hardship."

He put on the low-cut piqué waistcoat and drew his dress coat over it, the white silk lining caressing his hands as they passed through the sleeves.

"Let me see which buttons you chose," said Sieglinde. They were the amethyst ones; shirt-studs, cuff-links, and waistcoat buttons, a complete set.

She looked at him admiringly, proudly, adoringly, with a world of tenderness in her dark, shining eyes. He kissed the lips lying so softly on each other. They spent another minute on the chaise-longue in mutual caresses.

"Quite, quite soft you are again," said she, stroking his shaven cheeks.

"Your little arm feels like satin," said he, running his hand down her tender forearm. He breathed in the violet odor of her hair.

She kissed him on his closed eyelids; he kissed her on the throat where the pendant hung. They kissed one another's hands. They loved one another sweetly, sensually, for sheer mutual delight in their own well-groomed, pampered, expensive smell. The played together like puppies, biting each other with their lips. Then he got up.

"We mustn't be too late today," said he. He turned the top of the perfume bottle upside down on his handkerchief one last time, rubbed a drop into his narrow red hands, took his gloves, and declared himself ready to go.

He put out the light and they went along the red-carpeted corridor hung with dark old oil paintings and down the steps past the little organ. In the vestibule on the ground floor Wendelin was waiting with their coats, very tall in his long yellow paletot. They yielded their shoulders to his ministrations; Sieglinde's dark head was half lost in her collar of silver fox. Followed by the servant they passed through the stone-paved vestibule into the outer air. It was mild, and there were great ragged flakes of snow in the pearly air. The coupé awaited them. The coachman bent down with his hand to his cockaded hat while Wendelin ushered the brother and sister to their seats; then the door banged shut, he swung himself up to the box, and the carriage was at once in swift motion. It crackled over the gravel, glided through the high, wide gate, curved smoothly to the right, and rolled away.

The luxurious little space in which they sat was pervaded by a gentle warmth. "Shall I shut us in?" Siegmund asked. She nodded and he drew the brown silk curtains across the polished panes.

They were in the city's heart. Lights flew past behind the curtains. Their horses' hoofs rhythmically beat the ground, the carriage swayed noiselessly over the pavement, and round them roared and shrieked and thundered the machinery of urban life. Quite safe and shut away they sat among the wadded brown silk cushions, hand in hand. The carriage drew up and stopped. Wendelin was at the door to help them out. A little group of gray-faced shivering folk stood in the brilliance of the arc-lights and followed them with hostile glances as they passed through the lobby. It was already late, they were the last. They mounted the staircase, threw their cloaks over Wendelin's arms, paused a second before a high mirror, then went through the little door into their box. They were greeted by the last sounds before the hush—voices and the slamming of seats. The lackey pushed their plush-upholstered chairs beneath them; at that moment the lights went down and below their box the orchestra broke into the wild pulsating notes of the prelude.

Night, and tempest. . . . And they, who had been wafted hither on the wings of ease, with no petty annoyances on the way, were in exactly the right mood and could give all their attention at once. Storm, a raging tempest, without in the wood. The angry god's command resounded, once, twice repeated in its wrath, obediently the thunder crashed. The curtain flew up as though blown by the storm. There was the rude hall, dark save for a glow on the pagan hearth. In the center towered up the trunk of the ash tree. Siegmund appeared in the doorway and leaned against the wooden post beaten and harried by the storm. Draggingly he moved forward on his sturdy legs wrapped round with hide and thongs. He was rosy-skinned, with a straw-colored beard; beneath his blond brows and the blond forelock of his wig his blue eyes were directed upon the conductor, with an imploring gaze. At last the orchestra gave way to his voice, which rang clear and metallic, though he tried to make it sound like a gasp. He sang a few bars, to the effect that no matter to whom the hearth belonged he must rest upon it; and at the last word he let himself drop heavily on the bearskin rug and lay there with his head cushioned on his plump arms. His breast heaved in slumber. A minute passed, filled with the singing, speaking flow of the music, rolling its waves at the feet of the events on the stage. . . . Sieglinde entered from the left. She had an alabaster bosom which rose and fell marvelously beneath her muslin robe and deerskin mantle. She displayed surprise at sight of the strange man; pressed her chin upon her breast until it was double, put her lips in position and expressed it, this surprise, in tones which swelled soft and warm from her white throat and were given shape by her tongue and her mobile lips. She tended the stranger; bending over him so that he could see the white flower of her bosom rising from the rough skins, she gave him with both hands the drinking-horn. He drank. The music spoke movingly to him of cool refreshment and cherishing care. They looked at each other with the beginning of enchantment, a first dim recognition, standing rapt while the orchestra interpreted in a melody of profound enchantment.

She gave him mead, first touching the horn with her lips, then watching while he took a long draught. Again their glances met and mingled, while below, the melody voiced their yearning. Then he rose, in deep dejection, turning away painfully, his arms hanging at his sides, to the door, that he might remove from her sight his afflic-tion, his loneliness, his persecuted, hated existence and bear it back into the wild. She called upon him but he did not hear; heedless of self she lifted up her arms and confessed her intolerable anguish. He stopped. Her eyes fell. Below them the music spoke darkly of the bond of suffering that united them. He stayed. He folded his arms and remained by the hearth, awaiting his destiny.

Announced by his pugnacious motif, Hunding entered, paunchy and knock-kneed, like a cow. His beard was black with brown tufts. He stood there frowning, leaning heavily on his spear, and staring ox-eyed at the stranger guest. But as the primitive custom would have it he bade him welcome, in an enormous, rusty voice.

Sieglinde laid the evening meal, Hunding's slow, suspicious gaze moving to and fro between her and the stranger. Dull lout though he was, he saw their likeness: the selfsame breed, that odd, untram-meled rebellious stock, which he hated, to which he felt inferior. They sat down, and Hunding, in two words, introduced himself and accounted for his simple, regular, and orthodox existence. Thus he forced Siegmund to speak of himself—and that was incomparably more difficult. Yet Siegmund spoke, he sang clearly and with won-derful beauty of his life and misfortunes. He told how he had been born with a twin sister—and as people do who dare not speak out, he called himself by a false name. He gave a moving account of the hatred and envy which had been the bane of his life and his strange father's life, how their hall had been burnt, his sister carried off, how they had led in the forest a harried, persecuted, outlawed life; and how finally he had mysteriously lost his father as well. . . . And then Siegmund sang the most painful thing of all: he told of his yearning for human beings, his longing and ceaseless loneliness. He sang of men and women, of friendship and love he had sometimes won, only to be thrust back again into the dark. A curse had lain upon him forever, he was marked by the brand of his strange origins.

His speech had not been as others' speech nor theirs as his. What he found good was vexation to them, he was galled by the ancient laws to which they paid honor. Always and everywhere he had lived amid anger and strife, he had borne the yoke of scorn and hatred and contempt—all because he was strange, of a breed and kind hopelessly different from them.

Hunding's reception of all this was entirely characteristic. His reply showed no sympathy and no understanding, but only a sour disgust and suspicion of all Siegmund's story. And finally understanding that the stranger standing here on his own hearth was the very man for whom the hunt had been called up today, he behaved with the four-square pedantry one would have expected of him. With a grim sort of courtesy he declared that for tonight the guest-right protected the fugitive; tomorrow he would have the honor of slaying him in battle. Gruffly he commanded Sieglinde to spice his night-drink for him and to await him in bed within; then after a few more threats he followed her, taking all his weapons with him and leaving Siegmund alone and despairing by the hearth.

Up in the box Siegmund bent over the velvet ledge and leaned his dark boyish head on his narrow red hand. His brows made two black furrows, and one foot, resting on the heel of his patent-leather shoe, was in constant nervous motion. But it stopped as he heard a whisper close to him.

"Gigi!"

His mouth, as he turned, had an insolent line.

Sieglinde was holding out to him a mother-of-pearl box with maraschino cherries.

"The brandy chocolates are underneath," she whispered. But he accepted only a cherry, and as he took it out of the waxed paper she said in his ear:

"She will come back to him again at once."

"I am not entirely unaware of the fact," he said, so loud that several heads were jerked angrily in his direction. . . . Down in the darkness big Siegmund was singing alone. From the depths of his heart he cried out for the sword—for a shining haft to swing on that day when there burst forth at last the bright flame of his anger and rage, which so long had smoldered deep in his heart. He saw the hilt glitter in the tree, saw the embers fade on the hearth, sank back in gloomy slumber—and started up in joyful amaze when Sieglinde glided back to him in the darkness.

Hunding slept like a stone, a deafened, drunken sleep. Together they rejoiced at the outwitting of the clod; they laughed, and their eyes had the same way of narrowing as they laughed. Then Sieglinde stole a look at the conductor, received her cue, and putting her lips in position sang a long recitative: related the heart-breaking tale of how they had forced her, forsaken, strange and wild as she was, to give herself to the crude and savage Hunding and to count herself lucky in an honorable marriage which might bury her dark origins in oblivion. She sang too, sweetly and soothingly, of the strange old man in the hat and how he had driven the sword-blade into the trunk of the ash tree, to await the coming of him who was destined to draw it out. Passionately she prayed in song that it might be he whom she meant, whom she knew and grievously longed for, the consoler of her sorrows, the friend who should be more than friend, the avenger of her shame, whom once she had lost, whom in her abasement she wept for, her brother in suffering, her savior, her rescuer. . . .

But at this point Siegmund flung about her his two rosy arms. He pressed her cheek against the pelt that covered his breast and, holding her so, sang above her head—sang out his exultation to the four winds, in a silver trumpeting of sound. His breast glowed hot with the oath that bound him to his mate. All the yearning of his hunted life found assuagement in her; all that love which others had repulsed, when in conscious shame of his dark origins he forced it upon them—in her it found its home. She suffered shame as did he, dishonored was she like to himself—and now, now their brother-and-sister love should be their revenge!

The storm whistled, a gust of wind burst open the door, a flood of white electric light poured into the hall. Divested of darkness they stood and sang their song of spring and spring's sister, love!

Crouching on the bearskin they looked at each other in the white light, as they sang their duet of love. Their bare arms touched each other as they held each other by the temples and gazed into each other's eyes, and as they sang their mouths were very near. They compared their eyes, their foreheads, their voices—they were the same. The growing, urging recognition wrung from his breast his father's name; she called him by his: Siegmund! Siegmund! He freed the sword, he swung it above his head, and submerged in bliss she told him in song who she was: his twin sister, Sieglinde. In ravishment he stretched out his arms to her, his bride, she sank upon his breast—the curtain fell as the music swelled into a roaring, rushing, foaming whirlpool of passion—swirled and swirled and with one mighty throb stood still.

Rapturous applause. The lights went on. A thousand people got up, stretched unobtrusively as they clapped, then made ready to leave the hall, with heads still turned toward the stage, where the singers appeared before the curtain, like masks hung out in a row at a fair. Hunding too came out and smiled politely, despite all that had just been happening.

Siegmund pushed back his chair and stood up. He was hot; little red patches showed on his cheek-bones, above the lean, sallow, shaven cheeks.

"For my part," said he, "what I want now is a breath of fresh air. Siegmund was pretty feeble, wasn't he?"

"Yes," answered Sieglinde, "and the orchestra saw fit to drag abominably in the Spring Song."

"Frightfully sentimental," said Siegmund, shrugging his narrow shoulders in his dress coat. "Are you coming out?" She lingered a moment, with her elbows on the ledge, still gazing at the stage. He looked at her as she rose and took up her silver scarf. Her soft, full lips were quivering.

They went into the foyer and mingled with the slow-moving throng, downstairs and up again, sometimes holding each other by the hand.

"I should enjoy an ice," said she, "if they were not in all probability uneatable."

"Don't think of it," said he. So they ate bonbons out of their box—maraschino cherries and chocolate beans filled with cognac.

The bell rang and they looked on contemptuously as the crowds rushed back to their seats, blocking the corridors. They waited until all was quiet, regaining their places just as the lights went down again and silence and darkness fell soothingly upon the hall. There was another little ring, the conductor raised his arms and summoned up anew the wave of splendid sound.

Siegmund looked down into the orchestra. The sunken space stood out bright against the darkness of the listening house; hands fingered, arms drew the bows, cheeks puffed out—all these simple folk labored zealously to bring to utterance the work of a master who suffered and created; created the noble and simple visions enacted above on the stage. Creation? How did one create? Pain gnawed and burned in Siegmund's breast, a drawing anguish which yet was somehow sweet, a yearning—whither, for what? It was all so dark, so shamefully unclear! Two thoughts, two words he had: creation, passion. His temples glowed and throbbed, and it came to him as in a yearning vision that creation was born of passion and was reshaped anew as passion. He saw the pale, spent woman hanging on the breast of the fugitive to whom she gave herself, he saw her love and her destiny and knew that so life must be to be creative. He saw his own life, and knew its contradictions, its clear understanding and spoilt voluptuousness, its splendid security and idle spite, its weakness and wittiness, its languid contempt; his life, so full of words, so void of acts, so full of cleverness, so empty of emotion—and he felt again the burning, the drawing anguish which yet was sweet—whither, and to what end? Creation? Experience? Passion?

The finale of the act came, the curtain fell. Light, applause, general exit. Sieglinde and Siegmund spent the interval as before. They scarcely spoke, as they walked hand-in-hand through the corridors and up and down the steps. She offered him cherries but he took no more. She looked at him, but withdrew her gaze as his rested upon her, walking rather constrained at his side and enduring his eye. Her childish shoulders under the silver web of her scarf looked like those of an Egyptian statue, a little too high and too square. Upon her cheeks burned the same fire he felt in his own.

Again they waited until the crowd had gone in and took their seats at the last possible moment. Storm and wind and driving clouds; wild, heathenish cries of exultation. Eight females; not exactly stars in appearance, eight untrammeled, laughing maidens of the wild, were disporting themselves amid a rocky scene. Brünnhilde broke in upon their merriment with her fears. They skimmed away in terror before the approaching wrath of Wotan, leaving her alone to face him. The angry god nearly annihilated his daughter—but his wrath roared itself out, by degrees grew gentle and dispersed into a mild melancholy, on which note it ended. A noble prospect opened out, the scene was pervaded with epic and religious splendor. Brünnhilde slept. The god mounted the rocks. Great, full-bodied flames, rising, falling, and flickering, glowed all over the boards. The Walküre lay with her coat of mail and her shield on her mossy couch ringed round with fire and smoke, with leaping, dancing tongues, with the magic sleep-compelling fire-music. But she had saved Sieglinde, in whose womb there grew and waxed the seed of that hated unprized race, chosen of the gods, from which the twins had sprung, who had mingled their misfortunes and their afflictions in free and mutual bliss.

Siegmund and Sieglinde left their box; Wendelin was outside, towering in his yellow paletot and holding their cloaks for them to put on. Like a gigantic slave he followed the two dark, slender, furmantled, exotic creatures down the stairs to where the carriage waited and the pair of large finely matched glossy thoroughbreds tossed their proud heads in the winter night. Wendelin ushered the twins into their warm little silken-lined retreat, closed the door, and the coupé stood poised for yet a second, quivering slightly from the swing with which Wendelin agilely mounted the box. Then it glided swiftly away and left the theater behind. Again they rolled noiselessly and easefully to the rhythmic beat of the horses' hoofs, over all the unevennesses of the road, sheltered from the shrill harshness of the bustling life through which they passed. They sat as silent and remote as they had sat in their opera-box facing the stage— almost, one might say, in the same atmosphere. Nothing was there which could alienate them from that extravagant and stormily passionate world which worked upon them with its magic power to draw them to itself.

The carriage stopped; they did not at once realize where they were, or that they had arrived before the door of their parents' house. Then Wendelin appeared at the window, and the porter came out of his lodge to open the door.

"Are my father and mother at home?" Siegmund asked, looking over the porter's head and blinking as though he were staring into the sun.

No, they had not returned from dinner at the Erlangers'. Nor was Kunz at home; Märit too was out, no one knew where, for she went entirely her own way.

In the vestibule they paused to be divested of their wraps; then they went up the stairs and through the first-floor hall into the dining room. Its immense and splendid spaces lay in darkness save at the upper end, where one lustre burned above a table and Florian waited to serve them. They moved noiselessly across the thick carpet, and Florian seated them in their softly upholstered chairs. Then a gesture from Siegmund dismissed him, they would dispense with his services.

The table was laid with a dish of fruit, a plate of sandwiches, and a jug of red wine. An electric tea-kettle hummed upon a great silver tray, with all appliances about it.

Siegmund ate a caviar sandwich and poured out wine into a slender glass where it glowed a dark ruby red. He drank in quick gulps, and grumblingly stated his opinion that red wine and caviar were a combination offensive to good taste. He drew out his case, jerkily selected a cigarette, and began to smoke, leaning back with his hands in his pockets, wrinkling up his face and twitching his cigarette from one corner of his mouth to the other. His strong growth of beard was already beginning to show again under the high cheekbones; the two black folds stood out on the base of his nose.

Sieglinde had brewed the tea and added a drop of burgundy. She touched the fragile porcelain cup delicately with her full, soft lips and as she drank she looked across at Siegmund with her great humid black eyes.

She set down her cup and leaned her dark, sweet little head upon her slender hand. Her eyes rested full upon him, with such liquid, speechless eloquence that all she might have said could be nothing beside it.

"Won't you have any more to eat, Gigi?"

"One would not draw," said he, "from the fact that I am smoking, the conclusion that I intend to eat more."

"But you have had nothing but bonbons since tea. Take a peach, at least."

He shrugged his shoulders—or rather he wiggled them like a naughty child, in his dress coat.

"This is stupid. I am going upstairs. Good night."

He drank out his wine, tossed away his table-napkin, and lounged away, with his hands in his pockets, into the darkness at the other end of the room.

He went upstairs to his room, where he turned on the light—not much, only two or three bulbs, which made a wide white circle on the ceiling. Then he stood considering what to do next. The good-night had not been final; this was not how they were used to take leave of each other at the close of the day. She was sure to come to his room. He flung off his coat, put on his fur-trimmed house-jacket, and lighted another cigarette. He lay down on the chaise-longue; sat up again, tried another posture, with his cheek in the pillow; threw himself on his back again and so remained awhile, with his hands under his head.

The subtle, bitterish scent of the tobacco mingled with that of the cosmetics, the soaps, and the toilet waters; their combined perfume hung in the tepid air of the room and Siegmund breathed it in with conscious pleasure, finding it sweeter than ever. Closing his eyes he surrendered to this atmosphere, as a man will console himself with some delicate pleasure of the senses for the extraordinary harshness of his lot.

Then suddenly he started up again, tossed away his cigarette and stood in front of the white wardrobe, which had long mirrors let into each of its three divisions. He moved very close to the middle one and eye to eye he studied himself, conned every feature of his face. Then he opened the two side wings and studied both profiles as well. Long he looked at each mark of his race: the slightly droop- ing nose, the full lips that rested so softly on each other; the high cheek-bones, the thick black, curling hair that grew far down on the temples and parted so decidedly on one side; finally the eyes under the knit brows, those large black eyes that glowed like fire and had an expression of weary sufferance.

In the mirror he saw the bearskin lying behind him, spreading out its claws beside the bed. He turned round, and there was tragic meaning in the dragging step that bore him toward it—until after a moment more of hesitation he lay down all its length and buried his head in his arm.

For a while he lay motionless, then propped his head on his el- bows, with his cheeks resting on his slim reddish hands, and fell again into contemplation of his image opposite him in the mirror. There was a knock on the door. He started, reddened, and moved as though to get up—but sank back again, his head against his outstretched arm, and stopped there, silent.

Sieglinde entered. Her eyes searched the room, without finding him at once. Then with a start she saw him lying on the rug.

"Gigi, what ever are you doing there? Are you ill?" She ran to him, bending over with her hand on his forehead, stroking his hair as she repeated: "You are not ill?"

He shook his head, looking up at her under his brow as she contin- ued to caress him.

She was half ready for bed, having come over in slippers from her dressing-room, which was opposite to his. Her loosened hair flowed down over her open white dressing jacket; beneath the lace of her chemise Siegmund saw her little breasts, the color of smoked meerschaum.

"You were so cross," she said. "It was beastly of you to go away like that. I thought I would not come. But then I did, because that was not a proper good-night at all. . . . "

"I was waiting for you," said he.

She was still standing bent over, and made a little moue which brought out markedly the facial characteristics of her race. Then, in her ordinary tone:

"Which does not prevent my present position from giving me a crick in the back."

He shook her off.

"Don't, don't—we must not talk like that—not that way, Sieglinde." His voice was strange, he himself noticed it. He felt parched with fever, his hands and feet were cold and clammy. She knelt beside him on the skin, her hand in his hair. He lifted himself a little to fling one arm round her neck and so looked at her, looked as he had just been looking at himself—at eyes and temples, brow and cheeks.

"You are just like me," said he, haltingly, and swallowed to moisten his dry throat. "Everything about you is just like me—and so—what you have—with Beckerath—the experience—is for me too. That makes things even, Sieglinde—and anyhow, after all, it is, for that matter—it is a revenge, Sieglinde—"

He was seeking to clothe in reason what he was trying to say—yet his words sounded as though he uttered them out of some strange, rash, bewildered dream.

But to her it had no quality of strangeness. She did not blush at his half-spoken, turbid, wild imaginings; his words enveloped her senses like a mist, they drew her down whence they had come, to the borders of a kingdom she had never entered, though sometimes, since her betrothal, she had been carried thither in expectant dreams.

She kissed him on his closed eyelids; he kissed her on her throat, beneath the lace she wore. They kissed each other's hands. They loved each other with all the sweetness of the senses, each for the other's spoilt and costly well-being and delicious fragrance. They breathed it in, this fragrance, with languid and voluptuous abandon, like self-centered invalids, consoling themselves for the loss of hope. They forgot themselves in caresses, which took the upper hand, passing over into a tumult of passion, dying away into a sobbing. . . .

She sat there on the bearskin, with parted lips, supporting herself with one hand, and brushed the hair out of her eyes. He leaned back on his hands against the white dressing-chest, rocked to and fro on his hips, and gazed into the air.

"But Beckerath," said she, seeking to find some order in her thoughts, "Beckerath, Gigi . . . what about him, now?"

"Oh," he said—and for a second the marks of his race stood out strong upon his face—"he ought to be grateful to us. His existence will be a little less trivial, from now on."

Translated by Helen Tracey Lowe-Porter

Mario and the Magician

The atmosphere of Torre di Venere remains unpleasant in the memory. From the first moment the air of the place made us uneasy, we felt irritable, on edge; then at the end came the shocking business of Cipolla, that dreadful being who seemed to incorporate, in so fateful and so humanly impressive a way, all the peculiar evilness of the situation as a whole. Looking back, we had the feeling that the horrible end of the affair had been preordained and lay in the nature of things; that the children had to be present at it was an added impropriety, due to the false colors in which the weird creature presented himself. Luckily for them, they did not know where the comedy left off and the tragedy began; and we let them remain in their happy belief that the whole thing had been a play up till the end.

Torre di Venere lies some ten miles from Portoclemente, one of the most popular summer resorts on the Tyrrhenian Sea. Portoclemente is urban and elegant and full to overflowing for months on end. Its gay and busy main street of shops and hotels runs down to a wide sandy beach covered with tents and pennanted sand castles and sunburned humanity, where at all times a lively social bustle reigns, and much noise. But this same spacious and inviting fine-sanded beach, this same border of pine grove and near, presiding mountains, continues all the way along the coast. No wonder then that some competition of a quiet kind should have sprung up further on. Torre di Venere—the tower that gave the town its name is gone long since, one looks for it in vain—is an offshoot of the larger resort, and for some years remained an idyll for the few, a refuge for more unworldly spirits. But the usual history of such places repeated itself: peace has had to retire further along the coast, to Marina Petriera and dear knows where else. We all know how the world at once seeks peace and puts her to flight—rushing upon her in the fond idea that they two will wed, and where she is, there it can be at home. It will even set up its Vanity Fair in a spot and be capable of thinking that peace is still by its side. Thus Torre—though its atmosphere so far is more modest and contemplative than that of Portoclemente—has been quite taken up, by both Italians and foreigners. It is no longer the thing to go to Portoclemente—though still so much the thing that it is as noisy and crowded as ever. One goes next door, so to speak, to Torre. So much more refined, even, and cheaper to boot. And the attractiveness of these qualities persists, though the qualities themselves long ago ceased to be evident. Torre has got a Grand Hotel. Numerous pensions have sprung up, some modest, some pretentious. The people who own or rent the villas and pinetas overlooking the sea no longer have it all their own way on the beach. In July and August it looks just like the beach at Portoclemente: it swarms with a screaming, squabbling, merry-making crowd, and the sun, blazing down like mad, peels the skin off their necks. Garish little flat-bottomed boats rock on the glittering blue, manned by children, whose mothers hover afar and fill the air with anxious cries of *Nino!* and *Sandro!* and *Bice!* and *Maria!* Pedlars step across the legs of recumbent sun-bathers, selling flowers and corals, oysters, lemonade, and *cornetti al burro,* and crying their wares in the breathy, full-throated southern voice.

Such was the scene that greeted our arrival in Torre: pleasant enough, but after all, we thought, we had come too soon. It was the middle of August, the Italian season was still at its height, scarcely the moment for strangers to learn to love the special charms of the place. What an afternoon crowd in the cafés on the front! For instance, in the Esquisito, where we sometimes sat and were served by Mario, that very Mario of whom I shall have presently to tell. It is well-nigh impossible to find a table; and the various orchestras contend together in the midst of one's conversation with bewildering effect. Of course, it is in the afternoon that people come over from Portoclemente. The excursion is a favorite one for the restless denizens of that pleasure resort, and a Fiat motor-bus plies to and fro, coating inch-thick with dust the oleander and laurel hedges along the high road—a notable if repulsive sight.

Yes, decidedly one should go to Torre in September, when the great public has left. Or else in May, before the water is warm enough to tempt the Southerner to bathe. Even in the before and after seasons Torre is not empty, but life is less national and more subdued. English, French, and German prevail under the tent-awnings and in the pension dining-rooms; whereas in August—in the Grand Hotel, at least, where, in default of private addresses, we had engaged rooms—the stranger finds the field so occupied by Florentine and Roman society that he feels quite isolated and even temporarily *déclassé*.

We had, rather to our annoyance, this experience on the evening we arrived, when we went in to dinner and were shown to our table by the waiter in charge. As a table, it had nothing against it, save that we had already fixed our eyes upon those on the veranda beyond, built out over the water, where little red-shaded lamps glowed—and there were still some tables empty, though it was as full as the dining-room within. The children went into raptures at the festive sight, and without more ado we announced our intention to take our meals by preference in the veranda. Our words, it appeared, were prompted by ignorance; for we were informed, with somewhat embarrassed politeness, that the cozy nook outside was reserved for the clients of the hotel: *ai nostri clienti*. Their clients? But we were their clients. We were not tourists or trippers, but boarders for a stay of some three or four weeks. However, we forbore to press for an explanation of the difference between the likes of us and that clientèle to whom it was vouchsafed to eat out there in the glow of the red lamps, and took our dinner by the prosaic common light of the dining-room chandelier—a thoroughly ordinary and monotonous hotel bill of fare, be it said. In Pensione Eleonora, a few steps landward, the table, as we were to discover, was much better.

And thither it was that we moved, three or four days later, before we had had time to settle in properly at the Grand Hotel. Not on account of the veranda and the lamps. The children, straightway on the best of terms with waiters and pages, absorbed in the joys of life on the beach, promptly forgot those colorful seductions. But now there arose, between ourselves and the veranda clientèle—or perhaps more correctly with the compliant management—one of those little unpleasantnesses which can quite spoil the pleasure of a holiday. Among the guests were some high Roman aristocracy, a Principe X and his family. These grand folk occupied rooms close to our own, and the Principessa, a great and a passionately maternal lady, was thrown into a panic by the vestiges of a whooping cough which our little ones had lately got over, but which now and then still faintly troubled the unshatterable slumbers of our youngest-born. The nature of this illness is not clear, leaving some play for the imagination. So we took no offense at our elegant neighbor for clinging to the widely held view that whooping cough is acoustically contagious and quite simply fearing lest her children yield to the bad example set by ours. In the fullness of her feminine self-confidence she protested to the management, which then, in the person of the proverbial frock-coated manager, hastened to represent to us, with many expressions of regret, that under the circumstances they were obliged to transfer us to the annex. We did our best to assure him that the disease was in its very last stages, that it was actually over, and presented no danger of infection to anybody. All that we gained was permission to bring the case before the hotel physician—not one chosen by us—by whose verdict we must then abide. We agreed, convinced that thus we should at once pacify the Princess and escape the trouble of moving. The doctor appeared, and behaved like a faithful and honest servant of science. He examined the child and gave his opinion: the disease was quite over, no danger of contagion was present. We drew a long breath and considered the incident closed—until the manager announced that despite the doctor's verdict it would still be necessary for us to give up our rooms and retire to the *dépendance*. Byzantinism like this outraged us. It is not likely that the Principessa was responsible for the willful breach of faith. Very likely the fawning management had not even dared to tell her what the physician said. Anyhow, we made it clear to his understanding that we preferred to leave the hotel altogether and at once—and packed our trunks. We could do so with a light heart, having already set up casual friendly relations with Casa Eleonora. We had noticed its pleasant exterior and formed the acquaintance of its proprietor, Signora Angiolieri, and her husband: she slender and black-haired, Tuscan in type, probably at the beginning of the thirties, with the dead ivory complexion of the southern woman, he quiet and bald and carefully dressed. They owned a larger establishment in Florence and presided only in summer and early autumn over the branch in Torre di Venere. But earlier, before her marriage, our new landlady had been companion, fellow-traveler, wardrobe mistress, yes, friend, of Eleonora Duse and manifestly regarded that period as the crown of her career. Even at our first visit she spoke of it with animation. Numerous photographs of the great actress, with affectionate inscriptions, were displayed about the drawing-room, and other souvenirs of their life together adorned the little tables and étagères. This cult of a so-interesting past was calculated, of course, to heighten the advantages of the signora's present business. Nevertheless our pleasure and interest were quite genuine as we were conducted through the house by its owner and listened to her sonorous and staccato Tuscan voice relating anecdotes of that immortal mistress, depicting her suffering saintliness, her genius, her profound delicacy of feeling.

Thither, then, we moved our effects, to the dismay of the staff of the Grand Hotel, who, like all Italians, were very good to children. Our new quarters were retired and pleasant, we were within easy reach of the sea through the avenue of young plane trees that ran down to the esplanade. In the clean, cool dining room Signora Angiolieri daily served the soup with her own hands, the service was attentive and good, the table capital. We even discovered some Viennese acquaintances, and enjoyed chatting with them after luncheon, in front of the house. They, in their turn, were the means of our finding others—in short, all seemed for the best, and we were heartily glad of the change we had made. Nothing was now wanting to a holiday of the most gratifying kind.

And yet no proper gratification ensued. Perhaps the stupid occasion of our change of quarters pursued us to the new ones we had found. Personally, I admit that I do not easily forget these collisions with ordinary humanity, the naive misuse of power, the injustice, the sycophantic corruption. I dwelt upon the incident too much, it irritated me in retrospect—quite futilely, of course, since such phenomena are only all too natural and all too much the rule. And we had not broken off relations with the Grand Hotel. The children were as friendly as ever there, the porter mended their toys, and we sometimes took tea in the garden. We even saw the Principessa. She would come out, with her firm and delicate tread, her lips emphatically corallined, to look after her children, playing under the supervision of their English governess. She did not dream that we were anywhere near, for so soon as she appeared in the offing we sternly forbade our little one even to clear his throat.

The heat—if I may bring it in evidence—was extreme. It was African. The power of the sun, directly one left the border of the indigo-blue wave, was so frightful, so relentless, that the mere thought of the few steps between the beach and luncheon was a burden, clad though one might be only in pajamas. Do you care for that sort of thing? Weeks on end? Yes, of course, it is proper to the south, it is classic weather, the sun of Homer, the climate wherein human culture came to flower—and all the rest of it. But after a while it is too much for me, I reach a point where I begin to find it dull. The burning void of the sky, day after day, weighs one down;

the high coloration, the enormous naiveté of the unrefracted light—
they do, I dare say, induce light-heartedness, a carefree mood born
of immunity from downpours and other meteorological caprices.
But slowly, slowly, there makes itself felt a lack: the deeper, more
complex needs of the northern soul remain unsatisfied. You are left
barren—even it may be, in time, a little contemptuous. True without
that stupid business of the whooping cough I might not have been
feeling these things. I was annoyed, very likely I wanted to feel them
and so half-unconsciously seized upon an idea lying ready to hand
to induce, or if not to induce, at least to justify and strengthen, my
attitude. Up to this point, then, if you like, let us grant some ill will
on our part. But the sea; and the mornings spent extended upon the
the fine sand in face of its eternal splendors—no, the sea could not
conceivably induce such feelings. Yet it was none the less true that,
despite all previous experience, we were not at home on the beach,
we were not happy.

It was too soon, too soon. The beach, as I have said, was still in
the hands of a middle-class native. It is a pleasing breed to look at,
and among the young we saw much shapeliness and charm. Still,
we were necessarily surrounded by a great deal of very average
humanity—a middle-class mob, which, you will admit, is not more
charming under this sun than under one's own native sky. The voices
these women have! It was sometimes hard to believe that we were in
the land which is the western cradle of the art of song. *"Fuggièro!"* I
can still hear that cry, as for twenty mornings long I heard it close
behind me, breathy, full-throated, hideously stressed, with a harsh
open *e*, uttered in accents of mechanical despair. *Fuggièro! Rispondi
almeno!"* Answer when I call you! The *sp* in *rispondi* was pronounced like *shp*, as Germans pronounce it; and this, on top of what
I felt already, vexed my sensitive soul. The cry was addressed to a
repulsive youngster whose sunburn had made disgusting raw sores
on his shoulders. He outdid anything I have ever seen for ill-
breeding, refractoriness, and temper and was a great coward to boot,
putting the whole beach in an uproar, one day, because of his outrageous sensitiveness to the slightest pain. A sand-crab had pinched
his toe in the water, and the minute injury made him set up a cry
of heroic proportions—the shout of an antique hero in his agony—
that pierced one to the marrow and called up visions of some frightful tragedy. Evidently he considered himself not only wounded, but
poisoned as well; he crawled out on the sand and lay in apparently
intolerable anguish, groaning *"Ohi!"* and *Ohimè!"* and threshing

about with arms and legs to ward off his mother's tragic appeals and the questions of the bystanders. An audience gathered round. A doctor was fetched—the same who had pronounced objective judgment on our whooping cough—and here again acquitted himself like a man of science. Good-naturedly he reassured the boy, telling him that he was not hurt at all, he should simply go into the water again to relieve the smart. Instead of which, Fuggièro was borne off the beach, followed by a concourse of people. But he did not fail to appear next morning, nor did he leave off spoiling our children's sand-castles. Of course, always by accident. In short, a perfect terror.

And this twelve-year-old lad was prominent among the influences that, imperceptibly at first, combined to spoil our holiday and render it unwholesome. Somehow or other, there was a stiffness, a lack of innocent enjoyment. These people stood on their dignity—just why, and in what spirit, it was not easy at first to tell. They displayed much self-respectingness; toward each other and toward the foreigner their bearing was that of a person newly conscious of a sense of honor. And wherefore? Gradually we realized the political implications and understood that we were in the presence of a national ideal. The beach, in fact, was alive with patriotic children—a phenomenon as unnatural as it was depressing. Children are a human species and a society apart, a nation of their own, so to speak. On the basis of their common form of life, they find each other out with the greatest ease, no matter how different their small vocabularies. Ours soon played with natives and foreigners alike. Yet they were plainly both puzzled and disappointed at times. There were wounded sensibilities, displays of assertiveness—or rather hardly assertiveness, for it was too self-conscious and too didactic to deserve the name. There were quarrels over flags, disputes about authority and precedence. Grownups joined in, not so much to pacify as to render judgment and enunciate principles. Phrases were dropped about the greatness and dignity of Italy, solemn phrases that spoiled the fun. We saw our two little ones retreat, puzzled and hurt, and were put to it to explain the situation. These people, we told them, were just passing through a certain stage, something rather like an illness, perhaps; not very pleasant, but probably unavoidable.

We had only our own carelessness to thank that we came to blows in the end with this "stage"—which, after all, we had seen and sized up long before now. Yes, it came to another "cross-purposes," so evidently the earlier ones had not been sheer accident. In a word, we became an offense to the public morals. Our small daughter—eight years old, but in physical development a good year younger and thin as a chicken—had had a good long bathe and gone playing in the warm sun in her wet costume. We told her that she might take off her bathing-suit, which was stiff with sand, rinse it in the sea, and put it on again, after which she must take care to keep it cleaner. Off goes the costume and she runs down naked to the sea, rinses her little jersey, and comes back. Ought we to have foreseen the outburst of anger and resentment which her conduct, and thus our conduct, called forth? Without delivering a homily on the subject, I may say that in the last decade our attitude toward the nude body and our feelings regarding it have undergone, all over the world, a fundamental change. There are things we "never think about" any more, and among them is the freedom we had permitted to this by no means provocative little childish body. But in these parts it was taken as a challenge. The patriotic children hooted. Fuggièro whistled on his fingers. The sudden buzz of conversation among the grown people in our neighborhood boded no good. A gentleman in city togs, with a not very apropos bowler hat on the back of his head, was assuring his outraged womenfolk that he proposed to take punitive measures; he stepped up to us, and a philippic descended on our unworthy heads, in which all the emotionalism of the sense-loving south spoke in the service of morality and discipline. The offense against decency of which we had been guilty was, he said, the more to be condemned because it was also a gross ingratitude and an insulting breach of his country's hospitality. We had criminally injured not only the letter and spirit of the public bathing regulations, but also the honor of Italy; he, the gentleman in the city togs, knew how to defend that honor and proposed to see to it that our offense against the national dignity should not go unpunished.

We did our best, bowing respectfully, to give ear to this eloquence. To contradict the man, overheated as he was, would probably be to fall from one error into another. On the tips of our tongues we had various answers: as, that the word *hospitality,* in its strictest sense, was not quite the right one, taking all the circumstances into consideration. We were not literally the guests of Italy, but of Signora Angiolieri, who had assumed the role of dispenser of hospitality some years ago on laying down that of familiar friend to Eleonora Duse. We longed to say that surely this beautiful country had not sunk so low as to be reduced to a state of hypersensitive prudishness.

But we confined ourselves to assuring the gentleman that any lack of respect, any provocation on our parts, had been the furthest from our thoughts. And as a mitigating circumstance we pointed out the tender age and physical slightness of the little culprit. In vain. Our protests were waved away, he did not believe in them; our defense would not hold water. We must be made an example of. The authorities were notified, by telephone, I believe, and their representatives appeared on the beach. He said the case was *"molto grave."* We had to go with him to the Municipio up in the Piazza, where a higher official confirmed the previous verdict of *"molto grave,"* launched into a stream of the usual didactic phrases—the selfsame tune and words as the man in the bowler hat—and levied a fine and ransom of fifty lire. We felt that the adventure must willy-nilly be worth to us this much of a contribution to the economy of the Italian government; paid, and left. Ought we not at this point to have left Torre as well?

If we only had! We should thus have escaped that fatal Cipolla. But circumstances combined to prevent us from making up our minds to a change. A certain poet says that it is indolence that makes us endure uncomfortable situations. The *aperçu* may serve as an explanation for our inaction. Anyhow, one dislikes voiding the field immediately upon such an event. Especially if sympathy from other quarters encourages one to defy it. And in the Villa Eleonora they pronounced as with one voice upon the injustice of our punishment. Some Italian after-dinner acquaintances found that the episode put their country in a very bad light, and proposed taking the man in the bowler hat to task, as one fellow-citizen to another. But the next day he and his party had vanished from the beach. Not on our account, of course. Though it might be that the consciousness of his impending departure had added energy to his rebuke; in any case his going was a relief. And, furthermore, we stayed because our stay had by now become remarkable in our own eyes, which is worth something in itself, quite apart from the comfort or discomfort involved. Shall we strike sail, avoid a certain experience so soon as it seems not expressly calculated to increase our enjoyment or our self-esteem? Shall we go away whenever life looks like turning in the slightest uncanny, or not quite normal, or even rather painful and mortifying? No, surely not. Rather stay and look matters in the face, brave them out; perhaps precisely in so doing lies a lesson for us to learn. We stayed on and reaped as the awful reward of our constancy the unholy and staggering experience with Cipolla.

I have not mentioned that the after season had begun, almost on the very day we were disciplined by the city authorities. The worshipful gentleman in the bowler hat, our denouncer, was not the only person to leave the resort. There was a regular exodus, on every hand you saw luggage-carts on their way to the station. The beach denationalized itself. Life in Torre, in the cafés and the pinetas, became more homelike and more European. Very likely we might even have eaten at a table in the glass veranda, but we refrained, being content at Signora Angiolieri's—as content, that is, as our evil star would let us be. But at the same time with this turn for the better came a change in the weather: almost to an hour it showed itself in harmony with the holiday calendar of the general public. The sky was overcast; not that it grew any cooler, but the unclouded heat of the entire eighteen days since our arrival, and probably long before that, gave place to a stifling sirocco air, while from time to time a little ineffectual rain sprinkled the velvety surface of the beach. Add to which, that two-thirds of our intended stay at Torre had passed. The colorless, lazy sea, with sluggish jellyfish floating in its shallows, was at least a change. And it would have been silly to feel retrospective longings after a sun that had caused us so many sighs when it burned down in all its arrogant power.

At this juncture, then, it was that Cipolla announced himself. Cavaliere Cipolla he was called on the posters that appeared one day stuck up everywhere, even in the dining room of Pensione Eleonora. A traveling virtuoso, an entertainer, *"forzatore, illusionista, prestidigatore,"* as he called himself, who proposed to wait upon the highly respectable population of Torre di Venere with a display of extraordinary phenomena of a mysterious and staggering kind. A conjuror! The bare announcement was enough to turn our children's heads. They had never seen anything of the sort, and now our present holiday was to afford them this new excitement. From that moment on they besieged us with prayers to take tickets for the performance. We had doubts, from the first, on the score of the lateness of the hour, nine o'clock; but gave way, in the idea that we might see a little of what Cipolla had to offer, probably no great matter, and then go home. Besides, of course, the children could sleep late next day. We bought four tickets of Signora Angiolieri herself, she having taken a number of the stalls on commission to sell them to her guests. She could not vouch for the man's performance, and we had no great expectations. But we were conscious of a need for diversion, and the children's violent curiosity proved catching.

The Cavaliere's performance was to take place in a hall where during the season there had been a cinema with a weekly program. We had never been there. You reached it by following the main street under the wall of the *"palazzo,"* a ruin with a FOR SALE sign, that suggested a castle and had obviously been built in lordlier days. In the same street were the chemist, the hairdresser, and all the better shops; it led, so to speak, from the feudal past the bourgeois into the proletarian, for it ended off between two rows of poor fishing-huts, where old women sat mending nets before the doors. And here, among the proletariat, was the hall, not much more, actually than a wooden shed, though a large one, with a turreted entrance, plastered on either side with layers of gay placards. Some while after dinner, then, on the appointed evening, we wended our way thither in the dark, the children dressed in their best and blissful with the sense of so much irregularity. It was sultry, as it had been for days; there was heat lightning now and then, and a little rain; we proceeded under umbrellas. It took us a quarter of an hour.

Our tickets were collected at the entrance, our places we had to find ourselves. They were in the third row left, and as we sat down we saw that, late though the hour was for the performance, it was to be interpreted with even more laxity. Only very slowly did an audience—who seemed to be relied upon to come late—begin to fill the stalls. These comprised the whole auditorium; there were no boxes. This tardiness gave us some concern. The children's cheeks were already flushed as much with fatigue as with excitement. But even when we entered, the standing-room at the back and in the side aisles was already well occupied. There stood the manhood of Torre di Venere, all and sundry, fisherfolk, rough-and-ready youths with bare forearms crossed over their striped jerseys. We were well pleased with the presence of this native assemblage, which always adds color and animation to occasions like the present; and the children were frankly delighted. For they had friends among these people—acquaintances picked up on afternoon strolls to the further ends of the beach. We would be turning homeward, at the hour when the sun dropped into the sea, spent with the huge effort it had made and gilding with reddish gold the oncoming surf; and we would come upon bare-legged fisherfolk standing in rows, bracing and hauling with long-drawn cries as they drew in the nets and harvested in dripping baskets their catch, often so scanty, of *frutto di mare*. The children looked on, helped to pull, brought out their little stock of Italian words, made friends. So now they exchanged nods with the "standing-room" clientèle; there was Guiscardo, there Antonio, they knew them by name and waved and called across in half-whispers, getting answering nods and smiles that displayed rows of healthy white teeth. Look, there is even Mario, Mario from the Esquisito, who brings us the chocolate. He wants to see the conjuror, too, and he must have come early, for he is almost in front; but he does not see us, he is not paying attention; that is a way he has, even though he is a waiter. So we wave instead to the man who lets out the little boats on the beach; he is there too, standing at the back.

It had got to a quarter past nine, it got to almost half past. It was natural that we should be nervous. When would the children get to bed? It had been a mistake to bring them, for now it would be very hard to suggest breaking off their enjoyment before it had got well under way. The stalls had filled in time; all Torre, apparently was there: the guests of the Grand Hotel, the guests of the Villa Eleonora, familiar faces from the beach. We heard English and German and the sort of French that Rumanians speak with Italians. Madame Angiolieri herself sat two rows behind us, with her quiet, bald-headed spouse, who kept stroking his moustache with the two middle fingers of his right hand. Everybody had come late, but nobody too late. Cipolla made us wait for him.

He made us wait. That is probably the way to put it. He heightened the suspense by his delay in appearing. And we could see the point of this, too—only not when it was carried to extremes. Toward half past nine the audience began to clap—an amiable way of expressing justifiable impatience, evincing as it does an eagerness to applaud. For the little ones, this was a joy in itself—all children love to clap. From the popular sphere came loud cries of *"Pronti!" Cominciamo!"* And lo, it seemed now as easy to begin as before it had been hard. A gong sounded, greeted by the standing rows with a many voiced "Ah-h!" and the curtains parted. They revealed a platform furnished more like a schoolroom than like the theater of a conjuring performance—largely because of the blackboard in the left foreground. There was a common yellow hat stand, a few ordinary straw-bottomed chairs, and farther back a little round table holding a water carafe and glass, also a tray with a liqueur glass and a flask of pale yellow liquid. We had still a few seconds of time to let these things sink in. Then, with no darkening of the house, Cavaliere Cipolla made his entry.

He came forward with a rapid step that expressed his eagerness to appear before his public and gave rise to the illusion that he had already come a long way to put himself at their service—whereas, of course, he had only been standing in the wings. His costume supported the fiction. A man of an age hard to determine, but by no means young; with a sharp, ravaged face, piercing eyes, compressed lips, small black waxed mustache, and a so-called imperial in the curve between mouth and chin. He was dressed for the street with a sort of complicated evening elegance, in a wide black pelerine with velvet collar and satin lining; which, in the hampered state of his arms, he held together in front with his white-gloved hands. He had a white scarf round his neck; a top hat with a curving brim sat far back on his head. Perhaps more than anywhere else the eighteenth century is still alive in Italy, and with it the charlatan and mountebank type so characteristic of the period. Only there, at any rate, does one still encounter really well-preserved specimens. Cipolla had in his whole appearance much of the historic type; his very clothes helped to conjure up the traditional figure with its blatantly, fantastically foppish air. His pretentious costume sat upon him, or rather hung upon him, most curiously, being in one place drawn too tight, in another a mass of awkward folds. There was something not quite in order about his figure, both front and back—that was plain later on. But I must emphasize the fact that there was not a trace of personal jocularity or clownishness in his pose, manner, or behavior. On the contrary, there was complete seriousness, an absence of any humorous appeal; occasionally even a cross-grained pride, along with that curious, self-satisfied air so characteristic of the deformed. None of all this, however, prevented his appearance from being greeted with laughter from more than one quarter of the hall.

All the eagerness had left his manner. The swift entry had been merely an expression of energy, not of zeal. Standing at the footlights he negligently drew off his gloves, to display long yellow hands, one of them adorned with a seal ring with a lapis lazuli in a high setting. As he stood there, his small hard eyes, with flabby pouches beneath them, roved appraisingly about the hall, not quickly, rather in a considered examination, pausing here and there upon a face with his lips clipped together, not speaking a word. Then with a display of skill as surprising as it was casual, he rolled his gloves into a ball and tossed them across a considerable distance into the glass on the table. Next from an inner pocket he drew forth a packet of cigarettes; you could see by the wrapper that they were the cheapest sort the government sells. With his fingertips he pulled out a cigarette and lighted it, without looking, from a quick-firing benzine lighter. He drew the smoke deep into his lungs and let it out again, tapping his foot, with both lips drawn in an arrogant grimace and the gray smoke streaming out between broken and saw-edged teeth.

With a keenness equal to his own his audience eyed him. The youths at the rear scowled as they peered at this cocksure creature to search out his secret weaknesses. He betrayed none. In fetching out and putting back the cigarettes his clothes got in his way. He had to turn back his pelerine, and in so doing revealed a riding whip with a silver claw handle that hung by a leather thong from his left forearm and looked decidedly out of place. You could see that he had on not evening clothes but a frock coat, and under this, as he lifted it to get at his pocket, could be seen a striped sash worn about the body. Somebody behind me whispered that this sash went with his title of Cavaliere. I give the information for what it may be worth—personally, I never heard that the title carried such insignia with it. Perhaps the sash was sheer pose, like the way he stood there, without a word, casually and arrogantly puffing smoke into his audience's face.

People laughed, as I said. The merriment had become almost general when somebody in the "standing seats," in a loud, dry voice, remarked: *"Buona sera."*

Cipolla cocked his head. "Who was that?" asked he, as though he had been dared. "Who was that just spoke? Well? First so bold and now so modest? *Paura,* eh?" He spoke with a rather high, asthmatic voice, which yet had a metallic quality. He waited.

"That was me," a youth at the rear broke into the stillness, seeing himself thus challenged. He was not far from us, a handsome fellow in a woollen shirt, with his coat hanging over one shoulder. He wore his surly, wiry hair in a high, disheveled mop, the style affected by the youth of the awakened Fatherland; it gave him an African appearance that rather spoiled his looks. *"Bè!* That was me. It was your business to say it first, but I was trying to be friendly."

More laughter. The chap had a tongue in his head. *"Ha sciolto la scilinguágnolo,"* I heard near me. After all, the retort was deserved.

"Ah, bravo!" answered Cipolla. "I like you, *giovanotto.* Trust me, I've had my eye on you for some time. People like you are just in my line. I can use them. And you are the pick of the lot, that's plain to see. You do what you like. Or is it possible you have ever not done what you liked—or even, maybe, what you didn't like? What somebody else liked, in short? Hark ye, my friend, that might be a pleasant change for you, to divide up the willing and the doing and stop tackling both jobs at once. Division of labor, *sistema americano, sa!* For instance, suppose you were to show your tongue to this select and honorable audience here—your whole tongue, right down to the roots?"

"No, I won't," said the youth, hostilely. "Sticking out your tongue shows a bad bringing-up."

"Nothing of the sort," retorted Cipolla. "You would only be *doing* it. With all due respect to your bringing-up, I suggest that before I count ten, you will perform a right turn and stick out your tongue at the company here farther than you knew yourself that you could stick it out."

He gazed at the youth, and his piercing eyes seemed to sink deeper into their sockets. *"Uno!"* said he. He had let his riding whip slide down his arm and made it whistle once through the air. The boy faced about and put out his tongue, so long, so extendedly, that you could see it was the very uttermost in tongue which he had to offer. Then turned back, stony-faced, to his former position.

"That was me," mocked Cipolla, with a jerk of his head toward the youth. *"Bè!* That was me." Leaving the audience to enjoy its sensations, he turned toward the little round table, lifted the bottle, poured out a small glass of what was obviously cognac, and tipped it up with a practiced hand.

The children laughed with all their hearts. They had understood practically nothing of what had been said, but it pleased them hugely that something so funny should happen, straightaway, between that queer man up there and somebody out of the audience. They had no preconception of what an "evening" would be like and were quite ready to find this a priceless beginning. As for us, we exchanged a glance and I remember that involuntarily I made with my lips the sound that Cipolla's whip had made when it cut the air. For the rest, it was plain that people did not know what to make of a preposterous beginning like this to a sleight-of-hand performance. They could not see why the *giovanotto*, who after all in a way had been their spokesman, should suddenly have turned on them to vent his incivility. They felt that he had behaved like a silly ass and withdrew their countenances from him in favor of the artist, who now came back from his refreshment table and addressed them as follows:

"Ladies and gentlemen," said he, in his wheezing, metallic voice, "you saw just now that I was rather sensitive on the score of the rebuke this hopeful young linguist saw fit to give me"—"*questo linguista di belle speranze*" was what he said, and we all laughed at the pun. "I am a man who sets some store by himself, you may take it from me. And I see no point in being wished a good evening unless it is done courteously and in all seriousness. For anything else there is no occasion. When a man wishes me a good evening he wishes himself one, for the audience will have one only if I do. So this lady-killer of Torre di Venere" (another thrust) "did well to testify that I have one tonight and that I can dispense with any wishes of his in the matter. I can boast of having good evenings almost without exception. One not so good does come my way now and again, but very seldom. My calling is hard and my health not of the best. I have a little physical defect which prevented me from doing my bit in the war for the greater glory of the Fatherland. It is perforce with my mental and spiritual parts that I conquer life—which after all only means conquering oneself. And I flatter myself that my achievements have aroused interest and respect among the educated public. The leading newspapers have lauded me, the *Corriere della Sera* did me the courtesy of calling me a phenomenon, and in Rome the brother of *il Duce* honored me by his presence at one of my evenings. I should not have thought that in a relatively less important place" (laughter here, at the expense of poor little Torre) "I should have to give up the small personal habits which brilliant and elevated audiences had been ready to overlook. Nor did I think I had to stand being heckled by a person who seems to have been rather spoiled by the favors of the fair sex." All this of course at the expense of the youth whom Cipolla never tired of presenting in the guise of *donnaiuolo* and rustic Don Juan. His persistent thin-skinnedness and animosity were in striking contrast to the self-confidence and the worldly success of which he boasted. One might have assumed that the *giovanotto* was merely the chosen butt of Cipolla's customary professional sallies, had not the very pointed witticisms betrayed a genuine antagonism. No one looking at the physical parts of the two men need have been at a loss for the explanation, even if the deformed man had not constantly played on the other's supposed success with the fair sex. "Well," Cipolla went on, "before beginning our entertainment this evening, perhaps you will permit me to make myself comfortable."

And he went toward the hat stand to take off his things.

"*Parla benissimo*," asserted somebody in our neighborhood. So far, the man had done nothing; but what he had said was accepted as an achievement, by means of that he had made an impression. Among southern peoples speech is a constituent part of the pleasure of living, it enjoys far livelier social esteem than in the north. That national cement, the mother tongue, is paid symbolic honors down here, and there is something blithely symbolical in the pleasure people take in their respect for its forms and phonetics. They enjoy speaking, they enjoy listening; and they listen with discrimination. For the way a man speaks serves as a measure of his personal rank; carelessness and clumsiness are greeted with scorn, elegance and mastery are rewarded with social éclat. Wherefore the small man too, where it is a question of getting his effect, chooses his phrase nicely and turns it with care. On this count, then, at least, Cipolla had won his audience; though he by no means belonged to the class of men which the Italian, in a singular mixture of moral and æsthetic judgments, labels *simpatico*.

After removing his hat, scarf, and mantle he came to the front of the stage, settling his coat, pulling down his cuffs with their large cuff-buttons, adjusting his absurd sash. He had very ugly hair; the top of his head, that is, was almost bald, while a narrow, black varnished frizz of curls ran from front to back as though stuck on; the side hair, likewise blackened, was brushed forward to the corners of the eyes—it was, in short, the hair dressing of an old-fashioned circus director, fantastic, but entirely suited to his outmoded personal type and worn with so much assurance as to take the edge off the public's sense of humor. The little physical defect of which he had warned us was now all too visible, though the nature of it was even now not very clear; the chest was too high, as is usual in such cases, but the corresponding malformation of the back did not sit between the shoulders, it took the form of a sort of hips or buttocks hump, which did not indeed hinder his movements but gave him a grotesque and dipping stride at every step he took. However, by mentioning his deformity beforehand he had broken the shock of it, and a delicate propriety of feeling appeared to reign throughout the hall.

"At your service," said Cipolla. "With your kind permission, we will begin the evening with some arithmetical tests."

Arithmetic? That did not sound much like sleight-of-hand. We began to have our suspicions that the man was sailing under a false flag, only we did not yet know which was the right one. I felt sorry on the children's account; but for the moment they were content simply to be there.

The numerical test which Cipolla now introduced was as simple as it was baffling. He began by fastening a piece of paper to the upper right-hand corner of the blackboard; then lifting it up, he wrote something underneath. He talked all the while, relieving the dryness of his offering by a constant flow of words, and showed himself a practiced speaker, never at a loss for conversational turns of phrase. It was in keeping with the nature of his performance, and at the same time vastly entertained the children, that he went on to eliminate the gap between stage and audience, which had already been bridged over by the curious skirmish with the fisher lad; he had representatives from the audience mount the stage, and himself descended the wooden steps to seek personal contact with his public. And again, with individuals, he fell into his former taunting tone. I do not know how far that was a deliberate feature of his system; he preserved a serious, even a peevish air, but his audience, at least the more popular section, seemed convinced that that was all part of the game. So then, after he had written something and covered the writing by the paper, he desired that two persons should come up on the platform and help to perform the calculations. They would not be difficult, even for people not clever at figures. As usual, nobody volunteered, and Cipolla took care not to molest the more select portion of his audience. He kept to the populace. Turning to two sturdy young louts standing behind us, he beckoned them to the front, encouraging and scolding by turns. They should not stand there gaping, he said, unwilling to oblige the company. Actually he got them in motion; with clumsy tread they came down the middle aisle, climbed the steps, and stood in front of the blackboard, grinning sheepishly at their comrades' shouts and applause. Cipolla joked with them for a few minutes, praised their heroic firmness of limb and the size of their hands, so well calculated to do this service for the public. Then he handed one of them the chalk and told him to write down the numbers as they were called out. But now the creature declared that he could not write! *"Non so scrivere,"* said he in his gruff voice, and his companion added that neither did he.

God knows whether they told the truth or whether they wanted to make game of Cipolla. Anyhow, the latter was far from sharing the general merriment which their confession aroused. He was insulted and disgusted. He sat there on a straw bottomed chair in the center of the stage with his legs crossed, smoking a fresh cigarette out of his cheap packet; obviously it tasted the better for the cognac he had indulged in while the yokels were stumping up the steps. Again he inhaled the smoke and let it stream out between curling lips. Swinging his leg, with his gaze sternly averted from the two shamelessly chuckling creatures and from the audience as well, he stared into space as one who withdraws himself and his dignity from the contemplation of an utterly despicable phenomenon.

"Scandalous," said he, in a sort of icy snarl. "Go back to your places! In Italy everybody can write—in all her greatness there is no room for ignorance and unenlightenment. To accuse her of them, in the hearing of this international company, is a cheap joke, in which you yourselves cut a very poor figure and humiliate the government and the whole country as well. If it is true that Torre di Venere is indeed the last refuge of such ignorance, then I must blush to have visited the place—being, as I already was, aware of its inferiority to Rome in more than one respect—"

Here Cipolla was interrupted by the youth with the Nubian coiffure and his jacket across his shoulder. His fighting spirit, as we now saw, had only abdicated temporarily, and he now flung himself into the breach in defense of his native heath. "That will do," he said loudly. "That's enough jokes about Torre. We all come from the place and we won't stand strangers making fun of it. These two chaps are our friends. Maybe they are no scholars, but even so they may be straighter than some folks in the room who are so free with their boasts about Rome, though they did not build it either."

That was capital. The young man had certainly cut his eye teeth. And this sort of spectacle was good fun, even though it still further delayed the regular performance. It is always fascinating to listen to an altercation. Some people it simply amuses, they take a sort of killjoy pleasure in not being principals. Others feel upset and uneasy, and my sympathies are with these latter, although on the present occasion I was under the impression that all this was part of the show—the analphabetic yokels no less than the *giovanotto* with the jacket. The children listened well pleased. They understood not at all, but the sound of the voices made them hold their breath. So this was a "magic evening"—at least it was the kind they have in Italy. They expressly found it "lovely." Cipolla had stood up and with two of his scooping strides was at the footlights.

"Well, well, see who's here!" said he with grim cordiality. "An old acquaintance! A young man with his heart at the end of his tongue" (he used the word *linguaccia,* which means a coated tongue, and gave rise to much hilarity). "That will do, my friends," he turned to the yokels. "I do not need you now, I have business with this deserving young man here, *con questo torregiano di Venere,* this tower of Venus, who no doubt expects the gratitude of the fair as a reward for his prowess—"

"*Ah, non scherziamo!* We're talking earnest," cried out the youth. His eyes flashed, and he actually made as though to pull off his jacket and proceed to direct methods of settlement.

Cipolla did not take him too seriously. We had exchanged apprehensive glances; but he was dealing with a fellow countryman and had his native soil beneath his feet. He kept quite cool and showed complete mastery of the situation. He looked at his audience, smiled, and made a sideways motion of the head toward the young cockerel as though calling the public to witness how the man's bumptiousness only served to betray the simplicity of his mind. And then, for the second time, something strange happened, which set Cipolla's calm superiority in an uncanny light, and in some mysterious and irritating way turned all the explosiveness latent in the air into matter for laughter.

Cipolla drew still nearer to the fellow, looking him in the eye with a peculiar gaze. He even came halfway down the steps that led into the auditorium on our left, so that he stood directly in front of the troublemaker, on slightly higher ground. The riding whip hung from his arm.

"My son, you do not feel much like joking," he said. "It is only too natural, for anyone can see that you are not feeling too well. Even your tongue, which leaves something to be desired on the score of cleanliness, indicates acute disorder of the gastric system. An evening entertainment is no place for people in your state; you yourself, I can tell, were of several minds whether you would not do better to put on a flannel bandage and go to bed. It was not good judgment to drink so much of that very sour white wine this afternoon. Now you have such a colic you would like to double up with the pain. Go ahead, don't be embarrassed. There is a distinct relief that comes from bending over, in cases of intestinal cramp."

He spoke thus, word for word, with quiet impressiveness and a kind of stern sympathy, and his eyes, plunged the while deep in the young man's, seemed to grow very tired and at the same time burning above their enlarged tear-ducts—they were the strangest eyes; you could tell that not manly pride alone was preventing the young adversary from withdrawing his gaze. And presently, indeed, all trace of its former arrogance was gone from the bronzed young face. He looked open mouthed at the Cavaliere and the open mouth was drawn in a rueful smile.

"Double over," repeated Cipolla. "What else can you do? With a colic like that you *must* bend. Surely you will not struggle against the performance of a perfectly natural action just because somebody suggests it to you?"

Slowly the youth lifted his forearms, folded and squeezed them across his body; it turned a little sideways, then bent, lower and lower, the feet shifted, the knees turned inward, until he had become a picture of writhing pain, until he all but groveled upon the ground. Cipolla let him stand for some seconds thus, then made a short cut through the air with his whip and went with his scooping stride back to the little table, where he poured himself out a cognac.

"*Il boit beaucoup,*" asserted a lady behind us. Was that the only thing that struck her? We could not tell how far the audience grasped the situation. The fellow was standing upright again, with a sheepish grin—he looked as though he scarcely knew how it had all happened. The scene had been followed with tense interest and applauded at the end; there were shouts of "*Bravo, Cipolla!*" and "*Bravo, giovanotto!*" Apparently the issue of the duel was not looked upon as a personal defeat for the young man. Rather the audience encouraged him as one does an actor who succeeds in an unsympathetic role. Certainly his way of screwing himself up with cramp had been highly picturesque, its appeal was directly calculated to impress the gallery—in short, a fine dramatic performance. But I am not sure how far the audience were moved by that natural tactfulness in which the south excels, or how far it penetrated into the nature of what was going on.

The Cavaliere, refreshed, had lighted another cigarette. The numerical tests might now proceed. A young man was easily found in the back row who was willing to write down on the blackboard the numbers as they were dictated to him. Him too we knew; the whole entertainment had taken on an intimate character through our acquaintance with so many of the actors. This was the man who worked at the greengrocer's in the main street; he had served us several times, with neatness and dispatch. He wielded the chalk with clerkly confidence, while Cipolla descended to our level and walked with his deformed gait through the audience, collecting numbers as they were given, in two, three, and four places, and calling them out to the grocer's assistant, who wrote them down in a column. In all this, everything on both sides was calculated to amuse, with its jokes and its oratorical asides. The artist could not fail to hit on foreigners, who were not ready with their figures, and with them he was elaborately patient and chivalrous, to the great amusement of the natives, whom he reduced to confusion in their turn, by making them translate numbers that were given in English or French. Some people gave dates concerned with great events in Italian history. Cipolla took them up at once and made patriotic comments. Somebody shouted "Number one!" The Cavaliere, incensed at this as at every attempt to make game of him, retorted over his shoulder that he could not take less than two-place figures. Whereupon another joker cried out "Number two!" and was greeted with the applause and laughter which every reference to natural functions is sure to win among southerners.

When fifteen numbers stood in a long straggling row on the board, Cipolla called for a general adding match. Ready reckoners might add in their heads, but pencil and paper were not forbidden. Cipolla, while the work went on, sat on his chair near the blackboard, smoked and grimaced, with the complacent, pompous air cripples so often have. The five-place addition was soon done. Somebody announced the answer, somebody else confirmed it, a third had arrived at a slightly different result, but the fourth agreed with the first and second. Cipolla got up, tapped some ash from his coat, and lifted the paper at the upper righthand corner of the board to display the writing. The correct answer, a sum close to a million, stood there; he had written it down beforehand.

Astonishment, and loud applause. The children were overwhelmed. How had he done that, they wanted to know. We told them it was a trick, not easily explainable offhand. In short, the man was a conjuror. This was what a sleight-of-hand evening was like, so now they knew. First the fisherman had cramp, and then the right answer was written down beforehand—it was all simply glorious, and we saw with dismay that despite the hot eyes and the hand of the clock at almost half past ten, it would be very hard to get them away. There would be tears. And yet it was plain that this magician did not "magick"—at least not in the accepted sense, of manual dexterity—and that the entertainment was not at all suitable for children. Again, I do not know, either, what the audience really thought. Obviously there was grave doubt whether its answers had been given of "free choice"; here and there an individual might have answered of his own motion, but on the whole Cipolla certainly selected his people and thus kept the whole procedure in his own hands and directed it toward the given result. Even so, one had to admire the quickness of his calculations, however much one felt disinclined to admire anything else about the performance. Then his patriotism, his irritable sense of dignity—the Cavaliere's own countrymen might feel in their element with all that and continue in a laughing mood; but the combination certainly gave us outsiders food for thought.

Cipolla himself saw to it—though without giving them a name—that the nature of his powers should be clear beyond a doubt to even the least-instructed person. He alluded to them, of course, in his talk—and he talked without stopping—but only in vague, boastful, self-advertising phrases. He went on awhile with experiments on the same lines as the first, merely making them more complicated by introducing operations in multiplying, subtracting, and dividing; then he simplified them to the last degree in order to bring out the method. He simply had numbers "guessed" which were previously written under the paper; and the guess was nearly always right. One guesser admitted that he had had in mind to give a certain number, when Cipolla's whip went whistling through the air, and a quite different one slipped out, which proved to be the "right" one. Cipolla's shoulders shook. He pretended admiration for the powers of the people questioned. But in all his compliments there was something fleeting and derogatory; the victims could scarcely have relished them much, although they smiled, and although they might easily have set down some part of the applause to their own credit. Moreover, I had not the impression that the artist was popular with his public. A certain ill will and reluctance were in the air, but courtesy kept such feelings in check, as did Cipolla's competency and his stern self-confidence. Even the riding whip, I think, did much to keep rebellion from becoming overt.

From tricks with numbers he passed to tricks with cards. There were two packs, which he drew out of his pockets, and so much I still remember, that the basis of the tricks he played with them was as follows: from the first pack he drew three cards and thrust them without looking at them inside his coat. Another person then drew three out of the second pack, and these turned out to be the same as the first three—not invariably all the three, for it did happen that only two were the same. But in the majority of cases Cipolla triumphed, showing his three cards with a little bow in acknowledgment of the applause with which his audience conceded his possession of strange powers—strange whether for good or evil. A young man in the front row, to our right, an Italian, with proud, finely chiseled features, rose up and said that he intended to assert his own will in his choice and consciously to resist any influence, of whatever sort. Under these circumstances, what did Cipolla think would be the result? "You will," answered the Cavaliere, "make my task somewhat more difficult thereby. As for the result, your resistance will not alter it in the least. Freedom exists, and also the will exists; but freedom of the will does not exist, for a will that aims at its own freedom aims at the unknown. You are free to draw or not to draw. But if you draw, you will draw the right cards—the more certainly, the more willfully obstinate your behavior."

One must admit that he could not have chosen his words better, to trouble the waters and confuse the mind. The refractory youth hesitated before drawing. Then he pulled out a card and at once demanded to see if it was among the chosen three. "But why?" queried Cipolla. "Why do things by halves?" Then, as the other defiantly insisted, *"E servito,"* said the juggler, with a gesture of exaggerated servility; and held out the three cards fanwise, without looking at them himself. The lefthand card was the one drawn.

Amid general applause, the apostle of freedom sat down. How far Cipolla employed small tricks and manual dexterity to help out his natural talents, the deuce only knew. But even without them the result would have been the same: the curiosity of the entire audience was unbounded and universal, everybody both enjoyed the amazing character of the entertainment and unanimously conceded the professional skill of the performer. *"Lavora bene,"* we heard, here and there in our neighborhood; it signified the triumph of objective judgment over antipathy and repressed resentment.

After his last, incomplete, yet so much the more telling success, Cipolla had at once fortified himself with another cognac. Truly he did "drink a lot," and the fact made a bad impression. But obviously he needed the liquor and the cigarettes for the replenishment of his energy, upon which, as he himself said, heavy demands were made in all directions. Certainly in the intervals he looked very ill, exhausted and hollow-eyed. Then the little glassful would redress the balance, and the flow of lively, self-confident chatter run on, while the smoke he inhaled gushed out gray from his lungs. I clearly recall that he passed from the card tricks to parlor games—the kind based on certain powers which in human nature are higher or else lower than human reason: on intuition and "magnetic" transmission; in short, upon a low type of manifestation. What I do not remember is the precise order things came in. And I will not bore you with a description of these experiments; everybody knows them, everybody has at one time or another taken part in this finding of hidden articles, this blind carrying out of a series of acts, directed by a force that proceeds from organism to organism by unexplored paths. Everybody has had his little glimpse into the equivocal, impure, inexplicable nature of the occult, has been conscious of both curiosity and contempt, has shaken his head over the human tendency of those who deal in it to help themselves out with humbuggery, though, after all, the humbuggery is no disproof whatever of the genuineness of the other elements in the dubious amalgam. I can only say here that each single circumstance gains in weight and the whole greatly in impressiveness when it is a man like Cipolla who is the chief actor and guiding spirit in the sinister business. He sat smoking at the rear of the stage, his back to the audience while they conferred. The object passed from hand to hand which it was his task to find, with which he was to perform some action agreed upon beforehand. Then he would start to move zigzag through the hall, with his head thrown back and one hand outstretched, the other clasped in that of a guide who was in the secret but enjoined to keep himself perfectly passive, with his thoughts directed upon the agreed goal. Cipolla moved with the bearing typical in these experiments: now groping upon a false start, now with a quick forward thrust, now pausing as though to listen and by sudden inspiration correcting his course. The roles seemed reversed, the stream of influence was moving in the contrary direction, as the artist himself pointed out, in his ceaseless flow of discourse. The suffering, receptive, performing part was now his, the will he had before imposed on others was shut out, he acted in obedience to a voiceless common will which was in the air. But he made it perfectly clear that it all came to the same thing. The capacity for self-surrender, he said, for becoming a tool, for the most unconditional and utter self-abnegation, was but the reverse side of that other power to will and to command. Commanding and obeying formed together one single principle, one indissoluble unity; he who knew how to obey knew also how to command, and conversely; the one idea was comprehended in the other, as people and leader were comprehended in one another. But that which was *done,* the highly exacting and exhausting performance, was in every case his, the leader's and mover's, in whom the will became obedience, the obedience will, whose person was the cradle and womb of both, and who thus suffered enormous hardship. Repeatedly he emphasized the fact that his lot was a hard one—presumably to account for his need of stimulant and his frequent recourse to the little glass.

Thus he groped his way forward, like a blind seer, led and sustained by the mysterious common will. He drew a pin set with a stone out of its hiding place in an Englishwoman's shoe, carried it, halting and pressing on by turns, to another lady—Signora Angiolieri—and handed it to her on bended knee, with the words it had been agreed he was to utter. "I present you with this in token of my respect," was the sentence. Their sense was obvious, but the words themselves not easy to hit upon, for the reason that they had been agreed on in French; the language complication seemed to us a little malicious, implying as it did a conflict between the audience's natural interest in the success of the miracle, and their desire to witness the humiliation of this presumptuous man. It was a strange sight: Cipolla on his knees before the signora, wrestling, amid efforts at speech, after knowledge of the preordained words. "I must say something," he said, "and I feel clearly what it is I must say. But I also feel that if it passed my lips it would be wrong. Be careful not to help me unintentionally!" he cried out, though very likely that was precisely what he was hoping for. *"Pensez trè fort,"* he cried all at once, in bad French, and then burst out with the required words— in Italian, indeed, but with the final substantive pronounced in the sister tongue, in which he was probably far from fluent: he said *vénération* instead of *venerazione,* with an impossible nasal. And this partial success, after the complete success before it, the finding of the pin, the presentation of it on his knees to the right person— was almost more impressive than if he had got the sentence exactly right, and evoked bursts of admiring applause.

Cipolla got up from his knees and wiped the perspiration from his brow. You understand that this experiment with the pin was a single case, which I describe because it sticks in my memory. But he changed his method several times and improvised a number of variations suggested by his contact with his audience; a good deal of time thus went by. He seemed to get particular inspiration from the person of our landlady; she drew him on to the most extraordinary displays of clairvoyance. "It does not escape me, madame," he said to her, "that there is something unusual about you, some special and honorable distinction. He who has eyes to see descries about your lovely brow an aureola—if I mistake not, it once was stronger than now—a slowly paling radiance ... hush, not a word! Don't help me. Beside you sits your husband—yes?" He turned toward the silent Signor Angiolieri. "You are the husband of this lady, and your happiness is complete. But in the midst of this happiness memories rise . . . the past, signora, so it seems to me, plays an important part in your present. You knew a king . . . has not a king crossed your path in bygone days?"

"No," breathed the dispenser of our midday soup, her golden-brown eyes gleaming in the noble pallor of her face.

"No? No, not a king; I meant that generally, I did not mean literally a king. Not a king, not a prince, and a prince after all, a king of a loftier realm; it was a great artist; at whose side you once—you would contradict me, and yet I am not wholly wrong. Well, then! It was a woman, a great, a world-renowned woman artist, whose friendship you enjoyed in your tender years, whose sacred memory overshadows and transfigures your whole existence. Her name? Need I utter it, whose fame has long been bound up with the Fatherland's, immortal as its own? Eleonora Duse," he finished, softly with much solemnity.

The little woman bowed her head, overcome. The applause was like a patriotic demonstration. Nearly everyone there knew about Signora Angiolieri's wonderful past; they were all able to confirm the Cavaliere's intuition—not least the present guests of Casa Eleonora. But we wondered how much of the truth he had learned as the result of professional inquiries made on his arrival. Yet I see no reason at all to cast doubt, on rational grounds, upon powers which, before our very eyes, became fatal to their possessor.

At this point there was an intermission. Our lord and master withdrew. Now I confess that almost ever since the beginning of my tale I have looked forward with dread to this moment in it. The thoughts of men are mostly not hard to read; in this case they are very easy. You are sure to ask why we did not choose this moment to go away—and I must continue to owe you an answer. I do not know why. I cannot defend myself. By this time it was certainly eleven, probably later. The children were asleep. The last series of tests had been too long, nature had had her way. They were sleeping in our laps, the little one on mine, the boy on his mother's. That was, in a way, a consolation; but at the same time it was also ground for compassion and a clear leading to take them home to bed. And I give you my word that we wanted to obey this touching admonition, we seriously wanted to. We roused the poor things and told them it was now high time to go. But they were no sooner conscious than they began to resist and implore—you know how horrified children are at the thought of leaving before the end of a thing. No cajoling has any effect, you have to use force. It was so lovely, they wailed. How did we know what was coming next? Surely we could not leave until after the intermission; they liked a little nap now and again—only not go home, only not go to bed, while the beautiful evening was still going on!

We yielded, but only for the moment, of course—so far as we knew—only for a little while, just a few minutes longer. I cannot excuse our staying, scarcely can I even understand it. Did we think, having once said A, we had to say B—having once brought the children hither we had to let them stay? No, it is not good enough. Were we ourselves so highly entertained? Yes, and no. Our feelings for Cavaliere Cipolla were of a very mixed kind, but so were the feelings of the whole audience, if I mistake not, and nobody left. Were we under the sway of a fascination which emanated from this man who took so strange a way to earn his bread; a fascination which he gave out independently of the programme and even between the tricks and which paralysed our resolve? Again, sheer curiosity may account for something. One was curious to know how such an evening turned out; Cipolla in his remarks having all along hinted that he had tricks in his bag stranger than any he had yet produced.

But all that is not it—or at least it is not all of it. More correct it would be to answer the first question with another. Why had we not left Torre di Venere itself before now? To me the two questions are one and the same, and in order to get out of the impasse I might simply say that I had answered it already. For, as things had been in Torre in general: queer, uncomfortable, troublesome, tense, oppressive, so precisely they were here in this hall tonight. Yes, more than precisely. For it seemed to be the fountainhead of all the uncanniness and all the strained feelings which had oppressed the atmosphere of our holiday. This man whose return to the stage we were awaiting was the personification of all that; and, as we had not gone away in general, so to speak, it would have been inconsistent to do it in the particular case. You may call this an explanation, you may call it inertia, as you see fit. Any argument more to the purpose I simply do not know how to adduce.

Well, there was an interval of ten minutes, which grew into nearly twenty. The children remained awake. They were enchanted by our compliance, and filled the break to their own satisfaction by renewing relations with the popular sphere, with Antonio, Guiscardo, and the canoe man. They put their hands to their mouths and called messages across, appealing to us for the Italian words. "Hope you have a good catch tomorrow, a whole netful!" They called to Mario, Esquisito Mario: *"Mario, una cioccolata e biscotti!"* And this time he heeded and answered with a smile: *"Subito, signorini!"* Later we had reason to recall this kindly, if rather absent and pensive smile.

Thus the interval passed, the gong sounded. The audience, which had scattered in conversation, took their places again, the children sat up straight in their chairs with their hands in their laps. The curtain had not been dropped. Cipolla came forward again, with his dipping stride, and began to introduce the second half of the program with a lecture.

Let me state once for all that this self-confident cripple was the most powerful hypnotist I have ever seen in my life. It was pretty plain now that he threw dust in the public eye and advertised himself as a prestidigitator on account of police regulations which would have prevented him from making his living by the exercise of his powers. Perhaps this eye wash is the usual thing in Italy; it may be permitted or even connived at by the authorities. Certainly the man had from the beginning made little concealment of the actual nature of his operations; and this second half of the program was quite frankly and exclusively devoted to one sort of experiment. While he still practiced some rhetorical circumlocutions, the tests themselves were one long series of attacks upon the will power, the loss or compulsion of volition. Comic, exciting, amazing by turns, by midnight they were still in full swing; we ran the gamut of all the phenomena this natural–unnatural field has to show, from the unimpressive at one end of the scale to the monstrous at the other. The audience laughed and applauded as they followed the grotesque details; shook their heads, clapped their knees, fell very frankly under the spell of this stern self-assured personality. At the same time I saw signs that they were not quite complacent, not quite unconscious of the peculiar ignominy which lay, for the individual and for the general, in Cipolla's triumphs.

Two main features were constant in all the experiments: the liquor glass and the claw-handled riding whip. The first was always invoked to add fuel to his demoniac fires; without it, apparently, they might have burned out. On this score we might even have felt pity for the man; but the whistle of his scourge, the insulting symbol of his domination, before which we all cowered, drowned out every sensation save a dazed and outbraved submission to his power. Did he then lay claim to our sympathy to boot? I was struck by a remark he made—it suggested no less. At the climax of his experiments, by stroking and breathing upon a certain young man who had offered himself as a subject and already proved himself a particularly susceptible one, he had not only put him into the condition known as deep trance and extended his insensible body by neck and feet across the backs of two chairs, but had actually sat down on the rigid form as on a bench, without making it yield. The sight of this unholy figure in a frock coat squatted on the stiff body was horrible and incredible; the audience, convinced that the victim of this scientific diversion must be suffering, expressed its sympathy: *"Ah, poveretto!"* Poor soul, poor soul! *"Poor soul!"* Cipolla mocked them, with some bitterness. "Ladies and gentlemen, you are barking up the wrong tree. *Sono io il poveretto.* I am the person who is suffering, I am the one to be pitied." We pocketed the information. Very good. Maybe the experiment was at his expense, maybe it was he who had suffered the cramp when the *giovanotto* over there had made the faces. But appearances were all against it; and one does not feel like saying *poveretto* to a man who is suffering to bring about the humiliation of others.

I have got ahead of my story and lost sight of the sequence of events. To this day my mind is full of the Cavaliere's feats of endurance; only I do not recall them in their order—which does not matter. So much I do know: that the longer and more circumstantial tests, which got the most applause, impressed me less than some of the small ones which passed quickly over. I remember the young man whose body Cipolla converted into a board, only because of the accompanying remarks which I have quoted. An elderly lady in a cane-seated chair was lulled by Cipolla in the delusion that she was on a voyage to India and gave a voluble account of her adventures by land and sea. But I found this phenomenon less impressive than one which followed immediately after the intermission. A tall, well-built, soldierly man was unable to lift his arm, after the hunchback had told him that he could not and given a cut through the air with his whip. I can still see the face of that stately, mustachioed colonel smiling and clenching his teeth as he struggled to regain his lost freedom of action. A staggering performance! He seemed to be exerting his will, and in vain; the trouble, however, was probably simply that he could not will. There was involved here that recoil of the will upon itself which paralyzes choice—as our tyrant had previously explained to the Roman gentleman.

Still less can I forget the touching scene, at once comic and horrible, with Signora Angiolieri. The Cavaliere, probably in his first bold survey of the room, had spied out her ethereal lack of resistance to his power. For actually he bewitched her, literally drew her out of her seat, out of her row, and away with him whither he willed. And in order to enhance his effect, he bade Signor Angiolieri call upon his wife by her name, to throw, as it were, all the weight of his existence and his rights in her into the scale, to rouse by the voice of her husband everything in his spouse's soul which could shield her virtue against the evil assaults of magic. And how vain it all was! Cipolla was standing at some distance from the couple, when he made a single cut with his whip through the air. It caused our landlady to shudder violently and turn her face toward him. "Sofronia!" cried Signor Angiolieri—we had not known that Signora Angiolieri's name was Sofronia. And he did well to call, everybody saw that there was no time to lose. His wife kept her face turned in the direction of the diabolical Cavaliere, who with his ten long yellow fingers was making passes at his victim, moving backward as he did so, step by step. Then Signora Angiolieri, her pale face gleaming, rose up from her seat, turned right round, and began to glide after him. Fatal and forbidding sight! Her face as though moonstruck, stiff-armed, her lovely hands lifted a little at the wrists, the feet as it were together, she seemed to float slowly out of her row and after the tempter. "Call her, sir, keep on calling," prompted the redoubtable man. And Signor Angiolieri, in a weak voice, called: "Sofronia!" Ah, again and again he called; as his wife went further off he even curved one hand round his lips and beckoned with the other as he called. But the poor voice of love and duty echoed unheard, in vain, behind the lost one's back; the signora swayed along, moonstruck, deaf, enslaved; she glided into the middle aisle and down it toward the fingering hunchback, toward the door. We were driven to the conviction, that she would have followed her master, had he so willed it, to the ends of the earth.

"*Accidente!*" cried out Signor Angiolieri, in genuine affright, springing up as the exit was reached. But at the same moment the Cavaliere put aside, as it were, the triumphal crown and broke off. "Enough, signora, I thank you," he said, and offered his arm to lead her back to her husband. "Signor," he greeted the latter, "here is your wife. Unharmed, with my compliments, I give her into your hands. Cherish with all the strength of your manhood a treasure which is so wholly yours, and let your zeal be quickened by knowing that there are powers stronger than reason or virtue, and not always so magnanimously ready to relinquish their prey!"

Poor Signor Angiolieri, so quiet, so bald! He did not look as though he would know how to defend his happiness, even against powers much less demoniac than these which were now adding mockery to frightfulness. Solemnly and pompously the Cavaliere retired to the stage, amid applause to which his eloquence gave double strength. It was this particular episode, I feel sure, that set the seal upon his ascendancy. For now he made them dance, yes, literally; and the dancing lent a dissolute, abandoned, topsy-turvy air to the scene, a drunken abdication of the critical spirit which had so long resisted the spell of this man. Yes, he had had to fight to get the upper hand—for instance against the animosity of the young Roman gentleman, whose rebellious spirit threatened to serve others as a rallying point. But it was precisely upon the importance of example that the Cavaliere was so strong. He had the wit to make his attack at the weakest point and to choose as his first victim that feeble, ecstatic youth whom he had previously made into a board. The master had but to look at him, when this young man would fling himself back as though struck by lightning, place his hands rigidly at his sides, and fall into a state of military somnambulism, in which it was plain to any eye that he was open to the most absurd suggestion that might be made to him. He seemed quite content in his abject state, quite pleased to be relieved of the burden of voluntary choice. Again and again he offered himself as a subject and gloried in the model facility he had in losing consciousness. So now he mounted the platform, and a single cut of the whip was enough to make him dance to the Cavaliere's orders, in a kind of complacent ecstasy, eyes closed, head nodding, lank limbs flying in all directions.

It looked unmistakably like enjoyment, and other recruits were not long in coming forward: two other young men, one humbly and one well dressed, were soon jigging alongside the first. But now the gentleman from Rome bobbed up again, asking defiantly if the Cavaliere would engage to make him dance too, even against his will.

"Even against your will," answered Cipolla, in unforgettable accents. That frightful *"anche se non vuole"* still rings in my ears. The struggle began. After Cipolla had taken another little glass and lighted a fresh cigarette he stationed the Roman at a point in the middle aisle and himself took up a position some distance behind, making his whip whistle through the air as he gave the order: *"Balla!"* His opponent did not stir. *"Balla!"* repeated the Cavaliere incisively, and snapped his whip. You saw the young man move his neck round in his collar; at the same time one hand lifted slightly at the wrist, one ankle turned outward. But that was all, for the time at least; merely a tendency to twitch, now sternly repressed, now seeming about to get the upper hand. It escaped nobody that here a heroic obstinacy, a fixed resolve to resist, must needs be conquered; we were beholding a gallant effort to strike out and save the honor of the human race. He twitched but danced not; and the struggle was so prolonged that the Cavaliere had to divide his attention between it and the stage, turning now and then to make his riding whip whistle in the direction of the dancers, as it were to keep them in leash. At the same time he advised the audience that no fatigue was involved in such activities, however long they went on, since it was not the automatons up there who danced, but himself. Then once more his eye would bore into the back of the Roman's neck and lay siege to the strength of purpose which defied him.

One saw it waver, that strength of purpose, beneath the repeated summons and whip crackings. Saw with an objective interest which yet was not quite free from traces of sympathetic emotion—from pity, even from a cruel kind of pleasure. If I understand what was going on, it was the negative character of the young man's fighting position which was his undoing. It is likely that not willing is not a practicable state of mind; *not* to want to do something may be in the long run a mental content impossible to subsist on. Between not willing a certain thing and not willing at all—in other words, yielding to another person's will—there may lie too small a space for the idea of freedom to squeeze into. Again, there were the Cavaliere's persuasive words, woven in among the whip crackings and commands, as he mingled effects that were his own secret with others of a bewilderingly psychological kind. *"Balla!"* said he. "Who wants to torture himself like that? Is forcing yourself your idea of freedom? *Una ballatina!* Why, your arms and legs are aching for it. What a relief to give way to them—there, you are dancing already! That is no struggle any more, it is pleasure!" And so it was. The jerking and twitching of the refractory youth's limbs had at last got the upper hand; he lifted his arms, then his knees, his joints quite suddenly relaxed, he flung his legs and danced, and amid bursts of applause the Cavaliere led him to join the row of puppets on the stage. Up there we could see his face as he "enjoyed" himself; it was clothed in a broad grin and the eyes were half shut. In a way, it was consoling to see that he was having a better time than he had had in the hour of his pride.

His "fall" was, I may say, an epoch. The ice was completely broken, Cipolla's triumph had reached its height. The Circe's wand, that whistling leather whip with the claw handle, held absolute sway. At one time—it must have been well after midnight—not only were there eight or ten persons dancing on the little stage, but in the hall below varied animation reigned, and a long-toothed Anglo-Saxoness in a pince-nez left her seat of her own motion to perform a tarantella in the center aisle. Cipolla was lounging in a cane-seated chair at the left of the stage, gulping down the smoke of a cigarette and breathing it impudently out through his bad teeth. He tapped his foot and shrugged his shoulders, looking down upon the abandoned scene in the hall; now and then he snapped his whip backward at a laggard upon the stage. The children were awake at the moment. With shame I speak of them. For it was not good to be here, least of all for them; that we had not taken them away can only be explained by saying that we had caught the general devil-may-careness of the hour. By that time it was all one. Anyhow, thank goodness, they lacked understanding for the disreputable side of the entertainment, and in their innocence were perpetually charmed by the unheard-of indulgence which permitted them to be present at such a thing as a magician's "evening." Whole quarter-hours at a time they drowsed on our laps, waking refreshed and rosy-cheeked, with sleep-drunken eyes, to laugh to bursting at the leaps and jumps the magician made those people up there make. They had not thought it would be so jolly; they joined with their clumsy little hands in every round of applause. And jumped for joy upon their chairs, as was their wont, when Cipolla beckoned to their friend Mario from the Esquisito, beckoned to him just like a picture in a book, holding his hand in front of his nose and bending and straightening the forefinger by turns.

Mario obeyed. I can see him now going up the stairs to Cipolla, who continued to beckon him, in that droll, picture-book sort of way. He hesitated for a moment at first; that, too, I recall quite clearly. During the whole evening he had lounged against a wooden pillar at the side entrance, with his arms folded, or else with his hands thrust into his jacket pockets. He was on our left, near the youth with the militant hair, and had followed the performance attentively, so far as we had seen, if with no particular animation and God knows how much comprehension. He could not much relish being summoned thus, at the end of the evening. But it was only too easy to see why he obeyed. After all, obedience was his calling in life; and then, how should a simple lad like him find it within his human capacity to refuse compliance to a man so throned and crowned as Cipolla at that hour? Willy-nilly he left his column and with a word of thanks to those making way for him he mounted the steps with a doubtful smile on his full lips.

Picture a thickset youth of twenty years, with clipped hair, a low forehead, and heavy-lidded eyes of an indefinite gray, shot with green and yellow. These things I knew from having spoken with him, as we often had. There was a saddle of freckles on the flat nose, the whole upper half of the face retreated behind the lower, and that again was dominated by thick lips that parted to show the salivated teeth. These thick lips and the veiled look of the eyes lent the whole face a primitive melancholy—it was that which had drawn us to him from the first. In it was not the faintest trace of brutality—indeed, his hands would have given the lie to such an idea, being unusually slender and delicate even for a southerner. They were hands by which one liked being served.

We knew him humanly without knowing him personally, if I may make that distinction. We saw him nearly every day, and felt a certain kindness for his dreamy ways, which might at times be actual inattentiveness, suddenly transformed into a redeeming zeal to serve. His mien was serious, only the children could bring a smile to his face. It was not sulky, but uningratiating, without intentional effort to please—or, rather, it seemed to give up being pleasant in the conviction that it could not succeed. We should have remembered Mario in any case, as one of those homely recollections of travel which often stick in the mind better than more important ones. But of his circumstances we knew no more than that his father was a petty clerk in the Municipio and his mother took in washing.

His white waiter's coat became him better than the faded striped suit he wore, with a gay-colored scarf instead of a collar, the ends tucked into his jacket. He neared Cipolla, who however did not leave off that motion of his finger before his nose, so that Mario had to come still closer, right up to the chair seat and the master's legs. Whereupon the latter spread out his elbows and seized the lad, turning him so that we had a view of his face. Then gazed him briskly up and down, with a careless, commanding eye.

"Well, *ragazzo mio,* how comes it we make acquaintance so late in the day? But believe me, I made yours long ago. Yes, yes, I've had you in my eye this long while and known what good stuff you were made of. How could I go and forget you again? Well, I've had a good deal to think about. . . . Now tell me, what is your name? The first name, that's all I want."

"My name is Mario," the young man answered, in a low voice.

"Ah, Mario. Very good. Yes, yes, there is such a name, quite a common name, a classic name too, one of those which preserve the heroic traditions of the Fatherland. *Bravo! Salve!*" And he flung up his arm slantingly above his crooked shoulder, palm outward, in the Roman salute. He may have been slightly tipsy by now, and no wonder; but he spoke as before, clearly, fluently, and with emphasis. Though about this time there had crept into his voice a gross, autocratic note, and a kind of arrogance was in his sprawl.

"Well, now, Mario *mio,*" he went on, "it's a good thing you came this evening, and that's a pretty scarf you've got on; it is becoming to your style of beauty. It must stand you in good stead with the girls, the pretty pretty girls of Torre—"

From the row of youths, close by the place where Mario had been standing, sounded a laugh. It came from the youth with the militant hair. He stood there, his jacket over his shoulder, and laughed outright, rudely and scornfully.

Mario gave a start. I think it was a shrug, but he may have started and then hastened to cover the movement by shrugging his shoulders, as much as to say that the neckerchief and the fair sex were matters of equal indifference to him.

The Cavaliere gave a downward glance.

"We needn't trouble about him," he said. "He is jealous, because your scarf is so popular with the girls, maybe partly because you and I are so friendly up here. Perhaps he'd like me to put him in mind of his colic—I could do it free of charge. Tell me, Mario. You've come here this evening for a bit of fun—and in the daytime you work in an ironmonger's shop?"

"In a café," corrected the youth.

"Oh, in a café. That's where Cipolla nearly came a cropper! What you are is a cup-bearer, a ganymede—I like that, it is another classical allusion—*Salvietta!*" Again the Cavaliere saluted, to the huge gratification of his audience.

Mario smiled too. "But before that," he interpolated, in the interest of accuracy, "I worked for a while in a shop in Portoclemente."

He seemed visited by a natural desire to assist the prophecy by
dredging out its essential features.

"There, didn't I say so? In an ironmonger's shop?"

"They kept combs and brushes," Mario got round it.

"Didn't I say that you were not always a ganymede? Not always
at the sign of the serviette? Even when Cipolla makes a mistake, it
is a kind that makes you believe in him. Now tell me: Do you believe
in me?"

An indefinite gesture.

"A halfway answer," commented the Cavaliere. "Probably it is
not easy to win your confidence. Even for me, I can see, it is not so
easy. I see in your features a reserve, a sadness, *un tratto di malin-
conia* ... tell me" (he seized Mario's hand persuasively) "have
you troubles?"

"*Nossignore,*" answered Mario, promptly and decidedly.

"You have troubles," insisted the Cavaliere, bearing down the
denial by the weight of his authority. "Can't I see? Trying to pull
the wool over Cipolla's eyes, are you? Of course, about the girls—
it is a girl, isn't it? You have love troubles?"

Mario gave a vigorous head shake. And again the *giovanotto's*
brutal laugh rang out. The Cavaliere gave heed. His eyes were roving
about somewhere in the air: but he cocked an ear to the sound, then
swung his whip backward, as he had once or twice before in his
conversation with Mario, that none of his puppets might flag in their
zeal. The gesture had nearly cost him his new prey: Mario gave a
sudden start in the direction of the steps. But Cipolla had him in
his clutch.

"Not so fast," said he. "That would be fine, wouldn't it? So you
want to skip, do you, ganymede, right in the middle of the fun, or,
rather, when it is just beginning? Stay with me, I'll show you something nice. I'll convince you. You have no reason to worry, I promise
you. This girl—you know her and others know her too—what's her
name? Wait! I read the name in your eyes, it is on the tip of my
tongue and yours too—"

"Silvestra!" shouted the *giovanotto* from below.

The Cavaliere's face did not change.

"Aren't there the forward people?" he asked, not looking down,
more as in undisturbed converse with Mario. "Aren't there the
young fighting-cocks that crow in season and out? Takes the word
out of your mouth, the conceited fool, and seems to think he has

some special right to it. Let him be. But Silvestra, your Silvestra—ah, what a girl that is! What a prize! Brings your heart into your mouth to see her walk or laugh or breathe, she is so lovely. And her round arms when she washes, and tosses her head back to get the hair out of her eyes! An angel from paradise!"

Mario started at him, his head thrust forward. He seemed to have forgotten the audience, forgotten where he was. The red rings around his eyes had got larger, they looked as though they were painted on. His thick lips parted.

"And she makes you suffer, this angel," went on Cipolla, "or, rather, you make yourself suffer for her—there is a difference, my lad, a most important difference, let me tell you. There are misunderstandings in love, maybe nowhere else in the world are there so many. I know what you are thinking: what does this Cipolla, with his little physical defect, know about love? Wrong, all wrong, he knows a lot. He has a wide and powerful understanding of its workings, and it pays to listen to his advice. But let's leave Cipolla out, cut him out altogether and think only of Silvestra, your peerless Silvestra! What! Is she to give any young gamecock the preference, so that he can laugh while you cry? To prefer him to a chap like you, so full of feeling and so sympathetic? Not very likely, is it? It is impossible—we know better, Cipolla and she. If I were to put myself in her place and choose between the two of you, a tarry lout like that—a codfish, a sea urchin—and a Mario, a knight of the napkin, who moves among gentlefolk and hands round refreshments with an air—my word, but my heart would speak in no uncertain tones—it knows to whom I gave it long ago. It is time that he should see and understand, my chosen one! It is time that you see me and recognize me, Mario, my beloved! Tell me, who am I?"

It was grisly, the way the betrayer made himself irresistible, wreathed and coquetted with his crooked shoulder, languished with the puffy eyes, and showed his splintered teeth in a sickly smile. And alas, at his beguiling words, what was come of our Mario? It is hard for me to tell, hard as it was for me to see; for here was nothing less than an utter abandonment of the inmost soul, a public exposure of timid and deluded passion and rapture. He put his hands across his mouth, his shoulders rose and fell with his pantings. He could not, it was plain, trust his eyes and ears for joy, and the one thing he forgot was precisely that he could not trust them. "Silvestra!" he breathed, from the very depths of his vanquished heart.

"Kiss me!" said the hunchback. "Trust me, I love thee. Kiss me here." And with the tip of his index finger, hand, arm, and little finger outspread, he pointed to his cheek, near the mouth. And Mario bent and kissed him.

It had grown very still in the room. That was a monstrous moment, grotesque and thrilling, the moment of Mario's bliss. In that evil span of time, crowded with a sense of the illusiveness of all joy, one sound became audible, and that not quite at once, but on the instant of the melancholy and ribald meeting between Mario's lips and the repulsive flesh which thrust itself forward for his caress. It was the sound of a laugh, from the *giovanotto* on our left. It broke into the dramatic suspense of the moment, coarse, mocking, and yet—or I must have been grossly mistaken—with an undertone of compassion for the poor bewildered, victimized creature. It had a faint ring of that *"Poveretto"* which Cipolla had declared was wasted on the wrong person, when he claimed the pity for his own.

The laugh still rang in the air when the recipient of the caress gave his whip a little swish, low down, close to his chair-leg, and Mario started up and flung himself back. He stood in that posture staring, his hands one over the other on those desecrated lips. Then he beat his temples with his clenched fists, over and over; turned and staggered down the steps, while the audience applauded, and Cipolla sat there with his hands in his lap, his shoulders shaking. Once below, and even while in full retreat, Mario hurled himself round with legs flung wide apart; one arm flew up, and two flat shattering detonations crashed through applause and laughter.

There was instant silence. Even the dancers came to a full stop and stared about, struck dumb. Cipolla bounded from his seat. He stood with his arms spread out, slanting as though to ward everybody off, as though next moment he would cry out: "Stop! Keep back! Silence! What was that?" Then, in that instant, he sank back in his seat, his head rolling on his chest; in the next he had fallen sideways to the floor, where he lay motionless, a huddled heap of clothing, with limbs awry.

The commotion was indescribable. Ladies hid their faces, shuddering, on the breasts of their escorts. There were shouts for a doctor, for the police. People flung themselves on Mario in a mob, to disarm him, to take away the weapon that hung from his fingers—that small, dull-metal, scarcely pistol-shaped tool with hardly any barrel—in how strange and unexpected a direction had fate leveled it!

And now—now finally, at last—we took the children and led them toward the exit, past the pair of *carabinieri* just entering. Was that the end, they wanted to know, that they might go in peace? Yes, we assured them, that was the end. An end of horror, a fatal end. And yet a liberation—for I could not, and I cannot, but find it so!

Translated by Helen Tracey Lowe-Porter

The Tables of the Law

1

H is birth was irregular, hence it was he passionately loved order, the absolute, the shalt and shalt not.

In his youth, in a blazing fit of rage, he had killed a man; so he
knew, better than the innocent, that to kill is very fine but to have
killed is most horrible, and that it is forbidden to kill.

His senses were hot, so he craved the spiritual, the pure, the holy;
he craved the unseen, because he felt that the unseen was spiritual,
holy and pure.

Among the Midianites, a scattered desert folk, brisk and enterpris-
ing shepherds and traders, with whom after the slaying he had taken
refuge, fleeing from Egypt the land of his birth (more of that presently)—among the Midianites he had heard of a God you could not
see but who saw you, a mountain dweller who at the same time sat
invisible on a movable chest in a tent, where he dispensed oracles
by the casting of lots. To the children of Midian this numen, named
Jahwe, was merely one god among others. They made no great fuss
of him, doing his service by way of precaution and just in case. It
had struck them that among all the gods there might quite possibly
be one whom they did not see, one without a shape, so they sacrificed
to him in order not to leave anything out, offend anybody, or draw
down unpleasantness from any quarter whatever.

Moses, on the contrary, by reason of his craving for the pure and
holy, was deeply impressed by just this feature of Jahwe's invisibility.
He felt that no visible god could vie in sanctity with one not visible,
and he was amazed that the children of Midian set so little store by
a quality which seemed to him so full of incalculable implications.
He pondered long and weightily as he kept sheep in the desert for the
brother of his Midianite wife, shaken by inspirations and revelations
which, in one instance, even issued out of his own breast and took

shape in a blazing outward vision, a proper manifestation laying down the law, inexorably prescribing the task before him. And he arrived at the conviction that Jahwe was no other than El Elyon, the Unique and Highest, El roi, God Who seeth me—He who was already called El Shaddei, the God of the Mountain, El olam, the God of the world and of the eternities—in a word, no other than the God of Abraham, Isaac, and Jacob, the God of the Fathers and, by inference, of the fathers of the poor benighted folk that dwelt in the land of Egypt. They were enslaved, their traditions forgotten, their worship utterly disorganized; yet it was their very blood that on the father's side flowed in Moses' own veins.

Full of his discovery, with heavy-laden soul, quivering with eagerness to fullfil the command, Moses ended his many years' sojourn among the Midianites. His wife Zipporah, a woman of gentle birth, daughter of Reuel, priest-king in Midian, and sister of Reuel's herd-owning son Jethro, he set on an ass, together with his two sons Gershom and Eliezer, and took the seven days' journey westward through many deserts back into Egypt—or rather into the low-lying fallow land where the Nile divides and where in the district of Kos, also called Goshen, Gosen, and Gosem, dwelt the blood of his father, toiling and moiling.

And straightway wherever he went, into huts and, work sheds and brick yards, he began to explain to his father's blood this great discovery of his. His arms dangled along his sides and his fists shook in a way they had when he talked. He gave them to know that the God of their fathers was found anew; that He had made Himself known to him, Moshe ben Amram, on Mount Horeb in the desert of Sin, out of a flame of fire in the midst of a bush which burned and was not consumed. And told him that He was called Jahwe, which signified I Am That I Am forever and ever, but likewise a blowing air and a great noise of wind; and that He had a great mind toward their blood and was ready under certain conditions to make a Covenant with them and elect them for His own out of all peoples. The condition was, that they bind themselves to serve Him and to raise up a sworn brotherhood to the unique and imageless service of the invisible God.

And Moses did not cease to din all this into them, his fists shaking on his broad stone-mason's wrists as he harangued. Yet even so he was not quite straight with them, but kept back various things he had in his mind—yes, even the most important thing of all—lest he frighten them and put them off altogether. He said not a word about the implications of invisibility, the spirituality, purity, and sanctity, and he refrained from pointing out that as sworn servants of the Invisible they had got to be a folk set apart, of extra purity and holiness. He kept quiet for fear of alarming them; for this flesh and blood of his father was so downtrodden and debased, so confused in its worship, he mistrusted it even while he loved it. Yes, when he told his people that Jahwe the Invisible had a mind to them, he was ascribing to the Deity and attributing to Him what may have been true of the god but was certainly true of himself: namely, that Moses had a mind to his father's blood, as the stone mason has a mind to the uncut block out of which he thinks to carve a fine and lofty statue by the work of his hands. Hence his palpitating eagerness, which had filled him on his departure from Midian, together with the weight of the great burden laid on his spirit through the Lord's command.

For the rest, he kept back the second half of the command, which had been twofold. It had been to the effect not only that Moses should tell the tribes about his rediscovery of the God of their fathers and His mind to them; but also that he was to lead them out of the Egyptian house of bondage into freedom and through many deserts into the land of their fathers, the Promised Land. All this was dependent upon the promise and indissolubly bound up with it. God— and freedom to return; the Invisible—and the shaking off of the foreign yoke. For him these were one and the same; but to the people he said naught as yet, because he knew that the second half followed after the first, and also because he hoped that he himself, single-handed, would worm it out of Pharaoh, King of Egypt—to whom he stood in a certain not remote relation.

Perhaps the people did not care for his speech, for he spoke indeed rather badly, often hesitating for the right word. Or perhaps the way his fists shook made them guess that there was more to be said about the invisibility and the Covenant he offered and that he might be luring them on to dangerous courses beyond their strength. Any-how, they betrayed a lack of enthusiasm. When he persisted they looked worried and stubborn, glanced toward their Egyptian jailers, and muttered between their teeth:

"Why are you shouting like that? And what sort of things are you blurting out? And who made you a prince and a judge over us? We would not know."

That was no news to him. He had heard it before, when he fled to Midian.

2

His father was not his father, and his mother was not his mother—so irregular had been his birth. One day Ramessu the Pharaoh's second daughter was disporting herself with her maidens in the royal gardens on the Nile, protected by armed guards. She saw a Hebrew slave drawing water, and she lusted after him. His eyes were sad, he had a new little beard on his chin, and you could see the muscles on his arms when he drew up the water. He labored in the sweat of his brow, and his troubles were many; but to Pharaoh's daughter he was a dream of beauty and desire. And she ordered him to be sent to her into her pavilion. She ran her exquisite little white hands through his sweat-damp locks, kissed the muscles of his arms, and aroused his manhood until he took her—he, the foreign slave, took the child of the king. When he had had her she let him go. But he went not far. After thirty paces he was cut down and straightway buried, and the sun-daughter's pleasure was at an end.

"Poor thing!" she said when she heard. "You are all so officious. He would have kept quiet; he loved me." But she proved to be with child, and in nine months, though no one knew it, she bore a man-child, and her women put him in a little basket of rushes coated with pitch and hid it in the reeds at the edge of the water. After a while they found it there and made outcry, saying: "Oh, a miracle, a foundling exposed in the rushes, just like the old fairy-tales, where Akki the water-bearer finds Sargon in the reeds and brings him up in the goodness of his heart. It happens over and over. But what shall we do with our find? The most sensible thing would be to give him to a nursing mother of humble birth who has more than enough milk, and let him grow up as the son of her and her good husband." And they gave the child to a Hebrew woman, who took it down to the land of Goshen to Jochebed, wife of Amram, one of the Hebrew emigrés, a man of the house of Levi. She was suckling her own son Aaron and had too much milk. Moreover, she profited now and then by good things sent to her house from an exalted source. So in the goodness of her heart she brought up the nameless child with her own. Thus Amram and Jochebed became Moses' parents before men, and Aaron was his brother. Amram had fields and herds, and Jochebed was the daughter of a stone mason. They did not know what to call the unlikely little lad; in the end they gave him a half-Egyptian name, or rather half of an Egyptian name. For the sons of the land were often named Ptah-mose, Amen-mose, or Ra-mose: in other words, sons of those gods. Amram and Jochebed preferred to leave out the god-name and simply called the boy Mose, or just "son." The question was, Whose?

3

He grew up as a member of the migrant tribe and spoke in their tongue. Their forefathers had been allowed into Egypt at the time of a drought: "hungry Bedouins from Edom," Pharaoh's clerks called them. The frontier authorities had passed them into the land of Goshen, and the lowland had been given them for pasturage. If anyone imagine they could have pastured there under any other circumstances, he does not know the children of Egypt, their hosts. Not only had they to pay such high taxes on their cattle that it was a grievous burden; but all those strong enough among them had to give their labor as well: they had to work on the building operations of all sorts that were always going on in a country like Egypt. Particularly since Ramessu, second of his name, had been on the throne in Thebes, extravagant building had been his pleasure and his royal delight. Magnificent and costly temples he built all over the land, and down below in the Delta he not only widened and improved the long-neglected canal that connected the eastern branch of the Nile with the Bitter Lakes and thus linked the Great Sea with the tip of the Red Sea, but also he built two great warehouse cities at the edge of the canal, called Pithom and Raamses. And now the children of the immigrants, these Ibrim, were conscripted to bake bricks, to haul and stack them in the sweat of their bodies beneath the Egyptian rod.

This rod of Pharaoh's overseers was more symbolic than functional: the tribes were not wantonly beaten with it. And the laborers ate well: plenty of fish from the Nile branch, bread, beef and beer enough and to spare. But even so such toil was not in their line. They were of nomad stock, traditionally of a free and roving life. Work by the hour, till they sweated, went against their grain. But they could not get together over their grievances, not being enough aware of themselves as a group. Generation after generation they had tented in a transitional land between the home of their fathers and Egypt proper. Their souls were unformed, their spirits wavering, and of settled teaching they had none. They had forgotten much, half-remembered more; lacking in steadiness, they were also without belief in themselves, so that even their resentment was feeble and yielded readily to all the free fish and beef and beer.

Now Moses, passing for Amram's son, would probably have had to make bricks for Pharaoh like the rest as soon as he grew out of childhood. But that did not happen. For the youth was removed from his parents and sent to Upper Egypt to a sort of elegant boarding-school where the sons of Syrian city kings were brought up together with scions of the native nobility. Thither he was sent. For his real mother, Pharaoh's daughter, who had borne him into the reeds, a loose female enough to be sure, but not at all spiritless, had been mindful of him for the sake of his buried father, the sad-eyed water bearer with the little beard. She wanted him not to continue with the desert folk, but to be educated as an Egyptian and granted a Court appointment, by way of recognizing, even secretly, his divine blood on one side. So then Moses, dressed in white linen with a wig on his head, learned about countries and heavenly bodies, writing and the law. But he was not happy among the young fops in the elegant boarding school. He was a solitary among them, full of distaste for all the Egyptian refinements and the luxury to which in fact he owed his being. The blood of the buried one who had had to serve that luxury was stronger in him than the Egyptian half, and his soul held with the poor unformed ones in Goshen who had not even the courage of their resentments. He held with them against the looseness and empty pride of his mother's side.

"What is your name?" his schoolmates might ask him.

"Moses," he answered.

"Ahmose or Ptahmose?" they asked.

"Just Moses," he replied.

"That is very low, it is common and ugly," said the swaggering youth. And Moses was so enraged he would have liked to kill and bury them. For he knew that their questions were aimed at his illegitimate birth, of which everybody was vaguely informed. How could he not know that he was only a by-blow, the fruit of Egyptian luxury, when it was an accepted though not very specific fact in all circles, even the highest—the dalliance of his daughter being as little of a secret from Pharaoh as it was from Moses himself—that Ramessu the builder was his grandfather in the pleasant flesh, issue of a passion both loose and fatal? Yes, Moses knew it and knew that Pharaoh knew it; and when he thought of it he nodded threateningly in the direction of the throne.

4

After he had lived two years among the dandies of the Theban school, he could stand it no longer. He climbed the wall and ran away at night, and bent his steps homeward to Goshen to his father's kin. He moved about morosely among the tribes. One day by the canal, near Ramessu's new buildings, he saw an Egyptian overseer strike down with his staff one of the laborers who had probably been idle or stubborn. Moses went white. With blazing eyes he accosted the Egyptian, who for all answer hit him on the nose, so that the bone was smashed in and remained so all his life. But Moses snatched the overseer's staff and fetched him a frightful blow which broke the man's skull and killed him on the spot. He had not once looked round to see if anyone saw him. But it was a lonely spot; no one was near. So he buried the man alone, for he whom he had defended had fled; and after the slaying and burying he felt as though it was what he had always wanted.

His deed of violence remained hidden, at least from the Egyptians: they did not find out what had become of the overseer, and time passed. Moses kept moving about among his father's people, and annoyed them by meddling in their affairs. One day he saw two laborers of the Ibrim quarreling and nearly coming to blows. "What is the matter with you, quarreling and almost fighting?" he said. "Aren't you wretched and forlorn enough to stick together, instead of showing your teeth at each other? This man is wrong; I saw it. Let him yield and be content, and as for the other, let him not be stiff-necked."

But, as will often happen, suddenly they turned on him together, saying: "Why are you mixing in our affairs?" And the man Moses found in the fault was the more impudent of the two and shouted: "Well, that is the limit! Who are you to stick your goat's nose into things that don't concern you? Aha, you are Moses, son of Amram, but that is not saying much, for nobody really knows who you are, not even yourself. We are curious to know who made you a prince and a judge over us. Do you mean to kill me as you killed the Egyptian?"

"Be quiet!" said Moses in alarm. But to himself he thought: How did this become known? So next day he saw what he must do, and he crossed the border where it was not closed, by the Bitter Lakes, through the reedy shallows. Through many deserts of the land of

Sinai he came to Midian, to the Minaeans and their priest–king Reuel.

5

When he returned to Egypt, filled with his discovery of God and with his mission, he was a robust man at the height of his powers; with flattened nose, prominent cheekbones, a beard parted in the middle, wide-set eyes, and wrists that had a striking breadth about them, as one could see particularly when he covered his mouth and beard with his right hand, musing, as he often did. He went from hut to hut and work shed to work shed, shook his fists alongside his thighs, and spoke of the Invisible, the God of the Fathers expectant of the Covenant. But although he talked much, at bottom he could not talk. For his was altogether a pent-up, inhibited nature, and in excitement he inclined to be tongue tied. Moreover, he was not perfectly at home in any language and blundered about in all three when he talked. The Aramaic Syro-Chaldaean spoken by his father's people and learned from his parents had been overlaid by the Egyptian tongue he had had to conform to in school. Then there was the Midianitic Arabic he had used so long in the desert. He mixed them all up together.

His brother Aaron was very useful to him: a tall, mild man with a black beard, black locks in the back of his neck, and large full eyelids which he kept piously cast down. Moses had initiated him into all the mysteries and won him over completely for the Invisible, with all its implications. And as Aaron knew how to give tongue with fluency and unction from his bearded lips, he mostly went where Moses went on his mission of conversion and spoke in Moses' place. His voice to be sure was rather guttural and oily, and did not carry full conviction; so that Moses was always trying to contribute more fire to Aaron's words, shaking his fists and often interrupting in his own helter-skelter jargon of Arabic, Aramaic, and Egyptian.

Aaron's wife was named Elisheba, the daughter of Amminadab. She too was strong for the Covenant and the teaching, and so was Miriam, a younger sister of Moses and Aaron, a woman fired by the spirit, who could play on the timbrel and sing. But more than all these Moses favored a certain youth who for his part supported Moses body and soul in all his preaching and plans and stirred not from his side. His name was actually Hosea, son of Nun (which means fish) of the tribe of Ephraim; but Moses had given him the

Jahwe name of Jehoshua, or Joshua for short, and he wore it proudly—an upright, muscular young man with a curly head, prominent Adam's apple, and two distinct deep folds between his brows. In this whole business he had his peculiar point of view, and it was not so much religious as military. For to Joshua, Jahwe the God of their fathers was above all the God of battles, and the idea of escaping from the house of bondage had as a necessary sequel the conquest of new habitations for the Hebrew tribes. Somewhere they had to live; and no land, whether promised or not, would be just given to them.

Joshua, young as he was, had all the facts in that curly head of his that sat so straight on his shoulders and looked so directly out of its eyes. He discussed them endlessly with Moses, his elder, master, and friend. Without commanding the means for an exact census, Joshua had estimated that the strength of the tented tribes in Goshen and the factory towns of Pithom and Ramses, adding in the Hebrew slaves scattered throughout the country, might be around twelve or thirteen thousand souls in all. Their numbers were afterward exaggerated out of all reason; but Joshua knew them with fair accuracy and was not very well satisfied with the figure. Three thousand men was no great strength, even if you reckoned that once on the way their numbers would be likely to be increased by the adhesion of various vaguely allied stocks now roving about in the desert. But with no greater resources than these no large enterprises could be thought of; it would be impossible with no greater numbers to thrust forward into the Promised Land. Joshua could see as much; therefore his immediate hope was for some free space where the tribes could settle down and be left for a while under fairly favorable circumstances to their normal rate of increase, which, as Joshua knew his people, meant two-and-a-half to every hundred each year. So the youth was looking for covert and coverture, a retreat where more military strength could be bred and built up. He often discussed his ideas with Moses, displaying a clear knowledge of geography, for he had a sort of map in his head of the suitable sites, with distances and water supplies. He even knew who dwelt in them, and how militant the inhabitants were.

Moses well knew what he had in his Joshua; knew that he would need him, and loved his zeal, although its immediate objects interested him but little. Covering mouth and beard with his right hand, he listened to the youth's strategic outgivings, his mind dwelling on other matters the while. For Moses too, Jahwe meant, of course, the exodus; but not so much as a campaign to conquer land as a journey into freedom and segregation. Jahwe meant that he, Moses, would have to himself all this helpless, hapless flesh and blood, now hanging confused among many cultures, all these begetting men and childing women, groping youth and children with running noses, his father's own blood, in a place somewhere outside in the open to stamp upon them the holy invisible God, the pure and spiritual; to gather them into a nucleus and shape them in His image. They should put on a folk-shape distinct from all others, belonging to God, destined for the holy and spiritual life, distinguished from all others by reverence, awe, and abstention—in other words by fear before the ideas of purity, precept, and discipline. And since the Invisible was in truth the God of all the world, that fear would in the future bind all humanity; but first of all it would be proclaimed for them alone and be their claim to power among the heathen.

Such was Moses' mind to his father's blood. It was the mind of the maker, which to him was identical with God's favor and election, His zeal for the Covenant. He was convinced that this formative interlude must take precedence of all the enterprises which young Joshua had in his head. And for that purpose time was needed— free time outside in the open; so he did not mind the delay in Joshua's plans due to insufficient numbers of arms-bearing men. Joshua needed time, first for the tribes to multiply according to nature, and secondly in order that he himself might put on more years and be in a position to lead the armies when formed. And Moses needed time to form their souls, a divine work which in his own very soul he craved to commence. So from their different points of view Moses and Joshua were at one.

6

In the meantime he on whom the task was laid, together with his nearest followers, the eloquent Aaron, Elisheba, Miriam, Joshua, and a certain Caleb, of the same age as Joshua, and his bosom friend—a simple, brave, straightforward young man—in the meantime all these wasted not a moment, but went about spreading among their kin the gospel of Jahwe the Invisible and His flattering offer of the Covenant. At the same time they fomented the resentment of the tribes against their Egyptian taskmasters and labored to spread the idea of shaking off their yoke—the idea of the exodus. Each did it in his own way: Moses with halting words and shaking fists; Aaron with oily eloquence, Elisheba prattling persuasively, Joshua and Caleb with military brusqueness, and Miriam, who soon became known as the prophetess, in loftier vein to the sound of the timbrel. And their preachments did not fall on stony ground. The idea of vowing themselves to Moses' favoring God, of dedicating themselves to the Imageless and going out into freedom under His banner and his prophet's—it took root among them and began to be their united goal; the more so that Moses promised, or at least held out high hopes, that he would deal with the top authorities and get sanction for the exodus out of Egypt, so that it need not be carried out as a dangerous revolt, but in pursuance of an amicable agreement. They knew, vaguely, about Moses' half-Egyptian reed-birth, the aristocratic upbringing he had had in early years, and the personal relations he could command with the Court itself. His mixed blood, his position as it were with one foot in the Egyptian camp, had once been a source of mistrust and dislike. Now it became a cause of confidence and lent him added authority. Certainly he, if anyone, was the man to stand before Pharaoh and lead their enterprise. And so they commissioned him to the office of arranging their departure with Ramessu the builder, their taskmaster. Or rather, they commissioned him and his foster-brother Aaron. For Moses meant to take him along, first because he himself could not speak connectedly and Aaron could, but also because Aaron had a certain magic rod with which they hoped to make play at Court in Jahwe's favor. He could take a cobra and press its neck and make it stiff; then when he threw it to the ground it curled up and turned into a snake again. Neither Moses nor Aaron took account of the fact that Pharaoh's magicians knew the same trick, so that it would scarcely serve as an awe-inspiring instance of Jahwe's might.

They had no luck at all, anyhow; it was not in the cards, however craftily, after a council of war with the youths Joshua and Caleb, they went about it. It had been decided to ask the King merely for permission for the Hebrew people to assemble and go out a three days' journey into the wilderness, to feast and make sacrifice in obedience to the summons of the Lord their God, and then to come back to work. This was merely the mild and polite form of a petition to depart, and it was scarcely to be expected that Pharaoh would be deceived and believe they would come back. Indeed, he did not take kindly to it at all.

But at least the brothers did succeed in standing in the Great House and before Pharaoh's seat, and that not once but many times in the course of stoutly fought and protracted negotiations. Moses had not promised his people too much, standing as he did on the firm ground of his relation to Ramessu, his grandfather in the lust of the flesh. Each knew that the other knew. Thus Moses had in his hand the means of applying pressure. It was never quite strong enough to win the King's consent to the exodus; but it did procure serious attention, and time after time it got him entry to the All-Powerful, because the All-Powerful was afraid of him. Of course, the fear of a King is dangerous, and Moses was playing a dangerous game all the while. He had courage—how much, and what impression he made with it on his people, we shall soon see. Ramessu could easily have had him put out of the way and done away with all trace of his daughter's little side-step. But the princess still had a sweet memory of that quarter-hour's enjoyment and did not want her reed boy to come to any harm. She went on protecting him, however ungracious his response had been to her plans for his education and advancement.

So Moses and Aaron were permitted to stand before Pharaoh. But the idea of the excursion and sacrifice he curtly brushed aside. In vain Aaron cast down his rod and turned it into a snake; for Pharaoh's magician did the same thing without turning a hair, proving that the Invisible, in whose name the Hebrews spoke, enjoyed no superior authority and that Pharaoh did not need to hearken to the voice of these men.

"Pestilence and the sword will visit our people if we do not go out three days' journey into the desert and sacrifice to the Lord our God." But the King answered: "It moves us not. You are numerous enough—more than twelve thousand head—and could well do with the reduction of your numbers through pestilence and the sword or extreme toil. You, Moses, and Aaron—you are just aiding and abetting your people in idleness and getting them a holiday from the work they owe. I cannot and will not allow it; I have several vast temples in building; moreover, I intend to erect a third warehouse town besides Pithom and Ramses, and I require your people's arms for the work. I thank you for the present interview, and you, Moses, I dismiss, well or ill, with special favor. But let us hear no more talk about celebrations in the desert."

Thus the audience ended. And not only did no good come of it, but in the sequel actual ill. For Pharaoh, affronted in his building zeal and out of sorts because he could not have Moses strangled lest his daughter make trouble for him, ordered that the people of

Goshen be more sorely oppressed than ever and the rod not spared when they were idle. They must work the harder to get this idea out of their heads, and all idle thoughts about the feast in the desert should be sweated out of them. And so it was. The work grew daily harder after Moses and Aaron had spoken before Pharaoh. For instance, they got no more straw for the bricks they had to bake, but had to go into the stubble field to gather what they needed, that the tale of bricks might not be minished. Otherwise the cudgel should dance up and down on their poor backs. In vain the officers of the children of Israel made representations to the authorities. The answer was: "You are idle, idle are you, so you come and say: 'We want to go and make sacrifice.' But the fact remains: get your own straw and deliver the full tale of bricks."

7

For Moses and Aaron it was no small embarrassment. The head men said to them: "There you have it; and this is what we have got for the Covenant with your God and from Moses' connections. You have done nothing but to make a stink in Pharaoh's nostrils and his servants' and give the sword into their hands to slay us."

That was not easy to answer, and Moses had some bad quarter-hours in his private sessions with the God of the thornbush, where he represented to Him how he, Moses, had been from the first unwilling to be charged with the mission and had begged not to be sent upon it no matter who else was, since he could not even talk properly. But the Lord had answered him that Aaron was eloquent. So then Aaron had been the spokesman, speaking much too fawningly and showing what a mistake it was to undertake such an affair, for a man who was thick-tongued himself and had to let others speak for him. But God both consoled and rebuked him out of his very own bosom and answered him thence, he should be ashamed of such pusillanimity; moreover, that his excuses had been the sheerest affectation, for at bottom he had been as eager for the mission himself, having as much a mind to the children of Israel and the shaping of them as He, God, had. Yes, that his, Moses', predilection was in nothing different from God's own, being one and the same: it was the God-desire had set him at the work, and he should blush to faint now at the first check.

Moses had borne all this the better that Joshua, Caleb, and Aaron and the excitable women had decided in council that the new set-

back, whatever bad blood it made, had not been such a bad beginning when you really looked at it. For the bad blood was not only
against Moses, but even more against the Egyptians, and had made
the tribes more receptive for the summons of the savior God and
the idea of the exodus into the open. And it was so: the ferment
against the straw and the bricks increased among the workers, and
the reproach that Moses had made them a stench and only injured
them was accordingly forgotten in the desire that Amram's son
should exploit his connections further and go again before Pharaoh's throne.

That he did. This time not with Aaron but alone, let his tongue
stammer as it would; he shook with his fists, standing before the
throne, and demanded with halting and ejaculations permission for
the exodus of his people into the free !and, under color of the sacrifice in the desert. Not once he did this, but even ten times, for
Pharaoh could not exactly deny him audience, considering all the
facts. A hard and prolonged struggle ensued between the King and
Moses. Never did it get so far as to convert the King to Moses' view;
a more likely result would be that some day the people of Goshen
would be thrust out of a land only too glad to see the last of them.
About the struggle and the kind of pressure exerted on the stub-
bornly resisting King, much has been written and said, not without
plausibility, though all of it bears the marks of having been embel-
lished. There is talk of the ten plagues, with which Jahwe one after
the other afflicted Egypt to soften Pharaoh's heart, while at the same
time He deliberately hardened it in order to show His power afresh
by ever new plagues. Blood, frogs, vermin, wild beasts, murrain,
boils, hail, locusts, darkness, and death of the first-born: these were
the ten plagues, and not one of them impossible—though it is a
question whether any of them contributed anything to the result
excepting the last, which is very obscure and has never been entirely
explained. The Nile, under some circumstances, can assume a blood-
red color, its waters are temporarily foul, and the fish die. That
happens. It is possible for frogs to multiply in the marshes or lice
and flies to propagate to the proportion of a plague. There were still
many lions roving at the edge of the desert and lurking in the jungle
of the dead branch of the Nile. And if the number of ravening attacks
on men and beast were greatly on the increase, that too might be
considered a plague. How frequent are itch and mange in Egypt,
and how easily there might be eruptions due to uncleanliness which
would riot like a pestilence among the masses! In that land the sky

is mostly clear; so that a rare and violent storm must make the profounder impression, and the lightning thrust mingled with the coarse gravel of hail strike the crops and make the trees to writhe without having any special significance beyond the natural. The locust is an all-too-familiar guest, and men have sometimes found means of protection against its greedy hosts. Yet oftener they come on triumphant, and whole stretches of land are devoured and laid bare. Finally, whoever has witnessed the gloomy and sinister atmosphere accompanying an eclipse of the sun can understand that a people used to brilliant light might call such a darkness and gloom by the name of plague.

But with that the tale of the plagues is done; for the tenth, the death of the first-born, is not in the same category, being an incident closely connected with the exodus itself, very puzzling and perhaps better left unexamined. As for the others, any of them might have happened singly or, in a long enough span of time, have happened "all together." One has to regard them more or less as figures of speech for the one single form of pressure that Moses could exert against Ramessu: the fact that Pharaoh was his grandfather in the flesh and that Moses could always make it public. More than once the King came close to yielding, and in time he did make great concessions. He consented that the males might go out to the sacrifice and feast, the women and children, flocks and herds remaining behind. Moses did not agree. With young and old, sons and daughters, sheep and oxen they must go out, for this was to be a feast before the Lord. Then Pharaoh yielded the wives and children, keeping back only the cattle for a pledge. But Moses inquired where, if there were no cattle, the animals would come from for the slaughter and the burnt offering. No, not one single hoof might remain behind—and thus it became clear that here was no question of a leave, but of a leaving.

This matter of the cattle resulted in a last stormy scene between Egypt's Majesty and Jahwe's servant. Moses had displayed great patience throughout the interview, though his fists shook with his inward rage. Pharaoh at last brought things to a head and literally drove Moses out of the hall of audience. "Away!" he shouted, "and take care not to come before my face again! If you do you shall die the death." Then Moses, from high excitement got all at once perfectly calm. He answered: "You have said. I go, and I will come no more before your face." But beneath this frightful composure as he took his leave his thoughts were not pleasant to contemplate. He did not like them himself—but the young men, Joshua and Caleb, they did.

8

This is a dark chapter, to be set down only in half words and veiled. A day came, or rather a night, an evil vesper, when Jahwe, or rather his avenging angel, went about and visited the tenth plague upon the children of Egypt, or rather upon a part of them, the Egyptians among the dwellers in Goshen as well as in the cities of Pithom and Ramses; for those huts and houses whose doorposts had been marked with blood as a sign were spared and passed by.

What was He doing? He was causing a dying, the dying of the first-born of Egyptian stock—in which He met many secret wishes and helped many second-born to their rights, which might otherwise have been withheld. A distinction must be noted between Jahwe and His avenging angel. It was not Jahwe Himself who went about, but His avenging angel or probably more correctly a whole carefully chosen band of them. But if anybody is bent on reducing the multiplicity to one, then much goes to show that Jahwe's avenging angel took the shape of an upstanding youthful figure with curly hair, prominent Adam's apple, and well-marked brows, a type of angel which is at all times glad to make an end of fruitless negotiations and get down to action.

There had been no lack of preparations for decisive action during the protracted negotiations with Pharaoh. For Moses himself they had been limited to his anticipating serious trouble and sending back his wife and sons secretly to Midian, to his brother-in-law Jethro, so as not to be hampered by concern about them. But Joshua, whose relation to Moses unmistakably resembles that of the avenging angel to Jahwe, had behaved after his own lights; and as he had not the means, or even the authority, to put his three-thousand arms-bearing comrades on a war footing, he armed at least a chosen few, drilled them and kept them under discipline, so that in case of need they would do for a start.

The events of that long ago are shrouded in darkness—in the very darkness of the vesper which, in the eyes of the children of Egypt, was a feast night for the slaves who lived among them. These slaves, it seemed, wanted to make up for the forbidden sacrificial feast in the desert by a celebration where they were, with feasting, lights, and worship. They had even borrowed gold and silver vessels for the occasion from their Egyptian neighbors. But meanwhile, possibly instead of the feast, there came this going about of the avenging angel, the death of the first-born in all the houses not marked by the branch of hyssop dipped in blood. The visitation brought with it so great a confusion, such a sudden upset of stable conditions and legal rights, that from one hour to the next the Moses-people found that the way out of the country stood open—yes, and that they could not take it fast enough to please the Egyptians. Actually it seems that the second-born were less zealous to avenge the death of those whose place they took than the originators of their elevation were to depart. The story goes that the ten plagues at last broke Pharaoh's pride so that he let Moses' father's tribe go free from slavery. Yet he sent speedily in pursuit a division of troops, which then were miraculously destroyed.

Be that as it may, in any case the exodus took the form of an expulsion, and the haste in which it was performed is established by the known detail that nobody had time to raise bread for the journey. They could only provide themselves with unleavened cakes, and Moses made the circumstance a commemoration and feast for all time. For the rest, great and small were quite ready. While the avenging angel went about they had sat with girded loins by their loaded carts, their shoes on their feet, their staves in their hands. The gold and silver vessels they had borrowed from the natives they took along.

My friends, in the exodus out of Egypt both killing and stealing took place. But Moses had firmly resolved that it should be for the last time. How shall man rid himself once and for all of sin save by making himself thoroughly sinful to begin with? Moses now had them out in the open—this fleshly object of his pedagogic concern, this formless humanity, his father's blood. In freedom the work of sanctification could begin.

9

The pilgrim band, very much smaller than legend reports, but hard enough to handle, lead, and tend for all that, were quite enough burden for him who bore the responsibility for their fate. They took the only route they could take if they wanted to avoid the Egyptian fortifications that begin north of the Bitter Lakes. It led through the district of the Salt Lakes, into which runs the larger, more westerly arm of the Red Sea to make a peninsula of the land of Sinai. Moses knew this region; he had passed through it both on his flight to Midian and on his return. Better than to young Joshua, the lie of the land was familiar to Moses, and the nature of these reedy shallows which sometimes made a connection between the Bitter Lakes and the sea, and through which under some conditions one could cross over dry shod into the land of Sinai. That is, if a strong east wind were blowing, the waters would be driven back and afford free passage. It was in this state the fugitives found them, thanks to Jahwe's favoring dispensation.

Joshua and Caleb spread the news among the hosts that Moses, invoking God, had held his staff above the waters and induced them to withdraw and make a passage for the people. Probably he did hold out his staff, aiding the east wind with solemn gesture in Jahwe's name. Anyhow, the faith of the people in their leader could do with such strengthening, the more that just here, and here first, it was put upon a hard proof. For here it was that Pharaoh's pursuing hosts, troops and wagons, grim sickle wagons which they knew only too well, overtook the fugitives and came very near to putting a bloody terminus to their pilgrimage to God.

The news of their approach came from Joshua's rear guard and roused extreme panic among the people. Regret that they had followed "this man Moses" flared up at once, and a mass murmuring arose which, to Moses' bitter affliction, was to repeat itself at every fresh difficulty they got into. The women cried to heaven, the men cursed and shook their fists at their thighs just as Moses did when he was outraged. "Were there not graves in Egypt," they said, "where we could have been laid peacefully at our hour, if we had stopped at home?" All at once Egypt was "home," which had always been a foreign house of bondage. "It would be better for us to serve the Egyptians than to perish by the sword in the wilderness." A thousand times Moses heard it; it even embittered the joy of deliverance, overwhelming as that was. He was always "the man Moses who led us out of Egypt," and that was praise so long as things went right. But if things went wrong, then the tune changed and the words turned into a growl of reproach, from which the idea of stoning was not so remote.

Well, after the brief alarm, things went so incredibly well that the people were abashed. Now Moses, by God's favor, stood very high, and was "the man who led us out of Egypt"—only in the other sense. The tribes rolled through the dry fords, and after them the wagons of Egypt. Then the wind died down, the waters rushed back, man and steed perished with gurgles in the consuming flood.

The triumph was beyond everything. Miriam the prophetess, Aaron's sister, sang, leading the women in the dance: "Sing to the Lord, for He has triumphed gloriously, the horse and his rider has He thrown into the sea." She wrote it herself. It must be imagined sung to the timbrel.

The people were deeply moved. The words mighty, holy, frightful, wonderful, miracle-working did not cease to pour from their lips. And it was unclear whether the adjectives were applied to the Deity or to Moses the man of God, of whom one assumed that his staff had brought the devouring flood rolling back over the might of Egypt. This confusion always threatened. When the people were not actually complaining of Moses he had a hard time preventing them from taking him for a god—for Him whom he preached.

10

That was at bottom not so absurd. For what he now began to require of the poor creatures was beyond the powers of ordinary humanity. Indeed, it could hardly have occurred to the mind of a mere mortal. It made one gape. Directly after Miriam's song Moses forbade all further exultation over the destruction of Egypt. He announced that Jahwe's angelic hosts had been about to join in the song of triumph, when the Deity told them: "What, my creatures are sinking in the sea and you would sing?" Moses put about this brief but amazing tale. He added: "Thou shalt not rejoice at the fall of thy foe; the heart shall not be glad at his overthrow." It was the first time that the whole huddle of them, twelve thousand and some hundred head, including three-thousand arms-bearing men, had been addressed like that as "thou"—a form that took them all in and at the same time fixed its eye on each one singly: man and wife, gray beard and infant. It deeply moved each one of them, as though a finger had touched each breast. Thou shalt not shout with joy at the fall of thy foe: that was in the highest degree unnatural. But obviously this unnaturalness was connected with the invisible nature of Moses' God who wanted to be their God. It began to dawn upon the more mentally alert among the dark-skinned herd just what all this meant, and how uncanny and irretrievable it was to have vowed allegiance to an invisible God.

They were in the land of Sinai; in fact, in the desert of Shur, a dismal tract which they would leave only to enter another as dismal, the desert of Paran. There was no reason why this desert should have two names. The two tracts abutted aridly one on the other and were one and the same waterless, cropless, accursed flatland, running up into dead hills; three days' march long, or even four and five. Moses had done well to begin his shaping task at the moment when his prestige was highest, at the Red Sea. For presently he was "this man Moses who led us out of Egypt"—that is to say, into misfortune. Loud grumbling assailed his ears. After three days the water supply dwindled. Thousands were thirsty—over their heads the relentless sun, under their feet the barren, flinty waste, whether it still called itself Shur or already Paran. "What shall we drink?" They shouted it aloud without feeling for the suffering of their responsible leader. He wished he might be the only one not to drink, never again to drink if only they could, if only he might not hear "Why have you made us leave Egypt?" To suffer alone is slight in comparison with having to pay for the sufferings of such a host. Moses was a much troubled man, and remained so—troubled above all men on earth.

And very soon there was no more to eat; for how long could their hastily snatched supply of unleavened cakes hold out? "What shall we eat?" This cry too arose with weeping and railing, and Moses had heavy hours alone with his God, when he told Him how harsh He was to lay the whole burden of this people upon Moses, His servant. "Did I then conceive and bear them all," he asked, "that you can say to me 'Carry them in your arms'? Where shall I get food for all the people? They weep before me and say 'Give us meat that we may eat.' I cannot carry so many alone, it is too hard for me. Then rather slay me that I behold not my misfortune and theirs."

But Jahwe did not leave him quite in the lurch. As for drink, on the fifth day they reached a table land and, crossing it, found a spring with trees, called on the maps *Marah,* as Joshua knew. The water had a bad taste due to unpalatable minerals in it. Bitter disappointment followed and prolonged grumbling, until Moses, made inventive by necessity, contrived a sort of filter which largely did away with the bad taste. To his people it was a little miracle and turned railing into praise, greatly improving his reputation once more. The words "who brought us out of the land of Egypt" had again a mellow ring.

And as for the food, here too there came a miracle, which at first evoked joyous amaze. Wide stretches of the desert of Paran proved to be covered with an edible fungus, a sweet-tasting flake, small and round, that looked like coriander seed and was very perishable, beginning to smell if not eaten at once. But grated or pounded and baked in flat cakes it made a tolerable food, tasting rather like wafers and honey, some thought; others found it rather like seed cake made with oil.

That was the first, more favorable verdict. But it did not last. After a few days they got sick and tired of the manna. As their sole food it became repulsive to them, and they complained: "We remember all the fish we had in Egypt, the gourds and leeks and onions and garlic. Our souls are weary, for our eyes see naught but manna."

Moses heard and suffered. And heard, of course, the eternal question, Why have you made us leave Egypt? What he asked God was: What shall I do with this folk? They will eat no more manna. You will see, only a little more and they will stone me!

11

From that fate at least he was more or less protected by young Joshua and the body of troops he had already gathered to his standard in Goshen. They surrounded the Liberator whenever grumbling and threats increased among the masses. They had been but a small body at first, and young, but Joshua only awaited a proper occasion to make himself commander-in-chief and put all the arms-bearing men, the whole three-thousand, under his orders. And he was aware that such an occasion was at hand.

Moses was dependent on the young man, whom he had named with the name of God. There were times when he would have been lost without him. For Moses was a religious man, and his virility, sturdy and strong as it was, like that of a broad-wristed mason, was a spiritual virility, turned in upon itself, held in check by God, full of fanatic inward zeal, and in his preoccupation with holiness blind to outward appearances. He had a sort of flightiness in odd contrast to his habitual pose of brooding contemplation, with his mouth and beard covered by his hand. In all that he thought and did Moses had one single idea: that of getting his father's sect to himself that he might form it to his desire and carve out of this hapless, amorphous mass, which he so loved, the sacred image of the Deity. But he had thought little or nothing about the risks of freedom or the hardships of the desert or the trouble of getting such a horde as this through it in safety. He had not even much considered where he would take them afterward, nor had he at all prepared himself for the practical duties of leadership. So he could but be glad to have Joshua at his side; while for his part the youth worshipped Moses' religious fervor and put his own sturdy, forthright young manhood utterly at Moses' command.

It was due to Joshua that they moved in a straight line through the desert and did not go around in circles till they died. Joshua mapped their course by the stars, reckoned the daily march, and took care that they reached a water supply at tolerable, sometimes just barely tolerable, intervals. It was Joshua too who found out that the manna could be eaten. In a word he was a prop to the reputation of his master; and whenever the phrase "the man who led us out of Egypt" began to sound threatening he took steps to turn it into praise. He had the goal clear in his mind and steered thither direct, in agreement with Moses. For both of them felt that they needed an immediate goal, a settled even though not permanent habitation, a place where they could live and have time, quite a good deal of time: partly (this in Joshua's mind) that they might breed and produce the recruits for a larger body of troops; partly (this in Moses' view) that he might first mold this clay in God's likeness, might make something respectable and even pure and holy of it and dedicate the work of his hands to the invisible God, toward whom he yearned both in his soul and in his broad-wristed body.

The goal was the oasis of Kadesh. We have seen that the desert of Paran immediately adjoined the desert of Shur. But south of Paran lay still another, the desert of Sinai. Yet not quite so immediately, for at one point in between the two lay the oasis of Kadesh. It was a plain, beautiful by comparison with the desert—a green refreshment in the waterless waste, with three large springs and a number of smaller ones; a day's march long by half a march wide. It had good soil and was covered with fresh pasture. In short, it was an inviting stretch of land with ample food and game, large enough to lodge and feed a body like theirs.

Joshua knew of this attractive spot; it was well marked on the map he carried in his head. Moses knew about it too, but it was Joshua's idea that they should make for it. Here was his chance. A pearl like Kadesh did not, of course, lie there ownerless. It was occupied in strength; yet perhaps not too strongly, young Joshua hoped. Still, if they wanted it they must fight for it with those in possession—and that was Amalek.

It was some of the Amalekites who held Kadesh, and certainly they would defend it. Joshua made it clear to Moses that there must be war, a battle between Jahwe and Amalek, even if permanent enmity were the result from generation to generation. They had to have the oasis; it was the perfect site for their combined needs of physical and spiritual growth.

Moses hesitated. For him one of the implications of the invisible nature of God was that a man should not covet his neighbor's house, and he voiced the objection to his henchman. But Joshua answered: "Kadesh is not Amalek's house." For the youth was knowledgeable in time as well as in space, and he knew that historically Kadesh had been occupied—he did not indeed know when—by Hebrews, hence kinfolk, descendants of the fathers who had been driven out and scattered by the Amalekites. Kadesh, then, had been stolen, and it was fair enough to steal it back.

Moses doubted it. But he had his own grounds for thinking that Kadesh was a domain of Jahwe and belonged to those who were in a Covenant with Him. Kadesh meant "sanctuary," and the oasis was so called not alone on account of its natural advantages. In a sense it was a shrine of the Midianite Jahwe, whom Moses had confessed as the God of his Fathers. Not far off, eastward toward Edom, lay in a line with other mountains Mount Horeb, which Moses had visited from Midian and on whose slope God had revealed Himself in the burning bush. Horeb, the mountain, was Jahwe's seat—one of them, at least. His original seat, Moses knew, was Mount Sinai, in the range to the far south. But between Sinai and Horeb, the site of Moses' commission, there was close connection, in that Jahwe had His seat on both of them; you could put them on a par, you could call Horeb Sinai. And Kadesh was called what it was, a sanctuary, because, roughly speaking, it lay at the foot of the sacred mount.

Moses, then, accepted Joshua's plan and instructed him to prepare for the armed encounter between Jahwe and Amalek.

12

The battle took place; that is historic fact. It was a hard-fought battle, swaying to and fro. But Israel issued from it triumphant. This name, Israel, meaning "God fighteth," had been conferred by Moses on his people to strengthen them for the ordeal. He explained that it was a very old name, long forgotten: Jacob the patriarch had wrested it by struggle for himself and given it to his people. It did the tribes a great deal of good. The loose unorganized mass, being now all Israel, fought unitedly and well under the aegis of this name, ranged in order of battle and commanded by Joshua the youthful general and Caleb his second in command.

When the Amalekites beheld the approaching hosts they did not doubt the meaning of what they saw. Such a sight has but one meaning. They did not remain in the oasis and await the attack, but issued forth at once in great strength into the wilderness. They were more numerous and better armed than the Israelites, and the battle was joined between the two armies amid whirling clouds of dust, loud battle cries, and great tumult and din. It was still more unequal because Joshua's people were plagued with thirst and for some days had had only manna to eat. On the other hand, they were strong in their leaders, the clear-eyed youth Joshua and Moses the man of God.

Moses, indeed, at the beginning of the fray, had withdrawn, together with his half-brother Aaron and Miriam the prophetess, upon a hill where they could look down on the place of decision. His virility was not of the martial kind, but rather of a priestly nature; hence it was his vocation, unquestioned by any, to call upon God with uplifted arms and in words of fire—as for instance, "Rise up, Jahwe of the myriads, the thousands of Israel, and smite the foe, that they who hate Thee may flee and be scattered from before Thy face!"

They fled not and they scattered not, or they did so at first only locally and temporarily. For though Israel raged mightily, mad with thirst and disgust of manna, yet the myriads of Amalek were more, and after briefly falling back they again advanced, and even got dangerously close to Moses' own hill. But it turned out that as long as Moses held up his arms to heaven, Israel triumphed; but if he let them fall, then Amalek did. Of course, he could not hold them up all the time; so Aaron and Miriam supported him under the armpits and held his arms aloft. But what that meant one can measure by the fact that the battle lasted from morn to eve, and in all that time Moses had to sustain his painful attitude. So we see what a hard time spiritual virility had up there praying on its hill—very likely even harder than sturdy youth hacking away down in the melée.

Even so, Moses could not keep it up all day on end. His assistants had to let the master's arms down for a minute once in a while; and straightaway Jahwe's men lost blood and ground. Then they hoisted the arms up again, and those below drew fresh strength from the sight. Joshua's military talents also availed to bring about the favorable issue of the conflict. He had a real gift both for planned strategy and for brilliant inspiration, and invented novel maneuvers, quite unheard of before, at least in the wilderness; besides he had a strength of purpose that could look on undismayed at a temporary loss of ground. He assembled the best troops he had, a selected group—the avenging angels, in short—on the enemy's right wing, exerted great pressure there, forced it to fall back, and scored a local victory, though elsewhere the greater strength of Amalek was in the ascendant and gaining ground from Israel in violent lunges. However, by breaking through on the flank Joshua got into Amalek's rear, so that the latter had to turn around and fight him while still engaged with the main body of Israel's army, which had been close to surrender but now took heart afresh. Now Amalek lost his head; panic seized on him, and he gave up the fight. "Treason! Despair!" he cried. "All is lost! Jahwe is over us, a God of insatiable cruelty!" And with this despairing cry Amalek let fall his sword and was slain.

Only a few of his party succeeded in fleeing northward and joining the main group of their tribe. But Israel entered into the oasis of Kadesh, which proved to have a broad, swift stream running through it and to be planted with fruit trees and nut bushes and filled with bees, songbirds, quail and hares. Some of the children of Amalek had remained behind; these swelled the numbers of Israel's progeny, while Amalek's wives became the wives and servants of the Israelites.

13

Moses, though his arms were stiff long afterward, was a happy man. That he remained a much troubled one, tried above any other on earth, we shall soon see. But in the beginning he was very happy over the way things had turned out. The exodus had been accomplished, Pharaoh's avenging might was sunk in the reedy sea, the journey through the wilderness had gone off well and with Jahwe's help the battle of Kadesh was won. And now he stood before his father's people and was "the man Moses who has led us out of Egypt." He had needed just this success in order to begin his work, the work of purification and shaping in the sign of the Invisible; the work of chipping and chiseling at this flesh and blood, after which his soul had yearned. Happy he was to have this flesh now by itself in the open, in the oasis whose name meant sanctuary. Here was his workshop.

He showed the people the mountain visible among others at the back side of the desert east of Kadesh: Horeb, which one might also call Sinai. It was covered with bushes two-thirds of the way up, above that bare; and it was Jahwe's seat. The statement was not hard to credit; for it looked unusual, being distinguished from the others by a cloud that never went away, but lay at all times like a thatch on its head. In the daytime it looked gray, but at night it was lighted up. There, so his people heard, on the thicketed slope below the rocky peak, Jahwe had spoken to Moses out of the burning bush and commanded him to lead them out of Egypt. They listened with fear and trembling, which with them still took the place of awe and worship. Actually all of them, even the bearded men, trembled at the knees like savages and cowards when Moses pointed out the mountain in its abiding cap of cloud and told them the God sat there who had a mind to them and would be their only God. Moses, his fists shaking, scolded them for their pusillanimity and laid himself out to give them a better and more familiar attitude toward Jahwe by setting up a shrine for Him in the midst of them, at Kadesh itself.

For Jahwe, it seemed, had a movable presence; that, like so much else, fell together with His invisibility. He sat on Sinai, He sat on Horeb, and now Moses—directly they had got settled into the houses of the Amalekites at Kadesh—made Him a dwelling in their very midst, near Moses' own, which he called the tent of meeting or assembly, also the tabernacle, where were kept certain sacred articles which could be used about the Imageless and in His honor. They were chiefly things that Moses remembered as having to do with the cult of the Midianite Jahwe. First there was a sort of chest with carrying poles, on which, according to Moses (and certainly he ought to know) the God sat throned invisible and would be borne thus into the field and in the front of the battle if ever Amalek should return seeking revenge. A bronze staff with a serpent's head, in short the so-called brazen serpent, was kept beside the chest in memory of Aaron's well-intentioned trick before Pharaoh. It had now the added meaning that it might also stand for the staff that Moses had stretched out over the reedy shallows to divide the waters. Likewise the "Ephod" was kept in the Jahwe tent: a sort of bag for the drawing of lots, the "Urim and Thummim," the yes or no, right or wrong, which was appealed to in cases of difficulties and disagreement, to invoke Jahwe's judgment where man's failed.

But in most cases Moses did the judging himself. Indeed, almost the first thing he did at Kadesh was to set up a judgment seat, where on certain days he resolved disputes and gave out law, sitting beside the largest spring in the oasis, the Me-Meribah or water of judgment, already so called. Thence flowed the law, even as the water flowed out of the earth. But when one remembers that there were all together some twelve-thousand-five-hundred souls who applied to him for justice, one can measure the extent of Moses' tribulations. For they pressed about his seat at the fountain, the more so that the idea of "right" was something quite new to this lost, bewildered sect. Indeed, they scarce knew there was such a thing—and now they came to hear that the "right" was immediately associated with the invisibility of their God and His holiness, that it was under His direct protection. Further, they heard that in this new idea of right was included the idea of "wrong." And this the masses for a long time utterly failed to grasp. They thought that where the right flowed everyone must get his rights; they would not and could not believe that a man was getting his "rights" even when he was judged in the wrong and had to go away with his nose out of joint. Such a man, of course, cursed himself for not having settled the quarrel with his opponent in the natural way, with a stone, when the result might have been quite different. Only slowly did they learn from Moses that such ideas were not in harmony with the invisibility of God, and that nobody got his nose put out of joint who was judged unright by the law, for that the law was always both beautiful and austere in its holy invisibility, no matter whether it pronounced a man in the right or in the wrong.

So Moses had not alone to pronounce the law, but also to teach it, and was troubled indeed. He had studied it in his school in Thebes, the Egyptian legal rolls and the Codes of Hammurabi, the King on the Euphrates. That helped him to clear judgment in many of the cases that came up. For instance, if an ox had gored a man or a woman the ox should be stoned and his flesh not eaten, but the owner of the ox was innocent unless it was well known that the ox was used to push with his horns and the owner had not kept him in. In that case the owner too lost his life, unless he could redeem it with thirty silver shekels. Or if any man opened a pit and did not cover it properly, so that an ox or an ass fell in, then the owner of the pit must make it good by giving money to him, and the dead beast should be his. Or whatever happened of bodily injury, harm to slaves, breaking in and stealing, damage to fields, arson or abuse of trust; in all such cases and in a hundred others Moses found judgment, leaning on Hammurabi, and pronounced between right and wrong. But there were too many cases for one judge, and the seat by the fount of judgment was overrun. If the master investigated thoroughly one single case, he never got done, he had to postpone judgment, fresh cases came up; he was plagued over and above the lot of mankind.

14

So it was very good that his brother-in-law Jethro, from Midian, visited him at Kadesh and gave him a piece of advice, an idea that his own obstinate conscience would never have hit upon. Soon after he arrived in the oasis Moses had sent down to Midian to his father-in-law to have him send back his wife Zipporah and his two sons, for he had given them into his charge during the tribulations in Egypt. But Jethro was kind enough to come in person to hand over Moses' wife and sons, to embrace him and hear how things were going.

He was a portly sheik with a merry eye and easy gestures, a man of the world, prince of a developed and socially experienced people. He was welcomed with due ceremony and went in to Moses into his hut and heard, not without amazement, how one of his gods, the very one who was invisible among them, had conducted Himself so surprisingly toward Moses and his people and how He had known how to deliver them out of the hands of the Egyptians.

"Who would have thought it?" he said. "He is obviously much greater than we supposed, and what you tell me makes me afraid that we have been negligent in His service up till now. I must see to it that He receives greater honor among us." The next day public burnt offerings were appointed, such as Moses seldom commanded. He had no exaggerated ideas about offerings; they were not essential, he thought, before the Invisible; it was a custom practiced by other peoples, the peoples of the world. Whereas Jahwe had said: "Above all hearken to My voice; that is, to the voice of My servant Moses. For then I will be your God and you My people." But this time there were slayings and burnings for Jahwe's nostrils as well as in celebration of Jethro's visit. And on the next day early in the morning he took his brother-in-law with him to the judgment fount

254 · *Thomas Mann*

to be present at a sitting and see how Moses sat and judged the people. They clustered around him from morn to eve, and there was no end to it.

"Tell me, my dear brother-in-law," said the guest as they left the place together, "tell me, why on earth you give yourself all that trouble! Sitting alone and all the crowd standing around from morn to eve! Why do it?"

"I must do so," Moses answered. "The people come to me that I may judge between each one and his neighbor and show him God's justice and His laws."

"But, my dear fellow, how can you be so impracticable?" said Jethro again. "Is that a way to govern? Does a ruler let himself be skinned alive, doing everything himself? You are getting so worn out it is a shame; you can hardly see out of your eyes, you lose your voice—and your people are just as tired out as you are. That is no way to do it; you can't go on doing everything yourself, and it is not at all necessary. Just listen to me! If you represent God to the people and bring the most important things to His attention your-self—things which are of general concern—that is quite enough. Look around," he said with an easy wave of the hand, "among your people for upright and judicious men, a bit looked up to, and set them over the people to be rulers over a thousand, over a hundred, yes, over fifty and ten, and have them judge according to justice and the law you have given to the people. And only in a great matter shall they bring it to you, settling the lesser ones themselves. You don't need to know anything about it. That is the way we do, and it will greatly ease matters for you. I should not have had my fine little paunch, nor could I have got away to visit you, if I thought I had to know everything and do the way you do."

"But the judges will take presents," answered Moses gloomily, "and give the judgment to the godless. For presents make the seeing blind and wrench the true cause the false way."

"Yes, I know," responded Jethro. "Well I know. But you will have to stand a little of that sort of thing so long as justice more or less prevails and there is law and order, even if it gets a bit complicated with presents and such. You see, the ones that take presents are ordinary people; but after all, the people are just ordinary too. So for the ordinary it has meaning and is suited and agreeable to the community. Besides, if some man has his business judged ill by the judge over ten because the judge has taken presents from the unrigh-teous, then let him follow the usual routine and course of justice and appeal to the judge over fifty, and then over a hundred, and finally over a thousand. He gets the most presents of all, so he has a more open mind and the petitioner will get justice from him—if he has not got tired of the whole thing first."

Thus Jethro, with such soothing voice and gesture that it made life easier only to look at him; it was clear that he was priest-king of a developed and civilized desert folk. Moses listened pensively and nodded his head. He had the suggestible soul of the lonely, spiritual-minded man, who nods musingly at the wisdom of the world and perceives that it may well be right. And he did indeed take the advice of his experienced brother-in-law—there was really nothing else for him to do. He appointed lay judges to sit by the fountain and dispense petty justice, guided by his instructions. These men judged the ordinary day-to-day cases (as when an ass fell into a pit), and only the capital cases came up to him, the priest of God. The most important of all were decided by the sacred lots.

So now he was no longer involved beyond reason, but got his hands free for the educational program he proposed to carry out on the unformed mass of this folk, the theater for which had been fought for and won by the strategic-minded young Joshua, that is to say, the oasis of Kadesh. No doubt Justice was an important factor among all the implications of the Invisible; but, after all, it was only one—and how many factors there were! And what a task it was, how long and arduous, demanding both great patience and great fury! It would be hard enough to turn this uncivilized, ill-mannered horde into a decent ordinary folk fitting into the ordinary decent ways of life. That would be one thing; but quite another to make something extraordinary of them, a set apart and sanctified people, a purified community with its eyes fixed upon the Invisible and addressed to Him alone.

15

The kindred soon saw what it meant to have fallen into the hands of a man like Moses, a man of wrath and of infinite patience, a workman responsible alone for the invisible God. They saw that it had been only the beginning, that unnatural command to refrain from shouting for joy when the foe was drowned. In fact, even that beginning was premature. For it demanded of them an advanced stage of enlightenment resting on many premises of which they were ignorant. They had a long, long way to go before they could find it anything but utterly inhuman. They were, in short, nothing but raw material, flesh and blood, and the fundamental conceptions of purity and holiness entirely escaped them. So much is clear from the way Moses had to go to work from the very beginning and the pathetically primitive laws he had to instill into them. They did not like it: the block is not on the mason's side, but against him, and the first thing that happens in its shaping seems the most unnatural of all.

Moses was always among them, now here and now there, in this settlement and that; stocky, with flat nose and wide-set eyes. He shook his fists on their broad wrists; he nagged and nudged, he pushed and shoved, he bounced and bossed and rubbed and scrubbed at them, and always the invisibility of God was his text—Jahwe's, who had led them out of Egypt in order to make them His people, and who must have holy folk about him even as He Himself was holy. At the moment they were nothing but an unlicked crew, and they relieved themselves just wherever they happened to be. That was a shame and a nuisance. You must have a place outside, for you to go out to when you have need. And you must keep a little trowel by you and dig a little hole before you sit down and afterward you must cover it up. For in your dwelling the Lord your God moves about, and so it must be a pure and holy place so that He does not hold His nose and turn away. For godliness begins with cleanliness, and if there is purity even in the lowest things, then that is the lowly beginning of all purity. Do you understand that, Ahiman, and you, Naemi, his woman? Next time let me see everybody with a trowel, or the avenging angel will be after you!

Furthermore, you must be clean and bathe a great deal in running water for your health's sake; for without health there is no purity or holiness, and sickness is unclean. If you think that filth is healthier than cleanliness, then you are a fool, and you will be stricken with jaundice, fig boils, and the boils of Egypt. If you practice not cleanliness, then an evil black pox will break out and the seeds of pestilence go from blood to blood. Learn to distinguish between purity and impurity, or you cannot stand before the Invisible and are simply the scum of the earth. If a man or woman have a consuming eruption, an evil issue on the body, scab or itch, he or she shall be impure and not suffered in the dwelling place, but be put outside it, set apart in uncleanness, even as the Lord has set you apart to be pure. And whatever such a one has touched or lain upon, and the saddle he rode on, shall be burned. But if he becomes clean while set apart, he shall reckon seven days to see if he be verily clean, and bathe thoroughly with water: then he may come back.

Distinguish, I say to you, and be delicate in the sight of God or you cannot be holy as I would have you be. You eat everything regardless, without discrimination or shame, and it is an abomination to you. For you should eat one thing and not another, and feel both pride and disgust. Whatsoever parteth the hoof among the beasts and cheweth the cud, that shall ye eat. But what cheweth the cud and hath hoofs but divides them not, as the camel, it is unclean to you and you shall not eat it. Note that the good camel is not unclean, for he is God's creature; but he is not proper as food—as little as the swine, which likewise you shall not eat, for though it part the hoof, yet it does not chew the cud. So make a distinction! All that has fins and scales in the water may ye eat, but all that glides about without them, the tribe of newts, that is indeed from God too, but as food shall be an abomination to you. And among the fowls these are they you shall hold in abhorrence: the eagle, the hawk, the osprey, the vulture, and after their kind; every raven after his kind, the ostrich, the night owl, the cuckoo, the little owl, the swan, the great owl, the bat, the bittern, the stork, the heron, the crane, as well as the swallow. I forgot the hoopoe; that also shall you avoid. Who will eat the weasel, the mouse, the toad, or the hedge hog? Who is so low as to eat the lizard, the mole, or the blind worm, or anything that creeps upon the earth or crawls upon his belly? But you do it, and thereby make your souls an abomination. If ever again I see anyone eat a blindworm, I will see to it he does not do so again. Truly he will not die of it, nor is it harmful; but it is shameful, and much shall be shameful to you. So shall you eat no carrion; that is harmful, too.

So he made diet rules for them and restricted them in their eating—but not only therein. For he did the same in matters of love and lust; for here too they were very promiscuous, and their ways were vulgar in the extreme. You shall not break the bed vow, he told them, for it is a sacred bar. But do you know what it means, not to break the bed vow? It means a hundred restrictions, with respect to the holiness of God; and not alone that you shall not covet your neighbor's wife, for that is the least of it. You live in the flesh but are vowed to the Invisible and marriage is the whole content of all purity in the flesh before God's countenance. Therefore you shall not take a woman and her mother—to give you an example—for that is not fitting. And you must never lie with your sister to see her

258 · *Thomas Mann*

shame and she yours, for that is incest. Nor shall you even lie with
your aunt, for it is worthy neither of her nor of you, and you should
shrink from it. When a woman has her sickness you shall avoid her
and not approach the source of her blood. But if a man has a shameful issue in his sleep, he shall be impure until the next evening and
shall bathe thoroughly with water.

I hear you offer your daughter for a whore and take money from
her? Do not so, for if you persist I will have you stoned. And what
are you thinking of, to sleep with a boy as with a woman? That is
abnormal and an abomination among the people, and both shall die
the death. But if one do so with beasts, whether man or woman, they
shall be rooted out and shall be strangled together with the beast.

Imagine their consternation at all these restrictions! At first they
had the feeling that if one obeyed at all, life would not be worth
living. For Moses sprang about among them with his little chisel,
making the chips fly. Even literally: that about the punishments and
prohibitions proved to be no joke at all, for behind them stood
young Joshua and the avenging angels.

"I am the Lord your God," he said to them—and ran the risk of
having them take him at his word—"who led you out of the land
of Egypt and set you apart from all people. Therefore you shall also
separate the pure from the impure and not go whoring after other
peoples, but be sacred to Me alone. For I the Lord am holy and I
have set you apart to be Mine. The greatest uncleanness of all is to
trouble about any other God save Me, for I am a jealous God. The
worst of all is to make an image, let it look like man or woman, ox
or sparrow-hawk, fish or worm, for therewith you have already
fallen away from Me, even though the image should be of Me. Such
a one might just as well sleep with his sister or with a beast, for
there is no great difference, and one thing leads to the other. So take
care, for I am among you and I see all. He who whores after the
dead gods of Egypt, to him will I come home! I will hunt him into
the desert and cut him off like an outcast. In the same way whosoever sacrifices to Moloch, of whom, I well know, you still are mindful, and is smitten with his power, such a one is evil, and evilly will
I requite him. Therefore you shall not have your son or your daughter go through fire after the foolish old custom, nor shall you mark
the flight and cries of birds, nor mumble with soothsayers, augurs,
and interpreters of signs, nor question the dead nor meddle in magic
in My name. If a man be a villain and bring in My name to witness
in his mouth, that shall avail him least of all, for him will I consume.

But also to scratch or cut the face or shear the brows or mar the countenance in mourning for the dead, that is but cheap magic and an abomination. I will not have it."

How great was their consternation! So now they might not even mourn by making little cuts on the face; not even the least little bit of tattooing. So this was what it meant to have an invisible God! To covenant, they perceived, was to be limited extremely. Behind Moses' every prohibition stood the avenging angel; and since the people did not want to be driven into the desert, all the things that Moses forbade came to seem frightful to them. At first this was so only in connection with the punishment; but after a while the thing itself came to be thought of as an evil. And when a man broke the law it made him feel sick, even without thinking of the punishment.

Bridle your heart, so he told them, and cast not your eyes on another's goods to covet them, for that may easily lead to taking them, either by stealth, which is cowardly, or by murder, which is barbarous. Jahwe and I would have you neither cowards nor barbarians; the mean between them is what you must be—in other words, decent. Have you understood this much? Stealing is a skulking sin; but murder—whether out of rage or greed or greedy rage or raging greed—murder is a deed that cries to heaven. He who commits it, against him will I set My face, that he know not where he may hide himself. For he has shed blood, and, after all, blood is a great mystery, sacred and held in awe—an altar gift to Me and an atonement. Blood shall you not eat, and no flesh when blood is in it, for it is Mine. Now whosoever is smeared with man's blood, his heart shall shrink with cold horror, and I will hunt him until he runs from himself to the end of the earth. Say Amen!

And they all said Amen, hoping that when Moses used the word "murder" he meant literally killing, to which they had no great mind—or at least not often. But it turned out that Jahwe gave the word a meaning as broad as that which he had given to the breaking of the marriage vow. He meant by it all sorts of things, until murder and manslaughter ended by beginning with every injury one man did to another. Blood flowed, it appeared, in every overreaching or taking advantage—and to such nearly everybody had a mind. They must not deal falsely with each other, not bear false witness; they must give honest measure, full-weight pounds and bushels. It was all most unnatural; and for quite a while their natural fear of punishment was the only feature that seemed human at all.

A man must honor his father and his mother. Moses enjoined it upon them. But even this had a broader meaning than one would have supposed. Whoever lifted his hand against his begetter and cursed him—well, yes, such a one ought to be done away. But when the honoring extended to those who only might have been his father—? You must stand in the presence of gray hairs, cross your arms, and bow your simple head, you understand? Respect to God will have it so. The only consolation was that since your neighbor was forbidden to kill you, you had the prospect of getting old and gray yourself, so that the others would have to stand up and bow.

It came in the end to this: that age was a figure of speech for the old in general, for everything that was not of today or yesterday, but came from afar; for the pious and traditional, the usage of the fathers. To that one must pay honor and reverence. So shall you celebrate the day when I led you out of Egypt, the day of the unleavened bread, and always the day when I rested from the Creation. My day, the Sabbath, shall you not defile with the sweat of your brow; I forbid you. For I have led you out of the Egyptian house of bondage with mighty hand and outstretched arm, where you were a servant and a beast of burden, and My day shall be the day of your deliverance; that shall you celebrate. Six days shall you be a husbandman or a maker of plows, a potter or coppersmith, a cabinetmaker; but on My day shall ye put on fresh garments and be nothing but a man and open your eyes to the Invisible.

You were a slave there in Egypt, spent with toil—be mindful of it in your dealings with your own servants! You were a stranger among the children of Egypt—remember it in your treatment of the stranger among you, for instance, the children of Amalek whom God gave into your hands, and do not abuse them. Look on them as yourself and give them even-handed justice, or I will interfere, for they stand under Jahwe's shield. Make no such absurd and arrogant distinction between you and another man as to think that you alone are real and essential, while he is only a simulacrum. You have dear life in common, and it is only chance you are not he. Therefore love not yourself alone, but him as well, and do with him as you would he would do with you in his place. Be pleasant with each other and kiss the fingertips as you pass and bow politely and greet him, saying, I hope I see you well! For it is just as important that he is well as that you are. And if it be only out of mannerliness that you do so, and kiss your fingertips, yet after all the mere gesture must plant in your heart some feeling of the kind you should cherish for your neighbor.—Say Amen to all that!

16

But saying Amen did not get them very far. They only said it because he was the man who with luck had led them out of Egypt, sunk Pharaoh's wagons in the sea, and won the battle of Kadesh. It took a long time for his teachings and injunctions, his restrictions, commands, and prohibitions, to get under their skins or even to seem to do so. It was a big job he had undertaken: to raise up to the Lord out of these hordes a sanctified group, a cleansed community. In the sweat of his brow he worked on his mission, there in Kadesh his workshop. His wideset eyes were everywhere. He chiseled, blasted, planed, and smoothed at the rebellious block with sturdy patience, with repeated forbearance, often forgiving, sometimes blazing with scorn and lashing out ruthlessly. Even so he often despaired when this flesh on which he labored continued so willful, so forgetful, so unregenerate; when the people failed to use their little trowels or slept with their sisters or with the cow or ate blindworms or mutilated their faces, sat mumbling with soothsayers, committed petty thieveries, or even slew each other. "O beasts!" he said to them then, "you will see, the Lord will come down on you suddenly and blot you out." But to the Lord Himself he said: "What shall I do with this flesh, and why hast Thou removed Thy favor from me to lay upon my shoulders what I cannot bear? Rather will I clean the dung from a stall which seven years long has seen neither water nor spade, or clear a jungle with my hands to make a plowed field, than try to make a God-fearing people out of this filth. How do I come to be carrying this folk in my arms as if I had borne them? I am only half kin to them, on my father's side. So, I beseech You, make me glad of my life and let me off this task, for rather will I strangle myself!"

But God answered him out of his inmost self with so plain a voice that he heard it with his ears, and he fell on his face:

"Just because you are only half their kin, from the side of him buried, are you the man to work upon them for me and raise them up to me a seemly folk. For if you were in their very hearts and entirely one of them, you would not see them as they are and could not lay hand to them. But anyhow this lament of yours and your trying to beg off—all that is only pretense. For you surely see that a beginning has already been made with them; already you have made them a conscience, so that they are uncomfortable when they do wrong. So do not pretend to me that you have not the greatest zeal to your task. It is My zeal you have, Godly zeal, and without it your life would turn to disgust, as the manna to the people even after a few days. Of course, if I were to strangle you, then you could do without it; but no other way."

Moses, despite his misgivings, could see all that; he nodded at Jahwe's words as he lay on his face, and then again he stood up to his vow. But he was a man of grief, and that not only in his chosen task. For trouble and vexation reached into his family life; there was annoyance and envy and discord. It came through his own fault, if you like, for his senses were the cause of the affliction. The work left them raw and craving, and he fixed his heart on an Ethiopian; yes, the notorious Ethiopian female. For we know that at that time he lived with this woman, in addition to his first wife Zipporah, the mother of his sons. She was a person from the land of Kush, who had come as a child to Egypt, lived among the tribes in Goshen, and joined the exodus. No doubt she had already known more than one man; and still Moses took her to his bed. In her way she was a splendid piece of flesh, with towering breasts and rolling whites to her eyes; she had pouting lips, wherein to sink in a kiss might be an adventure to any man, and her skin smelled of spicery. Moses clung to her for her power to relax him, and could not part from her although he faced the hostility of his own family on her account: not only of his Midianitic wife and sons, but even more of his half-brother and sister, Miriam and Aaron. Zipporah indeed, having much of her brother Jethro's cosmopolitan poise, got on tolerably with her rival, especially as the woman took pains to hide her feminine triumph and behaved obsequiously toward the true wife. As for Zipporah, she treated the Ethiopian with more mockery than anger; and even to Moses himself she bridled her jealousy and behaved in the same spirit. The sons, Gershom and Eliezer, who were soldiers in Joshua's army, possessed too much feeling for discipline to contend against their father, though they did show some anger and chagrin over his behavior.

But things were different with Miriam and Aaron, the sanctimonious. Their hatred for the black woman was more venomous than the others' because it was by way of being an outlet for the deeper and more general anger that united them against Moses. Some time earlier they had begun to be jealous of his close relation to God, his spiritual leadership, his personal election, which they considered in great part imaginary. They thought they were just as good as he was, or better; saying to each other: "Does the Lord then speak by Moses only; speaks he not also by us? Who is this man Moses, that he should have raised himself so far above others?" Such emotions lay at the bottom of the offense they took at his relations with the black woman, and always when they attacked their brother and bitingly reproached him on account of his passionate nights, he knew to his sorrow that it was only the occasion for their real grievance; very soon they would go on to the injustice done them by his elevation.

One day they were with him in his house at sunset, tormenting him as usual with the black woman here and the black woman there, and how he clung to her black breasts, and what a scandal it was and what a slap in Zipporah's face, his first wife, and what an unmasking of himself, who claimed to be a spiritual lord and Jahwe's unique representative on earth. And so on.

"Claim?" said he. "What God has laid upon me to be, that I am. But how hateful of you, how really very hateful, to grudge me my pleasure and the relaxation I get on the breast of my Ethiopian girl! For it is no sin before God, and there is no prohibition among all those which he gave me, against lying with an Ethiopian. Not that I know of."

Oh, yes, they said. He made arbitrary rules and prohibitions, and it would not surprise them to hear that it was explicitly commanded to lie with Ethiopians, he being in his own eyes the only mouthpiece Jahwe had. But they, Miriam and Aaron, were genuine children of Amram, grandson of Levi, whereas he was, after all, only a foundling from the reeds and ought to learn a little humility. For his obstinacy about the Ethiopian, quite aside from the shame of it, was shocking because it sprang from his arrogance and conceit.

"Who can help his vocation?" said he. "And who can help it if he chance to see a burning bush? Miriam, I have always esteemed your prophetic gifts and never disputed your power with the timbrel."

"Then why did you forbid my song 'Horse and Rider'?" she asked, "and refuse to let me play before the women in dances because, forsooth, God had forbidden His hosts to rejoice at the destruction of Egypt? That was hateful of you."

"And you, Aaron," went on the hard-pressed man, "you I made high priest of the tabernacle and gave into your keeping the ark, the ephod, and the brazen serpent. So highly do I esteem you."

"It was the least you could do," responded Aaron, "for without my eloquence you would never have won over the people to Jahwe with your stammering tongue, nor have moved them to embark on the exodus. Yet you call yourself the man who brought us out of Egypt. Now if you do esteem us and do not in your vanity exalt yourself above the genuine brother and sister, why not listen to our words and open your ears to our warning that you bring our whole seed into danger with your black philanderings? For it is a bitter draft for Zipporah, your Midianitic wife, and you offend all Midian thereby, so that Jethro, your brother-in-law, will yet fall upon us, all on account of that black fancy of yours."

"Jethro," said Moses with great self-control, "is a well-balanced man of the world, who would, of course, understand that Zipporah, with all due respect to her name, can no longer afford a highly troubled and burdened man like me the needful relaxation. But the skin of my Ethiopian is like cinnamon and oil of carnation in my nostrils, and therefore I implore you, dear friends, grant her to me!"

But that they would not. They railed and demanded that not only should he part from the Ethiopian and she should void his bed, but that he should send her out without water into the desert.

Then Moses' angry vein began to swell, his fists to shake along his thighs. But before he could open his mouth in reply there came quite another shaking. For Jahwe intervened. He set His face against the hard-hearted brother and sister and took the side of his servant Moses, so that they never forgot it. Something frightful and unprecedented came to pass.

17

The foundations shook; the earth quaked and leaped and reeled under their feet so that they could not stand, but all three staggered to and fro in the hut, whose columns were shaken as by giant hands. The firm earth swayed, not only to one side, but to all sides at once, in a dizzying and confounding way, so that their sensations were horrible. And added to this came a subterranean bellowing and banging and, from above and without, a braying as of the loudest trumpets, accompanied by other groanings and thunderings and crashings. It is peculiarly confounding, when you are about to explode with wrath, to have the Lord take it right out of your mouth and do it Himself—only far more mightily than you could have done, shaking the whole earth whereas you could only have shaken your fists.

Moses was less alarmed than the others, being at all times steadfast in his God. But Aaron and Miriam were pallid with fright; and all three of them rushed out of the hut and saw that the earth had opened its mouth in a great crack just in front of them, which had obviously been intended for Miriam and Aaron, and they had escaped only by a few ells from being swallowed up. And lo, the mountain to the east, back in the desert—Horeb or Sinai: what was happening to Horeb, and what going on with Mount Sinai? It stood there wrapped in flame and smoke, flinging glowing fragments to heaven in a distant crash of explosions, while fiery rivers ran down its sides. Thick smoke, with lightnings within, darkened the stars above the desert, and a rain of ashes began to fall on the oasis Kadesh.

Aaron and Miriam fell on their foreheads, for the crack so clearly meant for them had terrified them sore, and the revelation of Jahwe on the mountain admonished them that they had gone too far and spoken as fools. Aaron cried out to Moses:

"Oh, my lord, this woman, my sister, has spoken foolishly and wantonly. Yet accept my plea and let the sin not rest upon her head that she has sinned against the Lord's anointed."

And Miriam too cried out and said: "My lord, no one could speak and utter more folly than my brother Aaron. Yet forgive him and let the sin not rest upon him, that God may not swallow him up because he taunted you with your Ethiopian."

Moses was not quite sure whether Jahwe's demonstration had really been addressed to his brother and sister on account of their hardness of heart, or whether it so came about that He just then summoned him to a council about the people and the work of education—for Moses was always expecting such a summons. He left it, however, as they had taken it, and replied:

"You see. But courage, children of Amram! I will speak a good word for you up there with God on the mount whither He summons me. For now shall you see, and all the people shall see, whether your brother is weakened by his black fancy or whether godly courage dwells in his heart as in no other. Upon the fiery mount I will go, alone, aloft to God, that I may hear His thoughts and fearless hold converse with the Frightful One, with thou and thou, far from men but upon their affairs. For long have I known that everything I have taught them to their salvation before Him the Holy One, He will collect together and sum up for all time, that I may bring it down to you from His mount and the people may possess it in the tabernacle together with the ark, the ephod, and the brazen serpent. Farewell! I may perish in God's tumult and in the fires of the mountain. That may well be; I must reckon with it. But if I return, I will bring you from His thunderings the final summing-up, the law of God."

Such indeed was his firm resolve, let the result be life or death. If he were ever to succeed in welding these froward, back-sliding tribes into a God-fearing community observing the divine law, nothing could be more effective to that end than that he should commit himself alone and unarmed unto Jahwe's terrors and bring down thence the decalogue. Then, he thought, they would be bound to keep it. They were running up now to his dwelling from all sides, their knees shaking in terror of the sign and the rendings and sway-ings of the earth, now dying away in fainter tremors. And he rebuked them for their uncivilized terror and recommended propriety and composure. God, he said, was summoning him on their account; he would go up to Jahwe upon the mountain and by God's will bring them something back. For their part, they should all go home and prepare for an excursion. They should dedicate themselves, and wash their clothes and themselves, and refrain from their wives; for on the morrow they were all to go out from Kadesh into the wilder-ness nearer to the mountain, and set up camp opposite it and wait for him there, until he came back from his frightful rendezvous and perhaps brought something to them.

So it came about, or more or less like that; for Moses, naturally, had thought only of their washing their clothes and refraining from their wives. But Joshua-ben-Nun the youthful strategist considered what else was requisite for such a mass excursion; and he and his troops took care for the needful to be taken along, water and food for thousands in the desert. He arranged for a service connecting Kadesh with the camp between it and the mountain. He left Caleb, his lieutenant, and a detachment of police in Kadesh with all those who could not or would not go out. But the rest, when the third day had come and all the preparations had been made, went out with carts and cattle, one day's journey and a half toward the moun-tain. And there Joshua made them an enclosure, still at a measurable distance from Jahwe's smoldering seat, and in Moses' name strictly forbade them to climb the mountain or even to touch its foot; for to the leader alone it was reserved to go so near to God. Besides, it was dangerous; and whosoever approached the mountain should be stoned or shot with bow and arrow. They listened unconcerned, for such a rabble has not much itch to get nearer to God, and to an ordinary man the mountain looked not at all inviting. Not by day, when Jahwe stood upon it in a thick cloud shot through with lightnings, and not by night, when the cloud glowed fierily and the whole peak as well.

Joshua was uncommonly proud of the godly intrepidity of his master, who on the very first day set out for the sacred mount on foot, before all the people. He held the pilgrim's staff and was provided only with an earthen flask, a few pieces of bread, and some tools—a hoe, a spade, a chisel, and a graving tool. Very proud was young Joshua of him and happy over the impression such dedicated bravery must be making on the people. But he was also concerned for his revered master and had earnestly implored him not to go right up close to Jahwe, and to be careful of the streams of lava running down the mountainside. However, he said, he would visit him now and again, so that the master might not lack for necessities in the God-possessed desert.

18

Accordingly Moses crossed the wilderness on his staff, his wide-set eyes bent on the mount of God, which was smoking like a chimney and often spewing out fire. It had an odd shape, the mountain: cracks and ridges ran round it, seeming to divide it into several storeys. They looked like paths running round it, but they were not: only terracelike gradations with yellow rear walls. By the third day the pilgrim had crossed the foothills to the rugged base; now he began to climb, his fist closed around his staff, which he set before him as he mounted pathless, trackless, blackened, scalded waste. Hours and hours he mounted, pace by pace, higher and higher into the nearness of God; as far as ever a human being could. For after a while the sulfurous vapors, smelling like hot metal, so filled the air that he gasped for breath and began to cough. Yet he got up to the topmost ridge just below the peak, where there was an extended view on both sides over the bare desert range and beyond the wilderness toward Kadesh. He could even see the little tribal encampment, closer in and far down in the depths.

Here Moses, coughing, found a cavity in the mountain wall, with a roof formed by a ledge of rock that should protect him from flying stones and molten streams. Here he set up his rest and took time to get his breath. And now he prepared to embark upon the task which God had laid upon him. Under all the difficulties (the metallic vapors oppressed his chest and even made the water taste of sulfur), the work was to take him forty days and forty nights.

But why so long? The question is an idle one. God's whole moral law, in permanently compact and compendious form, binding to all time, had to be composed and graven on the stone of His own mountain, in order that Moses might carry it down to his father's crude, confused, bewildered folk, down to the enclosure where they were waiting. It should be among them, from generation to generation inviolably graven as well in their minds and hearts, and their flesh and blood, the quintessence of human good behavior. God commanded him loudly from out of his own breast to hew two tables from the living rock and write the decrees on them, five on one and five on the other—in all, ten decrees. To make the tablets, to smooth them and shape them to be adequate bearers of the eternal law—that in itself was no small thing. One man alone, even though he had broad wrists and had drunk the milk of a stonemason's daughter, might not for many days accomplish it. Actually the making of the tables took a quarter of the forty days. But the writing itself, when he came to it, was a problem that might well bring Moses' stay on the hilltop to more than forty days. For how was he to write? In his Theban boarding school he had learned the decorative picture writing of the Egyptians and its cursive adaptation; also the cramped cuneiform of the formal script practiced in the region of the Euphrates and employed by the kings of the earth to exchange ideas on earthen shards. And among the Midianites he had got acquainted with a third kind of semantic magic expressed in symbols, such as eyes, crosses, beetles, rings, and various kinds of wavy lines. This kind of writing was used in the land of Sinai; it was a clumsy attempt to imitate Egyptian picture writing, but it did not manage to symbolize whole words and things—only syllables to be read together. Moses saw that no one of these three methods of putting down ideas would serve in the present case, for the simple reason that all of them depended on the language they expressed by signs. Not in Babylonian or Egyptian or the jargon of the Bedouins of Sinai—not in any one of these could he possibly write down the ten decrees. No, they must and could only be written in the tongue of the fathers' seed—the idiom it spoke, the dialect he himself used in his formative task; and that no matter whether they could read it or not. Indeed, how should they read it, when it could scarcely be written and there did not yet exist any semantic magic whatever for the tongue they talked in?

Fervently, with all his heart, Moses wished for it: for a kind of simple writing that they would be able to read quite quickly; one that they, children as they were, could learn in a few days—and it followed that such a one, God's help being nigh, could also be thought out and invented in no longer time. For thought out and invented a kind of writing had got to be, since it did not exist.

What a pressing, oppressive task! He had not measured it beforehand. He had thought only of "writing"—not at all of the fact that one could not just "write." His head glowed and steamed like a furnace; it was like the top of the peak itself, on fire with the fervor of his hopes for his people. He felt as though rays streamed from his head; as though horns came out on his brow for very strain of desire and pure inspiration. He could not invent signs for all the words his people used, nor for the syllables which composed them. The vocabulary of the people down there in the camp was small enough. But even so it would need so many symbols that they could not be invented in the limited number of days at his command; much less could the people learn to read them. So Moses contrived something else—and horns stood forth from his head out of sheer pride of his god-invention. He classified the sounds of the language: those made with the lips, with the tongue and palate, and with the throat; and he divided off from them the smaller group of open sounds which became words only when they were included in combinations with the others. Of those others there were not so very many—a bare twenty; and if you gave them signs which regularly obliged anyone pronouncing them to buzz or hiss, to huff or puff, or mumble or rumble, then you might adapt your sounds and combine them into words and pictures of things, paying no heed to those in the other group, which came in automatically anyhow. You could make as many combinations as you liked, and that not only in the language spoken by his father's people, but in any language whatever. You could even write Egyptian and Babylonian with them.

A god-inspiration! An inspiration with horns to it! It was like to its source, to the Invisible and Spiritual whence it came, who possessed all the world, and who, though He had especially elected the stock down below for His own, yet He was Lord everywhere and all over on earth. But it was also an inspiration peculiarly apt for Moses' immediate and urgent purpose and for the necessity out of which it was born—for the brief and binding text of the law. Of course, this was first to be impressed upon the seed which Moses had led out of Egypt, because God and he had a common love to it. But just as the handful of arbitrary signs might be used to write down all the words of all the tongues of all the people on earth, and just as Jahwe was omnipotent over all these, so also the text which Moses intended to set down by means of those signs should likewise be universal. It should be a compendium of such a kind as to serve everywhere on earth and to all the peoples on it as a foundation stone of morality and good conduct.

So, then, Moses—his head on fire—began by scratching his signs on the rocky wall in loose imitation of the sounds the Sinai people made, conjuring them up in his mind as he went. With his graving tool he scratched on the rock the signs he had made to represent the burrs and purrs and whirrs, the hisses and buzzes, the humming and gurgling of his father's native tongue. He set them down in an order that pleased his ear—and lo, with them one could set down the whole world in writing: the signs that took up space and those that took none, the derived and the contrived—in short, everything on earth.

And he wrote; I mean, he drilled and chiseled and scooped at the splintery stone of the tables; for these he had prepared beforehand with great pains, during the time he had spent cogitating his script. The whole took him rather more than forty days—and no wonder!

Young Joshua came up to him a few times, to fetch water and bread. The people did not need to know this: they believed that Moses sojourned up there sustained solely by God's presence and His words, and Joshua for strategic reasons preferred them to remain in this belief.

Moses rose with the dawn and labored till the sun set back in the desert. We must picture him there, sitting bare to the waist, his breast hairy, with the strong arms bequeathed him by his father the slain water bearer; with wide-set eyes, flattened nose, and parted grizzling beard; chewing a pancake, coughing now and then from the metallic vapors, and in the sweat of his brow hewing at the tables, filing and planing. Squatting before them as he leaned against the rocky wall, he toiled away with great attention to detail; first drawing his pot hooks, his magic runes, with the graver and then drilling them into the stone.

He wrote on the first table:

I, JAHWE, AM THY GOD; THOU SHALT HAVE NO OTHER GODS BEFORE ME.

THOU SHALT NOT MAKE UNTO THYSELF ANY GRAVEN
IMAGE.
THOU SHALT NOT TAKE MY NAME IN VAIN.
BE MINDFUL OF MY DAY TO KEEP IT HOLY.
HONOR THY FATHER AND THY MOTHER.

And on the other table he wrote:

THOU SHALT NOT KILL.
THOU SHALT NOT COMMIT ADULTERY.
THOU SHALT NOT STEAL.
THOU SHALT NOT AFFRONT THY NEIGHBOR BY BEARING
FALSE WITNESS.
THOU SHALT NOT CAST A COVETOUS EYE UPON THY
NEIGHBOR'S GOODS.

This was what he wrote, leaving out the vowels, which were taken
for granted. And while he worked it seemed to him as though rays
like a pair of horns stood out from the hair of his brow.

When Joshua came up for the last time he stayed a little longer
than before, in fact, two whole days, for Moses was not done with
his work, and they wanted to go down together. The youth admired
and warmly praised what his master had done, consoling him in the
matter of a few letters which, despite all Moses' loving care and
greatly to his distress, had got splintered and were illegible. Joshua
assured him that the general effect was unharmed.

As a finishing touch in Joshua's presence, Moses colored the letters
he had engraved. He did it with his own blood, that they might stand
out better. No other coloring matter was at hand; so he pricked his
strong arm with the tool and carefully let the drops of blood run
into the outlines of the letters, so that they showed red against the
stone. When the script was dry, Moses took a table under each arm,
handed to the young man the staff which had supported him on his
climb; and so they went down together from the mountain of God
to the tribal encampment opposite in the desert.

19

When they had got within hearing of the enclosure, though still
fairly far off, there came to their ears a distant squalling which they

knew not how to explain. Moses heard it first, but it was Joshua who spoke of it.

"Do you hear those strange sounds?" he asked, "—all that noise and hubbub? There is something the matter, I think; some kind of brawl, if I am not mistaken. And it must be considerable, and violent, for us to hear it from where we are. If it is as I think, then it is a good thing you are getting back."

"It is a good thing in any case," answered Moses. "But so far as I can make out, that is not a brawling I hear, but a noise of merrymaking, with something like singing and dancing. Don't you hear shrill yells among the bass, and crashing drums? Joshua, how do they come to be having a feast without my permission? Joshua, what has got into them? Let us hasten our steps."

He hoisted up his tables under his armpits and stepped out faster, and Joshua strode alongside, shaking his head. "Singing and dancing, singing and dancing," he repeated, more and more dismayed, at length in sheer alarm. For by now they could tell that this was no rough-and-tumble. They were not scuffling, one on top and one underneath. No, they were bawling in chorus. The only question was, what sort of song they were bawling.

Even that riddle was soon resolved. It was a most dreadful state of affairs. When Moses and Joshua hastened under the beam of the gate and entered the enclosure, they could see it in all its bald shamelessness. The tribes were out of bounds. They had flung aside all restraint, all the precepts which Moses had laid upon them for their souls' good, and all godly decorum. They had reverted, in short, and were wallowing with hair-raising abandon.

Just beyond the gate was an open assembly place; this was now the theater where they were celebrating their miserable freedom. They had all gorged their fill before the singing and dancing; the open space betrayed to any eye the marks of slaughtering and gluttony. And in honor of what had they slaughtered and stuffed? It was standing there. In the center of the open space, on a stone plinth, an altar base, an image stood, a crudely made thing, a misbegotten idol, a gilded calf.

It was no calf: it was a bull, the common stud bull of all the peoples of the world. It has been called a calf because it was only medium-sized, even rather small, badly cast, and ridiculously shaped, a clumsy abomination, but only too easily recognizable as the bull it was. Around the clumsy invention moved a ring a dozen deep, men and women hand in hand, dancing to the sound of cymbals and drums. Their heads were flung back, their eyes rolled up, their knees tossed up to their chins; they squalled, shouted and made coarse gestures of worship toward the image. They went round in opposite directions, one shameful circle moving to the right, the next to the left. And inside the inmost ring, in front of the calf, Aaron could be seen hopping up and down in the long-sleeved garment he wore in the service of the tabernacle; he had pulled it up so as to be able to fling his long, hairy legs the better. And Miriam, shaking her timbrel, was leading the women in the dance.

So much for the ring about the calf. In the space round about it there was fitting accompaniment to the sight. It is painful to describe the shamelessness that was there. Some were eating blindworms. Others were lying with their sisters, and that in public, in honor of the calf. Others again simply squatted and relieved themselves, guiltless of any little trowel. One saw men offering their strength to the bull. Somewhere a man was cuffing his own mother, right and left.

At this horrid sight Moses' angry vein swelled to bursting. With blazing face he pushed his way straight up to the calf, bursting through the ring of dancers, who came staggering to a stop and goggled at him with embarrassed grins as they recognized the master. He went straight to the heart, the source, the monstrous core of the crime. He lifted high one of the tables of the law in his mighty arms and smashed it down upon the ridiculous animal until it buckled at the knees; struck again and again with such fury that the tablet itself flew into pieces and the effigy was an almost formless mass. He swung the other table and gave the death blow to the abomination, smashing it utterly; and as the second tablet was still whole, he broke it upon the stone base. Then he stood there with quivering fists and groaned from the depths of his heart.

"You debased, you god-forsaken wretches! There lies what I brought you down from God and what He wrote for you with His own finger to be a talisman against your miserable state of ignorance. There it lies in bits among the ruins of your idol. What shall I do with you now before the Lord, that He consume you not?"

And he saw Aaron, who had been hopping up and down, standing near him with his eyes cast down and his greasy curls in his neck, inexpressibly awkward and foolish. Moses took him by the clothes in front and shook him, saying:

"How comes the gilded Belial here, the filthy beast? And what had the people done to you that you thrust them down to ruin while

I was on the mountain, and even prance and wanton before him
yourself, as though you were a goat?"

But Aaron answered: "Ah, my dear lord, let not your wrath mount
up against me and your sister, for we were forced to yield. You know
the wickedness of this people; verily, they forced us. You stayed away
too long and stopped on the mountain an eternity, so that we all
thought you were never coming back. Then the people assembled
against me and shrieked: 'No one knows what has become of this
Moses man who led us out of Egypt. He will not be coming back.
Probably the jaws of the mountain, out of which it spews, have
swallowed him up. Up, then, make us gods which can go before us
when Amalek returns! We are a people like another, and we want
to wanton before gods which are like other people's gods!' Thus
they spoke, my lord, for, by your leave, they thought they were rid
of you. But tell me what I could have done when they got together
against me? I told them to bring me all their gold earrings from their
ears, and I melted them down and made a mold and cast the little
calf for a god to them."

"And it was not even a good likeness," said Moses contemptuously.

"I was in such haste!" Aaron replied. "For even on the next day,
that is to say today, they wanted to have their debauchery before
good fleshly gods that they could understand. So I turned the cast
over to them, and you cannot assert that it has no likeness at all;
and they were glad, and said: 'These are your gods, O Israel, who
have led you out of Egypt.' And we built an altar, and they made
burnt offerings and thank offerings, and they ate, and then they
played and danced a little."

Moses left him where he stood and pushed back through the broken circle to the gate, where he placed himself under the crossbeam
with Joshua and cried with all his strength:

"To me, to me, all ye who belong to the Lord!" Then came many
to him who were sound at heart and had joined unwillingly, and
Joshua's youthful hosts gathered round the two.

"Unhappy creatures," said Moses, "what have you done, and how
shall I atone for your sin before Jahwe that He may not reject you
as incorrigibly evil and consume you altogether? To make to yourself
a gilded Belial the minute my back is turned! Shame upon you—
and upon me! Look at the ruins there! I don't mean the calf, may
perdition seize it: I mean the broken pieces! They are the present I
brought down to you: the everlasting, the brief and binding law, the

rock of right and decency. They are the decalogue which, together with God, I wrote for you in your script and wrote it in my own blood; with the blood of my father, with your blood, I wrote it. Now lies it there, that I brought, broken in fragments."

Many of them wept, and there was a great sobbing and sniffing in all the place.

"Perhaps it can be made good," said Moses. "For the Lord is long-suffering and of great mercy, and He forgives ill doing and transgression—and lets no one go unpunished!" he suddenly thundered, his blood rushing to his head and his vein swelling up. "For I will visit the ill-doing unto the third and fourth generation, like the zealot I am. Here shall judgment be held and a bloody purification, for with blood was it written. The ringleaders shall be put to death, who first shrieked for the gilded be given to the avenging angel, let them be who they may. They shall be stoned to death and die by shooting—and even were there three-hundred of them! But the rest shall put away all adornments and mourn until I return. For I will go again upon the mount of God and see what I can still do for you, O froward and perverse generation!"

20

Moses was not present at the executions which he had decreed on account of the calf; they were the business of the iron-handed Joshua. He himself was again on the mountain, in front of his cave under the echoing peak, while the people mourned; and he remained another forty days and forty nights up there alone in the poisonous vapors. But why so long, the second time? The answer is: It was not only because Jahwe directed him to make the tables again, and again to write the decrees on them. This time it went a bit faster, as he had had practice, and, even more importantly, he already had the script. No: it was because, before the Lord granted the renewal, Moses had a long struggle with Him—a wrestling in which anger and mercy, love and disgust fought together, and Moses had to use great persuasive powers and shrewd appeals to keep God from declaring the bond broken and disowning the incorrigible crew, destroying them altogether even as Moses in his wrath had destroyed the tables.

"I will not draw near to them," said God, "to lead them into the land of their fathers; do not ask it of Me, for I could not trust my patience. I am a zealot, and My wrath blazes up, and you shall see how some day I shall know Myself no more and devour them utterly."

And since the people were like the gilded calf, so badly cast and without hope of betterment, there was nothing left but to shatter and destroy them. He told Moses they should be destroyed root and branch as they stood. But that He would make him, Moses, a great people and live with him in the Covenant. But Moses could not bear it, and he said: "No, Lord, forgive them their sins; if not, then blot me too out of your book, for I will not survive and become a chosen people in my own person instead of them."

And he put God on His honor and said: "Consider, Holy One: if you slay these people as one man, then the heathen when they hear will cry, 'Fie upon the Lord! For He could not lead the people to the Promised Land as He had sworn—He was not able—and therefore has He slain them in the wilderness.' Will you have such things said of you by the peoples of the world? Therefore now let the might of the Lord wax great and be gracious to the transgression of these people in Thy mercy."

It was particularly with this argument that Moses won over the Lord and decided Him for forgiveness, even though with reservations. God declared that none of this generation should see the land of the fathers, excepting only Joshua and Caleb. "Your children," so the Lord decreed, "I will lead in. But those now more than twenty years old shall not see the Land, but their bodies shall lie down in the waste."

And Moses assented and agreed with the Lord that they would leave it at that. For the decision really coincided with his and Joshua's own purposes, so he did not argue against it. "Let me now renew the tables," he said, "and bring down to the tribes Thy brief and binding will. After all, it was no great loss that I broke the first ones: there were a few bad letters in them. I will confess to You now that I thought of it when I smashed them."

So he sat there a second time, with his food and drink secretly supplied by Joshua. He sharpened and chiseled, planed and smoothed, sat and wrote, wiping his brow with the back of his hand, drilling and graving the script into the tables, which were even better than the first ones. And afterward he once more painted the letters with his blood. Then he descended the hill with the Law under his arms.

Israel had been notified that it should end its mourning and should put on festal garments—of course excepting their earrings, for those had been melted down to an evil end. And all the people came before Moses that he might give them what he had brought: the message of Jahwe from the mountain, the tables with the decalogue.

"Take them, O blood of my father," he said, "and keep them holy in God's tent. But that which they say, that keep holy yourselves in doing and in leaving undone. For it is the brief and binding, the condensed will of God, the bedrock of all good behavior and breeding, and God wrote it in the stone with my little graving tool—the Alpha and Omega of human decency. In your speech He wrote it, but in signs with which if necessary all the languages of the world can be written; for He is Lord everywhere. Hence this ABC is His, and His speech, though it be addressed to you, O Israel, yet it is just as much a universal speech.

"In the stone of the mountains I engraved the ABC of human conduct, but no less shall it be graven in your flesh and blood, O Israel, so that everyone who breaks one of the ten commandments shall shrink within himself and before God, and it shall be cold about his heart because he overstepped God's bound. Well I know, and God He too knows well, that His commands will not be obeyed, but will be rebelled against over and over again. But everyone who breaks the laws shall from now on grow icy cold about the heart, because they are written in his flesh and blood and he knows the Word will avail.

"But cursed be the man who stands up and says: 'They are good no longer.' Cursed be he who teaches you: 'Up and be free of them, lie, steal, and slay, whore, dishonor father and mother and give them to the knife, and you shall praise my name because I proclaim freedom to you.' Cursed be he who sets up a calf and says: 'There is your God. To its honor do all this, and lead a new dance about it.' Your God will be very strong; on a golden chair will he sit and pass for the wisest because he knows the ways of the human heart are evil from youth upward. But that will be all that he knows; and he who only knows that is as stupid as the night is black, and better it were for him had he never been born. For he knows not of the bond between God and man, which none can break, neither man nor God, for it is inviolate. Blood will flow in streams because of his black stupidity, so that the red pales from the cheek of mankind, but there is no help, for the base must be cut down. And I will lift up My foot, saith the Lord, and tread him into the mire—to the bottom of the earth will I tread the blasphemer, a hundred and twelve fathoms deep, and man and beast shall make a bend around the spot where

I trod him in, and the birds of the air high in their flight shall swerve
that they fly not over it. And whosoever names his name shall spit
toward the four quarters of the earth, and wipe his mouth and say
'God save us all!' that the earth may be again the earth—a vale of
troubles, but not a sink of iniquity. Say Amen to that!" and

all
the
people
said
Amen.

Translated by Helen Tracey Lowe-Porter

ESSAYS

Freud and the Future

A speech delivered in Vienna, May 9, 1936,
on Freud's eightieth birthday

We are gathered here to do honor to a great scientist. And the question may very properly be raised: what justifies a man of letters in assuming the role of spokesman on such an occasion? Or, passing on the responsibility to the members of the learned society which chose him, why should they not have selected one of their own kind, a man of science, rather than an author, to celebrate in words the birthday of their master? For an author, my friends, is a man essentially not bent upon science, upon knowing, distinguishing, and analyzing; he stands for simple creation, for doing and making, and thus may be the object of useful cognition, without, by his very nature, having any competence in it as subject. But is it, perhaps, that the author in his character as artist, and artist in the field of the intellect, is especially called to the celebration of feasts of the mind; that he is by nature more a man of feast-days than the scientist and man of knowledge? It is not for me to dispute such a view. It is true, the poet has understanding of the feasts of life, understanding even of life as a feast—and here I am just touching, very lightly for the moment, upon a theme that may become a main motif in the chorus of homage which we are to perform this evening. But it is more likely that the sponsors of this evening had something else in mind in their choice: that is to say, the solemn and novel confrontation of object and subject, the object of knowledge with the knower—a saturnalia, as it were, in which the knower and seer of dreams himself becomes, by our act of homage, the object of dreamlike penetration. And to such a position I could not object, either; particularly because it strikes a chord capable in the future of great symphonic development. It will recur, more clearly accented and fully instrumented. For, unless I am greatly mistaken, it is just this confrontation of object and subject, their mingling and identification, the resultant insight into the mysterious unity of ego and actuality, destiny and character, doing and happening, and thus into the mystery of reality as an operation of the psyche—it is just this confrontation that is the alpha and omega of all psychoanalytical knowledge.

Be that as it may, the choice of an artist as the encomiast of a great scientist is a comment upon both. In the first place, one deduces from it a connection between the man of genius we now honor and the world of creative literature; in the second place, it displays the peculiar relations between the writer and the field of science whose declared and acknowledged master and creator the other is. Now, the unique and remarkable thing about this mutual close relation is that it remained for so long unconscious—that is, in that region of the soul which we have learned to call the unconscious, a realm whose discovery and investigation, whose conquest for humanity, are precisely the task and mission of the wise genius whose fame we celebrate. The close relation between literature and psychoanalysis has been known for a long time to both sides. But the solemn significance of this hour lies, at least in my eyes and as a matter of personal feeling, in that on this evening there is the first official meeting between the two spheres, in the acknowledgment and demonstration of their relationship.

I repeat that the profound sympathy between the two spheres had existed for a long time unperceived. Actually we know that Sigmund Freud, that mighty spirit in whose honor we are gathered together, founder of psychoanalysis as a general method of research and as a therapeutic technique, trod the steep path alone and independently, as physician and natural scientist, without knowing that reinforcement and encouragement lay to his hand in literature. He did not know Nietzsche, scattered throughout whose pages one finds premonitory flashes of truly Freudian insight; he did not know Novalis, whose romantic-biologic fantasies so often approach astonishingly close to analytic conceptions; he did not know Kierkegaard, whom he must have found profoundly sympathetic and encouraging for the Christian zeal which urged him on to psychological extremes; and, finally, he did not know Schopenhauer, the melancholy symphonist of a philosophy of the instinct, groping for change and redemption. Probably it must be so. By his unaided effort, without knowledge of any previous intuitive achievement, he had methodically to follow out the line of his own researches; the driving force of his activity was probably increased by this very freedom from special advantage. And we think of him as solitary—the attitude is inseparable from our earliest picture of the man. Solitary in the sense of the word used by Nietzsche in that ravishing essay "What Is the Meaning of Ascetic Ideals?" when he characterizes Schopenhauer as "a genuine philosopher, a self-poised mind, a man and gallant knight, stern-eyed, with the courage of his own strength, who knows how to stand alone and not wait on the beck and nod of superior officers." In this guise of man and gallant knight, a knight between Death and the Devil, I have been used to picture to myself our psychologist of the unconscious, ever since his figure first swam into my mental ken.

That happened late—much later than one might have expected, considering the connection between this science and the poetic and creative impulse in general and mine in particular. The connection, the bond between them, is twofold: it consists first in a love of truth, in a sense of truth, a sensitiveness and receptivity for truth's sweet and bitter, which largely expresses itself in a psychological excitation, a clarity of vision, to such an extent that the conception of truth actually almost coincides with that of psychological perception and recognition. And secondly it consists in an understanding of disease, a certain affinity with it, outweighed by fundamental health, and an understanding of its productive significance.

As for the love of truth: the suffering, morally conditioned love of truth *as psychology*—that has its origin in Nietzsche's lofty school, where in fact the coincidence of "truth" and "psychological truth," of the knower with the psychologist, is striking indeed. His proud truthfulness, his very conception of intellectual honesty, his conscious and melancholy fearlessness in its service, his self-knowledge, self-crucifixion—all this has psychological intention and bearing. Never shall I forget the deepening, strengthening, formative effect upon my own powers produced by my acquaintance with Nietzsche's psychological agony. In *Tonio Kröger* the artist speaks of being "sick of knowledge." That is true Nietzsche language; and the youth's melancholy has reference to the Hamlet-like in Nietzsche's nature, in which his own mirrored itself: a nature called to knowledge without being genuinely born to it. These are the pangs and anguishes of youth, destined to be lightened and tranquilized as years flowed by and brought ripeness with them. But there has remained with me the desire for a psychological interpretation of knowledge and truth; I still equate them with psychology and feel the psychological will to truth as a desire for truth in general; still interpret psychology as truth in the most actual and courageous sense of the word. One would call the tendency a naturalistic one, I suppose, and ascribe it to a training in literary naturalism; it forms a precondition of receptivity for the natural science of the psyche— in other words, for what is known as psychoanalysis.

I spoke of a second bond between that science and the creative impulse: the understanding of disease, or, more precisely, of disease as an instrument of knowledge. That, too, one may derive from Nietzsche. He well knew what he owed to his morbid state, and on every page he seems to instruct us that there is no deeper knowledge without experience of disease, and that all heightened healthiness must be achieved by the route of illness. This attitude too may be referred to his experience; but it is bound up with the nature of the intellectual man in general, of the creative artist in particular, yes, with the nature of humanity and the human being, of which last of course the creative artist is an extreme expression. "L'humanité," says Victor Hugo, "s'affirme par l'infirmité." A saying which frankly and profoundly admits the delicate constitution of all higher human- ity and culture, and their connoisseurship in the realm of disease. Man has been called *das kranke Tier* because of the burden of strain and explicit difficulties laid upon him by his position between nature and spirit, between angel and brute. What wonder, then, that by the approach through abnormality we have succeeded in penetrating most deeply into the darkness of human nature; that the study of disease—that is to say, neurosis—has revealed itself as a first-class technique of anthropological research?

The literary artist should be the last person to be surprised at the fact. Sooner might he be surprised that he, considering his strong general and individual tendency, should have so late become aware of the close sympathetic relations which connected his own existence with psychoanalytic research and the life-work of Sigmund Freud. I realized this connection only at a time when his achievement was no longer thought of as merely a therapeutic method, whether recog- nized or disputed; when it had long since outgrown his purely med- ical implications and become a world movement which penetrated into every field of science and every domain of the intellect: litera- ture, the history of art, religion and prehistory; mythology, folklore, pedagogy, and whatnot—thanks to the practical and constructive zeal of experts who erected a structure of more general investigation round the psychiatric and medical core. Indeed, it would be too much to say that I came to psychoanalysis. It came to me. Through the friendly interest that some younger workers in the field had shown in my work, from *Little Herr Friedemann* to *Death in Venice, The Magic Mountain,* and the *Joseph* novels, it gave me to understand that in my way I "belonged"; it made me aware, as probably behooved it, of my own latent, preconscious sympathies; and when I began to occupy myself with the literature of psychoanalysis I recognized, arrayed in the ideas and the language of scientific exactitude, much that had long been familiar to me through my youthful mental experiences.

Perhaps you will kindly permit me to continue for a while in this autobiographical strain, and not take it amiss if instead of speaking of Freud I speak of myself. And indeed I scarcely trust myself to speak *about* him. What new thing could I hope to say? But I shall also, quite explicitly, be speaking in his honor in speaking of myself, in telling you how profoundly and peculiarly certain experiences decisive for my development prepared me for the Freudian experience. More than once, and in many places, I have confessed to the profound, even shattering impression made upon me as a young man by contact with the philosophy of Arthur Schopenhauer, to which then a monument was erected in the pages of *Buddenbrooks.* Here first, in the pessimism of a metaphysics already very strongly equipped on the natural-science side, I encountered the dauntless zeal for truth that stands for the moral aspect of the psychology of the unconscious. This metaphysics, in obscure revolt against centuries-old beliefs, preached the primacy of the instinct over mind and reason; it recognized the will as the core and the essential foundation of the world, in man as in all other created beings; and the intellect as secondary and accidental, servant of the will and its pale illuminant. This it preached not in malice, not in the antihuman spirit of the mind-hostile doctrines of today, but in the stern love of truth characteristic of the century which combated idealism out of love for the ideal. It was so sincere, that nineteenth century, that— through the mouth of Ibsen—it pronounced the lie, the lies of life, to be indispensable. Clearly there is a vast difference whether one assents to a lie out of sheer hatred of truth and the spirit or for the sake of that spirit, in bitter irony and anguished pessimism! Yet the distinction is not clear to everybody today.

Now, Freud, the psychologist of the unconscious, is a true son of the century of Schopenhauer and Ibsen—he was born in the middle of it. How closely related is his revolution to Schopenhauer's, not only in its content, but also in its moral attitude! His discovery of the great role played by the unconscious, the id, in the soul-life of man challenged and challenges classical psychology, to which the consciousness and the psyche are one and the same, as offensively as once Schopenhauer's doctrine of the will challenged philosophical belief in reason and the intellect. Certainly the early devotee of *The World as Will and Idea* is at home in the admirable essay that is included in Freud's *New Introductory Essays in Psychoanalysis* under the title "The Anatomy of the Mental Personality." It describes the soul-world of the unconscious, the id, in language as strong, and at the same time in as coolly intellectual, objective, and professional a tone, as Schopenhauer might have used to describe his sinister kingdom of the will. "The domain of the id," he says, "is the dark, inaccessible part of our personality; the little that we know of it we have learned through the study of dreams and of the formation of neurotic symptoms." He depicts it as a chaos, a melting-pot of seething excitations. The id, he thinks, is, so to speak, open toward the somatic, and receives thence into itself compulsions which there find psychic expression—in what substratum is unknown. From these impulses it receives its energy; but it is not organized, produces no collective will, merely the striving to achieve satisfaction for the impulsive needs operating under the pleasure principle. In it no laws of thought are valid, and certainly not the law of opposites. "Contradictory stimuli exist alongside each other without canceling each other out or even detracting from each other; at most they unite in compromise forms under the compulsion of the controlling economy for the release of energy." You perceive that this is a situation which, in the historical experience of our own day, can take the upper hand with the ego, with a whole mass-ego, thanks to a moral devastation which is produced by worship of the unconscious, the glorification of its dynamic as the only life-promoting force, the systematic glorification of the primitive and irrational. For the unconscious, the id, is primitive and irrational, is pure dynamic. It knows no values, no good or evil, no morality. It even knows no time, no temporal flow, nor any effect of time upon its psychic process. "Wish stimuli," says Freud, "which have never overpassed the id, the impressions which have been repressed into its depths, are virtually indestructible, they survive decade after decade as though they had just happened. They can only be recognized as belonging to the past, devalued and robbed of their charge of energy, by becoming conscious through the analytic procedure." And he adds that therein lies preeminently the healing effect of analytic treatment. We perceive accordingly how antipathetic deep analysis must be to an ego that is intoxicated by a worship of the unconscious to the point of being in a condition of subterranean dynamic. It is only too clear and understandable that such an ego is deaf to analysis and that the name of Freud must not be mentioned in its hearing.

As for the ego itself, its situation is pathetic, well-nigh alarming. It is an alert, prominent, and enlightened little part of the id—much as Europe is a small and lively province of the greater Asia. The ego is that part of the id which became modified by contact with the outer world; equipped for the reception and preservation of stimuli; comparable to the integument with which any piece of living matter surrounds itself. A very perspicuous biological picture. Freud writes indeed a very perspicuous prose, he is an artist of thought, like Schopenhauer, and like him a writer of European rank. The relation with the outer world is, he says, decisive for the ego, it is the ego's task to represent the world to the id—for its good! For without regard for the superior power of the outer world the id, in its blind striving toward the satisfaction of its instincts, would not escape destruction. The ego takes cognizance of the outer world, it is mindful, it honorably tries to distinguish the objectively real from whatever is an accretion from its inward sources of stimulation. It is entrusted by the id with the lever of action; but between the impulse and the action it has interposed the delay of the thought-process, during which it summons experience to its aid and thus possesses a certain regulative superiority over the pleasure principle which rules supreme in the unconscious, correcting it by means of the principle of reality. But even so, how feeble it is! Hemmed in between the unconscious, the outer world, and what Freud calls the superego, it leads a pretty nervous and anguished existence. Its own dynamic is rather weak. It derives its energy from the id and in general has to carry out the latter's behests. It is fain to regard itself as the rider and the unconscious as the horse. But many a time it is ridden by the unconscious; and I take leave to add what Freud's rational morality prevents him from saying, that under some circumstances it makes more progress by this illegitimate means.

But Freud's description of the id and the ego—is it not to a hair Schopenhauer's description of the Will and the Intellect, a translation of the latter's metaphysics into psychology? So he who had been initiated into the metaphysics of Schopenhauer and in Nietzsche tasted the painful pleasure of psychology—he must needs have been filled with a sense of recognition and familiarity when first, encouraged thereto by its denizens, he entered the realms of psychoanalysis and looked about him.

He found too that his new knowledge had a strange and strong retroactive effect upon the old. After a sojourn in the world of Freud, how differently, in the light of one's new knowledge, does one reread the reflections of Schopenhauer, for instance his great essay "Transcendent Speculations on Apparent Design in the Fate of the Individual"! And here I am about to touch upon the most profound and mysterious point of contact between Freud's natural-scientific world and Schopenhauer's philosophic one. For the essay I have named, a marvel of profundity and penetration, constitutes this point of contact. The pregnant and mysterious idea there developed by Schopenhauer is briefly this: that precisely as in a dream it is our own will that unconsciously appears as inexorable objective destiny, everything in it proceeding out of ourselves and each of us being the secret theater manager of our own dreams, so also in reality the great dream that a single essence, the will itself, dreams with us all, our fate, may be the product of our inmost selves, of our wills, and we are actually ourselves bringing about what seems to be happening to us. I have only briefly indicated here the content of the essay, for these representations are winged with the strongest and most sweeping powers of suggestion. But not only does the dream psychology which Schopenhauer calls to his aid bear an explicitly psychoanalytic character, even to the presence of the sexual argument and paradigm; but the whole complex of thought is a philosophical anticipation of analytical conceptions, to a quite astonishing extent. For, to repeat what I said in the beginning, I see in the mystery of the unity of the ego and the world, of being and happening, in the perception of the apparently objective and accidental as a matter of the soul's own contriving, the innermost core of psychoanalytic theory.

And here there occurs to me a phrase from the pen of C. J. Jung, an able but somewhat ungrateful scion of the Freudian school, in his significant introduction to the *Tibetan Book of the Dead.* "It is so much more direct, striking, impressive, and thus convincing," he says, "to see how it happens to me than to see how I do it." A bold, even an extravagant statement, plainly betraying the calmness with which in a certain school of psychology certain things are regarded which even Schopenhauer considered prodigiously daring speculation. Would this unmasking of the "happening" as in reality "doing" be conceivable without Freud? Never! It owes him everything. It is weighted down with assumptions, it could not be understood, it could never have been written, without all that analysis has brought to light about slips of tongue and pen, the whole field of human error, the retreat into illness, the psychology of accidents, the self-punishment compulsion—in short, all the wizardry of the unconscious. Just as little, moreover, would that close-packed sentence of Jung's, including its psychological premises, have been possible without Schopenhauer's adventurous pioneering speculation. Perhaps this is the moment, my friends, to indulge on this festive occasion in a little polemic against Freud himself. He does not esteem philosophy very highly. His scientific exactitude does not permit him to regard it as a science. He reproaches it with imagining that it can present a continuous and consistent picture of the world; with overestimating the objective value of logical operations; with believing in intuitions as a source of knowledge and with indulging in positively animistic tendencies, in that it believes in the magic of words and the influence of thought upon reality. But would philosophy really be thinking too highly of itself on these assumptions? Has the world ever been changed by anything save by thought and its magic vehicle the Word? I believe that in actual fact philosophy ranks before and above the natural sciences and that all method and exactness serve its intuitions and its intellectual and historical will. In the last analysis it is always a matter of the *quod erat demonstrandum*. Scientific freedom from assumptions is or should be a moral fact. But intellectually it is, as Freud points out, probably an illusion. One might strain the point and say that science has never made a discovery without being authorized and encouraged thereto by philosophy.

All this by the way. But it is in line with my general intention to pause a little longer at the sentence that I quoted from Jung. In this essay and also as a general method which he uses by preference, Jung applies analytical evidence to form a bridge between Occidental thought and Oriental esoteric. Nobody has focused so sharply as he the Schopenhauer–Freud perception that "the giver of all given conditions resides in ourselves—a truth which despite all evidence in the greatest as well as in the smallest things *never* becomes conscious, though it is only too often necessary, even indispensable, that it should be." A great and costly change, he thinks, is needed before we understand how the world is "given" by the nature of the soul; for man's animal nature strives against seeing himself as the maker of his own conditions. It is true that the East has always shown itself stronger than the West in the conquest of our animal nature, and we need not be surprised to hear that in its wisdom it conceives even the gods among the "given conditions" originating from the soul and one with her, light and reflection of the human soul. This knowledge, which, according to the *Book of the Dead,* one gives to the deceased to accompany him on his way, is a paradox to the Occidental mind, conflicting with its sense of logic, which distinguishes between subject and object and refuses to have them coincide or make one proceed from the other. True, European mysticism has been aware of such attitudes, and Angelus Silesius said:

> *I know that without me God cannot live a moment;*
> *If I am destroyed He must give up the ghost.*

But on the whole a psychological conception of God, an idea of the godhead which is not pure condition, absolute reality, but one with the soul and bound up with it, must be intolerable to Occidental religious sense—it would be equivalent to abandoning the idea of God.

Yet religion—perhaps even etymologically—essentially implies a bond. In Genesis we have talk of the bond (covenant) between God and man, the psychological basis of which I have attempted to give in the mythological novel *Joseph and His Brothers.* Perhaps my hearers will be indulgent if I speak a little about my own work; there may be some justification for introducing it here in this hour of formal encounter between creative literature and the psychoanalytic. It is strange—and perhaps strange not only to me—that in this work there obtains precisely that psychological theology which the scholar ascribes to Oriental esoteric. This Abram is in a sense the father of God. He perceived and brought Him forth; His mighty qualities, ascribed to Him by Abram, were probably His original possession, Abram was not their inventor, yet in a sense he was, by virtue of his recognizing them and therewith, by taking thought, making them real. God's mighty qualities—and thus God Himself—are indeed something objective, exterior to Abram; but at the same time they are in him and of him as well; the power of his own soul is at moments scarcely to be distinguished from them, it consciously interpenetrates and fuses with them—and such is the origin of the bond which then the Lord strikes with Abram, as the explicit confirmation of an inward fact. The bond, it is stated, is made in the interest of both, to the end of their common sanctification. Need human and need divine here entwine until it is hard to say whether it was the human or the divine that took the initiative. In any case the arrangement shows that the holiness of man and the holiness of God constituted a twofold process, one part being most intimately bound up with the other. Wherefore else, one asks, should there be a bond at all?

The soul as "giver of the given"—yes, my friends, I am well aware that in the novel this conception reaches an ironic pitch which is not authorized either in Oriental wisdom or in psychological perception. But there is something thrilling about the unconscious and only later discovered harmony. Shall I call it the power of suggestion? But sympathy would be a better word: a kind of intellectual affinity, of which naturally psychoanalysis was earlier aware than was I, and which proceeded out of those literary appreciations which I owed to it at an earlier stage. The latest of these was an offprint of an article that appeared in *Imago,* written by a Viennese scholar of the Freudian school, under the title "On the Psychology of the Older School of Biography." The rather dry title gives no indication of the remarkable contents. The writer shows how the older and simpler type of biography and in particular the written lives of artists, nourished and conditioned by popular legend and tradition, assimilate, as it were, the life of the subject to the conventionalized stock-in-trade of biography in general, thus imparting a sort of sanction to their own performance and establishing its genuineness; making it authentic in the sense of "as it always was" and "as it has been written." For man sets store by recognition, he likes to find the old in the new, the typical in the individual. From that recognition he draws a sense of the familiar in life, whereas if it painted itself as entirely new, singular in time and space, without any possibility of resting upon the known, it could only bewilder and alarm. The question, then, which is raised by the essay, is this: can any line be sharply and unequivocally drawn between the formal stock-in-trade of legendary biography and the characteristics of the single personality—in other words, between the typical and the individual? A question negatived by its very statement. For the truth is that life is a mingling of the individual elements and the formal stock-in-trade; a mingling in which the individual, as it were, only lifts his head above the formal and impersonal elements. Much that is extrapersonal, much unconscious identification, much that is conventional and schematic, is nonetheless decisive for the experience not only of the artist but of the human being in general. "Many of us," says the writer of the article, "'live' today a biographical type, the destiny of a class or rank or calling. The freedom in the shaping of the human being's life is obviously connected with that bond which we term 'lived *vita*.'" And then, to my delight, but scarcely to my surprise, he begins to cite from *Joseph,* the fundamental motif of which he says is precisely this idea of the "lived life," life as succession, as a moving in others' steps, as identification—such as Joseph's teacher, Eliezer, practices with droll solemnity. For in him time is canceled and all the Eliezers of the past gather to shape the Eliezer of the present, so that he speaks in the first person of that Eliezer who was Abram's servant, though he was far from being the same man.

I must admit that I find the train of thought extraordinarily convincing. The essay indicates the precise point at which the psychological interest passes over into the mythical. It makes it clear that the typical is actually the mythical, and that one may as well say "lived myth" as "lived life." But the *mythus* as lived is the epic idea embodied in my novel; and it is plain to me that when as a novelist I took the step in my subject matter from the bourgeois and individual to the mythical and typical my personal connection with the analytic field passed into its acute stage. The mythical interest is as native to psychoanalysis as the psychological interest is to all creative writing. Its penetration into the childhood of the individual soul is at the same time a penetration into the childhood of mankind, into the primitive and mythical. Freud has told us that for him all natural science, medicine, and psychotherapy were a lifelong journey round and back to the early passion of his youth for the history of mankind, for the origins of religion and morality—an interest which at the height of his career broke out to such magnificent effect in *Totem and Taboo.* The word *Tiefenpsychologie* ("deep" psychology) has a temporal significance; the primitive foundations of the human soul are likewise primitive time, they are those profound time sources where the myth has its home and shapes the primeval norms and forms of life. For the myth is the foundation of life; it is the timeless schema, the pious formula into which life flows when it reproduces its traits out of the unconscious. Certainly when a writer has acquired the habit of regarding life as mythical and typical there comes a curious heightening of his artist temper, a new refreshment to his perceiving and shaping powers, which otherwise occurs much later in life; for while in the life of the human race the mythical is an early and primitive stage, in the life of the individual it is a late and mature one. What is gained is an insight into the higher truth depicted in the actual; a smiling knowledge of the eternal, the ever-being, and authentic; a knowledge of the schema in which and according to which the supposed individual lives, unaware, in his naive belief in himself as unique in space and time, of the extent to which his life is but formula and repetition and his path marked out for him by those who trod it before him. His character is a mythical role which the actor just emerged from the depths to the light plays in the illusion that it is his own and unique, that he, as it were, has invented it all himself, with a dignity and security of which his supposed unique individuality in time and space is not the source, but rather which he creates out of his deeper consciousness in order that something which was once founded and legitimized shall again be represented and once more for good or ill, whether nobly or basely, in any case after its own kind conduct itself according to pattern. Actually, if his existence consisted merely in the unique and the present, he would not know how to conduct himself at all; he would be confused, helpless, unstable in his own self-regard, would not know which foot to put foremost or what sort of face to put on. His dignity and security lie all unconsciously in the fact that with him something timeless has once more emerged into the light and become present; it is a mythical value added to the otherwise poor and valueless single character; it is native worth, because its origin lies in the unconscious.

Such is the gaze which the mythically oriented artist bends upon the phenomena about him—an ironic and superior gaze, as you can see, for the mythical knowledge resides in the gazer and not in that at which he gazes. But let us suppose that the mythical point of view could become subjective; that it could pass over into the active ego and become conscious there, proudly and darkly yet joyously, of its recurrence and its typicality, could celebrate its role and realize its own value exclusively in the knowledge that it was a fresh incarnation of the traditional upon earth. One might say that such a phenomenon alone could be the "lived myth"; nor should we think that it is anything novel or unknown. The life in the myth, life as a sacred repetition, is a historical form of life, for the man of ancient times lived thus. An instance is the figure of the Egyptian Cleopatra, which is Ishtar, Astarte, Aphrodite in person. Bachofen, in his description of the cult of Bacchus, the Dionysiac religion, regards the Egyptian queen as the consummate picture of the Dionysiac *stimula;* and according to Plutarch it was far more her erotic intellectual culture than her physical charms that entitled her to represent the female as developed into the earthly embodiment of Aphrodite. But her Aphrodite nature, her role of Hathor-Isis, is not only objective, not only a treatment of her by Plutarch or Bachofen; it was the content of her subjective existence as well, she lived the part. This we can see by the manner of her death: she is supposed to have killed herself by laying an asp upon her bosom. But the snake was the familiar of Ishtar, the Egyptian Isis, who is represented clad in a garment of scales; also there exists a statuette of Ishtar holding a snake to her bosom. So that if Cleopatra's death was as the legend represents, the manner of it was a manifestation of her mythical ego. Moreover, did she not adopt the falcon hood of the goddess Isis and adorn herself with the insignia of Hathor, the cow's horns with the crescent moon between? And name her two children by Mark Antony Helios and Selene? No doubt she was a very significant figure indeed—significant in the antique sense, that she was well aware who she was and in whose footsteps she trod!

The ego of antiquity and its consciousness of itself were different from our own, less exclusive, less sharply defined. It was, as it were, open behind; it received much from the past and by repeating it gave it presentness again. The Spanish scholar Ortega y Gasset puts it that the man of antiquity, before he did anything, took a step backward, like the bullfighter who leaps back to deliver the mortal thrust. He searched the past for a pattern into which he might slip as into a diving bell, and being thus at once disguised and protected might rush upon his present problem. Thus his life was in a sense a reanimation, an archaizing attitude. But it is just this life as reanimation that is the life as myth. Alexander walked in the footsteps of Miltiades; the ancient biographers of Cæsar were convinced, rightly or wrongly, that he took Alexander as his prototype. But such *imitation* meant far more than we mean by the word today. It was a mythical identification, peculiarly familiar to antiquity; but it is operative far into modern times, and at all times is psychically possible. How often have we not been told that the figure of Napoleon was cast in the antique mold! He regretted that the mentality of the time forbade him to give himself out for the son of Jupiter Ammon, in imitation of Alexander. But we need not doubt that—at least at the period of his Eastern exploits—he mythically confounded himself with Alexander; while after he turned his face westward he is said to have declared: "I am Charlemagne." Note that: not "I am like Charlemagne" or "My situation is like Charlemagne's," but quite simply:

"I am he." That is the formulation of the myth. Life, then—at any rate, significant life—was in ancient times the reconstitution of the myth in flesh and blood; it referred to and appealed to the myth; only through it, through reference to the past, could it approve itself as genuine and significant. The myth is the legitimization of life; only through and in it does life find self-awareness, sanction, consecration. Cleopatra fulfilled her Aphrodite character even unto death—and can one live and die more significantly or worthily than in the celebration of the myth? We have only to think of Jesus and His life, which was lived in order that that which was written might be fulfilled. It is not easy to distinguish between His own consciousness and the conventionalizations of the Evangelists. But His word on the cross, about the ninth hour, that *"Eli, Eli, lama sabachthani?"* was evidently not in the least an outburst of despair and disillusionment; but on the contrary a lofty messianic sense of self. For the phrase is not original, not a spontaneous outcry. It stands at the beginning of the Twenty-second Psalm, which from one end to the other is an announcement of the Messiah. Jesus was quoting, and the quotation meant: "Yes, it is I!" Precisely thus did Cleopatra quote when she took the asp to her breast to die; and again the quotation meant: "Yes, it is I!"

Let us consider for a moment the word *celebration* which I used in this connection. It is a pardonable, even a proper usage. For life in the myth, life, so to speak, in quotation, is a kind of celebration, in that it is a making present of the past, it becomes a religious act, the performance by a celebrant of a prescribed procedure; it becomes a feast. For a feast is an anniversary, a renewal of the past in the present. Every Christmas the world-saving Babe is born again on earth, to suffer, to die, and to arise. The feast is the abrogation of time, an event, a solemn narrative being played out conformably to an immemorial pattern; the events in it take place not for the first time, but ceremonially according to the prototype. It achieves presentness as feasts do, recurring in time with their phases and hours following on each other in time as they did in the original occurrence. In antiquity each feast was essentially a dramatic performance, a mask; it was the scenic reproduction, with priests as actors, of stories about the gods—as for instance the life and sufferings of Osiris. The Christian Middle Ages had their mystery play, with heaven, earth, and the torments of hell—just as we have it later in Goethe's *Faust;* they had their carnival farce, their folk mime. The artist eye has a mythical slant upon life, which makes it look like a farce, like a theatrical performance of a prescribed feast, like a Punch and Judy epic, wherein mythical character puppets reel off a plot abiding from past time and now again present in a jest. It only lacks that this mythical slant pass over and become subjective in the performers themselves, become a festival and mythical consciousness of part and play, for an epic to be produced such as that in the first volume of the *Joseph and His Brothers* series, particularly in the chapter "The Great Hoaxing." There a mythical recurrent farce is tragicomically played by personages all of whom well know in whose steps they tread: Isaac, Esau, and Jacob; and who act out the cruel and grotesque tale of how Esau the Red is led by the nose and cheated of his birthright to the huge delight of all the bystanders. Joseph too is another such celebrant of life; with charming mythological hocus-pocus he enacts in his own person the Tammuz–Osiris myth, "bringing to pass" anew the story of the mangled, buried, and arisen god, playing his festival game with that which mysteriously and secretly shapes life out of its own depths—the unconscious. The mystery of the metaphysician and psychologist, that the soul is the giver of all given conditions, becomes in Joseph easy, playful, blithe—like a consummately artistic performance by a fencer or juggler. It reveals his *infantile* nature—and the word I have used betrays how closely, though seeming to wander so far afield, we have kept to the subject of our evening's homage.

Infantilism—in other words, regression to childhood—what a role this genuinely psychoanalytic element plays in all our lives! What a large share it has in shaping the life of a human being; operating, indeed, in just the way I have described: as mythical identification, as survival, as a treading in footprints already made! The bond with the father, the imitation of the father, the game of being the father, and the transference to father-substitute pictures of a higher and more developed type—how these infantile traits work upon the life of the individual to mark and shape it! I use the word "shape," for to me in all seriousness the happiest, most pleasurable element of what we call education *(Bildung)*, the shaping of the human being, is just this powerful influence of admiration and love, this childish identification with a father-image elected out of profound affinity. The artist in particular, a passionately childlike and play-possessed being, can tell us of the mysterious yet after all obvious effect of such infantile imitation upon his own life, his productive conduct of a career which after all is often nothing but a reanimation of the hero under very different temporal and personal conditions and with very different, shall we say, childish means. The *imitatio* Goethe, with its Werther and Wilhelm Meister stages, its old-age period of *Faust* and *Diwan,* can still shape and mythically mold the life of an artist—rising out of his unconscious, yet playing over—as is the artist's way—into a smiling, childlike, and profound awareness.

The Joseph of the novel is an artist, playing with his *imitatio dei* upon the unconscious string; and I know not how to express the feelings that possess me—something like a joyful sense of divination of the future—when I indulge in this encouragement of the unconscious to play, to make itself fruitful in a serious product, in a narrational meeting of psychology and myth, which is at the same time a celebration of the meeting between poetry and analysis.

And now this word *future:* I have used it in the title of my address, because it is this idea, the idea of the future, that I involuntarily like best to connect with the name of Freud. But even as I have been speaking I have been asking myself whether I have not been guilty of a cause of confusion; whether—from what I have said up to now—a better title might not have been something like "Freud and the Myth." And yet I rather cling to the combination of name and word and I should like to justify and make clear its relation to what I have so far said. I make bold to believe that in that novel so kin to the Freudian world, making as it does the light of psychology play upon the myth, there lie hidden seeds and elements of a new and coming sense of our humanity. And no less firmly do I hold that we shall one day recognize in Freud's life-work the cornerstone for the building of a new anthropology and therewith of a new structure, to which many stones are being brought up today, which shall be the future dwelling of a wiser and freer humanity. This physicianly psychologist will, I make no doubt at all, be honored as the pathfinder toward a humanism of the future, which we dimly divine and which will have experienced much that the earlier humanism knew not of. It will be a humanism standing in a different relation to the powers of the lower world, the unconscious, the id: a relation bolder, freer, blither, productive of a riper art than any possible in our neurotic, fear-ridden, hate-ridden world. Freud is of the opinion that the significance of psychoanalysis as a science of the unconscious will in the future far outrank its value as a therapeutic method. But even as a science of the unconscious it is a therapeutic method, in the grand style, a method overarching the individual case. Call this, if you choose, a poet's utopia; but the thought is after all not unthinkable that the resolution of our great fear and our great hate, their conversion into a different relation to the unconscious which shall be more the artist's, more ironic and yet not necessarily irreverent, may one day be due to the healing effect of this very science.

The analytic revelation is a revolutionary force. With it a blithe skepticism has come into the world, a mistrust that unmasks all the schemes and subterfuges of our own souls. Once roused and on the alert, it cannot be put to sleep again. It infiltrates life, undermines its raw naiveté, takes from it the strain of its own ignorance, de-emotionalizes it, as it were, inculates the taste for understatement, as the English call it—for the deflated rather than for the inflated words, for the cult which exerts its influence by moderation, by modesty. Modesty—what a beautiful word! In the German (Bescheidenheit) it originally had to do with knowing and only later got its present meaning; while the Latin word from which the English comes means a way of doing—in short, both together give us almost the sense of the French savoir faire—to know how to do. May we hope that this may be the fundamental temper of that more blithely objective and peaceful world which the science of the unconscious may be called to usher in?

Its mingling of the pioneer with the physicianly spirit justifies such a hope. Freud once called his theory of dreams "a bit of scientific new-found land won from superstition and mysticism." The word won expresses the colonizing spirit and significance of his work. "Where id was, shall be ego," he epigrammatically says. And he calls analysis a cultural labor comparable to the draining of the Zuider Zee. Almost in the end the traits of the venerable man merge into the lineaments of the gray-haired Faust, whose spirit urges him

> to shut the imperious sea from the shore away,
> Set narrower bounds to the broad water's waste.
>
> Then open I to many millions space
> Where they may live, not safe-secure, but free
> And active. And such a busy swarming I would see
> Standing amid free folk on a free soil.

The free folk are the people of a future freed from fear and hate, and ripe for peace.

Translated by Helen Tracey Lowe-Porter

A Brother

Were it not for the frightful sacrifices which continue to be offered up to the fatal psychology of this man; were it not for the ever-widening circle of desolation which he makes, it would be easier to admit that he presents an arresting phenomenon. Yet, hard as it is, we must admit it; nobody can help being preoccupied by the deplorable spectacle. For he has chosen—in default, as we know, of capacity to wield any other—to use politics as his tool; and politics always magnify and coarsen the effect they produce. So much the worse for us all; so much the worse for Europe today, lying helpless under his spell, where he is vouchsafed the role of the man of destiny and all-conquering hero, and where, thanks to a combination of fantastic chances—or mischances—everything is grist that comes to his mill, and he passes unopposed from one triumph to another.

Even to admit all this, even to recognize the bald and sorry facts, comes close to being a moral self-flagellation. One has to force oneself. And after that one begins to fear lest one be pusillanimous enough to fall short in the hatred which is the only right reaction from those to whom our civilization is anywise dear. I tell myself that I do not fall short. Most sincerely do I hope that this public misfortune may meet a disgraceful end, as disgraceful and as speedy as his well-known caution can give us ground to hope for. And yet I feel that those are not my best hours in which I hate the miserable, if also portentous phenomenon. Happier and worthier are those other hours when my hatred is overcome by my need for freedom, for objective contemplation—in a word, for the irony which I have long since recognized as the native element of all creative art. Love and hatred are great emotions; yet it is strange how prone people are to underestimate, precisely as emotion, that attitude in which they both unite: I mean *interest*. And in underestimating it, they are underestimating at the same time its morality. For interest connotes a desire for self-discipline; it inclines to be humorous, ascetic; to acknowledge similarity, even identification with oneself; to feel a sense of solidarity. And all this I find morally superior to hatred.

The fellow is a catastrophe. But that is no reason why we should not find him interesting, as a character and an event. Consider the circumstances. Here is a man possessed of a bottomless resentment and a festering desire for revenge; a man ten times a failure, extremely lazy, incapable of steady work; a man who has spent long periods in institutions; a disappointed bohemian artist; a total good-for-nothing. And here is a people obsessed by powerful though far less justifiable feelings of defeat and inferiority, and unable to think of anything save how to retrieve its lost "honor." And then he—who had learned nothing, and in his dreamy, obstinate arrogance would learn nothing; who had neither technical nor physical discipline, could not sit a horse, or drive a car, or fly a plane, or do aught that men do, even to begetting a child—he develops the one thing needful to establish a connection between him and the people: a gift of oratory. It is oratory unspeakably inferior in kind, but magnetic in its effect on the masses: a weapon of definitely histrionic, even hysterical power, which he thrusts into the nation's wound and turns it around. He rouses the populace with images of his own insulted grandeur, deafens it with promises, makes out of the people's sufferings a vehicle for his own greatness, his ascent to fantastic heights, to unlimited power, to incredible compensations and overcompensations. He rises to such a pitch of glorification and awe-inspiring sanctity that anyone who in the past had wronged him, when he was unknown, despised, and rejected, becomes straightway a child of the evil one, meriting the most shameful and frightful death. He proceeds from the masses of Germany to the masses of Europe, and learns to apply in a larger setting the same technique of hysterical humbug and soul-paralyzing ideology which raised him to greatness in the smaller one. With masterly adroitness he exploits the weariness of the continent, its agony of fear, its dread of war. He knows how to stir up the people over the heads of their rulers and win large sections of opinion to himself. Fortune is his slave, all walls fall before him. The one-time melancholic ne'er-do-well, simply because he has learned—for aught he knows, out of patriotism—to be a political animal now bids fair to subjugate Europe, or, God knows, maybe the whole world. All that is unique. It is on a new scale; one simply cannot help granting the phenomenon the need of a certain shuddering admiration.

There are traits of the legendary about it all—distorted, of course; but then, how much degeneration and distortion are there not in Europe today? The motif of the poor, wool-gathering simpleton who wins the princess and the kingdom; the ugly duckling who becomes a swan; the Sleeping Beauty surrounded by a rose-hedge instead of Brunnhilde's circling flames and smiling as her Siegfried hero awakes her with a kiss. *"Deutschland erwache!"* It is ghastly, but it all fits in, as well as many another folk tradition, mingled with debased and pathological elements. The whole thing is a distorted phase of Wagnerism, as has been said long ago; we know the not unfounded if rather illegitimate reverence which our political medicine-man feels for the musician-artist whom, after all, Gottfried Keller called a hairdresser and a charlatan.

Ah, the artist! I spoke of moral self-flagellation. For must I not, however much it hurts, regard the man as an artist–phenomenon? Mortifyingly enough, it is all there: the difficulty, the laziness, the pathetic formlessness in youth, the round peg in the square hole, the "what ever *do* you want?" The lazy, vegetating existence in the depths of a moral and mental bohemia; the fundamental arrogance which thinks itself too good for any sensible and honorable activity, on the ground of its vague intuition that it is reserved for something else—as yet quite indefinite, but something which, if it could be named, would be greeted with roars of laughter. Then the bad conscience, the sense of guilt, the anger at everything, the revolutionary instinct, the unconscious storing up of mines of compensatory wishes; the obstinate need of self-justification, self-proof, the urge to dominate and subdue, the dream of seeing the whole world abased in fear and love, admiration and remorse, at the feet of the once despised! The thoroughgoingness of the fulfillment must not lead us to wrong conclusions about the volume and depth of the latent dignity which suffered so much from the dishonors of its chrysalis state, or about the extraordinary violence of the tension, in an unconscious which was maturing creations so impressive and grandiose. The alfresco, the grand historic style, is not a question of personality. It has to do with the medium and sphere of activity of the political or demagogic method which it wields to sway whole populations and the destinies of masses of people, with much accompanying noise and destructiveness. Its extrinsic scope proves nothing about the extraordinary character of the mental attributes or the actual greatness of this successful hysteric. But there is also present the insatiable craving for compensation, the urge to self-glorification, the restless dissatisfaction, the forgetfulness of past achievements, the swift abandonment of the prize once grasped, the emptiness and tedium, the sense of worthlessness so soon as there is nothing to do to take the world's breath away; the sleepless compulsion to make one's mark on something.

A brother—a rather unpleasant and mortifying brother. He makes me nervous, the relationship is painful to a degree. But I will not disclaim it. For I repeat: better, more productive, more honest, more constructive than hatred is recognition, acceptance, the readiness to make oneself one with what is deserving of our hate, even though we run the risk, morally speaking, of forgetting how to say no. That does not worry me. Anyhow, the moral sphere, insofar as it derogates from the innocent spontaneity of life, is really not altogether the artist's concern. It may be annoying, but after all it has its soothing side, to realize that despite all the psychoanalysis, all the progress we have made in learning how the human being's mind works, there is still absolutely no limit to the extent the unconscious can go in effective projection of itself upon reality.

We see this truth illustrated by the state of Europe today; the reduction to the primitive to which she has consciously and deliberately submitted herself. Indeed, the conscious and willing surrender, the treachery to the spirit and to the upper levels at which it had arrived, are themselves the severest possible indictment of the prevailing primitivism. For this primitivism is shameless. It is a wanton self-glorification, in the face of the developed civilization of our age. It is shameless as a philosophy, however much condoned as a reaction against arid intellectualism. It is, in the Old Testament phrase, a folly and an abomination. Even the artist, despite his position as ironic partisan of life, must turn away in disgust from the spectacle of such an utter collapse and betrayal. Lately, on the films, I saw a ritual dance of the Bali islanders. It ended in a complete trance condition, with frightful twitchings of the bodies of the exhausted youths. Where is the difference between these practices and the procedure in the European mass meeting? There is none. Or rather there is one: the difference between the exotic and the repellent.

When I was still very young, I described in *Fiorenza* how the sway of beauty and culture was once broken by the religious and social fanaticism of a monk who heralded the "miracle of regained detachment." In *Death in Venice* there is much of challenge to the psychologism of the age; much talk of a simplification and resolution of mind—though indeed in the story I made it come to a bad end. I did not lack contact with the tendencies and aspirations of the time, with ideas which twenty years later were to be the property of the man in the street. Who can wonder, then, that I paid no attention when they degenerated into the political sphere and wreaked their violence on a plane where professors enamored of the primitive and literary lackeys of the anti-intellectual pose were the only ones who did not fear to tread? Such activities make one disgusted with one's reverence for the sources of life. One feels compelled to hate them. But what is such hatred compared with that which the protagonist of the unconscious must feel for knowledge and mind? I have a private suspicion that the élan of the march on Vienna had a secret spring: it was directed at the venerable Freud, the real and actual enemy, the philosopher and revealer of the neuroses, the great disillusioner, the seer and sayer of the laws of genius.

Our notion of genius has always been shrouded in a superstitious haze. But I question whether today the haze is thick enough to prevent our calling this man a genius. And why not do so, if it pleases him? The intellectual man is almost as much interested in painful truths as the fool is in those which flatter him. If genius is madness tempered with discretion (and that *is* a definition!), then the man is a genius. One feels freer to admit it because genius, while it is a category, is not a class. It has no reference to rank or station, manifesting itself in the most various ways, and even at its lowest revealing the marks of its kind. I will not decide whether history has ever produced a specimen of mental and moral baseness accompanied by the magnetism we call genius, to compare with this one to which we are the amazed witnesses. In any case I am against allowing the particular manifestation to give us a distaste for the whole category. The phenomenon of the great man has after all been most often an aesthetic, not an ethical phenomenon. I admit that by overstepping our human limitations it has made humanity shudder before it; yet even so, and whatever the suffering involved, the shudder has nearly always been a thrill as well. We must make distinctions—they are very important. It annoys me when I hear people say today: "Napoleon was a boor too; we know that now." It is really going too far to speak in one breath of the great soldier and the blackmailing pacifist, the fighter and the coward whose role would be played out on the first day of actual armed conflict. That earlier figure is stamped forever on men's memories, a classic Mediterranean bronze. Hegel called him the "world-spirit on horseback." And shall we compare that all-embracing brain, that immense capacity for toil, that embodiment of the revolution and tyrant harbinger of liberty, with the pitiable idler and incapable, the fifth-rank visionary, the stupid foe of social revolution, the sly sadist and plotter of revenge, the representative of "temperament"?

I spoke of the distortions prevalent in Europe today. And truly our times have succeeded in distorting much; for instance, nationalism, socialism, myth, philosophy, irrationalism, faith, youth, revolution—and what not besides? To cap it all, we have the distortion of genius. We must reconcile ourselves to our lot; for today it is our fate to encounter genius in this one particular phase of all the phases possible to it.

An artist, a brother. But the bond, and the recognition of it, are an expression of art's contempt for itself—they do not want to be taken quite seriously. I like to think, yes, I am certain, that a future is now on the way in which art uncontrolled by mind, art as black magic, the issue of brainlessly irresponsible instinct, will be as much condemned as, in humanly frail times like ours, it is reverenced. Art, certainly, is not all sweetness and light. But neither is it all a brew of darkness, not all a freak of the tellurian underworld, not simply "life." More clearly and happily than ever will the artist of the future realize his mission as a white enchanter, as a winged, hermetic, moon-sib mediator between spirit and life. And mediation itself is spirit.

Germany
and the Germans

THE FOLLOWING IS THE TEXT OF AN ADDRESS DELIVERED BY DR.
MANN IN THE COOLIDGE AUDITORIUM IN THE LIBRARY OF CONGRESS
ON THE EVENING OF MAY 29, 1945.

As I stand here before you, a man of seventy, contrary to all expectations, an American citizen for more than a year, speaking English or at least making an effort to do so, a guest, no, an official member of the American state institution that invited you to listen to me—as I stand here before you I feel that life is indeed of such a stuff as dreams are made of. It is all so strange, so incredible, so unexpected. In the first place, I had never anticipated that I would attain patriarchal years, although at an early age I had regarded it as theoretically desirable. I thought and said that, once having been born into the world, it was a good and honorable thing to persevere a long time, to live a full, canonical life, and, as an artist, to be characteristically fruitful in all its stages. But I had very little confidence in my own biological qualification and soundness, and the endurance that I have nevertheless demonstrated, appears to me less a proof of my own vital patience than proof of the patience of the genius of life toward me—something unmerited, an act of grace. And grace is always astonishing and unexpected. He who experiences it thinks he is dreaming.

It seems like a dream to me to be and to be here. I should have to be something other than a poet to accept it as a matter of course. It takes but little fantasy to find life fantastic. How did I get here? What dream-wave swept me from the remotest nook of Germany, where I was born and where, after all, I belong, into this auditorium, on to this platform, to stand here as an American, speaking to Americans? Not that I regard it as inappropriate. On the contrary,

I fully approve—fate has seen to that. As things stand today, my type of Germanism is most suitably at home in the hospitable Panopolis, the racial and national universe called America. Before I became an American I had been permitted to be a Czech. That was very amiable and merited my gratitude, but it had little rhyme or reason. Similarly I only need to imagine that I had happened to become a Frenchman, an Englishman, or an Italian, in order to perceive with the greatest satisfaction how much more fittingly I became an American. Everything else would have meant too narrow and too definite an estrangement of my existence. As an American I am a citizen of the world—and that is in keeping with the original nature of the German, notwithstanding his seclusiveness, his timidity in the face of the world, and it is difficult to say whether this timidity is rooted in arrogance or in an innate provincialism, an international social inferiority complex—probably in both.

I am to speak to you today on Germany and the Germans— a risky undertaking, not only because the topic is so complex, so inexhaustible, but also because of the violent emotions that encompass it today. To deal with it purely psychologically, *sine ira et sine studio,* would appear almost immoral in view of the unspeakable that this unfortunate nation has done to the world. Should a German avoid this subject today? But I would scarcely have known what other subject to choose for this evening, and, beyond that, it is scarcely possible to conceive of any conversation rising above the purely personal today that would not inevitably turn to the German problem, the enigma in the character and destiny of this people which undeniably has given humanity much that is great and beautiful, and yet has time and again imposed fatal burdens upon the world. Germany's horrible fate, the tremendous catastrophe in which her modern history now culminates, compels our interest, even if this interest is devoid of sympathy. Any attempt to arouse sympathy, to defend and to excuse Germany, would certainly be an inappropriate undertaking for one of German birth today. To play the part of the judge, to curse and damn his own people in compliant agreement with the incalculable hatred that they have kindled, to commend himself smugly as "the good Germany" in contrast to the wicked, guilty Germany over there with which he has nothing at all in common—that too would hardly befit one of German origin. For anyone who was born a German *does* have something in common with German destiny and German guilt. Critical withdrawal from it should not be regarded as disloyalty. The truths that one tries to utter about one's people can only be the product of self-examination.

Already I have somehow slipped into the complex world of German psychology with the remark about the combination of expansiveness and seclusiveness, of cosmopolitanism and provincialism in the German character. I believe this observation, dating from my early youth, is correct. A trip out of the Reich, say across Lake Constance, into Switzerland, was a trip out of the provincial into the world—no matter how strange it may appear to regard the tiny country of Switzerland as "world" in comparison to the large and powerful German Reich with its gigantic cities. Still it was perfectly true: Switzerland, neutral, multilingual, under French influence, breathing western air—notwithstanding its miniature format—was actually far more European, far more "World," than the political colossus to the north, where the word "international" had long since been considered an insult and where arrogant provincialism had tainted the atmosphere and made it stagnant.

This was the modern nationalistic form of the old German world-seclusiveness and melancholy world-unfitness, which, along with a sort of philistine universalism, cosmopolitanism in a nightcap, so to speak, had made up the German picture. This state of mind, this unworldly, provincial, German cosmopolitanism, always had something scurrilously spooky, something hiddenly uncanny about it, a quality of secret demonism that I was particularly able to perceive on account of my personal origin. I think back to that corner of the German world that constituted the first frame of my existence, and from which the dream-wave of life swept me here: it was the ancient city of Lübeck, near the Baltic Sea, once the threshold of the Hanseatic League, founded before the middle of the twelfth century, and raised to the rank of a free imperial city by Barbarossa in the thirteenth. The exceptionally beautiful City Hall, which my father, as a senator, frequented, was completed in the very year in which Martin Luther posted his Theses on the portal of the Castle Church at Wittenberg, the beginning of the modern era. But just as Luther, the Reformer, had a good deal of the medieval man about him and wrestled with the Devil all his life, so we who lived in the Protestant city of Lübeck, even the Lübeck that had become a Republican member of Bismarck's Reich, moved in an atmosphere of the Gothic Middle Ages—and I am thinking not only of the skyline with its pointed towers, gates, and walls, of the humorously macabre thrills that emanated from the Dance of Death frescoes in St. Mary's

Church, of the crooked, haunted looking alleys that were frequently named after the old guilds, the Bell-founders, the Butchers, and of the picturesque burgher houses. No, in the atmosphere itself something had clung of the state of mind of, let's say, the final decades of the fifteenth century, the hysteria of the dying Middle Ages, something of latent spiritual epidemic. It's a strange thing to say about a sensibly sober, modern, commercial city, but it was conceivable that a Children's Crusade might suddenly erupt here, a St. Vitus Dance, an outbreak of religious fanaticism coupled with mystic processions of the people, or the like—in short, an anciently neurotic substratum was perceptible, an arcane spiritual state that was outwardly evidenced by the many "characters" to be found in such a city, eccentrics and harmless lunatics who live within its walls and who, in a sense, belong to its scene as much as the ancient buildings. There was, for example, a certain type of old woman with bleary eyes and a crutch, who was half humorously rumored to be a witch; a man, retired on a small income, with a scarlet, warty nose and some sort of nervous tic, with ludicrous habits, such as a stereotyped, involuntary bird-cry, a female with an absurd hairdo roaming through the streets in a trailing dress of obsolete style, with an air of insane superciliousness, and followed by a retinue of pug-dogs and cats. And the children, the street urchins, are a part of the picture, trailing these characters, mocking them, and running away in superstitious panic when they turn around. . . .

I really don't know why I am conjuring up these early memories here and now. Is it because I first experienced "Germany," visually and spiritually, in the form of this quaintly venerable city scene, and because I am trying to suggest a secret union of the German spirit with the Demonic, a thesis which is, indeed, part of my inner experience, but not easily defensible? The hero of our greatest literary work, Goethe's Faust, is a man who stands at the dividing line between the Middle Ages and Humanism, a man of God who, out of a presumptuous urge for knowledge, surrenders to magic, to the Devil. Wherever arrogance of the intellect mates with the spiritual obsolete and archaic, there is the Devil's domain. And the Devil, Luther's Devil, Faust's Devil, strikes me as a very German figure, and the pact with him, the Satanic covenant, to win all treasures and power on earth for a time at the cost of the soul's salvation, strikes me as something exceedingly typical of German nature. A lonely thinker and searcher, a theologian and philosopher in his cell who, in his desire for world enjoyment and world domination, bar-ters his soul to the Devil—isn't this the right moment to see Germany in this picture, the moment in which Germany is literally being carried off by the Devil?

It is a grave error on the part of legend and story not to connect Faust with music. He should have been musical, he should have been a musician. Music is a demonic realm; Søren Kierkegaard, a great Christian, proved that most convincingly in his painfully enthusiastic essay on Mozart's Don Juan. Music is Christian art with a negative prefix. Music is calculated order and chaos-breeding irrationality at once, rich in conjuring, incantatory gestures, in magic of numbers, the most unrealistic and yet the most impassioned of arts, mystical and abstract. If Faust is to be the representative of the German soul, he would have to be musical, for the relation of the German to the world is abstract and mystical, that is, musical—the relation of a professor with a touch of demonism, awkward and at the same time filled with arrogant knowledge that he surpasses the world in "depth."

What constitutes this depth? Simply the musicality of the German soul, that which we call its inwardness, its subjectivity, the divorce of the speculative from the sociopolitical element of human energy, and the complete predominance of the former over the latter. Europe always felt it and understood its monstrous and unfortunate aspects. In 1839 Balzac wrote: "If the Germans do not know how to play the great instruments of liberty, still they know naturally how to play all instruments of music." That is a good observation, and it is not the only striking remark of this kind that the great novelist made. In *Cousin Pons* he says of the German musician Schmucke, a wonderful figure: "Schmucke, who, like all Germans, was very strong in harmony, orchestrated the scores, while Pons supplied the melody." Correct, the Germans are primarily musicians of the vertical, not of the horizontal, greater masters of harmony, with which Balzac includes counterpoint, than of melody; they are instrumentalists rather than glorifiers of the human voice, far more inclined toward the learned and the spiritual in music than toward the melodically happy-making. They have given the western world perhaps not its most beautiful, socially uniting, but certainly its deepest, most significant music, and the world has not withheld its thanks and praise. At the same time it has felt and feels more strongly than ever today that such musicality of soul is paid for dearly in another sphere—the political, the sphere of human companionship.

Martin Luther, a gigantic incarnation of the German spirit, was exceptionally musical. I frankly confess that I do not love him. Germanism in its unalloyed state, the Separatist, Anti-Roman, Anti-European shocks me and frightens me, even when it appears in the guise of evangelical freedom and spiritual emancipation; and the specifically Lutheran, the choleric coarseness, the invective, the fuming and raging, the extravagant rudeness coupled with tender depth of feeling and with the most clumsy superstition and belief in demons, incubi, and changelings, arouses my instinctive antipathy. I should not have liked to be Luther's dinner guest; I should probably have felt as comfortable as in the cozy home of an ogre, and I am convinced that I would have gotten along much better with Leo X, Giovanni de' Medici, the amiable humanist, whom Luther called "The Devil's sow, the Pope." Moreover I do not even accept the necessity of the contrast of popular robustness and good manners, the anti-thesis of Luther and the refined pedant Erasmus. Goethe has outgrown this contrast and reconciles it. He represents well-mannered, civilized strength and popular robustness, urbane Demonism, spirit and blood at once, namely art. . . . With him Germany made a tremendous stride in human culture—or should have made it, for in reality she was always closer to Luther than to Goethe. And no one can deny that Luther was a tremendously great man, great in the most German manner, great and German even in his duality as a liberating and at once reactionary force, a conservative revolutionary. He not only reconstituted the Church; he actually saved Christianity. Europeans are in the habit of accusing the German nature of irreligiousness, of heathenism. That is very disputable. Germany certainly took Christianity more seriously than anyone else. In the German-Luther Christianity took itself childlikely and rustically serious at a time when it did not take itself seriously at all elsewhere. Luther's revolution preserved Christianity—in about the same way in which the New Deal is intended to preserve capitalistic economics—even if capitalism refuses to understand it.

No aspersions against Luther's greatness! It was his momentous translation of the Bible that really first created the German language which Goethe and Nietzsche finally perfected; and it was also he who, through the breaking of the scholastic fetters and the renovation of the conscience, tremendously promoted the freedom of research, of criticism, and of philosophic speculation. By the establishment of the direct relationship of man to his God he advanced the cause of European democracy; for "every man his own priest," that is democracy. German idealistic philosophy, the refinement of psychology by pietistic examination of the individual conscience, finally the self-conquest of Christian morality for reasons of morality—for that was Nietzsche's deed or misdeed—all of that comes from Luther. He was a liberating hero—but in the German style, for he knew nothing of liberty. I am not speaking now of the liberty of the Christian, but of political liberty, the liberty of the citizen—this liberty not only left him cold, but its impulses and demands were deeply repugnant to him. Four hundred years after his time the first president of the German Republic, a Social Democrat, spoke the words: "I hate revolution like sin." That was genuinely Lutheran, genuinely German. In the same way Luther hated the peasant revolt which, evangelically inspired as it was, if successful, would have given a happier turn to German history, a turn toward liberty. Luther, however, saw in it nothing but a distortion of his work of spiritual liberation and therefore he fumed and raged against it as only he could do. The peasants, he said, should be killed like mad dogs and he told the princes that they could now gain the kingdom of heaven by slaughtering the peasant beasts. Luther, the German man of the people, bears a good share of responsibility for the sad ending of this first attempt at a German revolution, for the victory of the princes, and for all its consequences.

At that time there lived in Germany a man who has my special sympathy, Tilman Riemenschneider, a master of religious art, a sculptor and wood-carver, widely famous for the faithful and expressive excellence of his works, his profound altar painting and chaste reliefs which ornamented the places of worship all over Germany. The master had won high regard, both as a man and as a citizen, in his immediate environs, the city of Würzburg, where he was a member of the Council. He never expected to take a hand in politics, in world affairs—the thought lay far from his natural modesty and from his love for his free and peaceful work. There was nothing of the demagogue about him. But his heart, that beat warmly for the poor and oppressed, forced him to take the part of the peasants, whose cause he recognized as just and pleasing in the sight of God, against the lords, the bishops and princes, whose favor he could easily have retained. Moved by the great and fundamental contrasts of the time, he felt compelled to emerge from his sphere of purely spiritual and esthetic artistic life and to become a fighter for liberty and justice. He sacrificed his own liberty for the cause that he held higher than art and the dignified calm of his existence.

It was his influence, chiefly, that determined the city of Würzburg to refuse military service to the "Burg," the Prince-Prelate, and, in general, to assume a revolutionary attitude against him. Riemenschneider paid dearly for it. For after the crushing of the peasant revolt, the victorious powers whom he had opposed took cruel revenge upon him; they subjected him to prison and torture, and he emerged from the ordeal as a broken man, incapable of awakening the beauties in wood and stone.

Such men we had in Germany too, at all times. But they are not the specifically and monumentally German type. That type is represented by Luther, the musical theologian. In the political realm he advanced only to the point of deciding that both parties, the princes and the peasants, were wrong, an attitude which soon led him to inveigh with berserk fury only against the peasants. His inwardness was in full agreement with St. Paul's admonition "Let every soul be subject unto the higher powers." But these words referred to the authority of the Roman World empire, which was the prerequisite and the political realm for the Christian world religion, while in Luther's case it was a question of the reactionary, petty authority of German princes. His antipolitical servility, the product of musical-German inwardness and unworldliness, was not only responsible for the centuries-old, obsequious attitude of the Germans toward their princes and toward the power of the state, it not only partly created and partly fostered the German dualism of boldest speculation on the one hand and political immaturity on the other. But it is also and chiefly typical in a monumental and defiant manner of the purely German sundering of the national impulse and the ideal of political liberty. For the Reformation, like the later uprising against Napoleon, was a *nationalistic* movement for liberty.

Let us speak for a moment of liberty: the peculiar perversion which this concept has suffered, and suffers to this day, at the hands of a people as important as the Germans, is food for serious thought. How was it possible that even National Socialism, now ending in disgrace, could adopt the name of a "German liberation movement," when, according to universal opinion, such an abomination cannot possibly have anything to do with liberty? This appellation was the expression not only of defiant insolence, but also of a fundamental misinterpretation of the concept of liberty, that had its effects in German history again and again. Liberty, in a political sense, is primarily a matter of internal political morality. A people that is not internally free and responsible to itself does not deserve external liberty; it cannot sit in the councils of freedom, and when it uses the sonorous word, the application is wrong. The German concept of liberty was always directed outward; it meant the right to be German, only German, and nothing else and nothing beyond that. It was a concept of protest, of self-centered defense against everything that tended to limit and restrict national egotism, to tame it and to direct it toward service to the world community, service to humanity. Stubborn individualism outwardly, in its relations to the world, to Europe, to civilization, this German concept of liberty behaved internally with an astonishing degree of lack of freedom, of immaturity, of dull servility. It was a militant slave mentality, and National Socialism went so far in its exaggeration of this incongruity between the external and internal desire for liberty as to think of world enslavement by a people themselves enslaved at home.

Why must the German urge for liberty always be tantamount to inner enslavement? Why did it finally have to culminate in an attack upon the liberty of all others, upon liberty itself? The reason is that Germany has never had a revolution and has never learned to combine the concept of the national with the concept of liberty. The "nation" was born in the French Revolution; it is a revolutionary and liberal concept that includes the humanitarian, internally it meant liberty, externally it meant Europe. All the ingratiating qualities of French political spirit are based upon this fortunate unity; all the constricting and depressing qualities of German patriotic enthusiasm rest upon the fact that this unity was never achieved. It might be said that the very concept of the "nation" in its historical affinity with that of liberty is foreign to Germany. It might be regarded as a mistake to call the Germans a nation, no matter whether they or others do it. It was wrong to use the word *nationalism* for their patriotic fervor—it is a misuse of a French idea and creates misunderstandings. One should not apply the same name to two different things. The German idea of liberty is racial and anti-European; it is always very near the barbaric if it does not actually erupt into open and declared barbarism, as in our days. The aesthetically repulsive and rude qualities that cling to its bearers and champions as early as the Wars of Liberation, to the student unions and to such types as Jahn and Massmann, are evidence of its unfortunate character. Goethe was certainly no stranger to popular culture; he wrote not only the classicistic *Iphigenie,* but also such ultra-German things as *Faust I, Götz,* and the *Aphorisms in Rhymes.* Yet, to the exasperation of all patriots, his attitude toward the wars against Napoleon was one of complete coldness, not only out of loyalty to his peer, the great Emperor, but also because he felt repelled by the barbaric-racial element in this uprising. The loneliness of this great man, who approved everything of a broad and generous nature, the supernational world Germanism, world literature,—his painful loneliness in the patriotically, "liberally" excited Germany of his day cannot be overemphasized. The determining and dominant concepts around which everything revolved for him, were culture and barbarism— and it was his lot to belong to a people whose idea of liberty turns into barbarism, because it is only directly outward, against Europe.

This is a misfortune, a curse, a perpetual tragedy, that finds added expression in the fact that even Goethe's disavowing attitude toward political Protestantism served only as a confirmation and a deepening of the Lutheran dualism of spiritual and political liberty throughout the nation and particularly among the intellectual leaders so that they were prevented from accepting the political element in their concept of culture. It is difficult to determine to what extent great men put their imprint upon the character of a people and mold its form,—and to what extent they themselves are its personification, its expression. This much is certain, that the German relation to politics is a negative one, a lack of qualification. Historical evidence lies in the fact that all German revolutions failed, that of 1525, of 1813, that of 1848 which was wrecked upon the rocks of the political impotency of the German bourgeois, and finally that of 1918. Further evidence also lies in the clumsy and sinister misconstruction that the Germans so easily place on the idea of politics whenever ambition drives them to engage in politics.

Politics has been called the "art of the possible," and it actually is a realm akin to art insofar as, like art, it occupies a creatively mediating position between the spirit and life, the idea and reality, the desirable and the necessary, conscience and deed, morality and power. It embraces much that is hard, necessary, amoral, much of expediency and concession to facts, much of human weakness and much of the vulgar. It would be hard to find a politician, a statesman, who accomplished great things without having to ask himself afterward whether he could still regard himself as a decent individual. And yet, just as mankind does not belong solely to the animal kingdom, so politics does not belong solely to the realm of evil. Without degenerating into something devilish and destructive, without being distorted into an enemy of mankind and perverting its concessive creativity into disgraceful and criminal sterility, it can never completely renounce its ideal and spiritual components, never deny the moral and humanly decent part of its nature, and reduce itself entirely to the immoral and vulgar, to lying, murder, deceit, and force. That would no longer be art and creatively mediating and actuating irony, but blind, inhuman nonsense that can never produce anything genuine, that achieves only transitory, terrifying success, and after even a brief span has a world-destroying, nihilistic, and finally self-destroying effect; for the totally immoral is by nature unfit to survive.

The peoples born and qualified for politics instinctively know how to guard the unity of conscience and action, of spirit and power, at least subjectively. They pursue politics as an art of life and of power that cannot be entirely freed from a strain of vitally useful evil, but that never quite loses sight of the higher, the idea, human decency, and morality: in this regard they feel politically, and they get along with themselves and with the world in this fashion. Such getting-along with life, founded on compromise, the German regards as hypocrisy. He was not born to get along with life and he proves his lack of qualification for politics by misunderstanding it in clumsily sincere manner. Not at all wicked by nature but with a flair for the spiritual and the ideal, he regards politics as nothing but falsehood, murder, deceit, and violence, as something completely and one-sidedly filthy, and if worldly ambition prompts him to take up politics, he pursues it in the light of this philosophy. When the German takes up politics he thinks he has to act in a fashion to dumbfound humanity, that's what he regards as politics. Since he thinks it is unalloyed evil, he believes he has to be a devil to pursue it.

We have seen it. Crimes were perpetrated that no psychology can excuse, and they are least of all excusable on the ground they were superfluous. For they were superfluous, they were not essential and Nazi Germany could have gotten along without them. She could have carried out her plans of power and conquest without their aid. In a world which knows trusts, cartels, and exploitation the idea of monopolistic spoliation of all other nations by the Goering Concern wasn't anything new and strange. The embarrassing thing about it was that it compromised the ruling system too greatly by clumsy exaggeration. Moreover, as an idea, it came a little too late—today when mankind is striving for economic democracy, struggling for a higher degree of social maturity. The Germans are always too late. They are late, like music which is always the last of the arts to express a world condition,—when that world condition is already in its final stages. They are abstract and mystical, too, like this, their dearest art—both to the point of criminality. Their crimes, I repeat, were not a necessary factor of their belated embarkment upon exploitation; they were a luxury in which they indulged from a theoretical predisposition, in honor of an ideology, the fantasm of race. If it did not sound like a detestable condonation, it might be said that they committed their crimes for dreamy idealism.

At times, particularly when contemplating German history, one has the impression that the world was not the sole creation of God but a cooperative work with someone else. One would like to ascribe to God the merciful fact that good can come from evil. But that evil so often comes from good, is obviously the contribution of the other fellow. The Germans might well ask why their good, in particular, so often turns to evil, becomes evil in their hands. Take, for example, their fundamental universalism and cosmopolitanism, their inner boundlessness, which may be regarded as a spiritual accessory of their ancient supernational realm, the Holy Roman Empire of the German Nation. This is a highly valuable, positive trait which, however, was transformed into evil by a sort of dialectic inversion. The Germans yielded to the temptation of basing upon their innate cosmopolitanism a claim to European hegemony, even to world domination, whereby this trait became its exact opposite, namely the most presumptive and menacing nationalism and imperialism. At the same time, they noticed that they were too late again with their nationalism because it had outlived its time. Therefore they substituted something newer, more modern, for it, the racial idol, which promptly led them to monstrous crimes and plunged them into the depths of distress.

Or take that quality of the Germans which is perhaps their most notable one, designated as inwardness, a word that is most difficult to define: tenderness, depth of feeling, unworldly reverie, love of nature, purest sincerity of thought and conscience—in short, all the characteristics of high lyricism are mingled in it, and even today the world cannot forget what it owes the German inwardness: German metaphysics, German music, especially the miracle of the German Lied—a nationally unique and incomparable product—these are the fruits of German inwardness. The great historical deed of German inwardness was Luther's Reformation—we called it a mighty deed of liberation and, as such, it was obviously something good. But it is evident that the Devil had his hand even in that deed. The Reformation brought about the religious schism of the Occident, a definite misfortune, and for Germany it brought the Thirty Years' War, that depopulated it, fatally retarded its culture, and, by means of vice and epidemics probably made German blood into something different and something worse than it had been in the Middle Ages. Erasmus of Rotterdam, who wrote the *Praise of Folly*, a skeptical humanist with very little inwardness, was well aware of the implications of the Reformation. "When you see terrible cataclysms arising in the world," he said, "then remember that Erasmus predicted it." But the venerable Lout of Wittenberg, tremendously charged with inwardness, was no pacifist; he was filled with true German acceptance of the tragic, and declared himself ready to take the blood that would flow, "on his neck."

German *Romanticism*, what is it but an expression of this finest German quality, German inwardness? Much that is longingly pensive, fantastically spectral, and deeply scurrilous, a high artistic refinement and all-pervading irony combine in the concept of Romanticism. But these are not the things I think of primarily when I speak of Romanticism. It is rather a certain dark richness and piousness—I might say: antiquarianism—of soul that feels very close to the chthonian, irrational, and demonic forces of life, that is to say, the true sources of life; and it resists the purely rationalistic approach on the ground of its deeper knowledge, its deeper alliance with the holy. The Germans are the people of the romantic counter-revolution against the philosophical intellectualism and rationalism of enlightenment—a revolt of music against literature, of mysticism against clarity. Romanticism is anything but feeble sentimentalism; it is depth, conscious of its own strength and fullness. It is pessimism of sincerity that stands on the side of everything existing, real, historical against both criticism and meliorism, in short, on the side of power against the spirit, and it thinks very little of all rhetorical virtuousness and idealistic disguising of the world. Herein lies the union of Romanticism with the Realism and Macchiavellianism that celebrated its triumphs over Europe in the person of Bismarck, the only political genius that Germany ever produced. The German desire for unity and empire, directed by Bismarck into Prussian paths, was misunderstood if it was interpreted according to the usual pattern as a movement for unification of national-democratic character. It tried to be just that at one time, around the year 1848, although even the Pan-German discussions of the St. Paul's Parliament had a tinge of medieval imperialism, reminiscences of the Holy Roman Empire. But it developed that the customary European, national-democratic road to unity was not the German road. Fundamentally Bismarck's empire had nothing in common with "nation" in the democratic sense of the word. It was purely a power structure aiming toward the hegemony of Europe, and notwithstanding its modernity, the empire of 1871 clung to memories of medieval glory, the time of the Saxon and Swabian rulers. This very thing was the characteristic and menacing factor; the mixture of robust timeliness, efficient modernness on the one hand and dreams of the past on the other, in a word highly technological Romanticism. Born in wars, the Unholy German Empire of Prussian Nation could never be anything but a war empire. As such it lived, a thorn in the side of the world, and as such it is now destroyed.

In the history of ideas the merits of the German Romantic counter-Revolution are invaluable. Hegel himself has a tremendous share in them by the fact that his dialectic philosophy bridged the gulf that rationalistic enlightenment and the French Revolution had opened between reason and history. His reconciliation of the reasonable with the real gave a mighty impetus to historical thinking and actually created the science of history, which had scarcely existed before that time. Romanticism is essentially submersion, especially submersion in the past; it is longing for the past and at the same time it is realistic appreciation of everything truly past in its own right, with its local color and atmosphere. No wonder that Romanticism was particularly favorable to the writing of history and actually inaugurated history in its modern form.

The contributions of Romanticism to the realm of the beautiful, as a science, as an aesthetic doctrine, are rich and fascinating. Positivism, intellectualistic enlightenment have no inkling of the nature of poetry; Romanticism alone imparted it to a world that was dying of boredom in virtuous academicism. Romanticism poetized ethics by proclaiming the right of individuality and of spontaneous passion. It raised the treasures of song and story from the depths of folk culture of the past; Romanticism was the genial patroness of the science of folklore that appears in its motley colors as a variety of exoticism. The priority over the rational which it grants to the emotional, even in its arcane forms of mystic ecstasy and Dionysiac intoxication, brings it into a peculiar and psychologically highly fruitful relationship to sickness; the late-Romanticist Neitzsche, for example, himself a spirit raised by illness to heights of fatal genius, was profuse in his praise of sickness as a medium of knowledge. In this sense even psychoanalysis, which represents a great advance toward the understanding of man from the side of illness, is a branch of Romanticism.

Goethe laconically defined the Classical as the heathy, the Romantic as the morbid. A painful definition for one who loves Romanticism down to its sins and vices. But it cannot be denied that even in its loveliest, most ethereal aspects where the popular mates with the sublime it bears in its heart the germ of morbidity, as the rose bears the worm; its innermost character is seduction, seduction to death. This is its confusing paradox: while it is the revolutionary representative of the irrational forces of life against abstract reason and dull humanitarianism, it possesses a deep affinity to death by virtue of its very surrender to the irrational and to the past. In Germany, its true home, it has most strongly preserved this iridescent dualism, as glorification of the vital in contrast to the purely moral, and likewise as kinship to death. As German spirit, as Romantic counterrevolution, it has contributed deep and vitalizing impulses to European thought; but on the other hand its life and death pride has disdained to accept any correcting instruction from Europe, from the spirit of European religion of humanity, from European democracy. In its realities power-political guise, as Bismarckianism, as German victory over France, over civilization, and by the erection of the German power empire, apparently blooming in the most robust health, it elicited the astonishment of the world, simultaneously confusing and depressing it. And as soon as the genius himself no longer stood at the helm of this empire it kept the world in a constant state of unrest.

Besides, the united power realm was a cultural disappointment. No intellectual greatness came from Germany that had once been the teacher of the world. It was only strong. But in this strength and in all its organized efficiency, the Romantic germ of illness and death lived and worked. Historical misfortune, the suffering and humiliation of a lost war, were its nourishment. And, reduced to a miserable mass level, the level of a Hitler, German Romanticism broke out into hysterical barbarism, into a spree and a paroxysm of arrogance and crime, which now finds its horrible end in a national catastrophe, a physical and psychic collapse without parallel.

The story I told you in brief outline, ladies and gentlemen, is the story of German "inwardness." It is a melancholy story—I call it that, instead of "tragic," because misfortune should not boast. This story should convince us of one thing: that there are *not* two Germanies, a good one and a bad one, but only one, whose best turned into evil through devilish cunning. Wicked Germany is merely good Germany gone astray, good Germany in misfortune, in guilt, and ruin. For that reason it is quite impossible for one born there simply to renounce the wicked, guilty Germany and to declare: "I am the good, the noble, the just Germany in the white robe; I leave it to you to exterminate the wicked one." Not a word of all that I have just told you about Germany or tried to indicate to you, came out of alien, cool, objective knowledge, it is all within me, I have been through it all.

In other words, what I have tried to give you here within the limits of time, was a piece of German self-criticism; and truly, nothing could have been more faithful to German tradition. The tendency toward self-criticism, often to the point of self-disgust and self-execration, is thoroughly German, and it is eternally incomprehensible how a people so inclined toward self-analysis could ever conceive the idea of world domination. The quality most necessary for world domination is naiveness, a happy limitation, and even purposelessness, but certainly not an extreme spiritual life, like the German, in which arrogance is coupled with contrition. Nothing that a Frenchman, an Englishman, or an American ever said openly about his people can remotely be compared to the pitiless truths that great Germans, Hölderlin, Goethe, Nietzsche, have uttered about Germany. In oral conversation, at least, Goethe went so far as to wish for a German Diaspora. "Like the Jews," he said, "the Germans must be transplanted and scattered over the world!" And he added: ". . . in order to develop the good that lies in them, fully and to the benefit of the nations."

This great good really exists, but it could not come to fruition in the traditional form of the national state. The immigration laws of the other states will probably categorically prevent that dispersion throughout the world which Goethe wished for the Germans and for which they will have a strong inclination after this war. But despite all drastic warnings against excessive expectations, that we have had from the past performance of power politics, may we not cherish the hope that after this catastrophe the first experimental steps may be taken in the direction of a world condition in which the national individualism of the nineteenth century will dissolve and finally vanish, and which will afford happier opportunities for the development of the "good" in the German character than the untenable old conditions? Should it not be possible after all that the liquidation of Nazism may pave the way for a social world reform which would offer the greatest prospect of happiness to Germany's very inclinations and needs. World economy, the minimizing of political boundaries, a certain depolitization of states in general, the awakening of mankind to a realization of their practical unity, their first thoughts about a world state, how could all this social humanitarianism—the true object of the great struggle—which far exceeds the bounds of bourgeois democracy, be foreign and repugnant to German character? In the seclusiveness of the German there was always so much longing for companionship; indeed at the bottom of the very loneliness that made him wicked lay always the wish to love, the wish to be loved. In the end the German misfortune is only the paradigm of the tragedy of human life. And the grace that Germany so sorely needs, my friends, all of us need it.

Acknowledgments

Every reasonable effort has been made to locate the owners of rights to previously published works printed here. We gratefully acknowledge permission to reprint the following material:

Essay: Harold Bloom's Introduction, *Modern Critical Views—Thomas Mann*, edited by Harold Bloom. By permission Chelsea House Publishers.

"Tristan," "Tonio Kröger," and "Death in Venice" from *Death in Venice and Other Stories* by Thomas Mann. Translated by David Luke, Translation copyright © 1988 by David Luke. Used by permission of Bantam Books, a division of Bantam Doubleday Dell Publishing Group, Inc.

"Mario and the Magician" and "Blood of the Walsungs" from *Death in Venice and Seven Other Stories* by Thomas Mann, trans., H. T. Lowe-Porter. Copyright 1930, 1931, 1936 by Alfred A. Knopf, Inc. Reprinted by permission of the publisher.

From *The Tables of the Law* by Thomas Mann, trans., H. T. Lowe-Porter. Copyright 1945 and renewed 1973 by Alfred A. Knopf, Inc. Reprinted by permission of the publisher.

"Freud and the Future" from *Essays of Three Decades* by Thomas Mann, trans., H. T. Lowe-Porter. Copyright 1929, 1933, 1937, 1947 by Alfred A. Knopf, Inc. Reprinted by permission of the publisher.

"A Brother" from *Order of the Day* by Thomas Mann, trans., H. T. Lowe-Porter. Copyright 1937, 1938, 1939, 1940, 1941, 1942 by Alfred A. Knopf, Inc. Reprinted by permission of the publisher. "Bruder Hitler" reprinted by permission S. Fischer Verlag. All rights reserved S. Fischer Verlag GmbH, Frankfurt am Main.

"Deutschland und die Deutschen." All rights reserved S. Fischer Verlag GmbH, Frankfurt am Main.